# Fundamental Web Design and Development Skills

**Rachel Andrew**

**Chris Ullman**

**Crystal Waters**

© 2002 glasshaus
Published by glasshaus Ltd,
Arden House,
1102 Warwick Road,
Acocks Green,
Birmingham,
B27 6BH, UK
Printed in the United States
ISBN 1-904151-17-5

# Fundamental Web Design and Development Skills

## Cover Image

Supplied by Tony Blessander

Tony was born and raised in a town called Västerås, located in the middle parts of beautiful Sweden. He has studied media and design for several years and feels that this is what he is here to do. Push the limits, experiment, look beyond the horizon, and solve every problem in the best way possible: that's what he does.

*Outside the life of graphic design I meet with friends, ride my skateboard,and enjoy every moment for what it is. I wish everyone could be as lucky as I am. Love to all my family and friends. Thanks for your time. Peace! / T.*

glasshaus

labor-saving devices for web professionals

© 2002 glasshaus

# Trademark Acknowledgments

# Credits

**Authors**
Rachel Andrew
Chris Ullman
Crystal Waters

**Additional Material**
Chris Mills

**Technical Reviewers**
Mike Brittain
Martin Honnen
Shefali Kulkarni
Sion Lee
Dan Maharry
Drew McLellan
Barbara Rhoades
David Schultz
Michael Walston

**Proof Reader**
Agnes Wiggers

**Commissioning Editor**
Simon Mackie

**Technical Editors**
Amanda Kay
Matthew Machell
Chris Mills
Daniel Walker

**Publisher**
Viv Emery

**Project Manager**
Sophie Edwards

**Graphic Editors**
Rachel Taylor
Pip Wonson

**Graphic Designer**
Dawn Chellingworth

**Indexer**
Adrian Axinte

# About the Authors

## Rachel Andrew

Rachel Andrew runs her own web solutions company in the UK, *http://www.edgeofmyseat.com*, the company web site also being home to various "web standards"-focused articles and Dreamweaver extensions. Rachel is a member of the Web Standards Project on the Dreamweaver Task Force, and hopes to encourage best practices in the support and use of W3C Standards in Dreamweaver.

When not writing code, or writing about writing code, Rachel spends time with her daughter, tries to encourage people to use Debian GNU/Linux, studies with the Open University, and enjoys a nice pint of beer.

*Thanks must go to everyone at glasshaus for making the process of working on this book enjoyable; to Drew McLellan for his constant love and support; and to my daughter Bethany, who thinks that all mummies are permanently attached to a computer. Thank you.*

## Chris Ullman

Chris Ullman is a Computer Science Graduate who worked for Wrox Press for six and a half years before branching out on his own. Now a father of a 13 month old baby, Nye, he divides his time between being a human punchbag for Nye, trying to write extra chapters with a baby on his lap and, in rare moments of spare time, either playing keyboards in psychedelic band the Bee Men, tutoring his cats in the art of peaceful co-existence and not violently mugging each other on the stairs, or hoping against hope his favorite soccer team, Birmingham City, can manage to stay more than a single year in the Premier League.

A selection of Chris's non-computer related writings on music, art, and literature can be found at *http://www.atomicwise.com*, while his band web site is at *http://www.beemen.com*.

## Crystal Waters

Crystal Waters has been writing about consumer-oriented technology since the 1980s, back when 5MB hard drives were a novel upgrade. She is author of two books, *Web Concept & Design* and *Universal Web Design* (New Riders), and of many articles. She has been an editor at a number of magazines and was director of MFWeb conferences, among other roles, and is a long-distance charity cyclist and avid kayak fisherman. She lives and fishes with her boyfriend Dwayne (who took this photo) and dog Nellie (pictured) in Vermont. Her sites are *http://www.typo.com* and *http://www.girlbike.com*.

# Table of Contents

# Chapter 3: Design and Process 53

# Chapter 4: Advanced Markup: HTML, XML, and XHTML 77

# Chapter 6: Traditional Page Layout Techniques    **111**

# Chapter 7: Navigation    **125**

## Chapter 10: Applying JavaScript in Your Pages          223

## Chapter 14: Techniques for Site Maintenance and Administration ......................................................... 331

# Chapter 15: Server-Side Scripting

**355**

# Introduction

So, you want to become a web professional? You want to design or develop web sites, and potentially make a living out of it? Well, you've come to the right place.

**Professional** is the important word in the above paragraph. As you cover the first few chapters of this book, you'll see how easy creating web pages with HTML really is. The tricky part is incorporating all the good design and coding principles that current web experts are using. This book will set you well on the way to this goal.

## Who Am I?

Perhaps you've come to a time in your life where you want a new challenge, or a new profession.

Maybe you've just finished school or college. You want to start a career, or gain some skills to get you started on a college course.

Perhaps you've already started playing with creating basic sites for your family – copying code from other people's pages? This may have sparked your interest to learn more about the subject, to open up a new avenue of possibilities.

## Where Will This Book Take Me?

Whatever your reason for wanting a new set of web design skills, this book will take you there. By the end of the book, you'll know:

- How to create sites that are great looking, as well as easily usable and accessible to those with disabilities

- How to upload your site to a server so it can be seen by the general public, and how to manage your site once it's online

● Where to go from here to learn more web skills or prepare yourself for a web professional career

The book is set out over a series of manageable-sized chapters. Each chapter is in a tutorial style, explaining exactly what you need to do and assuming nothing that wasn't covered in previous chapters. Each chapter ends with a summary, so you can check what you should have learned, and a list of other resources you may want to investigate for more information.

## What Do I Need to Begin?

The minimum you need to create the examples set out in this book is a plain text editor, such as Notepad for Windows or Simple Text for Macintosh. However, there are many tools that can be used to help make creating web pages easier. One such tool is Dreamweaver MX, trial versions of which can be found on the accompanying CD. While this book will not aim to teach you all the ins and outs of this product, it will be used to help explain some of the examples as we come across them. You do not need to have any experience of using Dreamweaver prior to reading the book.

## What Will Be Covered?

### Chapter 1: The Web and How It Works

The first thing we do in the book is to set the stage. We explore what the Web is, and explain the basic concepts upon which it is based, including browsers, hyperlinks, servers, clients, and HTML. We also take our first look at the various career opportunities and job roles that web professionals may aspire to.

### Chapter 2: Basic HTML

The task of creating a web page falls into two parts: designing what the page should look like, and implementing that page by actually creating the HTML that the browser will use. This second chapter looks at the latter role, while *Chapter 3* looks at the former.

Writing basic HTML is actually easy to get the hang of. By the end of this chapter, you'll be able to create basic sites that contain text, images, and links to other sites. We'll explain how to create these sites, using a plain text editor or Dreamweaver MX.

### Chapter 3: Design and Process

As mentioned above, design is one of the core skills you'll need when creating a site. In this chapter we'll discuss the processes you can use to turn your imagination and flair into well-designed site plans, and where to go for inspiration to get you started.

### Chapter 4: Advanced Markup: HTML, XML, and XHTML

Back with HTML, in this chapter we'll learn more about the language that we first encountered in *Chapter 2*. As well as learning more of the "vocabulary" you can use, we'll also look at a closely related language called XHTML.

HTML itself has changed over the years and appears in various versions. After version 4, a fairly large language change was decided on, including a name change to XHTML. So XHTML is basically the latest version of the HTML language. While many web sites are currently written using HTML, it is useful to know how to create sites in XHTML since this is the way the web world will go, given time.

## Chapter 5: Creating Graphics for the Web

While much of the content on the Web is textual, it would be nothing like as interesting without images. There are many types of formats for images, some of which are better than others for use on the Web. We'll explore the different formats here, as well as the many image techniques you can use on web pages to make them more interesting.

## Chapter 6: Traditional Page Layout Techniques

Actually implementing the layout of your site can now be done in a variety of ways, which generally fall into two camps. First there are the traditional layout techniques, such as using tables and frames. We'll discuss these aspects of the HTML language in detail here. Later, in *Chapter 8*, you'll discover a new way of laying out pages.

## Chapter 7: Navigation

As you'll know, most sites on the Web consist of more than just one page. They consist of a number of pages, each of which is linked to the others through a series of hyperlinks. There is a certain art to creating these hyperlinks in a way that makes them easy for users to find, and logical for them to follow. In this chapter we'll look at the various ways you can structure your navigation to ensure the user can find what they want.

## Chapter 8: CSS: Modern Layout and Style

Although HTML can tell the browser how the page should look (for example, what color it is, how it should be laid out, what the text should look like), this is not the spirit in which it was originally developed. Originally it was meant to describe the content of the page, rather than specify how it should be displayed.

In order to keep HTML for description rather than specifying presentation, a new language was developed: Cascading Style Sheets, or CSS. This can be used alongside HTML to provide instructions on how the page should look. We'll examine this language in detail here.

## Chapter 9: JavaScript Basics

HTML pages, on the whole, are fairly static. They do not change. But I'm sure you've seen pages that do change – perhaps images change when the mouse rolls over them, or your name appears at the top of the page? This type of functionality can be achieved using JavaScript, a low-level programming language particularly suited to the Web.

As well as explaining how JavaScript can be used, this chapter will cover most of the basic JavaScript syntax you'll ever need.

## Chapter 10: Applying JavaScript in Your Pages

Following on from *Chapter 9*, we now look at some bigger examples of what JavaScript can be used for. By walking through each example, you'll gain more familiarity with this useful language. You'll also find that the examples can be used within your own pages, either as is, or modified in some way to meet your own needs.

### Chapter 11: An Introduction to Usability

Much discussion has taken place amongst web professionals in recent years on the topic of usability. This basically means: "How easy is it for people to use your web site?" Through much discussion and investigation, some generic guidelines have been decided upon. While these won't prescribe exactly what you need to do to make your site easy to use, they will make you more aware about this issue.

Alongside usability is the topic of accessibility. This basically means: "How easy is it for users with a disability to use your site?" Many such users will not use one of the three mainstream browsers (IE, Netscape, and Opera), but one with built-in facilities making it easier for them to surf the Web. Making sure your sites are easily read and understood by such browsers is, at the very least, one way of differentiating yourself from the many other budding web professionals. However, in some circumstances, accessibility is a legal requirement of a web site in the US, Japan, Australia, and Europe.

### Chapter 12: Standards Compliance

Throughout the rest of the book, we discuss languages such as HTML, XHTML, CSS, and JavaScript. Behind each of these is a standard: a specified set of rules that describe how the language should be used. Although many browsers will let you bend these rules, there are many reasons why you should stick to the standards behind them. This chapter gives those reasons, as well as giving a little more background into the standards themselves.

### Chapter 13: Getting Your Site onto the Web

So, you now have a site that uses all the skills presented so far in this book. How do you get it onto the Web so others can view it? This chapter explains the intricacies of using an ISP (Internet Service Provider) to host your site. It will introduce the concept of FTP: a technique for transferring your site to the server on which it will be hosted.

### Chapter 14: Techniques for Site Maintenance and Administration

Now your site is on the Web, it isn't time to sit back and relax. It's likely that you will want to add to the site, or update it with more current content. Here we introduce many techniques for updating content, including a brief look at blogging – keeping an online diary.

### Chapter 15: Server-Side Scripting

Throughout the book, we have concentrated on client-side code – that is, HTML, CSS, and JavaScript that the browser can understand. However, the story doesn't stop there. There are other technologies, known as server-side technologies, that the browser does not understand. Instead, the server has to process the pages before they are sent to the browser. While we don't have room to teach these subjects in this book, here we give an overview of what they are and why you might use them, and point you in the direction of more information should you decide to learn more.

### Chapter 16: Where Do I Go from Here?

Finally, you've learned all the technology that this book can cover. Where should you go from here? This chapter provides sources of more learning, and also suggestions on how to get that all-important first web professional job.

## What's on the CD?

The CD that accompanies this book contains many useful things:

- All the sample code used within the book for you to test or to incorporate into your own pages.

- PC and Mac trial versions of visual design software for Macromedia Dreamweaver MX, Macromedia Fireworks MX, and Macromedia Flash MX.

- Sample chapters from some of our other glasshaus books. You may use these sample chapters to get a taster for other future learning directions.

- References to the sites mentioned throughout the book.

## Where Can I Get Help?

Although we aim for perfection, the sad fact of book publication is that a few errors will slip through. We would like to apologize for any that have reached this book despite our best efforts. If you spot such an error, please let us know about it using the e-mail address *support@glasshaus.com*. If it's something that will help other readers, then we'll put it up on the errata page at *http://www.glasshaus.com*.

This address can also be used to access our support network. If you have trouble running any of the code in this book, or have a related question that you feel that the book didn't answer, please mail your problem to the above address quoting the title of the book, the last 4 digits of its ISBN, and the chapter and page number of your query.

Note that we do not support the trial versions of the Macromedia products provided on the CD. Instead, try using the forums at *http://webforums.macromedia.com/dreamweaver/* or *http://www.mxzone.com/forum/*, or the *macromedia.dreamweaver* newsgroup.

### Web Support

Feel free to visit our web site at *http://www.glasshaus.com*. It features:

- Code Downloads: The example code for this, and every other glasshaus book, can be downloaded from our site.

- Galleries: The example code from some books is shown working on our site, including forms and menus.

- Authors: Interviews with the people who write our books.

- Books: Information on our other books and news about upcoming books.

# 1

- Brief history of the Web and Internet

- Hyperlinking through the Web

- Web browsers - what is available?

- Web career opportunities

**Author: Crystal Waters**

# The Web and How It Works

The Web, in its short lifetime, has changed the way we communicate, buy, sell, market, and control various parts of our business and personal life. It has truly become a worldwide phenomenon – web sites have sprung up from all corners of the planet, and anyone anywhere can access them. Luckily for you, as potential web professionals, the Web only shows signs of further growth, which means more potential for your creativity.

While we are sure that many of you have used the Web for a while, and may even remember a time without personal computers, we hope you'll take the time to read this brief history of the Internet and the Web. History was never one of this author's favorite topics, but it continues to amaze how this medium has grown so quickly.

The Web's history gives a perspective to the entire process that you have decided to embark upon: web design and development is far from being what it was when the Web first became an industry itself, and if we are to enter or continue a career in this field, we'll have to continue to grow just as quickly, and be able to adapt to the new challenges we are likely to face every day. We have to remain open-minded, willing to learn, flexible, and creative. Web designers and developers are the people who have driven much of the technology to its current level, and will continue to do so.

After our history lesson, we will take a look at the following basic topics, to give you a real feel for the web arena:

- How the Internet works – what happens when information (such as an e-mail or a web page) is sent across the Internet?

- Hyperlinking – linking from page to page – one of the main things that really makes the Web what it is.

- Browsers – the software that allows us to use the Web. What different ones are available, and how have they changed since the Web's inception?

- Jobs – what different career paths are available to aspiring web professionals in this day and age?

Lastly, at the end of the chapter you'll find a list of important terminology to know when you are getting to grips with the world of web design and development. A lot of these terms are used over the course of this chapter, so if you meet a term you do not understand, you will probably able to find an explanation of it at the end.

# A Brief History of the Web and the Internet

The Web hasn't been around that long in the grand scheme of things, having its origins in the work of Tim Berners-Lee (and others) at CERN in the early 1990s. The Internet's origins span a good deal further back than that, as we shall soon see. "But I thought they were the same thing!" I hear you cry. Well, the Web refers to the medium and process by which hypertext (that is, web pages) are transmitted. The Internet refers to not only to the medium and process by which web pages are transmitted, but also to all of the other methods of communication that are done across cyberspace too, like e-mail and news.

## The Origins of the Internet

The Internet has quite an interesting history full of significant technological and social milestones. If you search online to find out exactly when the Internet started (using *http://www.google.com* for example), you'll come up with a plethora of inconclusive answers. These answers span from 1858, when the first transatlantic cable was laid across the ocean floor, to what has arguably become one of Al Gore's most well-known misquotes (when he claimed to have created the Internet during his time as a US Congressman).

While the telegraph itself was patented in 1836, and Morse had invented Morse Code (a distant relative of binary code), it's the international aspect of this cable that makes it a significant step in today's communications. It was a landmark historical event put on the same pedestal as the Sputnik satellites launched a century later, and is considered by some to be the first "international network" (or "**inter-net**" for short), since it was the first time we were able to communicate with those across the ocean in an instant.

## War-Fed Technology

Without tying it down to any specific instance, it's generally accepted that the Internet as we know it today was created as a Cold War tool in the late 1950's, in response to the former USSR's launch of its Sputnik satellites. US President Dwight D Eisenhower allowed for the development of the **Advanced Research Projects Agency** (**ARPA**), whose team created the US's first successful satellite launches. The ARPA organization later moved its focus to communications technology and networking.

The massive, multi-connected web of communication networks was developed first as a guarantee that if one method of communication was cut off during a war, communications would bypass the "cut" and simply adopt another route through the network. It would be virtually impossible for an enemy to take out each and every one of these paths of communication. Whether the modern Internet could actually withstand a massive modern war is doubtful (according to those that study such things), but the same people will also point out that without the threat of war, the Internet may have never come into being.

In the 1960s, Dr. JCR Licklider, the head of US military computer technology research, determined that in order to best serve its purpose, ARPA had to move from the private sector to university networks. The resulting network of connections became the **ARPANET**. The first **node** or interconnection of branches of this network was set up at UCLA, then one at Stanford, then the University of California at Santa Barbara, and then the University of Utah. The network was born.

The first public showing of ARPANET at work was at the International Conference on Computer Communications in 1972, where delegates were allowed to try out applications running all over the US from the basement of the Washington Hilton Hotel. Soon after, "meeting" on the Internet was a regular activity for those who had access, including (there should be no surprise here) a group that discussed a text-based, online Star Trek game. Personal computers of today's capabilities weren't even imaginable at this time, but the Internet as many of us know it today was well under way.

Meanwhile, e-mail was invented in 1971 by Ray Tomlinson (who also picked the @ symbol for the e-mail addresses), and it's safe to say it will be around for quite a long time to come. Queen Elizabeth II of England sent the first royal e-mail in 1976, three years after the first international connections to the ARPANET were made at the University College of London (England) and Royal Radar Establishment (Norway).

In the 1970s (at Stanford, on the Pacific coast of the US), Vint Cerf and Bob Khan were busy defining some very important Internet **Protocols** – **TCP** (**Transmission Control Protocol**) and **IP** (**Internet Protocol**). They eventually refined these to **TCP/IP**, which we still use today – it is a reliable protocol, which ensures that our interconnected systems work with one another and exchange information successfully.

**Protocol**: an agreed upon format for transmitting data between two devices.

Cerf and Kahn figured out how the Internet could be used to send around "**packets**" of information. Basically, everything that we send or receive (for example, e-mail and web pages) is broken into packets, or parts, of the complete data. Each computer connected to the Internet is known as a **host**, and is given at least one **IP address** that uniquely identifies it from all the other host computers on the Internet (an IP address is simply a unique number that identifies your computer from all other computers on the Internet – it is also known as an **Internet Address**)

Note that there is always another protocol involved with the transfer of information across the Internet in addition to TCP/IP; it is the job of this other protocol to say what the kind of information is, and how the client and server involved should communicate (making sure they are speaking the same language), before giving it to TCP/IP to be broken up into packets and transmitted.

The nature of this other protocol depends on what type of information we are transmitting, for example, hypertext web pages are handled by **HTTP** (**HyperText Transfer Protocol**), whereas e-mail is handled by **SMTP** (**Simple Mail Transfer Protocol**.) Don't worry about the specifics of these protocols, as the procedure is basically the same, regardless of the type of information sent.

Let's look at an example. When you send an e-mail to someone, the e-mail (identified and handled by SMTP) gets cut up into packets by TCP/IP, and is sent from your computer (which could also be termed a **client** in this case – refer to the definitions at the end of the chapter) to the **server** (see the definition at the end of the chapter.)

Each packet, in addition to containing part of the e-mail message, also contains the sender's IP address and the receiver's IP address, so the server knows who sent the message, and who to send it on to. The packets are now forwarded to the recipient of your message, and then reassembled into the original message by TCP/IP, so the recipient can read it. The entire procedure looks something like this:

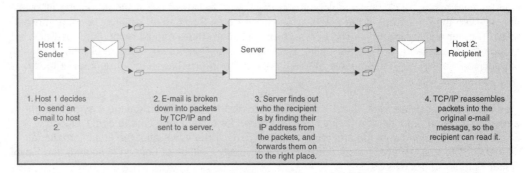

This is how all information is sent over the Internet. Note that the packets can get to their destination via completely different pathways across the Internet, and can arrive at their destination in a completely different order than they started in. This is the real power of TCP/IP – a watertight protocol that can reassemble this jumble of packets into the original data. Missing packets can cause the data to be totally unusable, so this is obviously important.

Basically, the Internet is a bunch of computers hooked together that sends billions of packets of information all over the world every day. This milestone set of protocols has earned Cerf and Khan the title of "fathers of the Internet" by those in academia and the industry.

## No Looking Back

Development of the Internet – the tools, protocols, networks, connections, and methods of communication – continued to grow exponentially. In 1977, the number of Internet servers (also known as Internet **nodes**) grew to over 100, and e-mail was a regular occurrence. **Telnet**, an application that gave people access to servers was born, as were **newsgroups** (**USENET**), and **MUDs (Multi-User Dungeons)** that gave people access to interactive adventure games and other cool activities. In 1984, nodes grew to over 1000 in number; in 5 years (1989), that number was over 100,000; in 1992, the number crossed the one million mark. Another 5 years (1997) and it was nearly 20 million. With the arrival of wireless Internet devices and an ongoing rise in users globally, this number is expected to grow to a billion or more within a few years.

In 1979, CompuServe became the first publicly accessible service to offer e-mail capabilities and technical support to regular people like us, who might have access to personal computers. It took another ten years, though, before it or other proprietary online services could send and receive mail from Internet locations.

**America Online** (**AOL**) was launched for Macintosh and Apple II computers in 1989, and was touted as the first visual-based online service; icons represented actions and content, and its subscribers didn't have to memorize codes and proprietary lingo to access its content and services. The aim of AOL has always been to bring the Internet to the masses, beyond the domain of the techies, and it has managed to do that quite well, right up to modern day. It is said to be designed to be used by anybody, from children to the elderly.

# Enter the Web

Let's fast forward some, and take a look at the Web itself. Tim Berners-Lee is usually the person credited with creating the World Wide Web, and rightly so. Back in 1989, Berners-Lee proposed what he terms "a global hypertext project." Based on a program he had written in order to organize his own work, this hypertext project was designed to be able to combine and link electronic-based work via **hypertext**. Hypertext came in being as simple HTML – text documents containing markup, which define styles, tables, and hyperlinks allowing you to jump from document to document. Around this time, the protocol HTTP was also invented, to allow hypertext to be transmitted over the Internet.

## HTML

The roots of HTML can be found in **Standard Generalized Markup Language** (**SGML**). But what is SGML? It is a very complicated syntax for defining languages for marking up documents (invented by Charles Goldfarb at IBM in 1969) – a meta language if you like (a language that describes languages).

Basically, HTML is based on SGML, defined using its rules, with the aim of creating a display-oriented markup language for marking up documents on the Web. When we say "markup text", we mean "apply rules to sections of text that define how they should be displayed" – for example, consider the following line of text:

```
This is the start of a long story.
```

We could mark it up using a simple HTML "rule" (as you will discover later, they are known as **elements**), that says that the word "start" should be displayed in a bolder typeface than the rest of the sentence:

```
This is the <strong>start</strong> of a long story.
```

HTML was first defined by Tim Berners-Lee and his team in the early 1990s, and has had many revisions since then, the newest version being HTML 4.01. For more details of how to implement HTML, see *Chapters 2* and *4* of this book.

HTML has always been called the "language of the Web" – it is the language that most web pages are written in, and this is not likely to change in the near future (however, there are a lot more web technologies to master, as you will see throughout the course of this book).

## How the Web Works

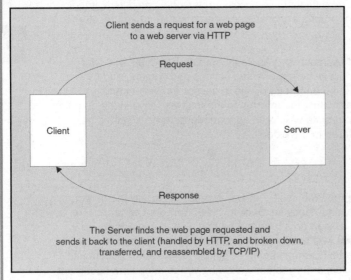

Client sends a request for a web page
to a web server via HTTP

Request

Client

Server

Response

The Server finds the web page requested and
sends it back to the client (handled by HTTP, and broken down,
transferred, and reassembled by TCP/IP)

We have already seen the basic theory of how data is sent over the Internet using TCP/IP, so now let's look at a simpler picture, of what happens when a client requests a web page. First, a web page is requested (the request is processed via HTTP) when a URL is typed into the address bar of a user's browser (or when a hyperlink is clicked on). This **request** is sent to the server where that information is held. The server then finds the page that the user has requested, and **responds** by sending the page back to the client (it is split up into packets by TCP/IP, sent, then reassembled as expected). This is sometimes called a **request/response** model.

## The Birth of Web Browsers

In February 1993, **NCSA (National Center for Supercomputing Applications)** released a browser called **Mosaic**, created by Netscape's future founder Marc Andreessen – this was the first widely distributed web browser available. You can still download Mosaic – the screenshot below shows the front page of Amazon (*http://www.amazon.com*), rendered in Mosaic version 1.0.3 (the earliest version I could find). It was very difficult to find any pages that showed up at all in the browser.

*Amazon.com displayed in Mosaic 1/0/3, one of the earliest web browsers available.*

It looks very basic, no? For comparison's sake, here is *Amazon.com* as displayed in Netscape 6.2:

Formatting, animated graphics, forms processing, layout tools, secure financial transactions – so many things have changed since the Web's early days. Being as spoiled as we are today with web features such as high-end motion graphics, multimedia, and fast connections at home, it's hard to picture a Web that was merely text and links.

*Amazon.com displayed in Netscape 6.2 – notice the difference!*

## Images on the Web

Marc Andreessen came to the fore again when he developed the functionality to allow images to be referenced from HTML so that we could have images as well as text within web pages.

When images could be posted along with text and links, the Web started to get a little more attention.

This author was working for an online branch of a publishing company when the novelty of what was the first real "**web cam**" became the hottest technical news fit to print. The program **XCoffee** was used as an internal tool before the Web was officially born – basically, a camera connected to a server was focused on a coffeepot, and would take images about three times a minute and post them "live" on the University of Cambridge Computer Laboratory server. The **Trojan Room Coffee Machine** project started as a tool for researchers in the building, allowing them to check if there was coffee in the pot before they walked up or down several floors to get a cup.

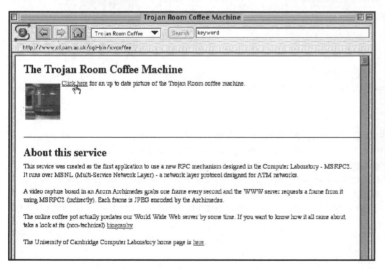

*The Trojan Room Coffee Machine, located at http://www.cl.cam.ac.uk/coffee/coffee.html*

*The Trojan Room Coffee Machine was the first web cam in history, making its debut in late 1993. It was turned off when the computer lab was to be moved to a new building; the pot was then auctioned off on eBay (http://www.ebay.com) to raise money for coffee facilities in the new computer lab. The pot was sold for £3350, or approximately $5150*

When HTML was first given the ability to handle images within web documents back in 1993, the original stand-alone XCoffee application was modified and the system was connected to the Web. Millions of people over the years checked out that coffee pot status until the Trojan Room Coffee Machine was turned off on August 22nd 2001.

## The Beginnings of Commercialism on the Web

WIRED magazine (see *http://www.wired.com/*) was launched in 1993, and its sister web site, HotWired (*http://hotwired.lycos.com/*), hit the Web in October 1994. Wired was the first commercial web site, complete with advertising. The commercialization of the Web hasn't paused since. (Web history buffs will be excited to find that the very first issue of **WIRED magazine**'s contents is online at *http://www.wired.com/wired/archive/1.01/.*)

## The Web Takes Off

In 1994, the **World Wide Web Consortium** (**W3C** see *http://www.w3.org/*) was founded by Berners-Lee and others with the mission of developing common protocols to help the Web evolve and grow. By creating web standards, the group intends to "lead the Web to its full potential..." by "developing technologies that will create a forum for information, commerce, inspiration, independent thought, and collective understanding". Since its inception, it has been a mainstay resource for web developers, and a leader in recommending standards by which the industry usually follows.

There are other organizations that drive towards the same kinds of goals, often working with the W3C. These include **WaSP** (**The Web Standards Project**), who promote standards and good practice on the Web, and **OASIS**, who maintain and promote e-business standards.

The next few years saw a whirlwind of activity. Magazines like **.net** (Future Publishing) in the UK encouraged *The* **Net** magazine (Imagine Publishing) in the US, and we saw (now defunct) magazines such as **Internet Underground** and **Internet World** hit the stands around 1994. These magazines flourished as guides to, and critiques of, web sites. Time saw more technical and specialized magazines take most of their places, or they evolved themselves to be magazines of the digital culture rather than web directories.

Other magazines included **Web Techniques** (1996), which is now **New Architect** magazine, **Yahoo Internet Life**, **Business 2.0**, and **Fast Company**. We saw digital media publications like **HOW** and **Communication Arts** start to cover web graphics issues. (While there is no longer a huge rush to bring web magazines to the stands, there are still plenty of specialty publications – mostly business-oriented – that cover the web market extensively.)

## The Internet Boom/Crash

Press coverage rises and falls with the market, so do web design firms. The Internet boom occurred in the mid to late 90s, simultaneously with the rise in web stock tickers – one fed off another. It seemed that everyone was working in the web industry or had a company developing a web site. Every warehouse in San Francisco housed a burgeoning start-up company, venture capital flowed into large and small firms like water, and kids in their 20s were buying million-dollar homes with their stock dividends.

These same millionaires rode skateboards through the hallways, played football during lunch, and worked 90-hour weeks coding e-commerce sites. It seemed that nearly any project that had a "dot com" stuck on the end of it could get over a million dollars and everyone lived happily every after.

Then came the crash. In 2000, the web market abruptly stopped being the golden child of investors, and the free-flowing venture capital jerked to a stop. Companies that were loaned millions of dollars one week went belly-up the next, and the kids had to sell their houses and go bankrupt in order to cover taxes. It seemed that everyone was out of work, or going to be laid off any minute.

The once cool and seemingly playful digital media creative organizations that survived the big web misadventure now have a distinct business feel. After the "crash," it's all business and zero skateboards, at least in front of clients.

Does this mean that people don't have fun doing web development any more? Absolutely not. But like any market that has had its legs shaken from under it, the market is now rather more serious and competitive than it used to be.

# The Concept of Hyperlinking

Hyperlinking is what makes the Web what it is: a mass of information that is connected by links to related documents via **hyperlinks** or **hypertext**. Without this feature, the Web would just be a collection of documents that were only accessible via their own URL, rather than a place where we can create documents that connect to others that may support or supplement the original.

Think about how you might have used this in print documents. Often in magazine articles, a story starts out in the middle of the magazine, only to be interrupted by another story and a line (called a **jump line** in publishing lingo) that instructs you to "*turn to page 102*" or simply tells you that it is "*continued on page 102*". We've seen this concept when we've read articles or academic papers that include footnotes or terms that we might not be familiar with – we're often instructed to "*see How to Prepare Asparagus, page 47*", or even told that the information we need should have been read previously ("*see last month's article on life jacket purchasing tips*") or will be available in the future ("*Be sure to buy next month's issue for instructions on how to carve soap!*"). Serial television shows tell us "*In last week's episode, the cow jumped over the moon*" and that next week "*Watch with us as we see what the dish will do under pressure from its peers*".

On television, we can't hop to next week's shows by clicking on anything; waiting is the only way to get to our "link". In print, we are limited to turning pages and seeking out the information we are told to jump to. The number of pages in the magazine limits the amount of information included in the current issue (or pile of issues) that we have immediate access to.

These examples of "linking" within print and television aren't that efficient because it is so much more limiting than being online. Hyperlinking in an electronic document works because there are a huge number of possible documents that can be linked to in a very small space of time. The reader (or site user) can access what information they like when they like. The user is in control.

So what is hyperlinking? When your browser retrieves and displays the contents of a web page, often there are highlighted items, such as buttons, images, or underlined text throughout the document. Clicking on these hyperlinks instructs your browser to go and retrieve the page that the hyperlink referred to, and then display that page onscreen. That page will most likely offer even more hyperlinks; if it comes from the same "site" as the first page, it may include a link back to that page. If it is a page from another "site", then they may not even know that their page is linked to from the first page. (See *Chapter 2* for information on how hyperlinks are implemented, and *Chapter 7* for a detailed look at web navigation.)

This linking process can take you to sites that you may never have found any other way. It's like a gossip circle, in a way – often, the most interesting of topics are found by a link from a link from a link from a link, and aren't anything you would have considered searching for in the first place! For example, consider the following navigation sequence:

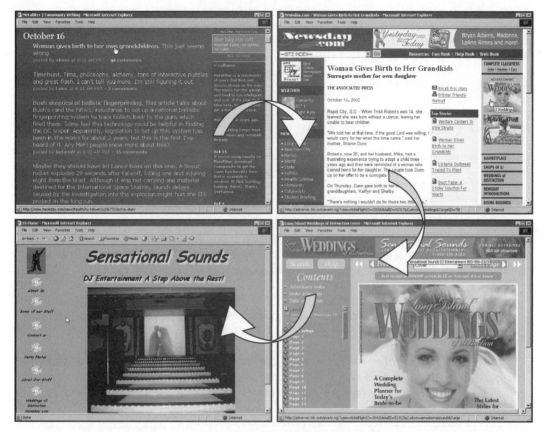

A typical navigation sequence: we have started on *metafilter.com*, a popular web-developer's blog/news site, and then gone to *newsweek.com*, a more general news site. From there, we have progressed to an online wedding magazine, and finished up on a site advertising DJs!

Following hyperlinks can obviously be a great distraction, and people new to the Web inevitably find themselves doing a lot more wandering around than they had originally intended. As a web professional, one of your goals is to make your site (or your client's) easily navigable and useful, to encourage people to wander around to other areas of your site and to explore other sites that support yours, rather than move off to a competitor's site (for more on navigation, see *Chapter 7*).

# Browsers

Ever since the first web designer role, it is the browser that has challenged and limited the web designer's work. As we saw earlier, since the Trojan Room coffee pot began brewing on the Web, and the Web wasn't written with much more than some simple HTML, more and more web technologies have come about, such as CSS and JavaScript. It is all well and good having these technologies to play with, but there is not much point laying out a site with glorious CSS styling and positioning, and using JavaScript to create a beautiful push-button menu, if your audience's browsers don't know how to interpret those technologies.

As new versions of these technologies are released, the web browsers are always some way behind in terms of adoption of them. In addition, even though new browser versions are released that support these new technologies, the rate at which web users adopt these new browser versions also becomes a limiting factor!

As you will see later in the book, making sure all of your site's audience can use your web site might be more difficult than you might think, for just these reasons. In this section we will take a brief look at the history of web browsers, and then look at what the major browsers are in the modern day, and how many people use them.

Browsers are our eyes on the Web, so keeping up with browser developments is key to keeping up with development and design standards. Nowadays it seems like browsers can show anything: from simple text like the old days, to full-motion video and interactive interfaces.

*There have been around 100 web browsers developed at different stages of the game, from those that only show text and associated links, to attempts at virtual reality browsers. There are browsers developed to assist those who are visually impaired with accessing the Web, such as pwWebSpeak and WebMedia's Talking Browser, as well as those developed specifically for young children, such as KidSafe and KidNet.*

*Proprietary browsers, such as AOL's original browser, have usually been replaced by more standards-supporting browsers (AOL owning Netscape helps in that department – take a look at http://webmaster.info.aol.com/ for AOL technical information.)*

*To get a taste of some of these many available browsers, past and present, we strongly recommend that you go and check out http://browsers.evolt.org/, where you can download them and try them for yourself.*

In the beginning, browsers only showed text. We have already seen Mosaic earlier on in the chapter, and MacLynx is shown here:

This may look woefully simple and inelegant, but this was what people were used to in the early days. In fact, only having to deal with text and hyperlinks could be seen as a bit of an advantage – it was very simple to provide browser support for this minimal feature set.

## Browser Support for Web Technologies

*As we saw above, HTML has always been called the "language of the Web", since its inception in the early 1990s. You can achieve a lot using HTML, but web developers quickly found that this was not enough. People wanted much more out of the Web than simple boring text, so support for images was added, as well as languages such as CSS and JavaScript.*

*As the new technologies are created, the development world has to wait for the browser manufacturers to catch up. This process is helped a lot if the browser manufacturers have a hand in creating the technologies in the first place. For example, the first real incarnation of JavaScript (which was called LiveScript, then before that, Mocha!), was invented by Netscape in 1995, in collaboration with Sun Microsystems, who invented the Java programming language. JavaScript was designed with the Netscape browser in mind, so Netscape supported it first, and it took Internet Explorer a while to catch up (and in fact, IE uses Microsoft's own interpretation of JavaScript, termed JScript, which has a few syntactical differences, and proprietary enhancements).*

*JavaScript support was first introduced in Netscape 2.0 (late 95-early 96), but IE didn't feature (JScript) support until IE 3 (late 1996). Support in those days was less than perfect. These days, both browsers have pretty good support for the technology.*

*Other, less manufacturer-dependent technologies have still followed similar paths, HTML being the most obvious one, introduced in the first versions of all browsers. CSS is another example (invented around 1994 by Håkon Lie at CERN), receiving some support in IE in version 3, and Netscape in version 4 (June 1997).*

*So as you can see, there is usually a fairly sizable gap between a technology proposal release, and support for the technology in browsers. This does not matter so much these days, as most of the technologies involved (especially the ones featured in this book) have stabilized a lot in recent years, allowing the browsers to catch up.*

However, as new technologies were released, and more people got on the Web, it turned into a race for supremacy between the browser manufacturers, to provide the best support, and win over the largest audience share, with browser manufacturers even implementing proprietary functionality in their browsers, so web sites coded specifically for their browsers would have a chance of not working properly in their competitor's browsers. This period was termed "**The Browser Wars**".

In the early days of the Web, keeping up with what all the browsers were and weren't supporting was practically a full-time job in itself. What looked right and acted right on Netscape Navigator, for example, would look horrible on the AOL original proprietary browser, and what looked correct on Microsoft Internet Explorer looked insane on Mosaic.

These days, however, the "browser wars" are virtually nonexistent, with better standards compliance overall, a move away from proprietary technologies, and the browser market being dominated by two main manufacturers: Microsoft **Internet Explorer** (or **IE**), and **Netscape Navigator** (also known as **Netscape**, or **NN**).

# Browsers Today

As said above, IE, Netscape, and Opera dominate the browser market today. On average, the usage figures for web browsers are something like the following:

| Browser | Percentage Market Share |
|---|---|
| Internet Explorer 6.x | 38% |
| Internet Explorer 5.x | 50% |
| Internet Explorer 4.x and below | 2% |
| Netscape 6.x | 2% |
| Netscape 4.x and below | 6% |
| Opera 5/6 | 1% |
| All other browsers | 1% |

*Rough estimates of modern browser market share*

So the message here is quite clear – IE has most of the browser market, with Netscape having a much smaller but still noticeable amount (it is useful to note that Netscape 7 is now available, although it currently has a negligible market share), and Opera being the only other browser with higher than negligible figures.

Netscape and IE may dominate the browser market, but that doesn't stop developers from making new browsers. Opera 6.05, shown below, is free, as long as you are happy to have advertisements displayed on the banner – otherwise you need to pay and register. Touted as the "world's fastest browser," Opera supports tons of standards for the Web and is a much smaller download than its two giant competitors.

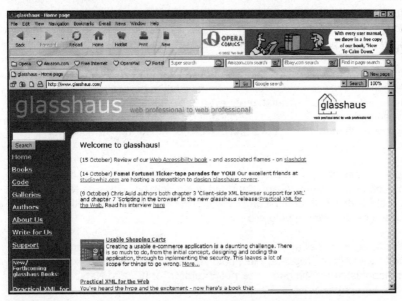

It is a good idea to check out the homepages of the major browsers regularly, for versioning updates, and bug fixes etc:

- http://www.microsoft.com/windows/ie/default.asp
- http://www.netscape.com
- http://www.opera.com

# A More Diverse Web

These days, browsing the Web is not just limited to desktop machines. There are many alternative devices available for surfing the net, including mobile phones, PDAs, and WebTV. This provides the web developer with even more of a challenge, if they want to support these devices (and their own specialized browsers) with their web sites – these devices don't have quite the power of a desktop PC, and often don't support the same web technologies, so you need to take measures such as making your site simple enough for the device to handle, or creating a special version of your site for the target device.

Let's have a quick look at a couple of examples of browsers for these kinds of devices.

### WebTV

WebTV is a fairly new technology allowing you to view the Web over a standard television, requiring nothing more than a special receiver box, and control peripherals (including keyboards and mice). There are various vendors selling this technology, for example, Microsoft's MSN TV (see *http://resourcecenter.msn.com/access/MSNTV/default.asp* for more details).

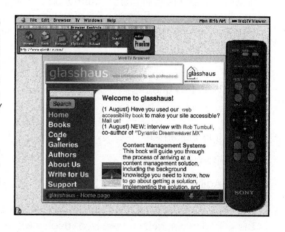

The WebTV Viewer seen below, developed by WebTV Networks, is a browser mocking another browser. It lets us browse our sites to see if they are WebTV-compatible.

### Mobile Phone Browsers

Mobile phones have come on in great leaps and bounds in the last couple of years, but are still inherently low power devices, hence their browsers can only display very simple sites. They often have their own markup language, which tends to be a really simple stripped-down language providing just the functionality you need to publish mobile-viewable content (for example, WAP-enabled phones use either WML or XHTML Basic – simplified XHTML – whereas the Japanese craze of iMode phones use cHTML, or compact HTML – a proprietary simplified version of HTML).

Here we can see a screenshot from the Nokia Mobile Internet Toolkit 3.1 (a mobile phone emulator – for more information, see *http://www.forum.nokia.com/main.html*).

# Web Career Opportunities

At the time of this writing, there are still plenty of jobs in the web-creative market. While companies aren't forming and hiring as frantically as in the late 1990s, and stock options aren't necessarily an attractive job benefit, talented people are still being actively sought for designing, building, and maintaining web sites. Like any career, the likelihood of your success depends not only on your talent but on your location, your gumption, and specialization.

## Web Creative Titles

Watching the Web grow and mature into a full-fledged industry all its own has been a fascinating experience, and watching how job titles and requirements change has been a captivating – and sometimes amusing – pastime. What started out as a field in which anyone who did anything about creating web pages was dubbed a webmaster (and some people still prefer this title), has split into various specialties and job titles to match.

Like the traditional print publishing world, the creative side of making web sites has split into roles much like its print editorial cousin. Now we see web design teams rather than webmasters who did everything, and these teams are made up of writers, editors, graphic artists, programmers, HTML experts, database designers, information architects, usability designers, and quality controllers. Additional team members consist of network specialists and system administrators; business sites include sales teams, business management experts, and marketing teams.

Here, we'll take a walk through the following typical job titles:

- Web Designer
- Web Developer
- Information Architect
- Content Engineer
- Artist

Note that the specific duties for these job titles are likely to vary slightly between organizations. The following diagram summarizes roughly where these roles fit into the development of an average web site:

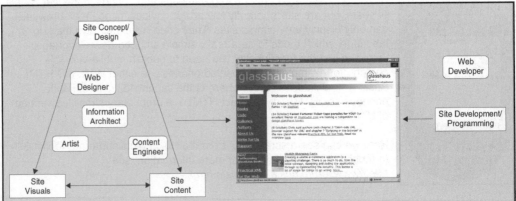

It is useful to think about the Site Concept/Design, the Site Content, and the Site Visuals as the three essential parts of producing a web site, up to the point where it actually gets coded and appears on the Web (the distance away from each point of the triangle of each job title indicates how much input they have on each part of the site's development, apart from the web developer of course, who has everything to do with the site coding, and limited, but sometimes essential input into the other tasks as a whole).

The Site Development/Programming tends to sit in its own reasonably separate box, although, through the course of creating a web site, the site design is often rethought numerous times, and various changes frequently fed back to the developer/programmer to implement. Although it would be great in an ideal world, it is very rare to see the site design at a completely rigid final stage, before its coding takes place (in fact, it is much better to give yourself scope and flexibility to allow change, as you never know when the clients will suddenly change their mind, or when a bug will be uncovered that requires a bit of redesigning to be done).

## Web Designer

"Web designer" is a title that has perhaps seen the most different meanings and definitions. At its simplest, it's someone who lays out web pages, much like a graphic designer lays out print pages in the traditional sense. What it's grown to mean on a larger scale is a team member who takes on the role of user-interface designing, perhaps writing pages to implement a design (or at least knowing HTML well enough that they know that their design can be implemented), and perhaps knowing some more advanced programming and scripting languages to help have power over the design.

To be a good web designer, you need the same core skills as a professional print graphic designer, as well as the basic proficiencies of a software interface designer. The design principles of creating a good-looking page are the same, both in print and electronically. However, designing web pages takes these skills one step further, as interface design skills are necessary to know how to best apply a smart design so that it works with the content and the technology behind implementing the design.

These days, it helps to know a good selection of software applications, many of which a graphic designer may already have skill in, such as Adobe Photoshop, Adobe Illustrator, Macromedia Freehand, as well as web-specific graphics applications such as Adobe Imageready or Macromedia Fireworks.

Next, knowing an HTML editor such as Macromedia Dreamweaver (by far the most popular), Microsoft FrontPage, or Adobe GoLive is crucial. To make yourself even more marketable, knowing HTML coding by hand is an advantage, as well as some more advanced techniques, such as JavaScript (see *Chapters 9* and *10* for more) and CSS (see *Chapter 8* for more).

## Web Developer

A term often coupled with "web design" is "web development." Generally though, the title of "web developer" holds more possible responsibility than that of "web designer": they are responsible for making sure the site is implemented correctly (either by coding it themselves, or by getting their team to do it), and they may also deal with business and overall planning aspects of a project. Since this role is so tied to that of designer, having a design background can be an added bonus if this is the role you're looking for.

As such, besides a feel for design, a web developer should have a more managerial background, along with advanced HTML knowledge, working knowledge of such technologies as JavaScript and CSS, as well as some knowledge of back-end programming languages (such as connecting databases to web sites).

In larger teams, this role can be split into roles such as "Project Managers", who make sure the project is managed properly and sufficiently on track, and "Developers" and "Web Programmers", who have less of a management insight, and mainly get stuck into the code. However, like any good team member, being able to work well under pressure, managing multiple elements of a project, and keeping open-minded and flexible while being productive, will take you further in these roles.

## Information Architect

When I was first handed a business card with the title "Information Architect" on it, I didn't have a clue what it meant. I was sure that the person who gave it to me just made it up because it sounded cool (which it did), but that it was a little over the top (which it was). Since then, though, the role of Information Architect has become a very real part of the web development process, and it's rare to find a web team without one. You will hear the term **information architecture** being rolled around the room when discussing site structure and organization.

An information architect is the person whose job is to decide upon a structure in which to present a site's content, and how the site's users will navigate that content. They are in charge of making sure that a site is well organized, accessible, and usable by potential site visitors, determine how to best lay a path for site growth and possible later design changes, and help to present this site plan and strategy to clients and the web design team at large. They seem to have input into most areas of the project at large.

The information architect very often is at the hub of a given project – they connect the web developers and designers, content producers, and managers. Knowing as much as possible about all of these roles is crucial. Without an information architect on board, the designer often works with the developer to cover this role.

## Content Engineer

Also know as Content Author/Designer/Developer/Manager, the content engineer is responsible for organizing the actual page content of the web site into how it should look, and putting it where it should be. In a larger team, it is sometimes split into two roles – a **content designer** plays the role of writer, and a **content developer** plays the role of editor, with the twist of having to know the boundaries and limitations of presenting text and images on the Web. Even today it is often the most overlooked part of the web process, and many otherwise well-designed sites suffer from poor content because of this.

Often, web site copy is written by people in the marketing department, especially if the site is sales-oriented. At other times, in many smaller teams, a specialized content person isn't titled as such, and the web designer or developer takes on the role of content creation. If that's the case, content developers may be contracted in an editorial role to assist the team to finish work, but may not be a part of the team through the entire process.

Content designers and developers not only work on the bulk of the body content after the site is designed, but work with the information architect in determining consistent site area names, words on menus that help with navigation, site map and help file wording, and so on.

Having a design background doesn't make someone a good writer, but knowing the concepts of web design and the way that people use and navigate the Web does help in content design and development. People read differently on screen, and sentence structure and story structure must accommodate shorter pages and links within text.

### Artist

The role of "artist" is another that can vary depending on the talents of the individual and the needs of the organization they work for. As in traditional media, an artist can be a freelancer hired to create specific pieces of artwork or illustration. Alternatively, they may not only create these illustrations but also implement them in a web design or page mock-ups, or go as far as creating presentations in an animation application like Flash.

# Summary

A lot has happened in the world of the Internet and the Web since its inception. The Web may take different faces these days, such as showing up on televisions and mobile phones, but it is still the Web: a collection of documents trillions strong, which needs people like you to make them well-designed and coded and therefore easy and pleasant to use by the intended audience.

There's no lack of web design and development job opportunities out there for those of us who want to seek them out. While it's not as easy to become an instant millionaire as it once was (and most likely will never be again), with solid training and specialization, open-mindedness and a willingness to continue to learn new technologies and methodologies, a web career is a solid one.

Throughout the rest of the book, we'll take this high-level overview of the area into much more depth, and learn how to design great web sites, use the technologies mentioned to implement them, get them up on the Web for all to see, and learn how to maintain them.

## Acronyms and Terms

The web world, like any technology area, is filled with acronyms and terms that you'll hear thrown around in the coffee room, in online user groups, in classes you take to further your career, and in this book. Here we list a few of the most important ones to get you started.

Note that some terms have found new meanings over the years, probably because we've all been using the acronyms instead of the words for so long. If the acronym has multiple interpretations, I've included them here.

Most of the acronyms are pronounced by saying each letter one after the other, for example HTTP is pronounced *atche tee tee pee*. However, if the acronym has a different pronunciation, I've included that in parentheses.

### ASCII (*azz key*)

Acronym for **American Standard Code for Information Interchange** – it basically refers to simple plain text content on your computer with absolutely no formatting. Think of Apple's Simple Text on a Mac, or Microsoft Notepad on a Windows PC – each comes with your respective operating system.

### Browser

The software on our device (be it a desktop PC or a mobile phone) that lets us view web pages. They are also often referred to as **client software** and **user agents**. We have already seen numerous examples of browsers in this chapter.

### Client

A client in the Internet world refers to a combination of the computer and software that allow us to retrieve various types of information from the Internet and the Web. In effect, a client exists to make use of a service, such as that provided by a web server.

So, web browsers are web clients, e-mail software packages are e-mail clients, and FTP sites are, as you might guess, FTP clients. Our experience as web users depends on the abilities of each individual client's abilities to receive and interpret the information requested.

Client software allows you to access and exchange files of a particular format.

### CSS

Acronym for **Cascading Style Sheets**. This is a technology that gives more control over the visual appearance of a web page and its contents. CSS gives designers power over such things as the size of typefaces, what kinds of fonts will be used, the position of paragraphs and other page elements on the page (HTML can do many of these kinds of tasks, but there are several distinct advantages to doing it with CSS instead – see *Chapter 8* for more details).

### DOM

Acronym for **Document Object Model**. Basically, this is a method of representing a markup document (such as HTML or XML) in a tree-like structure. You can then manipulate the branches of the tree (called **Nodes** in DOM-speak) using JavaScript, to do things such as adding or deleting elements from a markup document, or changing the values of the information contained within an HTML element.

**DHTML**
Acronym for **Dynamic HyperText Markup Language**. This is a popular term used to collectively describe HTML, CSS, JavaScript, and the DOM as a set of technologies for building dynamic, styled web pages.

**FAQ** (*eff a que* or *fack*)
Acronym for **Frequently Asked Questions**. It usually consists of a list of questions and answers that are most often asked about a site, a product, a file, etc. Creating an FAQ for your site or product saves your maintenance team time, since they won't have to spend work time replying to the same question dozens of times.

**FTP**
Acronym for **File Transfer Protocol**. This protocol is used to send and receive files from a server without interpretation – there is no reading or display of the file like in a browser, just sending or receiving the information. This protocol is used to upload your site to the Web, when putting your site "live". For more on FTP, see *Chapter 13*.

**GIF** (*giff* with a hard "g" or *jiff* – the debate never ends about its pronunciation)
Acronym for **Graphics Interchange Format**. This is an image compression format for flat-color images (not so good for handling photographs). See *Chapter 5* for more information about this and other graphics formats.

**GUI** (*gooey*)
Acronym for **Graphical User Interface**. When you are using a software application featuring icons and windows and the like (for example, Microsoft Windows), this is the part of the program that you directly interact with.

**HTML**
Acronym for **HyperText Markup Language**. This is the language that most web pages are written in. It contains special tags that determine the presentation of web information in our browsers. HTML is known as "the language of the Web", so is touched upon throughout the book, but we'll be looking at it most extensively in *Chapters 2 and 4*.

**HTTP**
Acronym for **HyperText Transport Protocol**. This protocol controls the transmission of web page information over the Internet. It basically defines how web clients and their servers should communicate.

**IT**
Acronym for **Information Technology**. IT covers most of the spectrum of computer technology and associated jobs: not only the world of web development/design, but also back-end technology for managing networks, desktop software application development, management of computer resources for companies, and computer support for end users, etc.

### Linux (*Lyn ucks*)

Linux is what is termed a UNIX-clone (see UNIX, later). It is a multi-user network-oriented operating system, originally developed by Finish-born developer **Linus Torvalds**. His aim was a free, open source alternative to proprietary UNIX, that could be installed on just about any PC you wanted. This work has now been taken up by thousands of other professional programmers around the world as a collaborative effort, and Linux can run on a wide range of devices, from handhelds to Mainframes. A number of clean and interactive GUIs exist to help you work with your Linux system in the same way as you would with a Mac or Windows PC.

### JavaScript

JavaScript is a scripting language – it allows you to insert chunks of script into HTML documents that allow more complicated functionality to be implemented than what is normally available with plain HTML, such as buttons that change as you roll your mouse pointer over them, and validation of the information users enter into forms on your site (for example, making sure that they have entered a valid e-mail address into the e-mail address textbox.) See *Chapters 9* and *10* for more on using JavaScript.

### JPEG (*jay peg*)

Acronym for **Joint Photographic Expert Group**. This method of storing an image in digital format is best used for photographs on the Web. See *Chapter 5* for more information about this and other graphics formats.

### MacOS X (*Oh-ess Ten*)

OS X is the newest operating system available for the Mac family of personal computers, and is growing in popularity. Like Linux, it is a UNIX operating system, and this is seen as one of its key selling points. Macs tend to be favored more by the design community, because they are very good at handling graphics. We will see more mentions of Macs (as well as PCs) as we traverse this book.

### OASIS

OASIS, like the W3C, is a non-profit organization dedicated to the maintenance and promotion of web standards. However, the standards they deal with are specifically associated with e-business. For more information, visit their web site at *http://www.oasis-open.org/*.

### Open Source

Open source is a term used to describe software that is released on a public license, and is fully modifiable/customizable. So, if you have the technical know-how, you can add the features you desire, and fix any bugs you find, without having to wait for a new version to come out. Because of this it has a reputation for reliability and security that commercial software often lacks, although some people are often intimidated by the fact that no commercial body exists to officially support it.

### PNG (*ping* or *pee en jee*)

Acronym for **Portable Network Graphics**. This is an alternative image compression format for both flat color and photographic images. While its compression and flexibility is impressive, it isn't as well supported by browsers as JPG or GIF images. *See Chapter 5* for more information about this and other graphics formats.

## Protocol
The specification of data communication methods, or how pieces of data are sent over a network or Internet connection – some protocol methods, such as TCP/IP, make sure that information is sent safely, and "reassembled" in the correct order for use on the receiving end.

## Server
Servers are the computers "out there" that provide the services that clients make use of (see "*Clients*".) For example, when we type a URL into our web browser, we are requesting that a server sends us a web page (of set of web pages) to use.

## SGML
Acronym for **Standard Generalized Markup Language**. This is a very complicated syntax for defining languages for marking up documents – a meta language if you like (a language that describes languages). It is the language that HTML and XML were derived from.

## TCP/IP
Acronym for **Transmission Control Protocol/Internet Protocol**. As we saw earlier, this set of protocols was developed by Vint Cerf and Bob Khan for controlling the transmission of data (as packets) over the Internet.

## UI
Acronym for **User Interface**. When you are using a software application, this is the part of the program that you directly interact with, be it a pretty graphical program with icons and windows (such as Microsoft Windows), or a simpler text-based system (such as DOS).

## UNIX (*yoo nix*)
Originally, UNIX was an operating system developed by **AT&T** in the early 1970's and does not actually exist anymore. The word 'UNIX' is now used to refer to a family of operating systems, which are descended from it. They are very popular in the business world for their power, flexibility, and cast-iron stability. For the Web, the only varieties you are ever likely to encounter, apart from Mac OS X and Linux, are **Solaris**, from **Sun Microsystems**, and **FreeBSD** (an open source initiative, similar to Linux). Generally, UNIX operating systems are fairly rare as desktop systems, because they are designed with network use in mind. Icon-driven GUIs do exist for virtually all of them, however.

## URL (*yoo are ell or earl*)
Acronym for **Uniform Resource Locator**. This is the address of a document on the Internet, and the information you type into your browser's address bar to get you to a web page (starting with *http://, ftp://,* etc.).

## WaSP
Acronym for the **Web Standards Project**. This is a non-profit coalition that fights for widespread adoption of web standards (such as those kept by the W3C), to make for a better developed, more future-proof Web. They do this by spreading the principles of good practice and design among their peers, browser manufacturers, and authoring tool makers. Go to their site at *http://www.webstandards.org* for more information.

### W3C

Short term for **World Wide Web Consortium**. This is a non-profit organization made up of industry experts (including **Tim Berners-Lee**) who maintain recommended standards for web site and technology development. The W3C can be found at *http://www.w3c.org*. This is a great site to query when looking into web standards, particularly when looking into the technology specifications themselves.

### Windows

You must have seen at least one version of Microsoft Windows – it is, without doubt, the most widely distributed client operating system in the world, and has become fairly ubiquitous with desktop PCs at home, and in most work situations (note however, that this is just on PCs – Mac users will be familiar with MacOS, see MacOS X.)

### WWW or W3

Short term for **World Wide Web**.

### XHTML

Acronym for **Extensible HyperText Markup Language**. XHTML is simply a reformulation of HTML as an XML vocabulary. This allows developers to apply all the advantages of XML (see below) to HTML, leading to more efficient, better coded, more versatile HTML.

### XML

Acronym for **Extensible Markup Language**. It is a language derived from SGML, specifically for marking up web documents. At first glance, XML is similar to HTML; however, using XML, you can make up your own markup languages, termed **XML Vocabularies**. There are many advantages of XML – XML deals only with the content of a document, and not its presentation, so it is very useful as an easily exchanged (across platforms and languages), easily styled data format. XML also has strict rules to follow when writing it, so promotes the coding of better-quality markup, leading to less errors, and smaller, more efficient documents. XML support in browsers is starting to become widespread, but it still a way off that available for HTML. For more discussion on XML, see *Chapter 4*.

The Web and How It Works

# 2

- Theory of HTML - how it works

- Tutorial: creating a basic page

- Adding images and hyperlinks

**Author: Crystal Waters**

# Basic HTML

Learning **HTML** (**HyperText Markup Language**) these days may seem trivial, and perhaps unnecessary, considering how far WYSIWYG web layout programs and HTML editors have come. The whole reason these web-making programs are so popular is that they can do complex stuff for us, so we (in *theory*) don't need to know a lick of HTML, nor do we have to ever expose ourselves to it if we don't want to. Why go to the trouble of learning how to write HTML if our program will do it for us?

Well, while it may be appropriate to say, "Because we said so!" in a very stern voice, it is more appropriate to say that you will be a better, more well-rounded designer because of learning it. You'll find that editing the HTML within your documents gives you much more control over a page's look, and you won't have to just stick to basic template designs from editors. You'll know your product better, you'll more easily understand the challenges and limitations of creating pages, and you'll be able to troubleshoot your work.

*You may also have heard of **XHTML (Extensible HyperText Markup Language)**, which is a reformulation of HTML as an XML vocabulary), which has now become the standard recommendation for creating web pages. Some would say that as a web designer, you should only learn XHTML, and leave HTML behind. However, knowing HTML principles and why it is structured the way it is gives you a glimpse of where we're trying to go with new standards. You will also run into many pages based on HTML for some time to come, so if you find yourself working on redesigns or site fixes, you'll want to at least know in general what it is you're looking at and working with. For these reasons, we won't discuss XHTML until Chapter 4.*

The HTML we will be building in this chapter will be markup at its simplest, in order to give you a feel for basic page structure. You don't need any expensive software: a simple text editor, such as Microsoft Notepad or Simple Text on the Mac, will do the trick. You'll also need a browser handy to be able to view the results of your work. You don't need to run out and take intensive courses in learning every HTML tag (that's what reference books are for), but I do recommend trying out these rudimentary lessons if you've never done any coding by hand.

# The Theory of HTML

Hypertext, as we learned in *Chapter 1*, was a concept introduced in order for researchers to share related documents via links that connected a word or phrase in one document to another document. That document can then go on to link to other documents, or link back to the original document – the possibilities are endless.

Creating links either with a program or by hand is only one part of what makes up a structure of a web page. For everyone to be able to view web sites, we must be presented with a common format so that all platforms, operating systems, and browsers can view the same information in the same way (or as similar as possible).

The goal in making the Web work the way it was intended is to make all information portable, viewable, and navigable among different systems, current ones and those developed in the future. The most basic level of document commonality is **ASCII** or **plain text**. It is guaranteed to be viewable on all platforms, from high-end super fast computers with monitors that support millions of colors, to small cell phone LCD screens.

Text by itself, while it can contain important content, isn't easily navigable, and accessing masses of text without structure can be unwieldy and tedious. This is where HTML comes in: as well as being a **plain text document**, it enhances text and the presentation of text and images through the use of special sequences of characters, as we will see shortly.

HTML and the standards of its structure (which are always being challenged, changed, and debated) are core to the Web and how it appears. Why is it challenged? Because, as browser manufacturers continue to battle out the war for supremacy, each browser needs to have something unique so that users can tell it apart from the others. Also, designers are continually pushing coding to its limits and asking for more and more features. Developers of new types of media want browsers to support their media. As a new feature is developed, it takes time for the various committees and browser companies to all agree on what becomes a "standard" – something that all browsers, ideally, will then support and be able to display on the majority of systems. Browser manufacturers are prone to introducing the new features before they are standardized, sometimes leading to features that are at variance with the standards. As web professionals, we are kept very much on our toes!

## Basic Rules of HTML

Before we get stuck in to creating an HTML page, we need to look at a few of the concepts and rules of HTML. At its most basic, HTML uses **tags** to mark up the text of a web page. These tags often surround some textual content and change its meaning or appearance; others give information about the page and its structure and contents.

The tags themselves come in two types: **opening tags** and **closing tags**. Opening tags consist of a sequence of characters that indicate the meaning of the tag, surrounded by angle brackets. For example, `<p>` is the opening tag that describes a paragraph. Closing tags are very similar, but contain a forward slash character (/). For example, the closing tag for a paragraph is `</p>`. This pair of opening and closing tags is used to surround text that should be set aside as a separate paragraph. For example:

```
<p>This is a new paragraph.</p>
<p>This is another paragraph.</p>
```

This complete construct (opening tag, text, and closing tag) is usually called an **element**.

In some cases, an element won't have any content. For example, if we want to specify a line break in the document, we use the tag `<br>`. Rather than open and close the tag without any content (`<br></br>`), we can use a **self-closing tag** (`<br />`). This tag has a forward slash before the final closing angle bracket.

*Note that often in HTML, you'll see tags that aren't closed. For example, you'll see paragraphs separated by single `<p>` tags, and line breaks specified by a single `<br>` tag. While this isn't precisely wrong, it is good practice to always close your tags, as we'll see in Chapter 4.*

Another concept that you need to know is that of **attributes**. An attribute is an addition to the element, to give the browser more information about it. It's specified using the **attribute name** followed by an equals sign and an **attribute value** within the opening tag of an element. For example, let's add the `align` attribute to our paragraphs. This tells the browser to what side of the browser window the text should be aligned:

```
<p align="left">This is a new paragraph.</p>
<p align="right">This is another paragraph.</p>
```

Note that HTML tags and attributes can be written using lowercase or uppercase letters – it's up to you. When hand coding in a simple text editor, it may be easier to use uppercase letters to help visually differentiate the text from the tags. However, sometimes HTML editors automatically color-code tags on your screen, or otherwise differentiate them from the text for you.

In some versions of XHTML, which you'll study more in *Chapter 4*, the case of tags does matter: all tags must be lowercase. For this reason, in this book, we will use lowercase tags throughout.

HTML coding is fairly easy to learn, because many of the tags are based on English words that most of us know, and therefore the tag meaning can usually be figured out or remembered easily. For example, the opening bold tag is `<b>` and the opening image tag is `<img>`.

As you might have guessed from the last paragraph, some tags specify how text should appear in the browser (bold or italic, for example). Others, such as the paragraph `<p>`, specify what the text *is* (paragraph or heading, for example). We'll be discussing this distinction further later in the chapter.

There are some HTML tags that appear in nearly every HTML document to give it structure. They tell the web browser that:

● The contained document is a web page (the `<html>` tag)

● The contained information is about the document rather than content (the `<head>` tag).

● The contained information is the content of the page to be displayed by the browser (the `<body>` tag).

We'll look in detail at these tags in the next section where we create a hand-coded web page.

# Creating a Basic Page

Let's hand code a simple page in our text editor. Open your text editor and type in:

```
<html>
</html>
```

As we mentioned above, these are the tags that hold the entire web page.

Next, add:

```
<html>
<head>
</head>
</html>
```

*It's a good habit to always write the opening and closing tags of an element before adding the content. That way, you can't accidentally forget to add a closing tag.*

The `<head>` element is where the title and other page information go. Information within the opening and closing `<head>` tags generally doesn't display within the web page since it mainly contains **metadata** – information that *describes* the page rather than adds to the content or appearance of the page.

Now we'll type in our first content, although it doesn't usually appear within the window of the browser. The `<title>` tag is used to specify the title of the document, and most browsers put this title up in the title bar of your browser (the bar at the very top of the browser window). Often overlooked in its significance, the wording within your title is key to site navigation and getting people back to your site. When someone bookmarks a page or adds it to their *Favorites* list, it's the title information – or whatever you type between the opening tag `<title>` and closing tag `</title>` – that will appear in this list.

In your editor, add:

```
<html>
<head>
<title>Practice Code</title>
</head>
</html>
```

Be sure to include the closing tag with its slash, so your browser will know where the `<title>` tag ends.

## Meaningful Titles

There are a few reasons to take some time to compose page `<title>` elements. When creating a personal site, for example, many people simply title a page "My Site", "My Home Page", "Welcome", or "Home". Besides being a sure sign of an unprofessional page, these kinds of vague titles don't differentiate your page from hundreds of thousands of other pages with the same name.

Let's say your company name is Carmen's Carpets. It would make sense to title the home page "Carmen's Carpets" or "Carmen's Carpets Home" – something fairly simple and descriptive. When someone bookmarks this page, what you write in the title is the information that shows up in their *Bookmarks* or *Favorites* list, and you want it to make sense when they come back to it.

If you want people to be able to use your page titles for navigation, be sure to write meaningful titles for interior pages that describe their content or content categories. Rather than titling every page in your site "Carmen's Carpets," add a bit more descriptive information. Try "Carmen's Carpets - About Us" or "Carmen's Carpets > Area Rugs > Hooked Rugs", or other titles that may give the visitor a better idea of what the page is about, and where they are in the layout of the site.

Here's a sample of a path I've taken through the *REI.com* site. Some of the titles (such as "*REI.com: Paddling on Sale*") give me an idea of where I am, both in content and in relation to the home page, so if I bookmarked these pages, I could go back to them later and have an idea of where I'd end up. Other titles don't make sense at all. This could be because the page developer didn't provide a title, or the page could be dynamically generated (from a search or other back-end database system) in which case its title may be the dynamically generated URL.

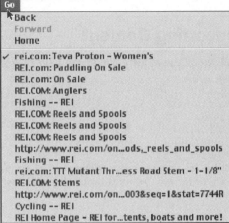
*A history list showing title information.*

## Saving the Document

At this point, let's save the document in whatever way your editor application saves.

It's important to save your site documents in a designated folder, so you know where to find them, so set up such a folder now. Later on, you may need to add folders inside this folder to contain images or other types of files that your site uses. When you come to make your site live (so it can be seen by the world at large), the folder structure will be duplicated on your server (discussed in detail in *Chapter 13*).

Give the document a simple name, like `index.htm` or `index.html`. Your web pages need either one of two these extensions (`.htm` or `.html`) for your browser to recognize them as HTML pages. In this book, we'll be sticking with `.html` extensions.

> *If you are using a word processor for your hand coding, be sure to "Save As Text" or you will end up with proprietary word processing code in your document and it may not work in your browser. This is one advantage that a simple text editor has over a word processor. Some word processors, like Microsoft Word, have an option to "Save As HTML". Don't use this, because it will turn the tags you've just typed in into content.*

Now open your file, `index.html`, by double-clicking on it or opening it through the web browser. It's not much to look at yet, but there's the title information you included.

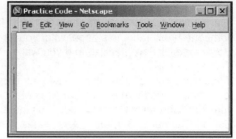

*The index.html page, containing just the title.*

## Inserting Content

We've only inserted a title so far. Let's now insert some content so that we can see how it looks in our page.

```
<html>
<head>
<title>Practice Code</title>
</head>
<body>
This is sample body content for my practice web site. This will show up in my
web page and be available for all to see.
</body>
</html>
```

First, type in the `<body>` and `</body>` tags. Then, on a new line between them, type in a couple of sentences. It's good practice to visually keep the tag separated from content by using separate lines. Save your document.

Open the document again in your browser. You should now see your page content appear, something like this:

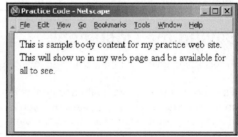

*The index.html page, now containing body content.*

## Adding Structure to Content

Type in two more paragraphs to your HTML page so that we'll have some text to work with and format. It doesn't matter what you type. There are a couple of returns between paragraphs to separate them:

```
<html>
<head>
<title>Practice Code</title>
</head>
<body>
This is sample body content for my practice web site. This will show up in my
web page and be available for all to see.
```

```
Hypertext, as we learned in Chapter 1, was a concept introduced in order for
researchers to share related documents via links that connected a word or phrase
in one document to another document. That document can then go on to link to
other documents, or link back to the original document &mdash; the possibilities
are endless.

Creating links either with a program or by hand is only one part of what makes
up a structure of a web page. For everyone to be able to view web sites, we must
be presented with a common format so that all platforms, operating systems, and
browsers can view the same information in the same way (or as similar as
possible).
</body>
</html>
```

Save the document `index.html` and take a look at it in your browser again. Without any HTML formatting, all of the text just runs together because the browser hasn't been instructed by HTML syntax about where to start a new paragraph or otherwise break up text. The browser ignores all line breaks and space we added between paragraphs in the HTML itself.

Also notice, about halfway down the text in the browser, the appearance of a large dash (an em-dash, —). If you look at the appropriate point in the code above, you'll see that this was created by the following sequence of characters: `&mdash;`. This was used because the em-dash is not part of basic ASCII text, so cannot appear in the text file as is. Instead, the sequence `&mdash;` is used, which the browser interprets as an em-dash.

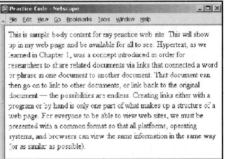

Such sequences (called **character entities**) are used for many other special characters. Ones that you may often come across are `&lt;` used for the < character and `&gt;` used for the > character. Although the < and > characters are part of ASCII text, using them in text would confuse the browser, since they are used to surround tags. Thus, if you want either character to appear on your page, you must use the `&lt;` and `&gt;` sequences of characters in your HTML code.

*The index.html page, with extra content added*

Here's our first formatting code put to use. The paragraph tags should be typed in around each separate paragraph.

```
<html>
<head>
<title>Practice Code</title>
</head>
<body>
<p>
This is sample body content for my practice web site. This will show up in my
web page and be available for all to see.
</p>
<p>
Hypertext, as we learned in Chapter 1, was a concept introduced in order for
researchers to share related documents via links that connected a word or phrase
in one document to another document. That document can then go on to link to
other documents, or link back to the original document &mdash; the possibilities
are endless.
```

```
</p>
<p>
Creating links either with a program or by hand is only one part of what makes
up a structure of a web page. For everyone to be able to view web sites, we must
be presented with a common format so that all platforms, operating systems, and
browsers can view the same information in the same way (or as similar as
possible).
</p>
</body>
</html>
```

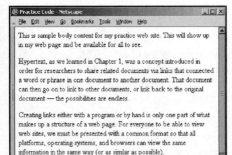

Save the page and view it in your browser.

Note the three distinct paragraphs that the addition of the `<p>` tags has caused.

*The index.html page, with added paragraph tags.*

Now let's add another formatting tag, the `<blockquote>`, around one of the paragraphs. This tag is used to format large blocks of text that is quoted verbatim. Take out the paragraph tags for the second paragraph: the `<blockquote>` tags will take care of spacing. Remember to include both a opening and closing tag.

```
<html>
<head>
<title>Practice Code</title>
</head>
<body>
<p>
This is sample body content for my practice web site. This will show up in my
web page and be available for all to see.
</p>
<blockquote>
Hypertext, as we learned in Chapter 1, was a concept introduced in order for
researchers to share related documents via links that connected a word or phrase
in one document to another document. That document can then go on to link to
other documents, or link back to the original document &mdash; the possibilities
are endless.
</blockquote>
<p>
Creating links either with a program or by hand is only one part of what makes
up a structure of a web page. For everyone to be able to view web sites, we must
be presented with a common format so that all platforms, operating systems, and
browsers can view the same information in the same way (or as similar as
possible).
</p>
</body>
</html>
```

Save and view in your browser.

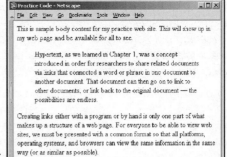

*The index.html page, with added blockquote tag.*

# Formatting Content

You've already had some experience of formatting paragraphs; now let's format a word or set of words. We're going to make the word "Hypertext" in the second paragraph bold, and the first part of the first sentence in the third paragraph italic. To do this, we use the `<strong>` and `<em>` tags.

```
<html>
<head>
<title>Practice Code</title>
</head>
<body>
<p>
This is sample body content for my practice web site. This will show up in my
web page and be available for all to see.
</p>
<blockquote>
<strong>Hypertext</strong>, as we learned in Chapter 1, was a concept introduced
in order for researchers to share related documents via links that connected a
word or phrase in one document to another document. That document can then go on
to link to other documents, or link back to the original document &mdash; the
possibilities are endless.
</blockquote>
<p>
<em>Creating links either with a program or by hand is only one part of what
makes up a structure of a web page.</em> For everyone to be able to view web
sites, we must be presented with a common format so that all platforms,
operating systems, and browsers can view the same information in the same way
(or as similar as possible).
</p>
</body>
</html>
```

The resulting bold and italic text are shown opposite.

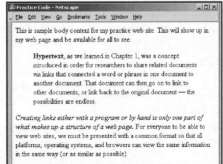

*The index.html page, with added strong and em tags.*

Now we're going to add a few more content formatting tags to the document.

```
<html>
<head>
<title>Practice Code</title>
</head>
<body>
<p>
This is <span style="color:#336699;">sample body content</span> for my practice
web site. <span style="font-size=x-large;">This will show up</span> in my web
page and be available for all to see.
</p>
<blockquote>
<strong>Hypertext</strong>, as we learned in Chapter 1, was a concept introduced
in order for researchers to share related documents via links that connected a
word or phrase in one document to another document. That document can then go on
to link to other documents, or link back to the original document &mdash; the
possibilities are endless.
</blockquote>
<p style="text-align=right;">
<em>Creating links either with a program or by hand is only one part of what
makes up a structure of a web page.</em> For everyone to be able to view web
sites, we must be presented with a common format so that all platforms,
operating systems, and browsers can view the same information in the same way
(or as similar as possible).
</p>
</body>
</html>
```

Note that the values specified for all attributes are within quotes. While most browsers will forgive you if you forget the quote marks, it's good practice to put them in to guarantee compatibility and accessibility.

In this pass through the document, we've added two <span> tags. These tags are used to surround a piece of text within a line of text that we can then manipulate in some way. In this case we use style attributes to change the color and size of the pieces of text. The values of these style attributes may look a little strange – they are inline CSS properties. Don't worry about these now, as we will make sense of these in *Chapter 8* on CSS.

We also added a style attribute to the final <p> tag. We use this attribute to make the paragraph right-aligned on the web page.

Here are the results of adding these tags and attributes.

Note that there are alternative ways to achieve these effects, in particular using `<font>` tags and the `align` attribute of `<p>`. However, the `<font>` element is deprecated, which basically means it is being phased out. Using the `style` attribute is a much more up-to-date, professional technique.

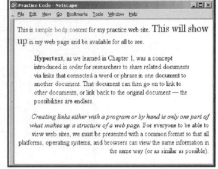

The index.html page, with added style attributes.

## Using Dreamweaver MX

Now that we've gone through the hard work of creating a web page by hand, let's see an example of what an HTML editor can create for you.

Launch Dreamweaver MX and choose *New* from the *File* menu. This launches the *New Document* dialog shown on the right. For now, we'll just pick *Basic Page* from the *Category* menu, and *HTML* from the *Basic Page* menu. Then click *Create*.

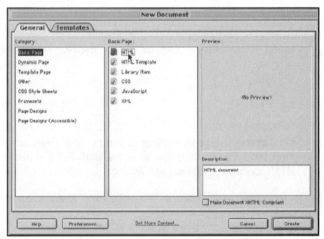

The Dreamweaver MX New Document dialog.

A new HTML document will be created for you to edit. Dreamweaver actually has three different ways for you to view this page. In *Code View*, you can see the HTML code: the tags and the content. In *Design View*, you see the page more or less as it would be seen on the browser. The final view allows you to see both *Code View* and *Design View* at the same time, by splitting the window into two panes.

You can toggle between these views of the page by clicking on the three buttons above and to the left of the viewing window. For now, to see the tags that are automatically created in Dreamweaver, click on the *Show Code View* button.

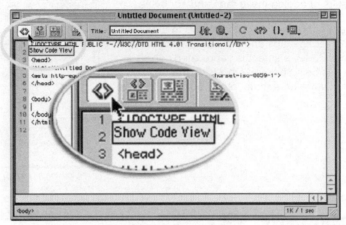

*The Dreamweaver MX Code View*

You should see the HTML below:

```
<!DOCTYPE HTML PUBLIC "-//W3C//DTD HTML 4.01 Transitional//EN">
<html>
<head>
<title>Untitled Document</title>
<meta http-equiv="Content-Type" content="text/html; charset=iso-8859-1">
</head>
<body>

</body>
</html>
```

Most of this should be familiar to you by now. There are just two lines that we have not yet discussed. The first line specifies the **DOCTYPE** – this gives more information about the type of HTML document that we are writing:

```
<!DOCTYPE HTML PUBLIC "-//W3C//DTD HTML 4.01 Transitional//EN">
```

There are actually three types of HTML document we could be writing, depending on what tags we want to use – Strict, Transitional, and Frameset. Each of these is specified by a **DTD** (**Document Type Definition**), which explains in full which tags can be used. The DOCTYPE instruction tells the browser which of these DTDs we expect the document to follow. You'll see more about this for XHTML in *Chapter 4* and a full discussion in *Chapter 12*. For now, all you need to know is what this looks like – it should appear at the top of each of your pages.

The other line is the following:

```
<meta http-equiv="Content-Type" content="text/html; charset=iso-8859-1">
```

This line is in the head of the document, so it describes the document rather than the content of the page. The `<meta>` tag is used to provide many different types of information about the document, but in this case it is explaining what character set the page uses, that is what set of characters are used to write the page.

# Structure vs. Presentation

While you might think from our previous hand-coded example that the purpose of HTML is to be able to make text better looking and more enticing than just plain text, its purpose from the beginning was actually to logically describe the **structure** and **meaning** of the information on a page so that browsers could then interpret the pages and give us its content in a logically designed way. We've already hinted at this division between tags for structure and tags for presentation in our earlier aside about the bold `<b>`, italic `<i>`, strong `<strong>`, and emphasis `<em>` tags. In fact, of the tags we've mentioned so far, `<p>`, `<blockquote>`, `<strong>`, and `<em>` define the structure and meaning of the content, while `<b>`, `<i>`, and `<font>` describe its presentation.

While the structural tags do tend to change the look of the text, these tags describe what the tagged text represents in function and meaning, and not a particular "look" or design. For example, a line tagged as a "heading" is meant to be a heading, not necessarily to have a particular font size or boldness. Within the HTML confines, the tags `<h1>`, `<h2>`, `<h3>`, `<h4>`, `<h5>`, and `<h6>` each describe levels of headers, with `<h1>` being the most important, or highest level, and `<h6>` being the least important, or lowest level. The browser usually interprets this level of significance by giving headings of higher significance a larger font size.

Let's add some headings and another paragraph to our example hand-coded page, `index.html`.

```
<html>
<head>
<title>Practice Code</title>
</head>
<body>
<h1>Introduction to Page Building</h1>
<p>
This is <span style="color=#336699;">sample body content</span> for my practice
web site. <span style="font-size=x-large;">This will show up</span> in my web
page and be available for all to see.
</p>
<h2>Simple Formatting Techniques</h2>
<blockquote>
<strong>Hypertext</strong>, as we learned in Chapter 1, was a concept introduced
in order for researchers to share related documents via links that connected a
word or phrase in one document to another document. That document can then go on
to link to other documents, or link back to the original document &mdash; the
possibilities are endless.
</blockquote>
<h3>Concept of Hyperlinking</h3>
<p style="text-align=right;">
<em>Creating links either with a program or by hand is only one part of what
makes up a structure of a web page.</em> For everyone to be able to view web
sites, we must be presented with a common format so that all platforms,
operating systems, and browsers can view the same information in the same way
(or as similar as possible).
</p>
<h1>The Next Step in Formatting</h1>
<p>
```

```
    While you might think from our previous hand coded example that the purpose of
    HTML is to be able to make text better looking and more enticing than just plain
    text, its purpose from the beginning was actually to logically describe the
    structure and meaning of the information on a page so that browsers could then
    interpret the pages and give us its content in a logically designed way.
    </p>
    </body>
    </html>
```

Here are the results of three levels of heading tags.

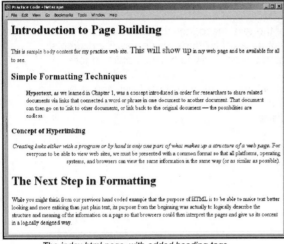

*The index.html page, with added heading tags.*

The easiest way to describe the significance of HTML "meaning" versus the visual changes the heading tags give to text, is to consider how **screen readers** (those programs that people with visual impairments use to access a web page) use the tags for easier navigation.

A sighted user is able to scan a page visually, and see headlines and subheadings that cue them to points on a page at which new sections begin and end. However, because a person with a visual impairment may not be able to differentiate these subheadings from the main body text visually, on improperly structured HTML pages they are forced to make the screen reader read the entire text out loud before they can find what they may (or may not) have been looking for within the page.

This might be tolerable if web pages were all short, but unfortunately, that's not the case. Long pages of text can easily become a frustrating frontier to visitors relying on screen readers or those using text browsers or low visual browsers, such as a LCD screen on a cell phone. Imagine reading this book if there were no headlines or subheadings, and all of the text ran from one paragraph to another without a break – what if you had to read it this way and you wanted to find out if any information within a chapter might be of interest?

If you use HTML well, you can save your audience such frustration. Screen readers generally take advantage of heading tags by giving the users who are visually impaired the option of an overview of the page structure. By directing the screen reader to read just the `<h1>` headings, for example, the users are able to scan the page for sections they may be interested in reading. If the other heading tags are used, then within a section, subsections can be scanned for an even more precise reading choice. If the users don't find a headline compelling after it is read aloud, they can instruct the screen reader to skip ahead to the next heading.

# Adding an Image

Text pages would be very boring if they only contained text, so let's have a look at adding images to the page.

In keeping with general site structure, before we add an image, it's a good idea to set up an *images* folder within the site folder. With one page and one image that may seem like overkill, but when you start getting into multiple pages that each have multiple images, you'll find it necessary to organize images separately if only to keep your sanity intact when you're trying to find your files! Once you've got the folder set up within your site folder, add an image to the folder to use as a sample. Here we're using a JPEG image called `jennie.jpg`.

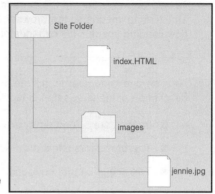

Folder structure of your practice site.

We then add the `<img>` tag to our `index.html` page, which tells the browser to find the image file and insert it into the page. (Note that we've only given the first few lines of the page here since the rest of the page stays the same as before.)

```
<html>
<head>
<title>Practice Code</title>
</head>
<body>
<h1>Introduction to Page Building</h1>
<img src="images/jennie.jpg">
<p>
This is <span style="color=#336699;">sample body content</span> for my practice
web site. <span style="text-size=x-large;">This will show up</span> in my web
page and be available for all to see.
</p>
```

The simplest way to use the `<img>` tag installs an image right where you insert it in the HTML, and it will displace the text below it. The syntax is:

```
<img src="n">
```

where `n` is the name and location of the image. Since our image is in a folder within the structure of the site, we use the value `"images/jennie.jpg"`. This instructs the browser to look in the folder `"images"` to find the file `"jennie.jpg"`.

Here's the result of the inserted image:

The index.html page, with added image.

To help browsers lay out the page faster, it's always recommended to add `width` and `height` attributes to images so the browser knows how much space on the page to reserve for the downloading image. This expands our tag to read:

```
<img src="images/jennie.jpg" width="216" height="292">
```

Also, always remember to include an `alt` attribute with your images. This is a short text description of the image that is displayed if:

- Images are turned off by a browser

- The browser is a text only browser

- The image cannot be found

If the image is large enough (and so takes long enough to download), the text supplied by the `alt` attribute information shows up before the image. Some browsers will show the `alt` attribute information if you put your mouse over the image, and this text is also what screen readers use to tell those who are visually impaired what's on the page (without `alt` information they just hear the word "image" read out loud). A sample `alt` attribute for this image could be written:

```
<img src="images/jennie.jpg" width="216" height="292"
     alt="Jennie with her horse, TommiBoy">
```

# Hyperlinks

Now on to the most integral part of HTML – the hyperlink. These are defined using the `<a>` tag, which stands for **anchor**.

To add a link to another web site, you'll need the URL for that page. This URL is placed in the `href` attribute of the `<a>` tag. For example:

```
This photo was used with <a href="http://www.dianeswebpage.com">Diane's</a>
permission.
```

A link to another page within the same site would be structured like this:

```
For more on hyperlinking, read
<a href="tutorials/hypertips.html">Hyperlinking Tips</a>
in our tutorial area.
```

This would link to a page called `hypertips.html` within a folder called *tutorials* within the main site folder.

In our example page, `index.html`, we'll add these links at the bottom of the page:

```
<h1>The Next Step in Formatting</h1>
<p>
While you might think from our previous hand coded example that the purpose of
HTML is to be able to make text better looking and more enticing than just plain
text, its purpose from the beginning was actually to logically describe the
structure and meaning of the information on a page so that browsers could then
interpret the pages and give us its content in a logically designed way.
```

```
</p>
<p>
This photo was used with <a href="http://www.dianeswebpage.com">Diane's</a>
permission.
</p>
<p>
For more on hyperlinking, read
<a href="tutorials/hypertips.html">Hyperlinking Tips</a>
in our tutorial area.
</p>
</body>
</html>
```

Here are our resulting links. Note that the URL or path of the link often shows up in the status bar on the bottom of the browser when the mouse hovers over the link. As you will have seen on many web pages, the default look for a link is to appear as underlined blue text.

*The index.html page, with added hyperlinks.*

Turning an image into a link is just as simple. Just put the `<a>` tags around the `<img>` tags, like this:

```
<a href="http://www.dianeswebpage.com/jennie.htm">
<img src="images/jennie.jpg" width="216" height="292"
     alt="Jennie with her horse, TommiBoy">
</a>
```

Here are the results of making an image into a link:

Note that the cursor turns into a hand when over the image and, by default, a blue border is added to the image to denote that it's a link. Again notice that the link destination is shown in the browser status bar, on the bottom of the page, telling the site visitor where they will go if they click.

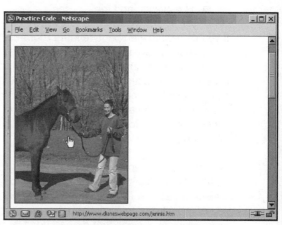

*An image that has been turned into a link.*

# Comments

Before we leave this chapter, there is one final construct we need to introduce, namely comments. These are used to add notes to your code that are not read or interpreted by the browser: they are wholly for the use of yourself or other developers who work on the HTML.

The comments you add to your HTML should start with the characters `<!--` and end with the characters `-->`. Anything in between is the text of your comment. For example:

```
<!-- This is a comment -->
<!-- This is another comment that
     goes over more than one line -->
```

Try adding these to the example we have built up – you'll see that there is no change to the output in the browser.

You'll find these especially useful to remind yourself (or tell other developers) why you made certain decisions while creating your code, so that you don't have to reinvent the wheel when you come back to it in a month or year's time.

# Summary

In this chapter we've covered the basic syntax of HTML pages, and the elements that make up an HTML page structure, namely `<html>`, `<head>`, and `<body>`. We've also introduced some of the main concepts and elements that make up a page:

- Text, and the `<p>` and `<h1>` to `<h6>` tags
- Images, and the `<img>` tag
- Hyperlinks, and the `<a>` tag

If you delve into web page layout programs, you may not do much hand coding, but even this most basic, rudimentary introduction should help you to get a better feel for what it is that you are actually creating, and what is going on behind the scenes. You don't need to become an HTML expert, but if you learn what you can, you'll be a more marketable designer and developer. If you plan to be in project management and never lay your hands on a web page, it will be beneficial to you and your workers to know what kinds of things you should be asking for and what you can expect a browser to be able to show. You'll have a better grasp of the concept of how easy or difficult a particular project may be.

Further on, in *Chapter 4*, we'll be looking at more advanced HTML, and you'll start to see pages that look more like the ones on the Web today. However, now that you've learned a little bit about making a page, in *Chapter 3* we want to give you a solid grounding in web design principles – how you go about designing a site using the process that a web developer typically uses. We'll also look at typical designs that do and don't work on the Web.

# 3

- Learning from print design

- Site structure and design process

- Reviewing and testing your site

Author: Crystal Waters

# Design and Process

Now that you've learned a little about the structure of a web page, we'll move on to take a look at the principles that are involved in designing a site. While this chapter won't teach you how exactly to implement design (since that is a fairly personal skill), it will introduce you to some of the typical processes that are integral to determining good design, to give you inspiration.

First, let's take a look at how we can get inspiration on how we want our site to look and the kinds of things it should contain. We will do this by comparing our task to that of traditional print media, and seeing how traditional print journals have managed their transition to the Web. There are many established features we can borrow from print media, which will greatly add to our web site.

## Learning from Print Design

There are obvious differences between designing layout for print and publication online. However, there are also certain principles that are universal. We can learn from our favorite books and magazines, and some of their successful elements can be translated to the Web.

It's possible to have no experience in print design and become a great web designer. However, even just a few hours browsing through publications (from fashion magazines to coffee-table travel books and automobile repair manuals) at a local bookstore can be priceless if you want to get the feel for the design elements that best serve a specific audience. Just as you can browse the Web to find good designs, you can take note of what magazine covers catch your eye, which tables of contents are easy to find, what makes you keep flipping pages, and what elements make a story or chapter easy to get to.

# Print Navigation

It may not at first be obvious that a newspaper or magazine has navigational challenges and design elements. However, if you take a look at a typical magazine, book, or newsletter, you'll notice that it has a distinctive logo or title, matching story or chapter title typefaces, and page numbers in the same place on every page. Pick up a copy of one of your favorite magazines, and flip through the pages. Once you've been a subscriber to the same magazine for a while (assuming the design has remained consistent), you become familiar with what columns you want to read and where to find them, either by knowing in what area of the magazine they can be found (news stories in the front, features in the middle, humor column on the last page), or by identifying the writer's picture, or even simply by knowing where to find the table of contents. At the most basic level, these navigational cues are much like menus or title bars on web pages. They are places we look at for finding out where we're going and where we are.

Page elements, such as font sizes, colors, and other visual signals, serve as navigational and identification cues for your viewers. Let's look at something obvious: if a typeface is larger on one headline than all others, then we generally expect that message to be more important than the others. Similarly, the closer to the top of the page, the more we expect to take notice of the material. We trust the editors to put the most compelling and important stories first. You'll see, for example, that newspapers put their most compelling news stories, headlines, and photos "**above the fold**". This means it is in the area of the newspaper that is seen when it is folded in a pile or in the newspaper vending machine. Compare this to a web page: designers try to keep the most important information, or the content they want viewers to see first, above the fold – meaning on the initial screen, before people need to scroll down to see more information. On web media, this is also known as "**above the scroll**".

# Design and Identity

Let's take a look at two well-known print publications, and see how this strong sense of branding serves to help the reader recognize the source of the material they're looking at and find their way around.

USA Today, a high-readership newspaper in the US, has a logo that its readers are familiar with, a table of contents in a consistent place, and a weather map that never moves, from issue to issue. Similarly, the Wall Street Journal print version is always black and white, with its trademark sketches on the front page, along with the public interest story column, which everyone generally reads first. Even if you're not regular readers of these titles, if you were given a copy of them, chances are you'd be able to distinguish one from the other because each carries a strong brand identity.

If we look at the online versions of these two publications, we can see that many of these elements have been carried over onto the web sites.

The USA Today web site retains the print newspaper's familiar four-color layout, with a dominant image and story on the front page, just like the printed version.

http://www.usatoday.com

The Wall Street Journal has added a hint of blue on their web site, but other than that, things are reassuringly familiar.

http://www.wsj.com.

While there are probably a lot of web publishers that don't consider their site a "magazine" or "newsletter", successful navigation and familiarity with a site depends on the same basic visual features that have made print publications successful. For example, headings or larger-than-body-text type tell you that you're about to embark on a new section. Text under an image or photograph explains what the picture is all about. A page, section, or chapter number gives you a hint about where you stand in the collection of pages that make up the publication. Tables of contents help you get to places in the publication, and indexes help you find more specific terms or phrases in a book.

## Nameplate

Generally the nameplate, or logo, of a site is the first and most prominent visual on the first, and possibly subsequent, pages. This should be distinctive, as it serves to establish a visual identity that viewers will (hopefully) remember. In the print world, this element is also referred to as a **banner**, but since banner ads are so prevalent in the web world, it might be confusing to call it that when talking to clients.

A good logo is recognizable at a glance, even if you don't remember a company's name. Have a look at the following sites and see how many logos you can identify.

- http://www.adidas.com
- http://www.mcdonalds.com
- http://www.nike.com
- http://www.mercedes.com
- http://www.coca-cola.com
- http://www.generalelectric.com
- http://www.wb.com
- http://www.kmart.com
- http://www.rollingstones.com
- http://www.yankees.com
- http://www.nbc.com
- http://www.mastercard.com

Note the logo placement, and how each page generally has the logo repeated, often in the same location on each page, to remind the viewer of the site's identity. Part of making a smart design and a memorable site is to give people something to recognize – in this case, a logo.

If your clients have an existing business, their business logos are an obvious starting point when designing the nameplate of their web site.

If you're creating a logo for a company that doesn't have a logo already, the rules of a good logo are that it be unique, stylish but not too trendy for the brand it identifies. Most of all, it must communicate what you want the audience to remember about the business. Advertising and marketing firms thrive off of the challenge of making memorable company logos, and a successful iconic symbol for a company is a real find.

# Design and Content

As you create your sites, utilizing elements of successful print publications makes for better structure and comprehension. While the names may be different, and the media would determine the placement of these items within the document, the parts of a well-oiled publication are the root of good design.

## Statement of Purpose

The statement of purpose, or **mission statement**, is a short description of what your site is about and what it's for. Look at print media: non-fiction books (like this one) often have a section at the beginning of the book that describes what it is about and who it is for. Adding a statement like this to your web site helps your viewers figure out, not just why your site was created in the first place, but also why they should bother to hang out there. Think of this as writing your objective on a résumé or as the answer to the question "What do I have that eight million other sites don't have?".

The statement of purpose should answer at least a few of the following questions:

- Who is the site for?

- What does the site offer those people that's helpful and/or unique?

- Who are you and why have you decided to create the site?

- And last but certainly not least, what is the purpose of the site?

This statement is often integrated in a site's *About Us* section, as we can see in the next illustration of the Pets Unlimited web site.

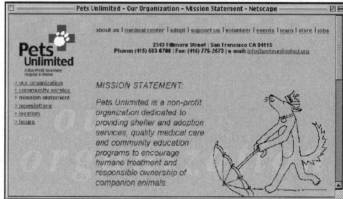

http://www.petsunlimited.org

## Table of Contents

The table of contents of a print publication is often the first step a reader (especially a first-time reader) takes in getting to grips with the content. It tells a reader what they'll find inside. In a book or newsletter, it is usually broken down in the linear order in which the chapters or stories follow each other.

Since there may not be a linear order that people will follow when going through a web site, you have a choice of creating lists of pages sorted alphabetically, by category, by the order in which you hope people will go through the site, or at random.

The equivalent of a table of contents on a web site is twofold: first, the **menu structure** of a site tells the user how the site is organized. Secondly, a **site map** can give a graphical representation of this structure, and show what information is found within each section.

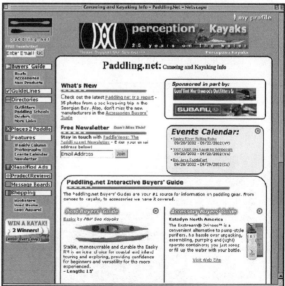

http://www.paddling.net

*Paddling.net*, shown above, uses a left-hand menu structure that looks much like a table of contents, as do most menu structures. Some, like this one, also break down main sections into subsections.

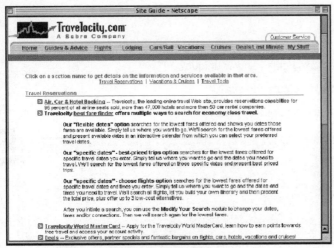

http://www.travelocity.com.

Travelocity adds another level of helpfulness, with a **site guide**. Each section of the site is explained in one or two sentences; just enough to give new users an overview.

## Publication Information

If your site is updated regularly, such as a news site, then a system of **issue and volume numbers**, or similar, can provide helpful cues. It also gives the impression of a professional site that continually offers something new. (Just make sure that you actually **do** offer something new.) You can either use the typical print *Issue 1, Volume 1* format, or a simple date label.

Other information can be provided to say who is responsible for running the site: a list of the people responsible for the site's content, design, and implementation. This is known as a **masthead**. A print magazine generally includes the publisher information, the names and positions of editors and designers, sales people, and others with roles relative to the publication. An expanded version of this for the Web could be a biography of each person in an "*About Us*" section of the site.

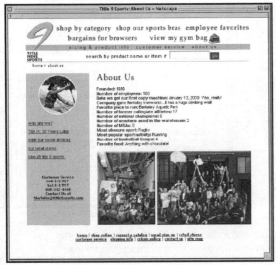

http://www.title9sports.com.

### About Us

No matter how big the company, the best thing as regards the "*About Us*" section is that it has the potential to give the site a human touch: a feeling that there is actually someone behind the screen. A masthead with people's names and pictures could also include e-mail or homepage links, for those who have them, or other details for each person, such as their work history, personal hobbies, or interests.

The Title 9 Sports site has an "*About Us*" page with a personal touch. While we don't get to meet every employee, we can see them all having fun.

# Contact Information

Another incredibly important piece of information that's surprisingly often missing from many commercial sites is basic contact information. You could include information such as:

- Company name
- Company postal address
- Company phone number
- Company fax number
- E-mail address(es) to contact for various information
- List of key personnel and their relevant contact information

Even if your site isn't commercial, if you're encouraging people to write to you or contribute their feedback, give them a way to do so. A simple `mailto:` link on the bottom of pages is all it takes. This is much like a normal hyperlink but, instead of taking you to a new page, it opens the browser's message composition window so site visitors can write a pre-addressed e-mail to you. To create a `mailto:` link, you would use anchor tags like so:

```
<a href="mailto:youremailaddress@yourdomain.com">Write to me!</a>
```

## Story Parts

Each story or article has various elements that set different parts of a story apart from each other. This holds true in print and online.

### Kickers

Kickers are short blurbs that help to introduce a story or categorize a headline. For example, perhaps you have a number of stories on your site about wool yarn products, broken down by category, such as:

- Knitting
- Weaving
- Customer Yarns
- Profiles
- "How To"s

You've written a story called *Fly Fishing With Wool Yarn* about a customer. To help give readers a clearer mental categorization of just what this story is about, you can place a kicker above the headline, such as *Profile of a Customer* or *A Step-By-Step How To*. You can see that, by choosing one or the other of these kickers, a different impression of the overall purpose of the story is given: a profile versus a hands-on tutorial.

## Headlines

In five words or less, can you describe this chapter? **Headlines** are perhaps the most difficult and the most fun part of an article to write, because they must convey as much as possible without being too lengthy or vague. The key tip for writing headlines is to explain the benefit to the viewer of following the link or reading the article. Note the difference among the following as a headline for a story about cooking eggplant:

- *Eggplant is Hard to Cook* (negative connotation; no cure).
- *Don't Wear Yourself Out Cooking Eggplant* (implies that there are easy ways to cook eggplant, but starts off with a negative phrase).
- *Eggplant Cooking the Easy Way!* (positive connotation; the benefit is that this story will make it easy).
- *5-minute Eggplant Recipes* (positive connotation; will save you time).

## Subheadings

If we took out all of the subheadings in this chapter, you'd still be able to find out the same amount of information from the text, but it would take a lot longer to do so. Subheadings break up the text and give viewers' eyes a place to rest, as well as serving as a navigational cue to what's to be found in a particular section.

## Lead-ins and Pull-quotes

Lead-ins and pull-quotes are similar to kickers because they give hints to what the main text is all about. **Lead-ins** are generally placed before the main body of text, while **pull-quotes** are placed within the body of text.

> *The easiest way to create a pull-quote or lead-in is to copy a witty or key sentence or quote from the main text, perhaps cutting it just enough...*

Their benefits are twofold. First, they give viewers a brief overview or tempter into the main text without forcing them to read the whole thing at once. Second, they also offer graphical pizzazz to your story, helping to break up what may otherwise be pages of brain-numbing text. The easiest way to create a pull-quote or lead-in is to copy a witty or key sentence or quote from the main text, perhaps cutting it just enough to tease the reader into delving into the whole story.

## Teasers

Teasers invite people further into your site from top-level pages (such as the home page) or from other areas of the site, such as the table of contents, captions under photos, or as additional links under a related story. The teasers "*Make a Million With Your Web Site*", "*A Profile of a Successful Web Designer*", and "*Free HTML Software!*" might follow a story about "*Web Sites Made Easy*" to lead readers through to other sections of the site.

## Artwork and Photographs

Images are not only cool in their own right, but they can help lead a reader into a story, or explain concepts that may otherwise take ten pages to explain. Since the Web lends itself to skim reading rather than reading in-depth, pictures can be more important than headlines for grabbing a visitor's attention.

There are certain rules that have to be followed with photos and other art, the most important of which is to make sure the file size is small while retaining the quality of the image. In terms of layout, placement is the key. A dominant piece of artwork or photo will tell your viewer where to look first. The easiest way to do this is to pick one image that is proportionally larger than the others, to tell readers where to look first. The dominant piece of artwork should appear "above the fold". As we said earlier, on the web page this term describes the content that is visible as the page first loads, without the viewer having to scroll to get to it.

### Captions

Imagine a newspaper full of photos with no text underneath them to tell you what the pictures are about. Like pull-quotes, captions also help to give viewers a capsulated view of what's in a story, as well as describing what's going on in an image or photo.

### Jumplines

In magazines and newspapers, we're used to following cues (or **jumplines**) that read *"continued on page 14"*, for instance, and going to the relevant page to read the rest of the story. The cool thing about hypertext documents is that if your document does span more than one page, a simple click on the jumpline should take you right to the top of the appropriate page. Often, the jumpline on a web page is simply the word *Next*.

Similarly, we also commonly see *"continued from page 2"* in print publications, giving us the clue that if the story first caught our eye while looking at page 14 (to use our earlier example), we could go back to page 2 to see the beginning. On web pages, this type of jumpline could read *Back* or *To the top*, giving the navigational options to go back a page or to the very top of a story or section.

### Page Numbers

Page numbers are very rarely used in the same way in web as in print publication. Page numbers serve in a linear print publication to give you an idea of where you are in the reading process, but web sites are rarely linear in structure. However, whether numeric, words, or icons, each web page should provide some sort of clue to the viewer as to where they are in a section of a site or the site as a whole. To make navigation easier, placement of this cue should be in the same or similar area on each page.

# Site Structure and Process

Now that we've drawn what we can from print design, let's turn our attention completely towards the design of web pages.

In the early days of the web design, anyone who created web sites generally did all of the steps themselves. They were the designer, writer, coder, publisher, illustrator, graphics expert, and technical support advisor. When some content needed to be changed, they were the one to do it; when there was a site redesign, they had to implement it. There are still people that do this, and there probably always will be, but generally the process for creating a web site has become like most other business processes: there is a place for everyone, and everyone in their place.

Luckily, though, like any good business, web site production companies that are successful don't simply farm tasks out to people sitting in separate cubicles. Ask any experienced web professional, and they'll tell you that the process is **organic**. There are some sites that started out as a technologically induced design idea, based on a new technology, such as Flash MX, rather than any idea about content. There are also sites that have been based on years of market research before launch.

For a site to be successful, it's generally agreed that the users have to be profiled, to some degree. Just like any other kind of product, we have to build sites that users will like, and want to use again and again. To do this, there are certain processes in the design phase that you should consider.

## Ask Questions

Before you begin to take on the process of the actual design of a site, there are a number of questions that you've got to ask either yourself, or your clients. The answers to these questions will have an effect on how you lay out a site, what content you decide on, and any of the processes that go into building it.

First of all, you've got to figure out the goal of your site (example answers are shown in parentheses).

- Who is the site for? (Young single mothers who want to finish college.)

- What is its purpose? (To assist users finding the right school with the right schedule, financial aid, and childcare.)

- What kind of impression do you want to make? (To promote trust, education, and inspiration.)

Once you figure out these answers, then you are ready to start brainstorming content and developing the site's integral structure. However, especially if you're tackling a project for a client, there are additional questions to ask. Among them are:

- What is your goal for this site? (To give more young single mothers a better chance to finish their higher education.)

- What do you want to achieve? (Better education, better jobs, and better chances.)

- What will you do to accomplish this goal, and what will I (or my firm) do? (Market research, preliminary site design, site structure, work with company to create content, user testing.)

- What are the deliverables? (A fully functioning web site.)

- When should it be done? (In six months.)

- What will we do once the structure is in place and the site launches? (A 30-day on-call follow-up, training office personnel basic content structure and uploading functions, other maintenance to be determined, etc.)

- How will we determine if the site is successful? (By traffic numbers, percentage of traffic that signs up, press coverage, successful graduates.)

Getting this information will help to create the focus of the site: the mission that you will keep at the forefront of your mind while creating design, determining content, and planning site changes and growth. Consider this as your task of building the mission statement we discussed earlier. If you look at your answers and know what the site is, what it does, and why you are doing it, without having to pause and rewrite the answer, then you're on the right track.

## Audience Profiling

It's crucial if you have access to your target audience that you tap into their experience with your company or product (or previous version of a web site). A useful aspect of having a captive market of people is that they are probably somewhat loyal to your organization, might have purchased products or services from you already, and most certainly have an opinion of their experience.

- Who are you?
- What do you want?
- How are we doing?
- What would you like us to do differently?

These questions are vague, but they are the basics that need to be answered. Before you can create a site or its structure, you need to know **what** you want it to portray, **who** you want to view and use it, and **how** they will use it.

Getting this information can be a simple as an informal poll of an existing customer base, or may mean hiring a professional marketing or polling firm that can do an in-depth, professional survey of those that may (or may not) visit your site.

Once armed with all of this information, though, what do you do with it? After you determine a general description of the type of person who may visit your site or who you wish to draw to its content (a process often called **profiling**), you can then use the information to help determine a number of design aspects. Here are some sample user attributes that a survey could provide you with and what those attributes can mean to your design.

### Age Range

How old your audience is could determine such things as your color scheme or how you style your text. You may want bright crazy colors for children-oriented sites, or larger text for older viewers with failing eyesight. The language you use, such as slang terms used in the 1960s or 2002 vernacular, will also be determined by the expected age of the visitor. Of course, the content of your site will vary depending on audience age too – some content may only legally be provided above a certain age. Also, what kind of people do you want to show in photographs or as endorsements for a particular age range of user?

### Family Status

The amount of time people have to use your site may well be determined by their family status. A person raising a family and holding down a job or two, is less likely to have much time to spend on the Web, whereas those with no children, or children who have left home for college, may find that they have more time to spend surfing. Those with less time would need to get to information that is easily digestible in short amounts of time.

Design and Process

Family status may also determine seasonal content; during the school season children may use the Web mainly for homework, whereas they'll use it for play during the off-school season. Parents may spend more time shopping around various vacations, and all could be spending more summer hours outdoors or away from home.

## Budget or Spending Level

If you're planning a storefront site, remember that how much money a site visitor has will obviously have some effect how much they buy. It could also determine what kind of equipment they are able to purchase: those with a smaller budget for computers may have older, slower systems with which to access the Web.

## Level of Computer Experience

How much technical experience your users have will influence how much you need to guide them through different activities on a site, such as how to download a file, how to add a plugin, or in some cases, how to get around the site in general. However, if they already have some technology background and experience with the Web, telling them how to use a *Back* button or forcing them to read instructions about how to click on buttons to get to a different area of the site is probably not a good idea! If you're not sure of their technical level, a separate, well-written, and navigable help file with links to reputable "how to use the Web" sites kills two birds with one stone.

## Access to the Web

Do your users access the Web from home or from work? Do they have to call long-distance to access the Web? What is their type and speed of connection – do they have fast cable modems or are they still using slow dial-up? Are they using **straight-ahead ISPs** (those that provide you with access to the Web, but nothing else) or do they access through proprietary services such as AOL or MSN?

All of these questions will help determine just how much time a person has to spend on the Web. (If at work, a boss may be looking over their shoulder; with a slow connection, they may have to spend more time accessing information.) Looking at these factors will also help determine how large graphics can be before they are intolerable and what kinds of extras can be added to your site (such as Flash or streaming audio).

## Type of Monitor Resolution/Computer Platform/Browser

While currently many users have monitors and systems that can handle millions of colors and demanding browser system requirements, this is still important information to find out. Each of these factors influences the resolution of graphics that is preferable and what content formats are best avoided or taken advantage of.

As we saw in *Chapter 1*, older browsers do not support some web technologies, and some old systems may not be able to run browsers that will support the technologies. Hardware is also an issue – if a lot of your audience only has access to slow modem connections, then it would be a bad idea to include lots of large graphics, movies, and sound tracks on your web sites.

# Location

The region of the world in which your audience resides could determine what content is legally presentable, what languages your site should use, or what software should be posted for download. If you're planning on selling products over the Web, these factors will also determine what kind of tax, shipping costs, shipping limitations, and other information must be provided. You'll also want to learn about the kinds of color schemes that may work for your audience: different combinations of colors could mean one thing in your home country, but a totally different thing somewhere else.

Many sites also neglect to mention where the actual business or warehouse is located, which can lead to confusion. For example, if you're in Australia and don't find out until the last page of the checkout process that the company doesn't ship outside the US, you'll naturally be very annoyed. Whether you choose to service international customers or not, be sure to provide this information up front. As necessary, allow for variations in form validation since postal codes and phone number length and structure vary from place to place.

## Preferred Way of Shopping

If you know that your audience is likely to have experience of shopping on the Web, or perhaps have never used the Web for shopping, this will help you assess how reassuring you should be during the shopping process on your site. It may also help you to determine what level of technical support you might need to offer via other communication media, such as a toll-free phone number.

Many users use the Web as a big catalog and price comparison opportunity rather than actually purchasing online. That said, finally finding a company's web site only to discover that they have no product information or pricing, no e-mail address for enquiries, and a demand that you phone for more information is a definite no-no.

## Accessibility Requirements

Some companies are required to meet certain accessibility standards for people with disabilities, and some simply want to be more conscious of making their content more accessible to as many people as possible. This will determine how certain information is presented, and whether or not a text or accessible version of the site is created.

*Accessibility* – the process by which sites are made to be usable by people with visual impairments, or other disabilities. This is not some esoteric design discipline – it can be achieved by following some simple guidelines, and observing some fairly obvious good design practices (for example, putting `alt` text descriptions on images so that users with visual impairments who use screen readers to read web sites out to them, will get a good description of what the images are; using HTML elements such as headings (`<h1>` etc.) for their proper purposes, so screen reader software find the text easier to understand).

*Bear in mind that accessibility is not only the right thing to do in a moral sense – it is also required by law in many situations (for example, it is illegal for public service providers such as government bodies and public hospitals to provide inaccessible web sites, thereby discriminating against users with disabilities). In addition, accessibility measures will generally result in sites that are more usable by non-disabled users too. For more on accessibility, see the Accessibility section in Chapter 11 of this book.*

## Other Access Methods

Whether users are going to be accessing your content through PDAs and cell phone screens will determine how many colors you can safely use on your pages, how many menu items per page are advisable, how long blocks of text can be, and what kind of content formats can be included.

Once you have a more solid idea of who is using your site, and how they will be using it, creating a design to uphold what your audience expects will be a lot easier than just making something up that you hope people will like. You'll have a better idea of the kinds of graphics, the color combinations, contrasts of type and backgrounds, what sorts of interactive features you'll need, and what media to create for. This will help you build a solid foundation on which the site architecture will be built.

# About Information Architecture

If the Web were just a mass of millions upon millions of documents without any structure or organization, then it would be nearly impossible to find any information we might want or need.

A web site, unlike a book or movie, is **multi-dimensional**. A book is linear: it's most often navigated from the first page to the last page, one numerically-ordered page following another numerically-ordered page. Longer books are most likely separated into sequential chapters, which are followed, as expected, in sequential order. Of course, readers always have the option of reading a book in any order that they may choose to – some readers of this book might have started with the table of contents, then moved on to *Chapter 4*, then skipped to *Chapter 10*, then skimmed through the *Index*, and then read the table of contents more thoroughly, before settling in to read the *Introduction*. A fictional book that relies perhaps more fully on previous chapters in order to better comprehend future chapters, is an example of how content may influence how a media is navigated.

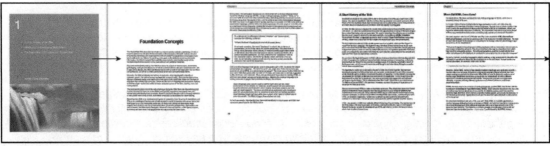

*A book is linear: it's most often navigated from the first page to the last page.*

A movie is also a linearly navigable media. Viewed in a theater or on television, the viewer must watch it from beginning to end to get all of its information and to make sense out of it. Viewed from a VCR or DVD player, the information may seem less linear since users can fast forward, rewind, or skip around at random to view the information. However, in making the movie, the information was structured linearly, and therefore that is generally the way that it is best comprehended.

So how are web sites structured? A web site is most often not linear. Pages spread out from the homepage, and those pages have links out to other pages, and often pages link from one level to another and back again.

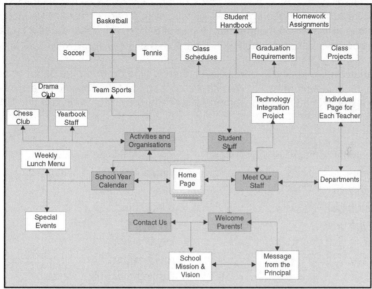

*The pages of a web site spread out in a non-linear way.*

It is generally accepted that structuring a site and its information is key to its success, and a good structure is preferable to users who seek information in its content.

**Information Architecture**, a term that came into being out of the growth and categorization of the web industry, is the art of organization and presentation of data to the user in a consistent, clear, and intuitive way. As mentioned in *Chapter 1*, an information architect is the person whose job it is to decide upon a structure in which to present a site's content, and how the site's users will navigate that content. They are in charge of making sure that a site is well-organized and accessible, determining how to best lay a path for site growth and possible later design changes, and helping to present this site plan and strategy to clients and the web design team at large.

Structuring a site has its challenges. If you've come up with a list 70 or 700 topics long, how do you begin to organize it? If you have hundreds of items to sell, how do you organize them? How do you organize all the stories you'll be writing for an online magazine?

The first thing we'll have to do is consider how the information is going to be used by site visitors, and try to categorize the information into, at most, six distinct categories. Any more than that and the site can get too littered with categories, defeating the goal of breaking down the information into specific chunks in the first place.

# Categorizing Practice

An easy way to get a feel for categorizing content is to first try it out on a sample site that you might build yourself, or have thought about building, such as one to support your kayaking hobby, or passion for fishing. You needn't have had any sort of big business plan spelled out already, just an idea for a site. When you start working professionally as a designer, you may come across companies that only have a goal of, "We want a web site, make it!". This practice session may be more valuable the less you've planned a site, for that very reason.

First, provide yourself with a pack of index cards or large sticky-backed notes, plus a pad of paper or a black or white board (if you're doing this exercise with a partner or team, a white or black board that you can all view works better than a pad of paper). Set aside at least a couple of hours when you won't be disturbed, preferably in a room that has some extra wall or table space.

Now, without analyzing or justifying or criticizing, start writing down on the paper or board anything and everything imaginable that has to do with the chosen topic. For example, let's say that you want to create a web site that serves women kayak-fishermen. Your brainstorming list might start out looking like this:

| | |
|---|---|
| kayaks | hard shell |
| women's personal flotation devices (PFDs) | specialty fishing kayaks |
| safety | inflatable kayaks |
| groups to fish with | hats |
| outfitting your kayak | sunglasses |
| fishing with the guys | dry tops |
| where to fish | kayak skirts |
| rods | rough water |
| reels | fighting motorboat wakes |
| rod holders | trolling |
| paddling when fishing | fishing with kids |
| trolling motors | fish recipes |
| anchors | health benefits of kayak fishing |
| challenges of kayak fishing | where to buy fishing kayaks |
| types of kayaks | make your own paddle leash |
| sit on tops | fishing in tournaments |

Once you are generally happy with the list (things can always be added later), the list topics should be transferred to the index cards or sticky notes, one topic per card or note.

Our index cards or sticky notes, adorned with one topic per card or note, are now puzzle pieces: it's our job to make the puzzle of this brainstorm list fit together into a logical, navigable structure. This isn't always easy, since you're faced with a blank canvas, but once you get started, obvious patterns should start to form. As you go along, you'll find that category topics emerge. Some you'll keep, some you'll put aside tentatively, and some you'll throw away. Chances are, you'll find that there is any number of ways that your information can be sorted. That's expected. As long as you stick to specific, well-defined categories with logical sub-categories, you should be able to find a combination of categories and a structure that not only works for you when planning, maintaining, and updating the site, but also works for site visitors when they start to visit, use, and navigate the site's content. It may take some time and wrangling at this point, but it will be much easier to do it now than after the site launches.

For example, for the kayaking site, we might decide that *"safety"* and *"challenges of kayak fishing"* go together in a general *"safety techniques"* category, as well as *"fighting motorboat wakes"*, *"rough water"*, and *"women's PFDs"*. We'll put those cards or notes together, either on the table or tacked up on the wall where all can be seen clearly. *"Kayaks"*, *"rods"*, *"reels"*, *"dry tops"*, *"kayak skirts"*, *"rod holders"*, *"trolling motors"*, *"anchors"*, and *"women's PFDs"* are all *"products and accessories"*; *"outfitting your kayak"*, *"fishing with the guys"*, *"where to fish"*, *"challenges of kayak fishing"*, *"fighting motorboat wakes"*, *"fishing with kids"*, and *"where to buy fishing kayaks"* might be *"tips and techniques"*.

As you will see fairly quickly, many categories often share topics, so you might find yourself creating new index cards with the same topic two or three times. You'll also probably find yourself changing the names of categories to better fit a grouping. Again, aim to create six or fewer main categories.

In this exercise, as your categories emerge, you are creating a rough visual conceptualization of your site's navigation and structure, as well as a categorical outline to which you can add information as you develop content. As you put topics in categories, take note if one category is getting half the cards and another category only has two or three cards – perhaps a different breakdown is necessary, perhaps not. In any case, the site architecture and flow is starting to form around a healthy amount of proposed content.

Of course, this exercise can be done with content topics already in a site when you are planning a site redesign – however, you've got to keep in mind that if your site has been very popular, previous visitors may be used to the current structure. It doesn't mean that there's no room for improvement: just remember that the improvements must actually be beneficial to warrant a new learning curve for a visitor.

# Creating Hierarchies

As you work with site topics and putting together the puzzle of your content, natural hierarchies emerge from the content. **Hierarchies** are maps that describe how different topics are related, and their relevant levels of importance. They are so specific to a site topic that it's difficult to teach how a hierarchy should be structured: this is exactly why people who are familiar with the topics should be involved in deciding how information should be broken down, which information is most important, and what should be at the top level of the hierarchy. If you are creating a site for a client, it's crucial that you involve them in deciding on topics and structure within the information, because they should know this information better than anyone else.

Consider that you are hired to make a site for a construction company that includes information for both its clients and employees. If the company throws out a number of topics and terms in its brainstorming session, could you categorize them without their assistance? Do you know which topics belong together logically if you're given a list including miter saws, shoring techniques, asphalt shingles, blocking, shotcrete, and fiberglass-reinforced polyethylene?

Within each section or category of the site, the hierarchy and structure should continue to be thought through. Depending on the kind of site and the number of relevant topics, subcategories within a top-level category (or the top of the hierarchy) should be determined in the same way that the original category was determined – with the aid of a consultant or expert in the field, who would have an educated estimation of how the company's users would want to access information.

This flowchart of information that you are creating is much like a company's organizational chart. Usually starting from the top (the president or CEO of a company, or the home page), the branches flow down (five vice presidents, with ten department heads below each of them), all the way down to junior janitor.

Structuring your site in a flowchart doesn't just help to give you the visual and navigational feel of a site: it's also a great way to help you organize the actual construction of a site. It provides good documentation of the site for future designs and developments.

## Design Process

The design of a site will depend on many factors, including the message and impression you want to give to users, the users themselves (as we discussed in the previous section on *Audience Profiling*), and the kind of site hierarchy that you've found emerge above. Before we can design a page visually, we have to determine what each page needs as far as user interaction and informational needs of your users is concerned. For a discussion of navigational issues, see *Chapter 7*.

Once this is determined, web designers will often create initial sketches of the different pages of the web site. These can be done on paper or through a piece of software on your computer. Often called **wireframes** or **storyboards**, these sketches are usually rough drafts of what the site pages will look like and, when laid out in the order in which the pages would appear, they give a better visual concept of what the site will start to feel like to a potential user, in terms of both look and feel of each individual page, and navigational routes through the site.

They are used by designers as draft documents. Once refined, these site sketches are usually presented to the client for approval, and then are used to create final designs.

The first image shown here is a basic pencil sketch; the second image was created in Photoshop (but can be made in any basic drawing program). Using a grid helps to align images, text, and other content.

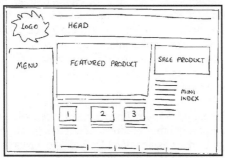

*A rough draft hand-drawn storyboard.*

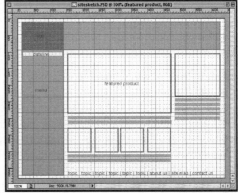

*The same storyboard, drawn using a graphics program.*

In a typical project design cycle, there will usually be many iterations of the design. They will probably start off very simple, as seen in the sketch, and will become more detailed through the course of the project, as more decisions are finalized about the site's content.

Once the design of the site's pages is fairly close to completion, the development team will usually be called in to make a site **prototype** – a working representation of the site that has as much of the functionality as possible implemented, so the development team and the client can get even more of a feel of what the final site will be like to use. Prototypes will usually be implemented in HTML, with working menus, navigation, and other main features. If the client is happy with how the prototype looks, then it will be fairly close to the final site, apart from some tweaks, and final graphics details.

Of course, there is always scope at this stage for more changes to be made to the design, in which case another prototype may be drawn up, and you might even have to go back to the wireframing stage, depending on how major those changes are.

Once everyone is happy with the design, site assets such as buttons, images, icons, illustrations, logos, and other graphic pieces are created to build the final site.

## Content Development Process

Content development is often done in parallel with site design, so that content is available once the design is finished. However, many sites will continue to add content to the site on a regular basis (whereas the basic site design itself will most likely stay as it is for a while), whether they are a publication site, such as an online magazine or newspaper, or a business site with a regular update for its customers.

While there's no fixed way that a site's content **workflow** (the set of steps needed in creating a piece of content) should be set up, there's a lot to be learned from traditional editorial workflow, such as for a magazine. This can be especially relevant if the site is to be regularly updated.

In print publishing, the members of the team include freelance writers, freelance artists, editor(s), copy editor(s), an art director, an art and production department, and a service bureau or printer. The flow of work often goes something like this:

- Article is conceived by editorial team
- Article assigned to writer by editor
- Writer writes article
- Writer turns in article to editor
- Editor reads article and edits it
- Editor turns article over to copy editor
- Copy editor returns article with changes back to editor
- Editor makes changes, and sends it to art department
- Editor, editor in chief, and art director discuss art and layout
- Art department prepares rough layout, plans art
- Art director assigns art

- Artist creates art and returns it to the department
- Art department prepares initial layout
- Editor reviews layout
- Editor approves layout
- Copy editor reads copy in layout form, returns changes to editor
- Editor approves changes and returns layout to art department
- Art department prepares new version of layout, using final art
- Copy editor re-reads story, makes any final changes (fitting text, filling in missing captions, and so on)
- Art department produces final layout
- Editor, copy editor, editor in chief, and art director approve final layout
- Files sent to service bureau/printer
- Service bureau/printer returns color proofs
- Editors and art department review proofs
- Proofs are approved
- Publication is printed

As the Web has matured, we see that members of a web publishing team often follow the same kind of structure as a print team. Its team members include: freelance writers, freelance artists, editor(s), copy editor(s), an art director, and an HTML production department. In the web world, we can also parallel many of the same steps in the workflow – however, since the medium is different, some changes may be reflected. For example, the design of the layout will be spread between the artists and the HTML production department, and the service bureau/printer is replaced by the HTML production team.

If you're a one-person "team" putting together a regularly updated site, then your flow may go more like this:

- Determine your story's content
- Write your story
- Re-read article and edit it
- Determine accompanying art
- Create art
- Prepare initial online layout
- Review layout

- Re-read copy in layout form
- Make editorial changes
- Prepare new version of layout
- Review new version of layout
- Make any final changes
- Put files on server
- Test files on server
- HTML files go live

# Site Review and Testing

At the end of the workflow discussed above is a stage that we haven't yet discussed: site testing. While this isn't really a part of *design*, it's an important part of the web site creation process so we'll discuss it a little here.

It's important to check out your site and how it works before all of the potential customers get their hands on the site. Besides taking some time to just get a feel for the site from the perspective of a user, it's important to proof and review content for accuracy, check design consistency, and get the ever-important final client approval. Here are some examples of what should be checked before showing off the final project to the client, and then rechecked before going live.

Your site may work great when it's running off your hard drive, but how will it work from your server or your service provider's server? The only way to find out is to upload it and try. It won't make you look reliable with your client and users if pages aren't showing up where they are supposed to, or if images are missing, or the site structure on the server doesn't match the site structure on your computer.

Your client's web site visitors are very likely to use various browsers (and versions of browsers) or media to access the site. So, it's crucial to check out how the site looks in various incarnations of browsers such as Netscape, Internet Explorer, and Opera, as well as whatever other kind of media may be predominant in the audience. If for some reason a majority of users still uses an older version of a browser or accesses the site through a proprietary service, this must be accounted for.

If you've designed your site on a Macintosh and tested it in browsers on the Mac, you'll still need to test the site in the Windows versions of the browsers. Graphics and some colors often show up darker when using Windows. You may want to go back to your graphics application and alter your images' contrast so that they are more easily viewed on various platforms.

If the text isn't readable for you, it probably won't be readable for your audience. Check contrast and image visibility before going live.

If pages are loading more slowly than expected, or nothing appears until an entire table is loaded, then the site has to be checked to make sure that there aren't tags out of place (improperly nested), tables that are too big and complex, and graphics that weren't accidentally saved at too high of a file size (that is, **unoptimized graphics**). If you know that the audience primarily uses 56k modems, turn off your cable modem, fire up your old dial-up connection, and try the site on for size.

> *Something like a misplaced tag can render a page nearly impossible to read.*

Are images appearing in the places that you thought you told them to? Is text wrapping around the images where you want them to wrap? Something like a misplaced tag can render a page nearly impossible to read.

Of all things, make sure that all links work. Test every text and image link that you have. Use the same link names and icons for a specific page throughout the site. For example, if you use a compass icon on one page to give people the option to view your site map, use the same icon for the same purpose on other pages. Also, check to make sure that the links you provide within text don't distract from the content: use the minimum number of links per sentence as possible for better readability. Consider putting all relevant links at the end of a story, in a sidebar, or below paragraphs that refer to the links.

If you're offering music clips and sound bytes from your site, try to keep file sizes down by experimenting with various formats. Full stereo sound is wonderful, but it takes up a lot more space than a mono sound byte. For narrative, low-end sound files are fine for most purposes.

These are just a few important examples. Site testing is a continual practice, and while it may take a significant amount of time before launch to go through the site and check details, it will save even more time in the long run. The reputations of both yourself and your client are on the line, and the product – the web site – may only have one chance to make an impression.

# Summary

The web design principles involved in designing a site, and the processes a web developer typically uses, aren't that different from the principles involved in any successful business. The more you learn, practice, and experience the flow of web design, the more you'll find the process is mostly organic. Balancing that organic creative process are "structure practices" based on previous media practices, such as storyboarding, navigational rules and techniques (see upcoming *Chapter 7*), and smart design principles.

In the next few chapters you'll see how this smart design may be tackled with more advanced HTML.

**Design and Process**

# 4

- XML and XHTML: what are they?

- More HTML and XHTML elements

- Markup in Dreamweaver MX

**Authors: Crystal Waters and Rachel Andrew**

# Advanced Markup: HTML, XML, and XHTML

Along with the growth of the Web came an evolution of HTML, the language upon which the Web has been built. With the advent of HTML 4.0(1) came more support for more media, including scripting languages, stylesheets, more accessibility features, and better document printing abilities. It also better supports frames, embedded objects, tables, and forms.

However, HTML's evolution didn't stop there. The next step was XML, which allows us to create our own markup languages, and it wasn't long before HTML was reformulated in XML, allowing the same ease of use enjoyed by HTML coders for years before, while at the same time taking advantage of XML's strict syntax rules and flexibility. This reformulation is known as XHTML.

In this chapter we'll take a look at the XML and XHTML standards, discuss what they mean for you as a designer, why you should learn more about them. Note that we will go deeper into the world of standards in *Chapter 12*, and see what other ones there are to take notice of.

## A Little More History

As we learned in *Chapter 1*, HTML grew out of SGML (Standard Generalized Markup Language). Let's have a little recap here, to refresh our memories, and help carry on with the story.

SGML is a **meta language**: not a markup or programming language in itself, but a collection of language rules that developers use as guidelines with which to create their own languages (for more on SGML, see *http://www.w3.org/MarkUp/SGML/*). HTML was one of those resulting languages, developed specifically for marking up documents for the Web in a common format, so they are portable, viewable, and navigable among different systems.

Another resulting product of SGML is **XML**, or **Extensible Markup Language**. Rather than being a straightforward markup language like its HTML sibling, XML is also a meta language– it can be used to define markup languages, which are referred to as **XML Vocabularies**.

**XHTML** (**Extensible HyperText Markup Language**) is basically HTML, only redefined as an XML vocabulary. The goal with XHTML is to bring back the strengths of HTML as a hypertext document structuring tool, rather than the overextended visual design tool it became.

## More Definitions

**DOCTYPE: Document Type Declaration** – the DOCTYPE needs to go at the top of your document. It declares which DTD you are using to validate this document and provides a link to where the DTD is outlined, usually on the W3C web site (*http://www.w3.org*).

**DTD: Document Type Definition** – a set of rules that defines which elements and attributes are allowed in the markup document the DTD is associated with. Different DTDs allow different sets of attributes and elements to be used within a document. If you do not put the correct DTD in a DOCTYPE at the start of your document, you have no guarantee that the browser or device will be able to display your document as you intended.

**Meta language:** A language that defines another language, for example, the meta language XML has been used to define XHTML.

**Schema:** In general terms, this refers to a structured framework or plan that defines something, for example, a document or a database. Document type definitions (see above) could be classified as schemas for markup documents, as could W3C XML Schemas (another kind of schema for defining markup documents – see later in the chapter).

**Structured data:** data that comprises of a standard set of fields defining enclosed information, such as a database, an address book, or a spreadsheet.

**Syntax:** the structure of a language. For example, in spoken language the rules for proper syntax are our grammatical guidelines.

**Validation:** the act of checking a markup document to make sure that it complies with the rules specified in the document's schema, be it a DTD or an XML Schema.

# XML

Learning just what XML is can be a challenge, especially if you go online and try to read specifications and standards, most of which were written by developers, for developers. What it *isn't* is a predefined set of elements, like the standard HTML elements (`<head>`, `<body>`, `<p>`, etc.). Instead, you can define whatever elements you want – if you wanted, you could have a `<fruit>` element, a `<banana>` element, and an `<apple>` element, etc. It all depends on how you want to structure your data.

When working in XML, a developer can create a DTD for their document, which includes the elements they wish to use. This is most often used in facilitating data transfer since, as long as the script or application which is importing the data knows where the DTD is, it will know what to do with the tags it receives.

**Web resources for XML information:**

- *http://www.xml.org* is one of the top resources online for XML information, resources, FAQs, and networking contacts.

- *http://xml.coverpages*.org publishes weekly news updates about XML, SGML, and other schemas applicable to web publishing.

- *http://www.4guysfromrolla.com/webtech/xml.shtml*. XML Articles on 4 Guys from Rolla – useful real-world tutorials and examples.

What might be the simplest way of describing XML would be to say that it was developed as a set of rules that can be applied to understandable elements that *you* (or the standards-setters in your organization) define. It allows easy structuring of data for many purposes, such as viewing on the Web, and data transferal between platforms and applications. Let's have a look at a simple example:

```
<?xml version="1.0"?>
<products>
   <product id="320">
      <name>dinner plate</name>
      <price>$2.00</price>
   </product>
   <product id="167">
      <name>cutlery set</name>
      <price>$8.00</price>
   </product>
   <product id="456">
      <name>frying pan</name>
      <price>$9.00</price>
   </product>
</products>
```

Anyone should be able to look at the XML document above and say "Oh, OK, that piece of data is a product name", or "that represents the field with price data". It differentiates whatever is in its markup from other information.

**Advanced Markup: HTML, XML, and XHTML**

While this example has taken pains to be 'human-readable' – easily understood by a person looking at the raw XML file – XML does not need to be written as such. If the purpose of your file is for it to be parsed or processed by a script, then you may opt for very short names to cut down on file size, both in your XML documents and in the scripts you are writing to process them.

What is defined as an element isn't important as long as the structural rules are applied. The rules have to be followed, or all this extra work won't be worth it. If the rules are followed, this information is defined and ready to work with other applications, other media viewers (phones, web-toasters, and so on).

## Structured Data

Let's have a look at how databases and XML are related, to aid understanding. As we have discussed above, structured data is information that has a standard set of fields, such as a database, an address book, or spreadsheet. For example, if you were to set up a database of a store's inventory of products, each product would have specific information assigned to it, such as a SKU code, wholesale cost, retail price, product name, manufacturer, description, measurements, sizes, or whatever other specifics that may be applicable. A human resources database may include each employee's name, title, hiring date, birth date, salary, company division, tax status, and insurance coverage, among other information.

| | A | B | C | D | E | F | G | H |
|---|---|---|---|---|---|---|---|---|
| 1 | PRODUCT | MANUFACTURER | SKU | WHOLESALE | RETAIL | SIZE | COLOR | IN STOCK |
| 2 | logo sweatshirt | Russell | 349-A45 | 10.00 | 22.00 | M | blue | 120 |
| 3 | logo sweatshirt | Russell | 349-A46 | 10.00 | 22.00 | L | blue | 43 |
| 4 | logo sweatshirt | Russell | 349-A47 | 12.00 | 25.00 | XL | blue | 66 |
| 5 | t-shirt | Hanes | 249-B31 | 4.00 | 9.00 | L | red | 110 |
| 6 | t-shirt | Hanes | 249-B32 | 4.00 | 9.00 | XL | red | 74 |
| 7 | bucket hat | Hat Co. | 655-D11 | 6.00 | 14.00 | S/M | beige | 59 |
| 8 | bucket hat | Hat Co. | 655-D12 | 6.00 | 14.00 | L/XL | beige | 77 |

If you've worked with databases, simple spreadsheets, address books, or any other kind of application that has fields of data with specific labels (like the store product inventory database here), then you have worked with structured data.

Let's look at the first two records of the above database table, represented in XML:

```
<?xml version="1.0" encoding="iso-8859-1"?>
<inventory>
  <item>
    <product>logo sweatshirt</product>
    <manufacturer>Russell</manufacturer>
    <sku>349-A45</sku>
    <wholesale>10.00</wholesale>
    <retail>22.00</retail>
    <size>M</size>
    <color>blue</color>
    <in_stock>120</in_stock>
  </item>
  <item>
    <product>logo sweatshirt</product>
```

*Note: XML markup looks a lot like HTML markup at first glance, since all the markup is in brackets, surrounding the text that it defines. This XML defines the content of the page, not the rank and appearance of the text. In its purest sense, XML and HTML have little to do with one another.*

```
      <manufacturer>Russell</manufacturer>
      <sku>349-A46</sku>
      <wholesale>10.00</wholesale>
      <retail>22.00</retail>
      <size>L</size>
      <color>blue</color>
      <in_stock>43</in_stock>
    </item>
</inventory>
```

Each one of these tags is written to be understandable by someone who might open up the file and need to transfer the data to another system, whether it is to post to a catalog on a web site, or import into a spreadsheet or database. As the developer of this XML document, you can decide what your tags are. For example, if you'd rather have "`product_name`" than "`roduct`" or "`who_makes_it`" rather than "`manufacturer`", that's totally up to you.

Now let's have a look at how raw XML data appears in web browsers. In some browsers, such as Netscape 6, the data appears in a pure form:
By looking at our XML in this browser, we can see that marking the data up in XML has had no effect on the appearance of the data or design of the page. It doesn't replace HTML.

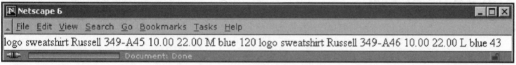

*Our XML example viewed in Netscape 6.*

However, some browsers apply styling to the XML markup, to show the data in a tree-like structure. If you view the XML markup in Internet Explorer, you will see something like this:

*Our XML example viewed in Internet Explorer 6.*

# How Does XML Relate to HTML?

Although you can call your elements anything you like, something that your XML has to adhere to, if you want it to be of any use, is the strict set of XML structure rules. Like HTML markup, XML uses angle brackets to enclose tags and quotes to enclose attribute values. Other than that, it has little in common with HTML markup. Consider the following example:

```
<p style="color:blue; font-size:large">Hello</p>
```

In HTML, this element would tell the browser to make "Hello" blue and large. In XML, it would instead simply designate a field called "p", with a value of "Hello" (to continue with the database analogy). The `style` attribute would simply provide some kind of meta information about the field value.

So, by now you will have gathered that XML is not the easiest thing to explain. Because XML gives us more power over our data, we also have the responsibility of using that power properly by using sensible, logical labels to identify the different parts of our information, and sticking to the rules governed by XML.

# The Rules of XML

XML markup is far fussier than HTML markup.

A lot of the sloppy coding that you can get away with in HTML (such as not closing elements properly, and not putting attribute values in quotes) is due to browsers being coded to be more forgiving – they have extra code in them to recognize sloppy HTML, and work out what the author of the markup intended. In this section, we will look at the rules of XML, including some things you can't get away with, that used to be "acceptable" in HTML.

Note that if an XML document does follow all these rules, then it is termed as being **well-formed**.

## An XML Declaration Must Be Included at the Very Top of the Document

A valid XML document must begin with an XML declaration which specifies which version of XML you are using:

```
<?xml version="1.0"?>
```

When we talk about valid documents we mean one which validates against its DTD – in the case of XHTML you have a valid document when you can run it through the validator on the W3C web site and it returns no errors. More on this in *Chapter 12*.

## The Document Should Have One Root Element

If a document is well-formed, then it should be a correct XML document with one **root element** (sometimes called the **document element** – this means the element that contains all others), with all other tags being correctly nested (as we describe below). For an XHTML document, being "well-formed" means that it must include the following tags, nested correctly:

```
<html>
<head>
  <title>The title</title>
</head>
<body>
  Content here
</body>
</html>
```

In an XHTML document, the root element is `<html>`.

## Elements Must Be Properly Nested

In the following line of HTML, the elements are not properly nested – note that the closing `</em>` tag is between the opening `<strong>` tag, and the closing `</strong>` tag:

```
<em>emphasised text, <strong>and some bold, emphasized text.</em></strong>
```

This would not be acceptable in XML. Instead, it would have to be like this:

```
<em>emphasized text, <strong>and some bold, emphasised text.</strong></em>
```

Now the `<strong>` element is clearly nested inside the `<em>` element.

## Elements Must Be Properly Closed

Another common rule that HTML could get away with breaking was the closing of elements (this was touched on in *Chapter 2*). For example, in HTML you could split a block of text into paragraphs as follows. We've also included a line break tag:

```
This is my first paragraph.<br> Let's break this line
<p>This is my second paragraph.
<p>This is my third paragraph.
```

In XML, this would not be allowed – the rules of XML dictate that elements need to be properly closed, like so:

```
<p>This is my first paragraph.<br/> Let's break this line</p>
<p>This is my second paragraph.</p>
<p>This is my third paragraph.</p>
```

You will have noticed that the above rules apply to both empty and non-empty elements. A non-empty element is an element such as the `<p></p>` tag. It will contain something between the opening and closing tag. In HTML, empty elements are those that did not have any closing tag, such as `<br>` and `<hr>`. In XHTML these too need to be closed, this time by adding a slash before the closing angle bracket, like so – `<br/> <hr/>` (these are merely shorthand for `<br></br>` and `<hr></hr>`.)

## Attribute Values Must Be Enclosed in Quotes

In HTML, you can also get away with not putting quotes around attribute values that do not contain a unit of measurement. For example:

```
   ...
<body bgcolor=#CC9966>
   ...
<td rowspan=2>
   ...
```

For XML to be well-formed, all attribute values must be quoted, whether they are numbers or letters:

```
   ...
<body bgcolor="#CC9966">
   ...
<td rowspan="2">
   ...
```

## No Attribute Minimization

Attributes in valid XML documents cannot be minimized. Attribute minimization refers to the practice of only writing an attribute name and not its value. All attributes should be written as name-value pairs even where this means that the value is the same as the name. The example below uses XHTML to show a common situation where in HTML we would see minimization of an attribute – checked.

Incorrect:

```
<input type="checkbox" name="checkbox" id="checkbox" value="True" checked />
```

Correct:

```
<input type="checkbox" name="checkbox" id="checkbox" value="True"
       checked="checked" />
```

## XML Naming Rules

There are some specific naming rules in XML that you need to take heed of, when deciding what to call your elements and attributes. Let's go over them briefly here:

- XML is case-sensitive. In HTML you can write your tags in uppercase or lowercase, or in a mixture of these. This is perfectly legal. XML is case-sensitive `<pizza>` is not the same as `<PIZZA>` or as `<Pizza>`, these three would all be seen as entirely different tags in XML. When you are working in XHTML you will find that all tags need to be in lowercase, as the DTD uses lowercase for the tags.

- XML names can only start with letters or an underscore ( _ ). No other punctuation of numbers is allowed.

- An exception to the 2nd bullet is that XML names can't start with the letters `xml`, in uppercase or lowercase.

The rules discussed above are simple, but must be obeyed – this could be a reason why more people haven't begun to embrace XML/XHTML. Also, XML names can't contain spaces.

# XHTML: The Happy (But Strict) Medium

There will be no further versions of HTML, instead the W3C have developed the XHTML specifications. XHTML 1.0, the reformulation of HTML 4.01 as XML, is the first step towards newer and more powerful implementations of the markup language used for the web.

On first glance, XHTML doesn't offer any extra exciting functionality that HTML doesn't, or any immediate benefits over HTML. So why bother looking into XHTML? The answer is, because the ever-forward movement of the Web, web media, and growth demands it. Taking the time to learn XHTML and complying with its standards will make you a better designer or developer, who will learn some principles of XML, and be able to grow into learning more about how information will best be presented on current and future platforms.

*W3C: **The World Wide Web Consortium** (http://www.w3.org) maintains documentation for and tracks the official status of such projects as XHTML, XML, HTML, XML Schemas, and many more. It is a very informative site to look at, but be warned that the material contained within the site consists of very thorough, complicated specifications, which are not the easiest of documentation to learn from.*

Designers on average have grown used to using HTML as a visual design tool, pushing it to its limits. In the process, HTML has lost its original purpose in the first place: to be a tool that structures information for use on the Web. For example, elements such as the heading elements (`<h1>`, `<h2>`, and so on), which were developed in order to structure your headings logically within a document, have been misused wherever people wanted larger text, and `<blockquote>` is frequently seen used because indentation was required.

If you have learned HTML markup, then you're more than ready to take on XHTML. XHTML doesn't add any new markup to your library; it simply ensures that you create markup to strict rules. While it is possible to create HTML documents that are well structured and marked up in a logical way, the fact that HTML is less strict about how you use the markup can lead to sloppier coding in some (although not all) cases. The XHTML rules are similar to the rules that HTML should follow anyway, but they have fallen by the wayside because browsers have evolved into more forgiving display media. With XHTML, there's no leeway – if a rule isn't followed, the document will be likely to not work as you intended, if at all.

Of course, remember that there is no scope to make up your own elements in XHTML – you must use the elements defined in the HTML 4.x spec.

## Using an XHTML 1.0 DTD

We very briefly saw a DTD in *Chapter 2* – a DTD is a set of rules that you can apply to a markup document, that specifies what elements you are allowed to use in your document. It can be said that you **validate** your document against the DTD. As we saw in *Chapter 2*, there are three types of HTML 4.01 DTD – **strict**, **transitional**, and **frameset**.

You'll be pleased to know that XHTML 1.0 also has strict, transitional, and frameset DTDs, so if you can get your head around one set, then the other should be easy to understand. The DTDs are very similar, but it is necessary to have two different sets, now that we have HTML 4 documents, and XHTML 1.0 documents on the Web – confusion could easily be caused otherwise; the DTDs help to tell them apart. We'll see some XHTML DTDs in action later on in this chapter, in the section on *Dreamweaver MX and XHTML*.

There are also some other DTDs for XHTML, but we won't worry about those now – we will look at these in more detail in *Chapter 12;* for now let's have a look at what the three basic types are, and how you actually reference them from your documents.

### Deprecated and Obsolete Elements

*Elements are described as **deprecated** when they are to be removed in future specifications – if you see that an element has been deprecated it is best not to use it unless you absolutely have to, as in a future specification the element may not exist and so browser and device support may be patchy or non-existent for it in the future.*

*Obsolete elements are those that have been removed from the specification.*

## Strict XHTML 1.0

The strict XHTML 1.0 DTD only allows you to use current elements, attributes, and character entities that are found within the XHTML 1.0 specification and does not allow the use of any deprecated or obsolete elements. The strict XHTML 1.0 declaration is as follows:

```
<!DOCTYPE html PUBLIC "-//W3C//DTD XHTML 1.0 Strict//EN"
        "http://www.w3.org/TR/xhtml1/DTD/xhtml1-strict.dtd">
<html xmlns="http://www.w3.org/1999/xhtml">
```

## Transitional XHTML 1.0

A transitional XHTML 1.0 document is more lenient, and lets us use deprecated elements, except frameset elements. It is very much equivalent to the HTML 4.01 Transitional DTD, just following the XML rules we discussed above:

```
<!DOCTYPE html PUBLIC "-//W3C//DTD XHTML 1.0 Transitional//EN"
        "http://www.w3.org/TR/xhtml1/DTD/xhtml1-transitional.dtd">
<html xmlns="http://www.w3.org/1999/xhtml">
```

## Frameset XHTML

The frameset DTD is meant for, as you might have guessed, frameset documents. It is similar to the transitional DTD, but allows you to use framesets:

```
<!DOCTYPE html PUBLIC "-//W3C//DTD XHTML 1.0 Frameset//EN"
        "http://www.w3.org/TR/xhtml1/DTD/xhtml1-frameset.dtd">
<html xmlns="http://www.w3.org/1999/xhtml">
```

# More HTML/XHTML Elements

Now we are aware of how to create an XHTML document and the basic rules we need to stick to in order to write valid XHTML, let's look at some more of the elements that make up the HTML 4 and XHTML 1.0 specification, and how to use them properly.

We already looked at many of the basic elements in *Chapter 2* – let's look at some of the other elements you will commonly encounter in your work, and how they are used.

## Character Encoding, and <meta> Tags

When you create an XHTML document you need to declare the character encoding – if you do not then it will not validate properly. You can declare the encoding either in the XML declaration at the very top of the document (before the DOCTYPE), like so:

```
<?xml version="1.0" encoding="iso-8859-1"?>
```

or in a `<meta>` tag:

```
<meta http-equiv="Content-Type" content="text/html; charset=iso-8859-1" />
```

Meta tags are tags that contain useful information about the markup document you are creating from the character encoding, as seen here, to search terms, which will help your site to be found easier by search engines such as Google. All `<meta>` tags are empty elements and therefore should be closed with a space slash.

## Form Elements

Form elements are the standard way of collecting data from users of a web site: for example, address details and payment details on an online shopping site. A typical form looks something like this:

Form elements in XHTML have some major changes – for a start, they all need to have an `id` attribute for purposes of identification by scripting (as we shall see in *Chapter 10*, scripting is definitely required to make use of the data entered into forms). In addition, many form elements are empty tags, so we need to make sure that they are closed properly.

### The <form> Element

The tags `<form></form>` mark the opening and closing of a form. You can use any other tags within the form, including of course your **form elements**. (Note that the term "form elements" does not just refer to the `<form>` element, but also to the other elements used to make up the form, which we will discuss shortly.) The `<form>` element requires two attributes, `method` and `action`. `method` explains how the form will be processed, and `action` is the location of the script or application that will process the form.

## The &lt;input&gt; Element

The `<input>` element allows you to create most of your **form controls** (this term refers to any of the objects in your form that you use for entering data, such as checkboxes, radio buttons, textfields, and so on.) You use the `type` attribute to say what kind of control each tag is.

```
<input type="radio" name="radiobutton1" id="radiobutton1" value="1" />
<input type="text" name="text1" id="text1" value="Enter Name" />
<input type="checkbox" name="checkbox1" id="checkbox1" value="1"
       checked ="checked" />
<input type="submit" name="Submit" id="Submit" value="Submit" />
```

The above example creates the following form controls:

If you wish to manipulate the form fields using scripting (to perform JavaScript validation for instance – see *Chapter 10* for more on this) you will need to give each element a unique `id` attribute (this can be and is often the same as the `name` attribute). You will also see that we have closed all fields with a space slash, and used `checked="checked"` in the checkbox example to avoid attribute minimization, which is common in HTML forms.

## The &lt;select&gt; and &lt;option&gt; Elements

The `<select>` element allows you to create a list of items from which the user can select one or more. Between the `<select>` and `</select>` tags, you will need to place your options, enclosed in `<option>` `</option>` tags. The `value` attribute of `<option>` is what will be sent to your script should that item be selected. The text enclosed by the `<option>` elements is the text that the user will see and make their choice from.

Note that the default size of the list is 1. Since there is more than one option, the options are presented as a drop-down list (see the screenshot on the left below.) If we modified the code below so that the `<select>` element had a `size` attribute with a value of "3", the box size would expand so that all the options would be displayed at once (as seen in the right-hand screenshot below).

```
<select name="select">
    <option value="1" selected="selected">item one</option>
    <option value="2">item two</option>
    <option value="3">item three</option>
  </select>
```

## The <textarea> Element

The `<textarea>` element allows you to create a multi-line input area for the user to type in longer text than would be appropriate for the `<input type="text" ... >` tag. It is a non-empty element, and should be closed with `</textarea>`. You can also put default text inside the `<textarea>` tags for the user to see, delete, or edit, and the `rows` and `cols` attributes can be used to specify the size of the textarea (measured in number of characters). For example:

```
<textarea name="comments" id="comments" rows="5" cols="20">Add your comments
here</textarea>
```

This code looks as follows, when viewed in a browser:

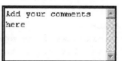

For more complete coverage of forms, see *Chapter 10*.

# List Elements

In XHTML (as in HTML 4.01), there are three non-deprecated list definitions to choose from: ordered list, unordered list, and definition list. The difference between an HTML 4.01 list and an XHTML list is simply that you can't get away with not closing all the `<li>` elements (list items) when working in XHTML.

So this wouldn't be acceptable in XHTML:

```
<ul>
   <li>list item one
   <li>list item two
</ul>
```

But this would:

```
<ul>
   <li>list item one</li>
   <li>list item two</li>
</ul>
```

It is also important to use the correct type of list when entering your information and not simply choose one or other for visual effect; if you are going for a certain "look" then you should use CSS to achieve it (see *Chapter 8* for more on CSS).

The three list definitions are as follows:

## Ordered List

For a list of items numbered in sequential order, useful for a list of step-by-step instructions or ranked items:

```
<ol>
   <li>list item one</li>
   <li>list item two</li>
   <li>list item three</li>
</ol>
```

Note that "`ol`" stands for "ordered list", and "`li`" stands for "list item" – this makes it easier to remember.

This looks as follows when viewed in a browser:

```
1.  list item one
2.  list item two
3.  list item three
```

## Unordered List

For a list of unordered items, useful for lists of attributes ("`ul`" stands for "unordered list"):

```html
<ul>
   <li>list item one</li>
   <li>list item two</li>
   <li>list item three</li>
</ul>
```

This looks like so:

```
•  list item one
•  list item two
•  list item three
```

## Definition List

Use a definition list if you have a list of items and explanations. By using this type of list you make it clear to someone using a screen reader (or other device that can only see the structure of the document) that the list contains items and their definition. If you make this kind of list just by altering the presentational aspects of the page, your intentions may not be clear to someone who cannot see that presentation. The definition list (`<dl>`) includes elements for terms (`<dt>`) and definitions (`<dd>`).

```html
<dl>
   <dt>the term</dt>
   <dd>the definition</dd>
   <dt>another term</dt>
   <dd>another definition</dd>
</dl>
```

This looks like so:

```
the term
        the definition
another term
        another definition
```

## The <object> Element

The `<object>` element allows you to insert an object such as a Flash movie, applet, image map, ActiveX, or other component into your document. It also allows you to set any parameters necessary for the running of this item. You can also add text within the element that will be viewable if the user's browser cannot display the object. The following example will insert a Flash movie called `myMovie.swf` onto your web page.

```
<object classid="clsid:D27CDB6E-AE6D-11cf-96B8-444553540000"
codebase="http://download.macromedia.com/pub/shockwave/cabs/flash/swflash.cab#vers
ion=5,0,0,0" width="71" height="42" title="My Movie">
    <param name="movie" value="myMovie.swf" />
    <param name="quality" value="high" />
    <param name="scale" value="exactfit" />
    This is a flash movie
</object>
```

Note that we won't be covering any of these kind of objects in this book.

# More Text Formatting Elements

We have already seen how to use many of the more basic text formatting elements in *Chapter 2* – now let's have a look at some of the other ones available:

- `<abbr>`: Any text enclosed within this element is defined as an abbreviation of a word or phrase.

- `<acronym>`: You should enclose acronyms with this tag.

- `<address>`: The text enclosed by this element is defined as an address. You can use other tags within this area, for example:

  ```
  <address>
  <p>1 The Lane
  <br />The Town
  <br />The State
  <br />The Country</p>
  </address>
  ```

- `<caption>`: Allows you to give a table a caption (see Chapter 6 for a detailed discussion of tables, and the elements that make them up).

- `<cite>`: This element enables you to indicate that the text is a citation, or a quote. Unlike <blockquote> (which will put the quote in a separate paragraph), <cite> keeps the text inline and within the normal flow of the document.

- `<sup>` and `<sub>`: <sup> (superscript) and <sub> (subscript) do what you'd expect them to do, and they are useful for displaying footnotes, scientific equations, mathematical formulas etc. For example:

  ```
  22<sup>nd</sup> October 2002<br />
  H<sub>2</sub>O
  C<sub>2</sub>H<sub>6</sub>
  ```

  Will appear in a browser like so:

  22$^{nd}$ October 2002
  $H_2O$ $C_2H_6$

- `<hr />`: This is the horizontal rule element. Where included, it causes a horizontal line to be drawn across the page.

# What Is Deprecated or Not Allowable in HTML/XHTML?

The following elements and attributes are those that are flagged as deprecated in XHTML. You can still use these tags if you are validating to the Transitional DTD, but not in the Strict DTD. Even if you are working in XHTML 1.0 Transitional, you would be advised to avoid using these tags and attributes except where you find no other option (for the sake of backwards-compatibility) as they are being gradually phased out of use.

| Element | Description |
|---|---|
| `<applet>` | Java applets |
| `<basefont>` | font properties defined as default |
| `<bgsound>` | background sound tag |
| `<blink>` | make text blink on and off |
| `<center>` | align a block of text |
| `<embed>` / `<noembed>` | embed an applet etc. |
| `<font>` | assign font size or color |
| `<layer>` / `<ilayer>` / `<nolayer>` | Netscape positionable layer tags |
| `<marquee>` | scrolling text |
| `<menu>` | a menu list |
| `<s>` | strike-through text |
| `<strike>` | struck-out text |
| `<u>` | underlined text |

| Attribute | Description / Example |
|---|---|
| `align` | `<td align="right">` `<div align="right">` |
| `alink, vlink, link` | as applied to the `<body>` element to color links within the document. |
| `background` | as applied to the `<body>` element to apply an image background to a document |
| `bgcolor` | `<body bgcolor="...">` `<td bgcolor="...">` |
| `border` | `<img border="0" ... >` |
| `clear` | as applied to the `<br />` tag |
| `color` | `<font color="...">` |
| `face` | `<font face="...">` |
| `height` | `<td height="...">` |
| `noshade` | `<hr noshade>` |
| `nowrap` | `<td nowrap>` |
| `size` | `<hr size="..." ... >` `<font size="..." ... >` |
| `width` | `<td width="..." ... >` `<hr width="..." ... >` |

# XHTML, XML, and Design: Why?

So what's the benefit? If we're losing some of the tricks we've managed with non-fussy HTML for so long, why the need for XHTML? These are good questions, so let's look further at why moving to XHTML is a good idea, besides being a good choice in terms of following standards.

The first benefit is concerned with the fact that the Web isn't just for desktop computers anymore. Today, it is common for cell phones and PDAs to have web access. However, these small devices have much less processing power available to them than a desktop machine, so can't deal with processing standard HTML, and especially not all the sloppy markup of yesteryear. Instead, you need to have streamlined, concise code. XML allows for this with its strict rules, and even allows the creation of cut-down markup subsets, specially designed to be viewed on small devices. For example, **WML (Wireless Markup language)** and **cHTML (Compact HTML)** are XML vocabularies especially for viewing on mobile phones and the like. Even without using one of the specific DTDs for such devices, you will find that well marked-up pages display well in many of the commonly used PDAs and phones on the market.

Working to a strict standard such as XHTML means that browser and device manufacturers have a greater chance of displaying or reading the content appropriately. Ideally, if you or your client's goal is to develop content that will conform to current and future platforms, XHTML will be the stepping-stone to that goal.

Another benefit to accepting and using the XHTML 1.0 standards are that it will be easier to introduce new elements and attributes to the schema. XHTML supports current media, and as it evolves, so will the kinds of media and supported documents. For more of a discussion on the benefits of using standards, see *Chapter 12*.

# XHTML Support Available

Thankfully, for those of us who can't bear the thought of keeping track of all these rules and schemas, many of the web development applications available include support for working in XHTML. These include large visual development environments such as Dreamweaver MX (XHTML support being new in this latest version of Dreamweaver), HTML editors such as Homesite, and also other tools – TopStyle CSS editor includes a capable XHTML editor in its latest version.

You can of course write your XHTML directly into a simple text editor; however, you may find that you can work faster in one of the development environments above. It's really up to personal preference.

For a look at the support available in web development applications for standards in general, see *Chapter 12*.

# Dreamweaver MX and XHTML

Macromedia Dreamweaver MX includes a wealth of great features to allow easier creation of XHTML 1.0 documents. The first major feature occurs when you first create a new document. As seen below, there is a *Make Document XHTML Compliant* checkbox – when checked, it adds the appropriate DTD (document type definition) reference within the DOCTYPE, telling it which collection of XHTML rules you've decided to follow and changes the opening HTML tag to `<html xmlns="http://www.w3.org/1999/xhtml">`.

Once you have started out with an XHTML document within Dreamweaver, all the markup and JavaScript that Dreamweaver uses will be XHTML 1.0 Transitional compliant.

*Note that you can make all your documents XHTML-compliant by default by going into Edit > Preferences, then the New Document panel, then checking the Make Document XHTML Compliant checkbox (by default, Dreamweaver chooses the XHTML Transitional DTD).*

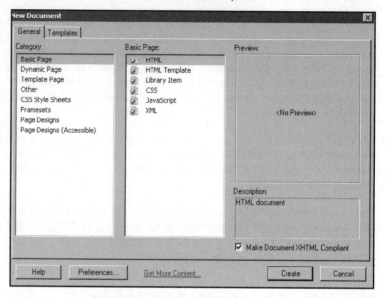

You can also set preferences for the validator by going to *Edit > Preferences* (see below.) You will see an option to validate as XHTML Strict, Transitional, or Frameset. Dreamweaver itself creates XHTML Transitional markup (or Frameset if you are using frames within your document) but if you are hand-coding to XHTML Strict, you could set the preference here. One way to move a document from XHTML Transitional to Strict is to change the DTD that you are validating against to Strict, run it through the validator, and then remove or change any attributes that cause an error.

To validate an XHTML document in Dreamweaver, first make sure that you have set your validator preferences to the XHTML DTD that you are working to – in this case XHTML Transitional.

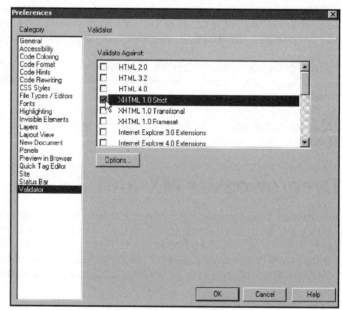

To validate an XHTML document, either click the green arrow in the results pane and select *Validate Current Document as XML*, or select *File > Check Page > Validate as XML*.

Let's have a look at a new XHTML 1.0 document in Dreamweaver MX. If you create one, your code should look like this:

```
Untitled Document (Untitled-2) (XHTML)
1  <?xml version="1.0" encoding="iso-8859-1"?>
2  <!DOCTYPE html PUBLIC "-//W3C//DTD XHTML 1.0 Transitional//EN" "http://www.w3.org/TR/xhtml1/DTD/xhtml1-transitional.dtd">
3  <html xmlns="http://www.w3.org/1999/xhtml">
4  <head>
5  <title>Untitled Document</title>
6  <meta http-equiv="Content-Type" content="text/html; charset=iso-8859-1" />
7  </head>
8
9  <body>
10 </body>
11 </html>
```

When you create a new XHTML document in Dreamweaver MX, your DOCTYPE is already written for you. It defaults to XHTML Transitional:

```
<!DOCTYPE html PUBLIC "-//W3C//DTD XHTML 1.0 Transitional//EN"
"http://www.w3.org/TR/xhtml1/DTD/xhtml1-transitional.dtd">
```

Note that the DTD web address reference is also included. This points the document to the URL where the XHTML 1.0 Transitional DTD is kept. If you now work within Dreamweaver to create your markup visually, it will use XHTML rather than HTML to do so – following the rules of XML as we discussed above. If you are working in code view and are unsure as to whether your markup is correct XHTML or includes some things that are incorrect (such as unclosed tags), then you can always ask Dreamweaver to check for you.

Paste the following markup within the `<body></body>` tags of a new XHTML document in Dreamweaver MX:

```
<h1>The Flash Usability Guide: Interacting with Flash MX</h1>
<p><img src="flash_usability.jpg" alt="The Flash Usability Guide" width="216"
height="260"></p>
<p>By members of the <a href="http://www.friendsofed.com">Friends of Ed</a>
Author Team</p>


<h2>Summary of Contents</h2>
<ul>
<li>Introduction
<li>Flash vs. Usability
<li>Whose contribution counts where?
<li>Choosing Flash
<li>Choosing usability
<li>Conventions and metaphors
<li>Structuring Flash 6
<li>Usable interactions
<li>Showing users respect
<li>Think Accessibility
```

```
<li>First impressions
<li>Offline Flash User testing
<li>Appendix: Resources and Articles on the Web
</ul>
```

(See `SampleDMXcode.html` in the code on the CD for this markup.)

You will notice that there are a number of things that break the XML rules in this bit of markup, so let's fix them, the quick way. After pasting this code into your document, select *Commands > Clean up XHTML* and you should see the following dialog:

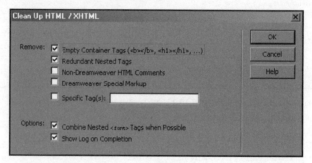

Click *OK* and Dreamweaver MX will fix all the syntax errors – on finishing, it will pop up an alert saying *XHTML Syntax Fixed*. Our code will now look like this:

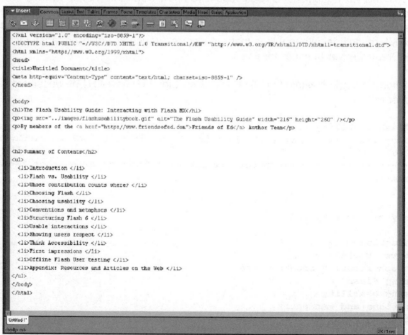

This technique can be very useful if you are pasting in large amounts of markup from somewhere else as it will go through and quickly fix those things that break the basic rules of XHTML. For example, it will:

- Convert all element and attribute names to lowercase.

- Quote all attributes.

- Close non-empty elements – such as <p></p>.

- Close "empty" elements with a space slash (for example, <br />).

- Convert minimized attributes (such as checked="checked".)

*Note: It is not required to leave the extra space before closing tags such as `<br>` – both `<br/>` and `<br />` are legal XHTML – but without the additional space some older browsers may fail to interpret the tag correctly.*

# Summary

Moving from HTML to XHTML may require a little work on our part, but it brings many benefits. XHTML brings back the strengths of HTML's original goals of making information accessible to as many platforms as possible, and the rules we have to follow ensure that our code is more streamlined, and more flexible than ever before. In this chapter we have covered the following:

- XML, and in particular its application as XHTML: the reformulation of HTML in XML.

- The main differences between working in HTML and XHTML.

- Why you might want to use XHTML.

- How to work in XHTML in a development environment such as Dreamweaver MX.

Advanced Markup: HTML, XML, and XHTML

# 5

- Bitmap image formats: GIF and JPEG

- Vector graphic formats: SVG and Flash

- Graphics software packages

Author: Crystal Waters

# Creating Graphics for the Web

As we mentioned in *Chapter 1*, graphics were not part of the initial HTML specification. However, it's hard to imagine the Web now without them. All you have to do is remember the infamous coffee pot mentioned in *Chapter 1* to see what an impact images can make. Can you imagine eBay or Amazon without any graphics?

The aim of having graphics on a web page is to enhance a site, making it more aesthetically pleasing and exciting, and more comprehensible by site visitors. A picture can quite literally take the place of a thousand words in its ability to communicate a message or make a first impression. Also, many web surfers skim web pages for the information they need – graphics may grab their attention more than words do.

There are now many different formats that graphics can take, whether they are static graphics formats or animated ones. In this chapter, we'll take a look at:

- The differences between the various graphics formats
- The factors that make "good" web graphics
- The tools available for creating graphics – from free to expensive

Before all this, however, we'll take a quick look at one particular aspect of images: color.

## Color

We've already seen some use of color in this book – recall the first HTML example in *Chapter 2* where we changed the color of some text:

```
<span style="color=#336699;">sample body content</span>
```

Alternatively, in older pages, you may see the deprecated `<font>` tag used like this:

```
<font color="#336699"> sample body content</font>
```

In both cases, we're setting the `color` to the value `#336699`. What does this mean?

This value is in **RGB Hexadecimal format**, where RGB stands for Red Green Blue. After the first `#`, the next two characters relate to an amount of red, the second two characters relate to an amount of green, and the third two characters relate to an amount of blue. When these amounts of red, green, and blue are mixed together, you get your final color. Since it is a hexadecimal format, the characters used range from `0` to `f`, with `00` being the smallest two-character value and `ff` being the largest. Thus, `#000000` corresponds to black (the absence of all color) and `#ffffff` corresponds to white.

There are also sixteen common color names that can be used as values for the `color` property/attribute, since they are specified within the HTML and XHTML recommendations. These are `black`, `green`, `silver`, `lime`, `gray`, `olive`, `white`, `yellow`, `maroon`, `navy`, `red`, `blue`, `purple`, `teal`, `fuchsia`, and `aqua`.

## Web-Safe Colors

*Dithering is a technique where various patterns of different colors are used to appear as other colors, especially when seen from a distance.*

In the early days of web design, sticking to what was dubbed the **web-safe color palette** of 216 colors was a crucial technique to master. This was the limited matrix of colors that the majority of browsers and graphics cards could support at the time without **dithering**. Books were written wholly based on creating with these colors, theories of various palettes discussed, and workarounds developed. However, with the majority of users now using monitors and their accompanying graphics cards that can display more than 256 colors, it's much less of a priority. Some argue there's no need to discuss it at all.

As a designer, you may have to design for PDA screens and cell phones that are still limited in their color depth, and so may want to at least be conscious of the existence and importance of the web-safe color palette. Those that are required to design accessible web sites may also want to stick to the lowest common denominator of designing for low-end monitors, and will want to keep their palettes limited to this library of colors for best visual and legal results.

Fortunately, there is still good support for the web-safe color palette in modern graphics packages. For example:

- To access the web-safe color palette in Fireworks MX (trial version available on the CD that accompanies this book), open the Colors panel, click on the Options drop-down menu in the upper right-hand corner, and choose Color Cubes from the menu.

- To access the web-safe color palette in Photoshop 7.0, open the Colors palette, click on the Swatches tab, and then click on the arrow in a circle in the upper right-hand corner to open the drop-down Options menu. Choose Web Safe Colors, Web Spectrum (colors sorted by spectrum), Web Hues (colors sorted by hue), or either of the Visibone palettes from the menu.

## Gamma and Graphics

Gamma is a term that refers to the way that the midtones of an image relate to the dark and light parts of an image, as well as the image's relation to its surroundings. It was initially a term that applied to television screens, since it was a setting that manufactures had to adjust because people watched televisions in dimly lit rooms at home, rather than bright showrooms in which they were purchased.

These days when we hear the word gamma, it is in reference to our computer monitors. It is generally known that images appear lighter on Macintosh computers than on Windows computers. Depending on the web site, it may be no big deal or may make a page look significantly different. In a media in which standardization is an aim, this is a difficult challenge to take on.

If designers make all their images on a Macintosh, and the majority of their clients and site visitors view the Web through a PC, the site could look so different as to make it unreadable or unattractive. Hues in images may appear in non-realistic shades, perhaps more red or green or blue being added to an image than was originally designed, or there may be a resulting lack of contrast on a page, making it difficult to read.

See *Chapter 11* for a further discussion of gamma.

# Bitmap Web Graphics Formats

The graphics formats we will mainly look at in this chapter are:

- GIF (Graphics Interchange Format)
- JPEG (Joint Photographic Experts Group)
- PNG (Portable Network Graphics)

These are all **bitmap formats**. Basically, this means that they are built up as rows and columns of dots or pixels, for each of which a color is specified.

In creating web graphics, the priority is to make graphic files (and therefore, the entire web page) smaller in size, in order to give fast access to content. The design community, used to creating huge graphics files for high-resolution printing, first found this teeny-file-making to be a challenge, especially given the initial limitations of screen and browser resolutions back in the early days of the Web. Much of the difference between the various bitmap graphic formats revolves around how they **compress** images in file size.

## GIFs

**GIF (Graphics Interchange Format**, pronounced with either a hard or soft G depending on who you ask) images are made with what is called **substitution compression**, or **LZW** compression (after Lempel-Ziv-Welch). For the non-algorithmic among us, here's a simplified explanation of its algorithm.

If the GIF algorithm comes across several parts of an image that are sequentially the same, it substitutes them with just one of the parts, and stores a key to (or description of) the substitution it has made with the image. When viewed, the GIF image is "decoded" and we can see it.

Clear as mud? Let's look at an example, but remember that this explanation isn't meant to replace a technical white-paper explanation of GIF algorithms by any means; it's simply to illustrate in layman's terms how space is saved. Say our image is represented by numbers, rather than pixels:

```
111111111111111122222
222222111111111333311
4343433333333344444
5555552222222333344
1111111111111555555
12345123451234512345
```

If we think of this in English, anywhere a pattern emerges, whether it's a series of the same numbers in a row, or a sequence of numbers that has been repeated, we can save space by "describing it" rather than "repeating it". For example, we can say the first line of our example above is:

*one one one one one one one one one one one one one one one two two two two two*

or we can substitute that by saying

*15 ones, 5 twos*

This obviously takes up a lot less space!

The resulting size of a GIF depends on the amount of repetition within an image. Therefore, even if two images have the same number of colors and have the same dimensions, the image with more pixels in sequence (the **flatter** image) will be a smaller file when saved as a GIF.

 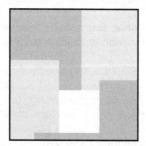

Both of these examples are 300 by 300 pixels, made up of the same three colors. However, the flowery one is about three times the size of the blocky one. The simpler sequence of pixels (and therefore the amount of information necessary to explain and display it) in the second image results in a more compressed image.

The lesson to learn here is that the GIF's compression scheme works ideally on images with flat colors, rather than photographs or images with a lot of dithering, which compress better with other methods.

Other points to note about GIF compression are:

- It is 8-bit, meaning that it can contain a maximum of 256 colors.

- It is lossless – no colors are lost after the image is compressed.

- It allows transparency – the image's background color can be set as transparent, allowing anything underneath it to show through.

## To GIF, or Not to GIF?

GIF formatted images have been used for years, long before the Web became a household entity. It was developed by CompuServe as a graphics compression method back in the late 1980s. CompuServe released GIF as an open and free specification in 1987, and it quickly became accepted worldwide as an ideal way to save images so that they would transfer more quickly over slow modems between CompuServe users and others online. It also became a standard for developers of image creation/manipulation software, who added its compression scheme to their libraries for common use.

However, GIF uses someone else's compression scheme. Unisys, a technology services company, holds the patent on the LZW algorithm, and after some investigation, it appeared that neither the folks at CompuServe that developed GIF (or anyone else for that matter) knew that there was a patent on LZW until Unisys brought it to their attention. In December 1994, CompuServe and Unisys announced that developers would have to pay a license fee in order to continue to use technology that supported the GIF format.

GIF isn't the only compression standard that uses LZW, and Unisys had never pursued licensing of its algorithm before. However, what became the first widespread online graphics format, and the first format to hit the Web, was soon threatened with removal unless paid for – or so the public thought. While the statement never said that GIF images had to be destroyed or taken down from online libraries or web pages, or that user of software that saved in GIF format needed to pay, numerous online libraries were purged of GIF files out of fear. In protest, there were passionate uproars of dissent from the online and development community.

After lots of confusion and back-and-forth negotiations, it was decided that those developers of software that save images to GIF format (or other formats that use the LZW compression algorithm, such as TIFF), such as Macromedia and Adobe, are the targets of the Unisys licensing fee.

## PNGs to the Rescue?

In reaction to the whole "LZW patent" controversy, in January 1995 CompuServe affirmed its objective to coordinate the development of GIF24, a freely usable successor to GIF, capable of 24-bit (16.7-million-color) lossless compression. Intent on solving the Unisys patent problem, several developers delved into projects and eventually came up with a convergence of GIF24 and other projects into what became **PNG**, or **Portable Network Graphics**. In light of the patent problem, some developers proclaimed that PNG also stands for "**P**NG is **N**ot **G**IF".

The most impressive feature of PNG graphics is their support for **alpha transparency**, which allows designers to include effects like drop-shadows and anti-aliasing against any background, unlike GIF or JPEG. PNG is now supported by most of the recent browser versions, although Internet Explorer (the most popular of browsers) still doesn't support its alpha channel features. As a result of this, PNG still isn't a high priority for web designers, with GIF still taking center stage, even though the W3C officially endorsed PNG as the format to replace GIF quite a while ago.

*Anti-aliasing is a method for reducing jagged lines within images that should, in reality, be straight.*

In addition, GIF got another big hurrah when the major browsers added support for GIF animations back in the mid 1990s. **GIF animations** (simple animations that are built with a series of GIF images) caught on like wildfire and we are still inundated with GIF-animated banners, buttons, and gimmicks nearly every time we land on a web page, commercial or not. Even though **MNG** files, or **animated PNGs**, were then developed in response, it was too little too late — the simplicity of creating a GIF animation along with the slow adoption of PNG-based formats by browsers practically makes it seem like PNG is non-existent.

## JPEGs

**JPEG** is an acronym of **Joint Photographic Experts Group**, pronounced jay-peg.

One of the reasons for choosing JPEG format images over GIF format images is that it lets you save images with millions of different colors (it is 24-bit, meaning 16.7 million colors), rather than just 256 or less. JPEG also generally compresses a file much smaller than a GIF, which means faster downloading time.

That's all well and good, but there are some downsides. First, unlike GIF, JPEG does not support transparency or animation. Second, and more importantly, JPEG uses **lossy compression**.

Lossy compression means that the image literally loses colors in order to compress an image, and does its best to use the remaining colors as a substitute. The more you compress a JPEG, the more colors it will lose, and therefore the fuzzier or wobblier the image looks. For this reason, the format works best with photographs or other graphics with many subtle changes in color, since the scope of colors that can be removed is larger. It doesn't work well for things like "blocky" images or images containing text.

Let's look at an example. Here is an image of Lance Armstrong in the Lance Armstrong Foundation's Kids' Fun Race at 100 percent quality. The file is a 208K JPEG, and very high quality.

In most applications that save JPEGs, we are able to specify the percentage quality we require (which the software interprets as a level of compression wanted in the image). At 50 percent quality, the image still looks great. However, its size is significantly smaller – only 50K. This is still a bit big for slower online connections, such as dial-up modems. At 20 percent quality, it is very apparent that the quality of the image is being sacrificed, but the image is 30K.

Finally, here you can see the same image at 5 percent quality, to demonstrate how bad a GIF can get. The image is now only 18K, but note the blockiness of the shadows, and the bad edges of the windows and buildings.

Is a larger file size worth the better quality? This is the kind of consideration you have to make when deciding on the quality of images. Of course, the level of blockiness at lower quality will be different for each image, but in general, the lower the percentage of saving quality, the lower the visual quality.

Just to compare, here's the high-quality image saved as a web-safe GIF at its highest possible quality. At 119 colors, it weighs in at 94K:

Depending on the photo, the GIF may not look all that bad until you take a look up close. Not the most flattering image we've seen:

Looking closely at the high-end JPEG, we can see that it's blocky, but the detail is much smoother than the GIF:

Take a close-up look at the low-end JPEG: it's easier to see the differences between the qualities of the JPG images here:

This is subjective, of course: some would still prefer the low-end JPEG over the GIF, and some would prefer the other way around. This is why it is worth while spending time with images, seeing which look best at what levels, how colors match up to the original, and so on. The image itself is the first deciding factor, and your judgment is the final deciding factor.

### JPEG-Like Formats

**Progressive JPEGs** are a variation of the JPEG format in which the image seems to "fade in" gradually from a fuzzy bunch of blocks to a more detailed image, rather than being drawn on screen from top to bottom. The benefit is that the user can generally figure out what the image is before its full detail is drawn on the page, and therefore offers better and faster understanding of the page's content.

A newly proposed standard JPEG format is **JPEG2000**, an image-coding system that uses compression techniques based on wavelet technology. Given its resulting smaller images with better quality, the new compression scheme is intended to be used not only on the Web, but in digital camera image storage, digital pre-press, high-end medical imaging, and other image-dependent fields and uses. However, ongoing patent disputes and disagreements about its specs may keep JPEG2000 out of the picture for a while. Keep up with its developments at *http://www.jpeg.org*.

# Vector Graphics: Beyond Bitmaps

Vector graphics differ from bitmap graphics in a very fundamental way: rather than specifying every single pixel within an image, the **coordinates** of specific points of the image are given. This has the great advantage of being easy to resize without losing any quality of the image and without increasing the file size. As the image "grows" in size, the coordinates of specific points of the image may change, but the number of points specified does not. The description of how the image looks in relation to the specified points remains the same as before.

Let's look at a very simple example: a straight line. A bitmap image would have to specify all the points on the line, so if we increase the size of the image, the number of points specified would increase. A vector graphic, however, would only need to specify the coordinates of the end points of the line and then say "join up these two points". If the image is increased in size, the end point coordinates will change, but the description of "join up these two points" won't.

Obviously, the larger the number of "end points" of an image, the more description is necessary. A file with more points to specify will be bigger, but generally it won't be as big as the corresponding bitmap file.

As I said above, vectors have the benefit over bitmap images that they can be resized without any loss in image quality. For example, consider the following image:

If the image was stored in a vector format (such as SVG), and then resized, it would look like the image on the near right – it retains its original quality. However, if the image was stored in a bitmap format (such as GIF), and then resized, it would look like the image on the far right:

Now we have looked at how vector graphics work, let's look at some of the formats available to produce them. We will look at:

- Macromedia Flash
- SVG (Scalable Vector Graphics)

There are other formats available, including **SMIL (Synchronized Multimedia Integration Language**, see *http://www.w3.org/AudioVideo/*), but adoption of these is currently not very widespread.

## Macromedia Flash

**Flash** has arguably been the most phenomenal software wave to hit the web-creative market in the last few years. Introduced first as FutureSplash, it became Flash in 1996. As a vector-based application that was developed along with its own web plugin for displaying its files, it soon became the pet of many a designer.

However, as designers tend to do, we pushed Flash technology to its limits, and thereby created larger-than-huge web sites based on Flash. With its amazing capabilities to combine animation, text, and full-fledged stereo disco techno-beat soundtracks, it was hard to resist putting in every element that we could possibly fit into our files.

So for a while, Flash wasn't fulfilling its promise, at least to web users. The plugin took a long time to download and a large proportion of Flash files were multi-megabytes, which added up to a long wait when on a modem connection. Quite a few sites that used the same old *bmphditty bmphditty bmph* soundtrack accompaniment to an annoying superfluous intro movie soon made us scramble for the *skip intro* link, if the designer had deemed to include it. Flash remained a favorite of designers, but there were a number of accessibility and usability challenges to overcome.

Luckily for us, many of them have now been overcome. These days, smart designers apply the same principles of design and content presentation and management to Flash as they do to other content, and sites based on Flash become cool again.

## SVG

**SVG** (**Scalable Vector Graphics**) is a language for describing two-dimensional graphics using an XML vocabulary. While not something you'll probably be working with any time soon on a regular basis, there are mentions of it often enough to warrant attention, and it has been recommended as a standard for web graphics by the W3C (see *http://www.w3.org/Graphics/SVG/*). Applications that create SVG images are still few and far between, but among them are Jasc WebDraw, Adobe GoLive, Adobe Illustrator, and CorelDraw 10.

Like CSS and other text-based standards, SVG is created using plain text that can then be embedded into HTML files. The benefit of describing images in this fashion makes for smaller overall web page download sizes, and faster loading pages. And again, because SVG images are vector format graphics, rather than bitmaps, they can be made larger or smaller and still retain their good looks.

Compared to the Macromedia Flash Player, however, Adobe's SVG Viewer – the one plugin that supports SVG on the Web—has an almost non-existent user base. Flash boasts nearly 98 percent of all web users have a version of Flash Player installed, whereas Adobe's SVG Viewer is one of those applications most haven't heard of.

# Graphics Applications

There are various applications available to help us create graphics for the Web.

**Fireworks MX** is Macromedia's graphics application, a trial version of which is included on the accompanying CD. It has the advantage over other software that it allows you to create, edit, and resize both vector images *and* bitmap images, retaining quality throughout.

**Adobe Photoshop** has been the most popular image manipulation program for designers since way back in 1990. In the past couple of major versions, Photoshop has added features such as web-safe color palettes, automated GIF animation creation, image map and rollover assistance, *Save for Web* optimization, and now partners up with Adobe Image ready to add web-specific features such as Web Photo Gallery. This automates the process of creating basic web-based photo and image galleries. Its major downfall is its expense. At a suggested list price of over $600 US, it's a sizable investment for the lone designer. Photoshop is available for both Windows and Macintosh platforms – see *http://www.adobe.com* for more information.

**Adobe Photoshop Elements** is billed as a "digital camera companion" software package by Adobe, and includes a few features that are web publishing-specific, borrowed from full-fledged Photoshop. At $99 suggested US list price, Photoshop Elements is quite a bit more affordable than Photoshop. It's available for both Windows and Mac, and 30-day free trial versions are available for download from *http://www.adobe.com*.

**Jasc Paint Shop Pro** was among the first Windows applications to get a lot of web designer customers. Like Photoshop, Paint Shop Pro has a long history as a well-respected image manipulation program that found itself being used by designers to create quality images for the Web. Among other interesting options are patterned and graduated paint brushes, output to GIF, JPEG, and PNG, image slicing, rollover tools, GIF animation creation, and the ability to create and define image maps. Its main limitation is that it is only available for Windows. One of its best features, however, is that it's very inexpensive: at just over $100 US, it's tremendous value. Jasc Software offers 30-day free trial downloads at *http://www.jasc.com*.

Unlike the other applications mentioned here, **the GIMP** runs on Linux as well as having Mac and Windows versions. And to top it off, it's free. It also gives the pay-for software a run for the money. Besides a full paint palette, GIMP supports GIF, JEPG, PNG, TIFF, MPEG, PDF, BMP, and many other file formats. It can be used as a full photo-image enhancement tool, as well as a web-graphics creation and manipulation tool. For more information or to download a copy of The GIMP, go to *http://www.gimp.org* or *http://www.macgimp.org*.

# Summary

No matter how you slice them, graphics are one of the most important aspects of the Web. The challenge of the early days to make images small and retain their quality hasn't changed, but applications and years of experimentation by designers have made reaching the goal a lot easier. While we haven't delved into every application developed to create web graphics (it would take a book on each to be fair!), it's important to note that there are a multitude of tools available for a designer, whether with a large or small budget. Knowing how to best take advantage of an application and create what a client wants with the tool you have is more crucial than purchasing the most expensive software. Be willing to experiment with various formats to achieve the best quality for your intended audience.

**Creating Graphics for the Web**

# 6

- Using tables for page layout

- The art of frames

- GIF spacers and image slicing

**Authors: Crystal Waters and Rachel Andrew**

# Traditional Page Layout Techniques

In this chapter, we'll cover some of the traditional HTML techniques for laying out our sites. These methods of web design are not considered best practice these days, hence we advise that you do not consider using these techniques in new projects if at all possible. However, they are methods you are likely to come across if you come to work on an old site that someone else has already developed.

The primary methods we will look at are the use of **layout tables** and **frames**. The use of tables for layout, and to some extent frames, was driven by the desire of early web designers to replicate printed media. The first web sites were nothing more than documents placed online and, as the web developed, designers really stuck to this principle of replicating their print designs online.

Many designers were trained in print techniques – of course, no-one was at that point trained in web design, and the aim was to create pages that attempted to emulate the 'pixel-perfect' positioning of printed media. Additionally, designers used to seeing their design printed exactly as they had designed it, wanted to ensure that their pages looked identical across all browsers (at this point Netscape and Internet Explorer had more or less an equal market share, and there were fewer alternative devices and browsers available).

As the Web has developed, it has become impossible to design something that will look the same in all browsers and devices: your page as displayed in a mainstream web browser on a computer screen will look very different on a PDA, or on WebTV, so this goal of pixel-perfect design is seen to be a misguided one. Instead, the aim seems to have shifted to accessible content in all browsers and devices (**functionality** across devices, rather than **form**).

As we will discuss later in this book, the abilities that we have at our disposal these days mean that graphic-intensive pages are often unnecessary and look dated in comparison to fluid, quick to load CSS-based designs, which only rely on actual images for such things as logos and finishing touches.

That said, it is possible that you will encounter older sites during the course of your work. Clients sometimes simply want someone to 'tidy up' or add a new section to an existing site and have no intention of paying for a redesign, so it is worth understanding these older techniques and what to do with sites that use them. The process of updating an old site in this fashion is sometimes referred to as **retrofitting**, and the old sites themselves are sometimes referred to as **legacy sites**.

# Tables and Layout

The original purpose of tables was, rather logically, to display tabular data on web sites. However, web designers soon found an alternative use for them. Tables make it possible to divide text into columns, and to separate blocks of text and graphics into either columns of a specified pixel-width, or a percentage width relative to the other columns in the table.

They soon became widely used to lay out sections of text and graphics – in imitation of how this is done in printed media. Indeed, it eventually became the case that tabular layout had gone too far. Rather than using a single table to define their site's layout, web designers were nesting tables inside of other tables, and the value of the `<table>` element for its original purpose had been undermined.

Using tables to lay out a visual design is problematic on many fronts. Tables were never designed for such a thing, and a large amount of markup has to be employed to produce the required effect, particularly where no CSS is used at all. Such things as nesting one table inside another to produce a border have been commonly used techniques, but the same effect can now be created with CSS, thus removing the need for all that additional markup. Nested tables used for layout are very complicated to change, for example when the client suddenly decides that the menu should be on the left of the screen rather than the right.

You should still familiarize yourself with the use of tables for layout, in order to know how to work with them on sites you come across in your professional work, but you should avoid their use on new sites yourself, if you can, instead employing CSS. We mention CSS a number of times in this chapter – for more detail on CSS, see *Chapter 8*.

## Table Basics

Tables work in a manner similar to a spreadsheet: information is set up and presented in **columns** and **rows**. The square that forms the intersection of a column and a row is referred to as a **cell**.

Here is a basic three-column, two-row table, and below is the HTML markup that produces it:

| This is cell A | This is cell B | This is cell C |
| This is cell D | This is cell E | This is cell F |

```
<table border="1">
  <tr>
    <td>This is cell A</td>
    <td>This is cell B</td>
    <td>This is cell C</td>
  </tr>
  <tr>
    <td>This is cell D</td>
```

```
      <td>This is cell E</td>
      <td>This is cell F</td>
   </tr>
</table>
```

The elements used are as follows:

- `<table>` is the container for all the table content.

- `<tr>` and `</tr>` (tr = "table row") mark out the rows of the table. Although some browsers are forgiving when you forget to include a closing `</tr>` at the end of each table row, some just assume the table row goes on. Always use an end tag rather than letting the browser guess: it's good practice to support standards that make a site more accessible.

- `<td>` and `</td>` mark out the individual cells of the table (td = "table data").

In the previous example, no information is given about the table cell sizes, so, by default, the cells are sized just as large as they need to be to contain their content. Two cells next to each other expand or decrease in size depending on the width of the browser page and the amount of text or size of the image within the cell.

However, attributes can be used on various table elements in order to resize the cells, rows, or columns. For example, some of the key attributes of the `<table>` element are as follows:

- `cellpadding`: specifies the space needed between the edges of a cell and its contents (this should now be replaced by applying a CSS rule to the cell using `padding`).

- `cellspacing`: specifies the space needed between individual cells in the table (this is now replaced with a CSS rule – `margin`).

- `width`: fixes the width of the whole table.

Another common attribute of the `<table>` element, which we used in the above example, is the `border` attribute. The value set for this attribute is the size of the border required around the table itself and all the individual cells. However, `border` is a deprecated attribute and it is advisable in new sites to replace this with the CSS `border` rule.

## More Complex Tables

Certain definitions of row and column widths and heights can make for an interesting combination of cell shapes and sizes – this is how we would construct a layout using a table. The `rowspan` and `colspan` attributes of the `<td>` element direct cells to span more than one row or column. Take the following table:

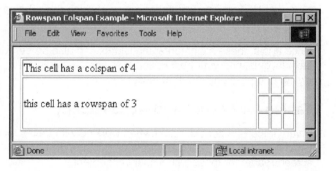

This table was produced using the following markup (see `RowspanColspan.html` on the CD):

```
<table width="400" border="1">
  <tr>
    <td colspan="4">This cell has a colspan of 4</td>
  </tr>
  <tr>
    <td rowspan="3">this cell has a rowspan of 3</td>
    <td> </td>
    <td> </td>
    <td> </td>
  </tr>
  <tr>
    <td> </td>
    <td> </td>
    <td> </td>
  </tr>
  <tr>
    <td> </td>
    <td> </td>
    <td> </td>
  </tr>
</table>
```

*Note that we have used another character entity in this example (we first met these in Chapter 2) – ` `. This creates a blank space character. `nbsp` stands for "non-breaking space".*

I've added a border to the above example so that you can see where the cells are. This simple structure could easily be the beginning of a traditional design laid out with tables. We can add widths to any of our table cells by using the `width` attribute, and align the text to the top, middle, or bottom of the cell using `align` and `valign`:

```
<td width="120" rowspan="3" valign="top">this cell has a rowspan of 3</td>
```

The values for the `width` attribute can either be given as percentage or a fixed number of pixels. If we wanted our table to fill the entire screen we would give the `<table>` tag a `width` of `100%`:

```
<table width="100%">
```

If I wanted a cell to always span `20%` of the width of the user's browser window we would use:

```
<td width="20%">
```

The values for `align` (which aligns the contents horizontally within the table cell) are `left`, `center`, or `right`. The values for `valign` (which does the same for vertical alignment) are `top`, `middle`, `bottom`, or `baseline`.

Once again, these alignments and widths can also be set with CSS, and if you need to work with table layouts then your best option is to combine a very simple tabular layout with CSS for all the styling and positioning of that layout.

## Tables for Layout and Accessibility

A very important consideration when working with tables for layout is what happens to that table when it is read by a browser that does not support tables or a non-graphical browser, such as a screen reader for those with visual impairment.

Browsers will automatically presume that the table is being used for tabular data (such as that which appears in a spreadsheet) and will read it starting from the top left hand cell, moving along the cells to the right and then starting on the next line. This is called **linearization** of the table. To understand how this would affect someone who doesn't have any visual clues as to how the information should be understood, consider the following example:

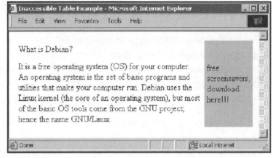

This image shows a construction not uncommon on the Web, as viewed in IE 6 – a content area (which is actually split into two table cells) and a right-hand column used for an advertising message. The table markup for this looks like so (see `InaccessibleTable.html` on the CD):

```
<table width="100%" cellpadding="5">
  <tr>
    <td width="80%">What is Debian?</td>
    <td rowspan="2" bgcolor="#99CCFF">free screensavers, download here!!!</td>
  </tr>
  <tr>
    <td width="80%">It is a free operating system (OS) for your computer.
      An operating system is the set of basic programs and utilities that make
      your computer run. Debian uses the Linux kernel (the core of an operating
      system), but most of the basic OS tools come from the GNU project; hence
      the name GNU/Linux. </td>
  </tr>
</table>
```

It is easily understood by anyone using a graphical browser that the answer to the question "What is Debian?" is to be found directly underneath the question. However, a text-only browser or device (or a screen reader) will read the right-hand column before reading the answer. In Lynx (a popular text-only browser) it looks like this:

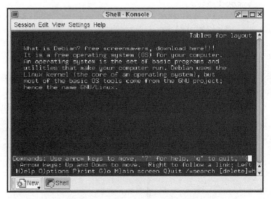

Now we're not sure if Debian is free screensavers or an operating system! This is a very simple demonstration, and perhaps isn't *that* incomprehensible, but imagine a site with multiple tables nested inside each other and you can imagine how quickly a page could become totally incomprehensible once read by a non-graphical browser or device.

If you must use tables for layout, or are tidying up a legacy site that does, then make sure that they are understandable once linearized. You can test them in the Lynx emulator found at *http://www.delorie.com/web/lynxview.html* or download Lynx itself from the *Evolt.org* browsers site at *http://browsers.evolt.org/*.

# Frames and Frame Building

Frames allow a web page to be split into two or more independent documents within the browser window (almost like you have different windows open within one browser window). As with other things that are mentioned within this chapter, frames in their current form are deprecated, and it is not expected that you would be using frames in the creation of new sites. However, as coming across your first framed site can be slightly confusing, it is worth discussing them here.

So how do we create a framed page? We use the `<frameset>` and `<frame>` elements instead of the `<body>` element. The `<frameset>` element defines the position of each frame within the browser window. A typical frameset layout with two frames might have one fixed frame that holds the logo and the main menu choices, and a main content window in which the choices made on the menu will appear. For example (see `SimpleFrameset.html`, `menupage.html`, and `contentpage.html` on the CD that accompanies this book):

```
<!DOCTYPE HTML PUBLIC "-//W3C//DTD HTML 4.01 Frameset//EN"
"http://www.w3.org/TR/html4/frameset.dtd">
<html>

<head>
   <title>A document containing frames</title>
</head>

<frameset cols = "130,*">
   <frame src="menupage.html">
   <frame src="contentpage.html">
</frameset>
<noframes>
   <body>
     This is what will appear on the screen if the person viewing the site
     isn't using a browser that supports frames.
   </body>
</noframes>

</html>
```

This page looks like so when viewed in a browser that supports frames:

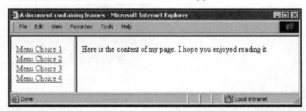

Note that the `<noframes>` element contains content that will display if the page is viewed using a browser that doesn't support frames (see the section on `<noframes>` later for more information).

In the markup, the `<frameset>` element takes a `cols` attribute, which indicates that the frames contained will act as "columns" within the main browser window. The value of the `cols` attribute is a comma-delimited list of the widths these columns will each take. One of the widths is usually set as variable (`*`), since we don't know how wide the user's browser window will be.

A width could be specified as an integer value (from example `"80"`) for the number of pixels, a percentage value (for example `"20%"`), for the percentage of the window width occupied, or a mathematical value such as `"2*"`, which in this case indicates that the frame is twice the size of the other frame (in other words, the 2 tells it that element should be 2:1 in proportion to the other element). In the previous example, the first frame is set to 130 pixels wide, while the other frame column is given a width of `"*"`, which tells the browser that the element is to take up the rest of the browser window – no matter what size it is.

The `<frameset>` element could alternatively have taken an attribute of `rows`, in which case the frames contained would be specified as rows within the main frameset. The same system of setting the row heights is then used.

Inside the frameset itself are the `<frame>` elements. These each have a `src` attribute that indicates the name of the HTML page that should be loaded into that frame within the browser.

## Nested Framesets

It is possible to nest framesets inside one another. In a nested frameset, the frameset markup will first tell the browser that there are two rows of frames. For example, here we have one fixed 80 pixel high frame, and the second row will take up the rest of the browser window:

```
<frameset rows="80,*" cols="*">
  <frame src="headline.html" name="topFrame">
```

Now we're going to nest another frameset inside our primary frameset. This markup tells the browser that there are two columns, and tells it what will be inside each one by default:

```
<frameset rows="80,*" cols="*">
  <frame src="headline.html" name="topFrame">
  <frameset cols="80,*">
    <frame src="menupage.html" name="leftFrame">
    <frame src="contentpage.html" name="maincontentFrame">
  </frameset>
</frameset>
```

This creates a page layout like this (see `NestedFrameset.html`):

### Dreamweaver MX Frameset Designs

Dreamweaver MX provides many templates – skeleton HTML pages that you can adjust to your own needs. The frameset designs can be accessed by selecting *File > New* and choosing *Framesets* from the *General* tab.

Playing around with the Dreamweaver MX framesets will give you a basic understanding of how frames actually work, in case you come across them at some point.

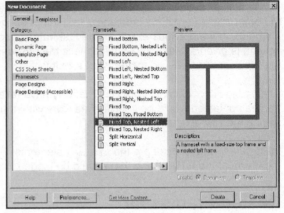

## The <noframes> Element

If you are using frames, then it is important to include `<noframes></noframes>` tags within the document so that browsers without frame support, such as screen readers, mobile phones, PDAs, and search engines, are able to read or index your pages. The `<noframes>` content should provide a way for people to navigate your main content pages without relying on navigation that is held within another inaccessible frame.

As we saw above, the `<noframes>` elements are placed in the HTML like so:

```
<noframes>
  <body>
    This is what will appear on the screen if the person viewing the site
    isn't using a browser that supports frames.
  </body>
</noframes>
```

## Problems with Frames

Frames are deprecated, and bring with them many disadvantages. Frames as we know them today do not appear in the XHTML 1.1 specification; therefore any site using them will need to be aware that they could find support for frames dropped in future browsers.

In most cases, the outermost frameset's `<title>` element content is what will show in the browser window title bar. This title remains there, no matter what content is called up into the subframes. This means that people cannot see where they are on your site so easily, and may be unable to bookmark individual pages. Despite this, you should always give each document its own individual `<title>` element.

Frames are not particularly search engine-friendly: many engines cannot index your pages effectively, and those that can may provide direct links to documents that are within your content frame and so visitors will arrive at that document but have no means of navigating around the rest of your site (you will not be presented with the full frameset). Some engines will only index the `<noframes>` content.

Alternative devices may be totally unable to read frames: to get around this problem your `<noframes>` content will need to be very comprehensive so, in effect, you are almost building two sites. This begs the question, why use frames in the first place when you could build one site that is accessible to all users, on all browsers and devices?

# GIF Spacers

GIF spacers are transparent GIF images that have traditionally been used to help keep things in line, to indent text, to nudge over an image, or to help align elements on a page. However, we can now use CSS for precise positioning, therefore it is not expected that you would build a new web site using these techniques. However, as you may come across existing sites that do use them, it would be unwise for us to totally ignore their existence.

To use this method you would need to create a 1 pixel by 1 pixel, transparent image (easily done in a graphics package such as Fireworks). You would then save it, and call it something obvious, such as `spacer.gif` or `transparent.gif`.

Ordinarily, when you place an image into an HTML page, you give the image the correct dimensions for the image you are using. However, when using a 1 pixel GIF for spacing, you give the GIF the size that you need for your effect. As an example of how this works, the following example shows two images placed side by side with very little spacing between them.

To create more space between these images, we can use a spacer GIF to space them 40 pixels apart. However, we do not need to create a spacer image 40 pixels wide: instead, we simply resize our 1 pixel GIF to the required width.

```
<?xml version="1.0" encoding="iso-8859-1"?>
<!DOCTYPE html PUBLIC "-//W3C//DTD XHTML 1.0 Transitional//EN"
"http://www.w3.org/TR/xhtml1/DTD/xhtml1-transitional.dtd">
<html xmlns="http://www.w3.org/1999/xhtml">
<head>
<title>Spacers</title>
<meta http-equiv="Content-Type" content="text/html; charset=iso-8859-1" />
</head>

<body>
<img src="dreamweavermx.gif" width="120" height="153"
     alt="Dynamic Dreamweaver MX" />
<img src="spacer.gif" alt="" width="40" height="1" />
<img src="dreamweaverphp.gif" width="120" height="153"
     alt="Dreamweaver MX: PHP" />
</body>
</html>
```

The images will now display in the browser like so (see GIFspacing.html on the CD):

These days, a new site would use the CSS rules for padding and margins to accomplish this task – you will discover how to do this in *Chapter 8*. If you find yourself having to tidy up a site that uses these methods, remove spacer GIFs and use CSS to produce the same effects wherever you can.

If you have to leave spacers in, ensure that each image that is there purely for layout purposes has a blank alt attribute (that is, alt=""), as in the above example. Otherwise, screen readers and non-graphical browsers will read or print "*IMAGE*" each time they come across a spacer GIF, which can be very frustrating for the user.

# Slicing

Slicing a page is another old-fashioned way of creating a page layout. The aim was to optimize the various elements of the page layout as either GIF or JPG files, depending on what works best for that part of the page. However, the effect of this on file size is negotiable since, as you chop up a page layout into small images and optimize each one to hopefully improve quality and cut down on file size, you take up more disk space in bloated and unnecessary table markup, needed to retain the original layout design.

Working in this way again stems from the desire to replicate print design, as we discussed at the beginning of this chapter. In the current climate, using a sliced-up image as your HTML page would make your new site look very dated. It also has repercussions for accessibility (as screen readers cannot read text contained within images, and users who need to resize text to read it cannot do so), and for search engines that will not be able to index your site.

Graphics packages such as Fireworks and Photoshop contain tools that will slice an image and turn it into an HTML page. If you come across a very messy web site/page with very little text, you have probably found something created by one of these applications. They generate an HTML file automatically, including the appropriate <img> and <table> elements (including rowspan and colspan attributes, where appropriate, as we showed you earlier), as well as outputting the image files themselves, in the formats chosen.

Basically, slicing an image is like creating a puzzle out of a layout. The resulting files are the picture pieces and the markup that puts it all back together in HTML. The only point at which you should ever consider slicing an image these days would be in order to create a banner or similar, which needs to be carefully lined up with the rest of the page.

The image is created within a graphics application and then the application's slicing tool is used to literally cut it up into many pieces.

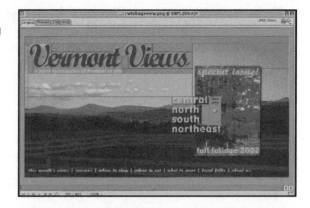

Here we can see how such a page will load in a browser – very slowly! Each of the rectangular areas you can see here is an individual table cell.

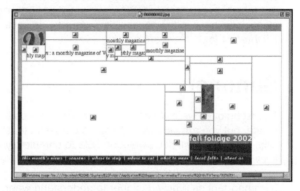

Each of these individual table cells contains an image which has to be loaded into the browser. There are likely to also be many spacer GIFs used in the construction of such a page, which is very unlikely to make any sense at all when viewed with a non-graphical browser.

## What Should You Do If You Have to Work with This?

If you need to work on a site such as this you will need to be careful. Because the original designer created the page in this manner, there are likely to be some very convoluted table arrangements used within it and it will be quite easy to break. If you have the time you might be able to take the layout and simplify it somewhat.

Use text and CSS (as we will discuss in *Chapter 8*) for the text parts of the document, and use background-colors instead of images for parts of the image that are block color. Also, ensure that any images that are purely for the visual layout use empty (`alt=""`) `alt` attributes, and that any image that contains important descriptive text has good, descriptive `alt` attribute content (of no more than 50 characters) so that someone not on a graphical browser can understand the page. What will happen is that the `alt` attribute content will be read out, or printed out in place of the image.

As time goes on, we should see fewer pages created in this manner, and you will hopefully never have to work in this way. However, it is worth being aware of such legacy methods, as there are many sites still active that are three or four years old, and may have had such methods employed in their creation.

# Dreamweaver Page Layouts

As we discovered when discussing frames, Dreamweaver MX includes a variety of page layouts, which you can use to familiarize yourself with these techniques. When you choose *File > New* in Dreamweaver MX, a dialog comes up with a number of choices for page layout. Among them are:

- Frame layouts
- Table-based page layouts
- Table-based accessible page layouts

All templates are modifiable within Dreamweaver if you choose to do so, and you can also save designs you've created as templates. Working with these simple layouts will help you to understand how frame- and table-based layouts are produced and, if you are creating pages that use tables as opposed to CSS for layout, it will be worth your while looking at the techniques used (especially those in the accessible page layouts section, but see also the *Accessibility* section of *Chapter 11* for some more details).

# Summary

The techniques we have covered here are not recommended for use in new web sites you may create, but you are very likely to come across at least some of them in your work on older web sites. Since you will not always be able to completely redesign such web sites, it is a good idea to know what was in the minds of the web designers when they built the site originally.

It is important as a new designer to understand where the Web has come from and to be able to work with older designs. However, if you are starting out at this point in the Web's history, you should focus your learning on new techniques, such as those discussed elsewhere in this book. By learning up-to-date techniques you may even find that you have a head start in some ways over more experienced designers, simply because you are not having to unlearn legacy mainstays such as those described here.

Traditional Page Layout Techniques

# 7

- Navigational structure and design
- Overview of types of navigation
- Ten navigation tips

Author: Crystal Waters

# Navigation

In a broad sense, navigation is how we move between web pages, but there are actually two definitions closely related to this idea. **Structural navigation** refers to the way that the many pages of a site are structured relative to one another and how someone is able to move through the site, from page to page. **Navigational design** refers to the way in which menus, directives, visuals, text instructions, and other parts of a page are designed to direct us to other pages, or other parts of the same page.

We'll explore various navigation options in this chapter, both popular and more unconventional. We'll take a look at what kinds of choices we have when structuring our site, and then go on to look at specific navigational methods most commonly used on the Web. We'll visit successful sites, popular layouts, and methods of determining layout and applying it to our site design plans.

## Structural Navigation and Navigation Design

While designers may know that a site they are working on has thousands of pages, no matter what the site structure, a user often can only see a web site one page at a time. In contrast, if you're handed a book, you can flip through it to get a feel for the way it flows, and simply heft it to see how much there is to navigate through. A movie is always marked with its length, so we know that it will take, for example, 112 minutes of our day to watch it from end to end.

Without navigational structure and a navigational design that gives guidance to a site visitor, the site – from the very beginning – is disorienting. What do I do? Where do I go? How do I get there? Where am I? These are questions that should be easily answered by a user at any given time. Therefore, navigational structure and navigational design must work hand in hand.

# Structural Navigation

In this section we will take a look at the different types of navigation structures commonly experienced, not only on the Web, but also in everyday life. Through exploring these various types of structure, you should get a feel for what will work best for your design ideas and those of your clients.

## Linear Navigation

**Linear navigation** basically works in a straight line. There's a start page, an end page, and sequential pages in between.

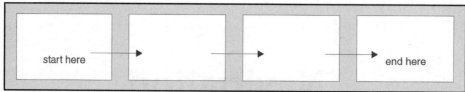

*Linear navigation.*

Many types of media, such as books or television and movies, tend to employ linear navigation – the story line starts, the story happens, the story ends. Although with any one of these types of media we can start where we want and stop when we want, it's not common (or expected) that someone reading a book will start in the middle and read pages backwards or in random order. Those watching a movie or television show will usually want to see the beginning before they see the end. The same goes for sound files: generally, a listener wants to hear a piece (be it music or narration) from beginning to end, rather than moving around within a broadcast or song to listen to parts in the middle before hearing the beginning, and so on. Even if we are given the option of skipping around, either with fast forward or flipping pages, it is generally desirable by both designer and user not to do so.

While mostly used for traditional media, we see samples of linear navigation online all the time:

- Any movie-based instruction or video, or Flash-based site that requires us to watch the full film in order to enter a site or navigate any further, is a sample of linear navigation.

- A site that features stories that must be read in order is utilizing linear navigation. Visit W3Schools.com (http://www.w3schools.com/) where tutorials are split over many pages: each page can be browsed to in a linear fashion from the previous page.

- The many people who have utilized Blogger (http://www.blogger.com) to keep personal online diaries have their content presented in chronological order, latest entry first.

## Cyclical Navigation

**Cyclical navigation** works in a similar fashion to linear navigation, although the theme or story line comes back to the beginning as part of its navigational flow. A good non-webbased real-life example of cyclical navigation could be a shopping mall: You start from the door you enter the mall by, go around the aisles collecting your shopping, pay for your goods, and end up back at the same door in order to exit, and go search for your car.

Web-based examples include sites that allow you to proceed from an index of a set of pages through each page in turn before returning you to the index (for example, an art gallery site that allows you to link through the many pages containing images). Web-based forums also often use this type of navigation in part. You may start at a page that lists the posts to a particular forum, click on a message to view that message, and click on *Reply* to send a reply to the message. Once you send your reply, you will often be navigated back to the first page containing a list of the posts to the forum.

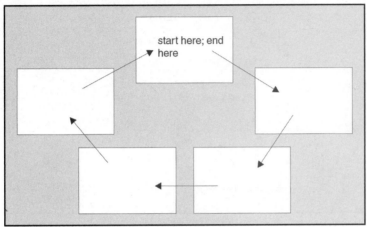

*Cyclical navigation.*

## Hierarchical Navigation

**Hyper** or **hierarchical navigation** is what most web sites use and what we associate the Web with most.

We are presented with a homepage, or sometimes an introductory splash page, when first arriving at a web site. From there, we are usually presented with multiple destination choices. Once we make a choice, then perhaps make a choice from the submenu of related areas, or make another choice from the main menu. At nearly every point (if the site is designed well) we should be able to get to a subarea on the site, or back to an area we came from, with only a few clicks at the most.

A typical path that a user might take in a hierarchical site is unpredictable in general. We might design a site that nudges users to go to our online store, for example, in order to persuade them to make a purchase, but the user has the option to go to whatever section of the site they wish, and should be able to get to other areas of the site from wherever they are. Consider your experiences in the non-web world: you visit a library or bookstore to find a specific book. You could go to the library or store, then to the bookshelf for the relevant topic, then to the book itself. Or you could just go straight to a bookshelf, and look at several different books, before noticing the one you really want. You might, instead, go to the librarian or bookstore information booth and ask them to find the book for you. However, you may also get completely distracted by a whole different section of books and end up in an area of the library or store that you didn't intend to be in, and get a whole different book altogether.

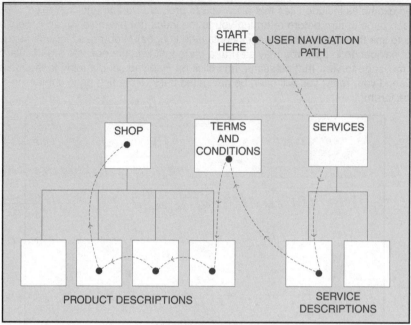

*Hierarchical navigation.*

There's also a relative to hierarchical navigation structure dubbed **web-like navigation** – suitably named for a method used on the Web, but not necessarily the first choice for web site design. A web-like navigation would also be hierarchical navigation, because we have to start somewhere when entering a site. However, areas of the site branch out from the homepage in random order, like branches of a tree, not necessarily in relation to one another. Basically, this is generally referred to as navigation without hierarchical organization.

## Navigation Design

In previous chapters, we've talked at length about the theory of hypertext and how it was developed to make finding relative documents and information easier for the user. A well-placed link can bring us to information that, in other media, might force us to search through a stack of documents, or a shelf of books.

However, getting that link in the right place is the challenge. Single links aren't generally much of a concern to us as designers: most of us will be dealing with multiple links per page, multiple site sections, and perhaps thousands of pages. To be successful, a site needs to be organized and structured in a consistent fashion that allows its users to find what they are looking for.

Read any article about successful web design and you'll probably find that the concern of many designers and information architects is **Human-Computer Interface** (**HCI**) interaction, or the way that people interact with a specific user interface design. The goal of these web professionals is to pursue the designs that make users more comfortable and productive with an application, whether it's a serious business site or a funky entertainment site. If a person can't work out how to operate or navigate a site, then they are not likely to be very productive or happy.

These average, unhappy users aren't alone in their struggles. Even highly experienced web users can have difficulty navigating a web site that is new to them. Having used a number of sites, experienced users may come to prefer certain navigational standards to others for their ease of use and functionality, and they develop certain expectations when using other sites. This doesn't necessarily mean that "you can't teach an old user new tricks" but it does mean that, if experienced users can't get something from your site in a manner that is intuitive or productive to them, they are likely to go somewhere else to find the services that they want, and you've lost another user.

Someone who is comfortable getting around your site will probably spend more time there, and enjoy the experience that bit more. They are probably more likely to explore the site beyond the scope of information they were originally looking for. So the moral is: no matter how innovative, beautiful, or informative your site's content is, if it doesn't serve the person using it because they can't get to it, it's no good.

You'll find that nearly every part of your navigational structure – menus, icons, navigational bars, overall design – will base its success on four key elements:

- Familiarity: How acquainted is your audience with this navigational design, chosen icons, or site structure?

- Consistency: Is there cohesion among the parts of the page? Do the images work well together, and do text menu names make sense? Do they mean the same thing in the same areas? Are similar pages designed in similar ways so that menus and elements can be found without a struggle?

- Simplicity: Is your site and navigational message distinct, clear, and uncomplicated?

- Clarity: Is it clear what your icons and other navigational aids represent? Or, do you have to explain them at length?

Applying these elements to your overall navigational design plan will make for a better experience for users, and keep your design cohesive and comprehensive.

## The Argument About Search Functions

Some think that a good search function in place on a site can take the place of smart navigational design, or use it to hide bad navigational design. However, while a good search function will almost certainly come in handy to help a user find something that may not otherwise be obvious, forcing the user to count on searching to find their way around can be detrimental to their experience. It forces them to do the navigational work; they may not be able to get back to where they came from; they probably won't know where they are in the site structure if they've searched in order to get there.

There are some sites with hundreds of categories, like eBay (*http://www.ebay.com*) or other auction or store sites, which really depend on their search functions for navigation. Given that there are so many items to choose from, it may take hours to wade through menus of categories, even if you had at least a vague description of what you're looking for.

While not ideal, it is possible to navigate around eBay using menu items – menu functionality is provided in addition to the search. The way in which the categories for each menu are organized makes this as easy as possible, considering the sheer number of them.

On eBay, the search engine is one of the first things presented on the page, so users have easy access to it (see below). This is also of added important because eBay users come from all levels of technological know-how, and guidance is available from the first point of contact – another triumph for this site design:

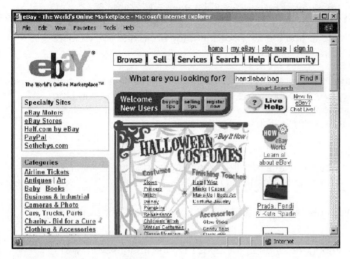

Here we do a search for "handlebar bag," hoping to find one for a bicycle. Without the search function, we'd have to look through all of the menu option categories on the left, trying to figure out what category this topic would be under. We'd then have to find a suitable subcategory, and so on.

Our search comes up with a number of results, and gives us a number of navigational options and clues (see left). If we look at the menu along the very top of the page, we can see that we are in the subcategory *find items*, under *Search*. On the left (in the *Matching Categories* box), we can see what subcategories our discoveries were found in. We can also choose to continue searching or refine our search (see the *Basic Search* box). In the main content of the page, the results of our search give links to found products.

If we click on one of the items in the list, we may find that it's not really the type of bag we want. However, eBay includes another feature to help us work out where we are – a link that describes the subcategory of items to which this particular item belongs.

In this case the link's text is: *Item located in: Parts & Accessories > Boats & Watercraft > Gear & Accessories > Personal Watercraft Gear*.

Clicking on this link will take us to a page (not shown here) that lists all items within that subcategory. Within that page is a useful navigation feature: a **breadcrumb trail**. This provides a series of links to pages that lie between the current page and the home page. In this case the links are:

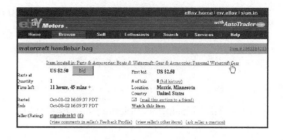

Home > All Categories > Parts & Accessories > Boats & Watercraft > Gear & Accessories > Personal Watercraft Gear

We could follow that path back to the homepage, or choose another level of the path. However, we wanted a bicycle handlebar bag, so we know this is not what we're looking for. We also know just where we are – to go back to the search list, we click the *Back* button twice in our browser.

In the search results list, we can now find a product more along the lines of what we're looking for. Again, the link that shows the path to this item is one we can follow to see all other products within the same category, if this particular item is not quite what we wanted. Note also how the menu at the top of the page shows that we are in *item view* within the *Browse* menu.

## Many Ways to Move

As with eBay, almost all sites have several ways that a site visitor can navigate, often more ways than they are aware of. For example, the following site has seven navigational options, as well as three options provided by the browser itself:

The options are as follows:

1. Using the browser's *Back* or *Forward* buttons, or using the *History* to go back to a page already visited.

2. Typing in a new URL.

3. Using the site's top-level navigation menus.

4. Using the search function to find a product.

5. Choosing from one of the *Shop By* options provided by a drop-down menu (in this case, allowing you to search by brand name).

6. Following the breadcrumb trail links back the way we came.

7.  Choosing from the *Categories* menu on the left.

8.  Clicking and holding down the mouse button on a Mac or clicking the right mouse button on a Windows PC, so that the navigational pop-up window appears. You can then make a choice to go *Back* or *Forward*.

9.  Utilizing the page's *Back* to link.

10. Making a choice among the text-link menu choices along the bottom of the page.

Clearly, we have many ways of moving from this page to others we may want to access. We can start at the top again, do a search, choose from various menus, or leave the site altogether. It's obvious that we have a challenge at hand, giving people enough options to find what they want easily and efficiently, and keeping them interested in content they find as they navigate through the site. There is no "right" or "wrong" number of options per se – giving someone ten navigation options doesn't mean that they are sure to go shooting off to another part of the site. The content and design of a particular page is what catches the user's eye, and keeps them there (or doesn't). The navigational options are what get people there in the first place.

# Types of Navigation

Now that we've seen that there are a number of different navigation design options available, let's take a look at some of them in more detail.

*As we saw in Chapter 3, **wireframing** is a term used to describe blocking out a page design into the parts that will eventually be filled with content. In this section, we'll be wireframing some existing sites to get a clearer view of the way the navigational structure and page layout works. Most sites contain a lot more elements than what you'll see here, such as advertisements, search forms, a secondary navigational menu, feature stories, or company news flashes, but you should start with just the basic structures at first.*

## Basic Navigation Bars

Navigation bars are usually thin menus that give the user the option to click to another area of the site. Each menu item may be simply a textual link, or an image link (sometimes called a **button**). We saw how the HTML for both these types of links works, back in *Chapter 2*.

An important factor in the success of your navigation bar is to use consistent placement. If it's at the top of the page in one area, and then the bottom of the page in another area, you're demanding unnecessary work from your users: they have to find the navigation bar before they can use it.

The navigation bar may be horizontal or vertical, depending on what is best for the site design as a whole:

```
<a href="AboutUs.html">About our Company</a> |
<a href="ProductInfo.html">Product Information</a> |
<a href="SalesInfo.html">Sales Information</a> |
<a href="Contact.html">Contact Us</a>
```

| About our Company | Product Information | Sales Information | Contact Us |

```
<a href="AboutUs.html">About our Company</a>
<br />
<a href="ProductInfo.html">Product Information</a>
<br />
<a href="SalesInfo.html">Sales Information</a>
<br />
<a href="Contact.html">Contact Us</a>
```

About our Company
Product Information
Sales Information
Contact Us

Navigation bars that are unobtrusive not only help people get around, but they assist in orientation, reminding the user where they happen to be in the whole scheme of things. For example, when a user clicks on a button to go to a new site location, that particular button's appearance might be changed (perhaps to be grayed out) on the new page, to remind the user that they are in that part of the site.

## Standard Layouts

It could be argued that there is no such thing as a "typical" web layout, but as the Web grows older, standards have begun to emerge. Some sites use horizontal navigation bar menus across the top of the page; other sites use vertical menus down one side of the page (usually the left). However, most use a combination of both of these menus. Most often, top-level company or organization information is in the horizontal menu, while content-specific menus are vertical.

### Horizontal Menus

CapitalOne.com (*http://www.capitalone.com/*) utilizes two levels of horizontal menus along the top part of its screen, one text-based and one graphics-based. It does have a vertical menu of sorts along the left-hand edge, but this changes dramatically depending on what page of the site you are on.

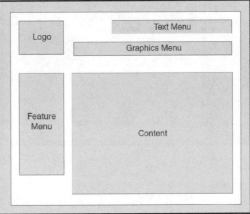

## Vertical Menus

*Zoic.com* (*http://zoic.com/*) only uses a left-aligned vertical menu throughout its site. However, on some pages of the site, the menu options are repeated as a horizontal textual menu at the bottom of the content being displayed.

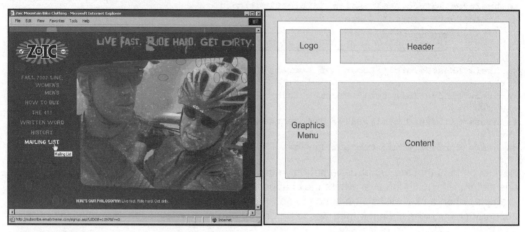

## Horizontal and Vertical Menus

REI-Outlet.com (*http://www.rei.com/*) uses a horizontal menu for general information and a left-aligned menu for information about particular categories. These menus are consistent throughout the site.

The site also provides plenty of navigational choices within its main content area, and a tabbed horizontal menu too. We'll talk more about tabbed menus in the next section.

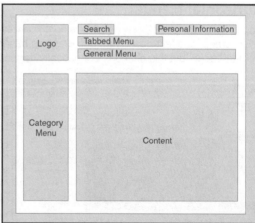

# Tabbed Menus

Tabbed menus are much like other menus. The only difference is that they give the reader a three-dimensional perspective on the choices they make, being similar to the physical tabs on dividers for paperwork.

Many sites make use of tabs, including Rei.com, which we looked at above. One of the more well-known tabbed navigation sites is Amazon.com (*http://www.amazon.com*), which uses tabs along the top of the screen layout, with subcategories and menu options below.

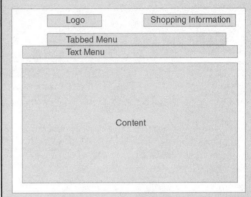

Follow a path into any area of the site, (for example, *BOOKS > BROWSE SUBJECTS > Awards > Best Books of All Time: Non-fiction*). Note that we are given a breadcrumb trail to show where we've come from. Also note that the tabbed menu choice we've made, *BOOKS*, is a different color (in this example, green) than other choices. The text of the submenu in which we are located, *BROWSE SUBJECTS*, is also a different color than the other submenu choices. Thus, the user knows both visually and textually where they are located.

*In Chapter 8, we'll be exploring ways in which to change the appearance of links depending on whether the link has been visited or the mouse is hovering over it, through the medium of CSS. We'll also take a look at ways in which to change images as we move our mouse over them using JavaScript in Chapter 10.*

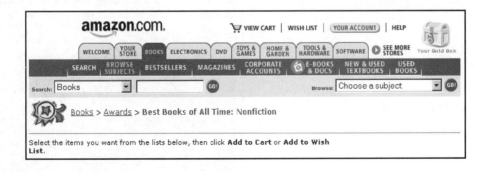

# Drop-Down Menus

So far, all menu choices that we have looked at have changed the content of the page when they are clicked. However, it is possible to create menus that are dynamic in some way. When the user clicks on a menu item (or perhaps simply rolls their mouse over the menu item), more associated menu choices are displayed without reloading the page. Usually these secondary menu choices will change the content of the page when clicked. This type of menu is often called a drop-down menu. We'll be seeing an example of how to create these with JavaScript in *Chapter 10*.

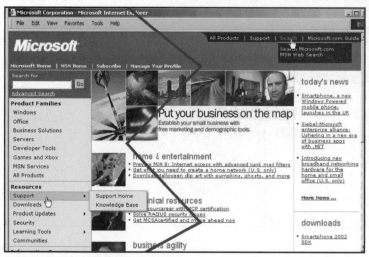

As an example, consider the Microsoft.com site. The menu choices in the top right-hand corner cause another menu to appear when the mouse hovers over them. The menu choices to the left that have an arrowhead next to them, also cause other menus to appear.

# Unconventional Menus

Aside from the more standard navigation types we have looked at so far, some sites use more imagination with their navigation.

For example, the folks over at Surly Bikes (*http://www.surlybikes.com*) use an amplifier for their top-level navigational interface, and images of their products as menu choices. The site is a two-part frameset: the top-level navigational menu is in one frame along the top of the browser window, and the main content shows up in the bottom frame. This unconventional design works well for this site, and all areas are available from within sub content areas.

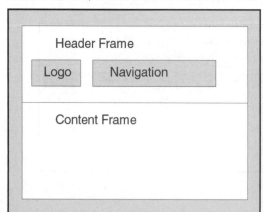

For another imaginative use of navigation see the Toy Box site (*http://www.toy-box.dk* – not shown here). This has lots of controls and sliders: a design that complements its techno-disco music. However, few of the design elements actually have a function other than perhaps some visual feedback (for example, you can turn switches "on" and "off", but nothing actually happens). While menu choices aren't necessarily obvious, this site is designed more to entertain than to serve as a standard business site.

The interfaces among the CBS reality TV shows seen below (*http://www.cbs.com/amazingrace*, *http://www.cbs.com/bigbrother*, *http://www.cbs.com/survivor*) are unconventional, yet fans of one show should be able to easily navigate the others, since they use the same basic layout and navigational functions.

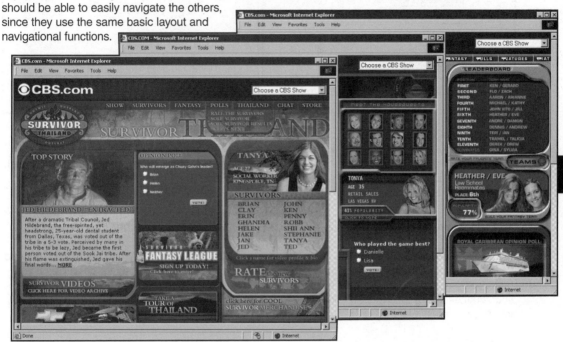

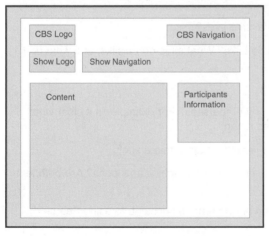

Here's the CBS reality show page layout wireframe. Consistency is a key to navigational success for CBS reality show fans.

Finally, take a look at the Brain Technologies Corporation (*http://www.thebrain.com*). They publish WebBrain, a navigational tool, which is also used on its own site for navigation.

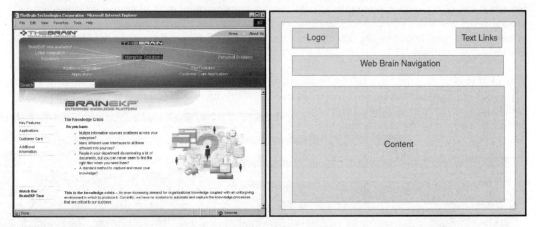

The window at the top houses the navigational system. Rather than a vertical or horizontal menu, WebBrain draws out the actual structure of the site as a "spider diagram", and users navigate by clicking on an area at the end of a "leg". The current page is highlighted in the center of the spider, and linked pages are branched off of the current page. Once a menu choice (such as *Enterprise Solutions* in this case) is clicked, it will move to the center of the navigational screen.

## What Navigation Design Should You Choose?

If you don't have a feel for the kind of preferences your site's audience have for navigation, how do you choose what to implement on your site? There are three good resources for good ideas: your own bookmarks, highly successful sites like Amazon and eBay, and your competitor's sites. Ask yourself these questions as you take time to really pay attention to how you view, navigate, and interact with each site:

- Which sites do I use – really use – most often? Why? What do I like (and dislike) about their navigational options?

- Do I always know where I am within my favorite sites?

- Of other sites I've looked at, which ones do I like? What sites do I dislike, and what do I dislike about them?

- What catches my eye first on the page?

- Do I need help learning how to navigate any of the sites? For example, is it clear what different menu items or content categories mean?

- Are there different ways of navigating to the same page within a site?

- Are the menus and navigation text-based, or are there graphics and icons? Are both text and graphics used?

- Do I know how to get around using menus or do I tend to succumb to using Search?"

Taking your answers into consideration, you have a wealth of design choices and options at hand with which to learn, practice with, and gain inspiration.

# Top Ten Navigation Tips

Now let's summarize what we have learned in this chapter into a checklist to go through when you become more experienced at designing navigation systems.

## Use Understandable Naming Conventions

The text used in navigation, whether it is in the form of text-based links, text within an image used as a link, or the value of the `alt` attribute of the `<img>` tag, should be decided upon before you create your navigation design. The text should be:

- **Intuitive**. The user should know exactly what to expect when they click on the link. For example, if you are linking to a page of product details, it is much more sensible to label the link "Products for Sale", or simply "Products", rather than "Stuff".

- **Consistent**. There should be a one-to-one relation between pages and the text used on links. For example, if you call a menu item that will take you to the information about the company "About Us" on the homepage, then all links that take you to that page should be labeled "About Us". If you use the text "Company Info" or "About our Company", it can cause confusion both to users and to site content editors.

## Use Breadcrumb Trails

As we've seen, breadcrumb trails on the Web serve as a guideline back to where a user started, as well as a reminder of where in the hierarchy they are at the moment. We saw them in use on Amazon.com and eBay earlier in this chapter, but you are likely to find them on many other sites.

> *Where does the term **breadcrumb trail** come from? Hansel and Gretel used breadcrumbs to mark their path home in a Hans Christian Andersen fairy tale. They were, in fact, unsuccessful, since the breadcrumbs were eaten by birds, but the idea is what counts!*

## Don't Hide Information

Keep all the information that your site provides readily available to the users:

- Make navigation links to other areas of the site conspicuous – make sure the navigation does not get lost within the content of the page.

- Keep popular information as few clicks as possible from the homepage. Hiding what might otherwise be a popular page under ten layers of clicks is a sign of bad navigation and bad content architecture, since users will have a hard time finding their way there again.

# Help Users Out

Site help can come in small or large packages. You probably don't need to provide lessons on how to use a web site in general, but you should include easily accessible information that explains terms and navigational structures that are exclusive to your site. This can be as simple as including a technical support page or creating a Frequently Asked Questions (FAQ) page.

# Include a Site Map

As we saw in *Chapter 3*, a site map, like a book's table of contents, is an easy way to give people guidance and an idea of your content structure. A well-organized site map enables people to find things quickly and to navigate quickly to deeper levels in the site's hierarchy. If your site has hundreds of pages, then you may not want to include the title of every page, but you will want to include a few levels of information. Like a book, you wouldn't want to have a table of contents that listed every paragraph, but you would want every chapter, and the first few heading levels of each chapter, to help you find information more readily.

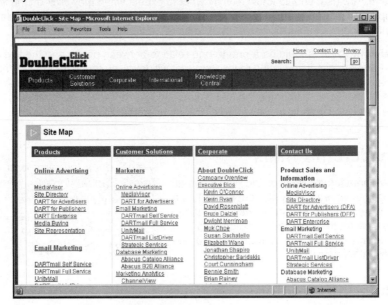

# Don't Count on Search Facilities

A search function can be crucial to a large site with many categories and pages, such as an online store, directory, or portal site (remember the classic example of eBay we looked at earlier). However, too many sites with poor navigation count on a search function to take the place of any loopholes in poor navigational design. A search function *can* fill in the gaps, but in planning a site's navigation, try to design in such a way that users will not need to resort to the search function. (Even if your site is going to have a search facility, when designing the navigation, design it as if you aren't going to have one.)

# Use alt Attributes

Including alt attributes in the `<img>` tags for your graphics, especially those used for menus or icons, is a necessary step for aiding navigation. There are many situations in which the user will not be able to make use of the graphics, such as:

- The browser does not support graphics, for example a text-based browser like Lynx or a screen reader.

- The user has turned off graphics in their browser, so they don't have to wait for them to download.

- The graphics are missing from the site, or are taking too long to download.

In these cases, the user will be dependent on alt attribute values in order to know where the links will take them. Try to use the same rules for deciding on alt text as you would use for textual links. For example, for a link to information about the company or organization, use an alt value of "*About Us*" or "*Information about us*" rather than "*This link takes you to information about our company*".

# Include a Text Menu

A text version of the top-level menu above or below the main page content has become a standard of page design. Some sites include them in both places, so users don't have to scroll around as much to have access to navigational options. Remember to keep the text menu options in the same order as the graphics menu options, and keep this order consistent throughout the site.

# Give Users Choice

Imagine a restaurant menu with only one or two items. Imagine that you absolutely love these two items, but the restaurant is only open from 2-4 pm on Tuesday afternoons. After a while, you'll probably stop playing hooky from work in order to eat there.

More options often make for a better experience. Overkill isn't necessary – offering one graphically based navigational system in combination with one text-based system will make a site all that much more accessible to all.

# Use the Four Key Elements

Remember: **familiarity**, **consistency**, **simplicity**, and **clarity**.

# Support in Web Development Tools

You'll be glad to hear that many web development tools come equipped with help for creating navigation links. For example, Dreamweaver MX has navigational "snippets" – ready-made breadcrumb trails and other navigational trinkets for your site. These won't do all of the work for you, but they'll give you a good start.

In Dreamweaver MX, access the *Snippets* tab of the *Code* panel. Under *Navigation*, you'll see various pieces of functionality that you can add to your page. For example, selecting the angle bracket delimited breadcrumb trail and clicking *Insert* will add the following code to your page:

```
<table width="100%" border="0" cellspacing="0" cellpadding="4">
  <tr>
    <td><a href="#">Lorem</a></td>
    <td>&gt;</td>
    <td><a href="#">Ipsum</a></td>
    <td>&gt;</td>
    <td><a href="#">Dolar</a></td>
    <td>&gt;</td>
    <td width="100%">Amit</td>
  </tr>
</table>
```

 You may have noticed the words Lorem Ipsum Dolar Amit used a lot by Dreamweaver MX or other tools. These are, in fact, the first few words of a piece of "nonsense text" (reported to be a garbled version of a Latin text) that is used by print and web developers alike when designing layouts before any real text is available.

# Summary

Logic plays a key role in creating a well-designed navigational system for your site. Take a look at your own experiences with applications – even non-computer examples, such as street signs, road maps, and VCR instructions. What makes sense and is helpful? What leaves you wondering where to go next?

In this chapter, we've taken a look at many different types and styles of navigation: text menus, graphic menus, tabbed menus, drop-down menus, and more exotic menus. Matching a style of navigation to the purpose and audience of your own site. (See *Chapter 3* for more detail about knowing your audience.)

We also looked at ten top navigation tips. Overarching all these is the general moral of good navigational structure and navigational design: **the more comfortable users are with your site, the better they can find what they want, and the more time they'll spend there**.

# 8

- CSS tutorial
- Styling text and hyperlinks
- Page layout with CSS

**Author: Rachel Andrew**

# CSS: Modern Layout and Style

In *Chapter 6*, we looked at the older style page layouts employed on the Web in the past. Now it's time to look at the recommended modern way of laying out pages (and styling text) – **Cascading Style Sheets** (**CSS**).

A good understanding of CSS is essential for the modern web designer or developer, and (as with most things on the Web), while the usage of CSS can be taken to highly complex and advanced levels, the basics of this language are easily grasped. In this chapter we will discover what CSS is and how to create consistent text styling for our web sites by using it. We will also explore some practical implementations of slightly more advanced CSS usage such as creating text and navigation buttons, attractive forms, stylesheets for print, and the use of CSS in page layout.

## What Is CSS?

CSS is a language that defines how page elements marked up with HTML or XHTML are displayed in the web browser or on other devices (for example, how a page is printed). You can think of CSS as being a "template" that defines the way that each HTML element looks when displayed.

### A Brief History of CSS

As HTML developed and became widely used, people wanted more and more control over the way their documents looked in the browser. They began to make use of tags that related to style and presentation of information rather than (or as well as) tags that described the content. For example, in order to create a document where headings are green and use the font Verdana and the regular text also uses Verdana but is blue, they may use the following markup:

```
<!DOCTYPE html PUBLIC "-//W3C//DTD XHTML 1.0 Transitional//EN"
  "http://www.w3.org/TR/xhtml1/DTD/xhtml1-transitional.dtd">
<html>
<head>
  <title>Example of styling using font tags</title>
</head>
<body>
<h1>
  <font color="#339900" face="Verdana">
    hello world!
  </font>
</h1>
<p>
  <font color="#003399" face="Verdana">
    This is how we used to mark up our documents.
  </font>
</p>
</body>
</html>
```

However, this was unsatisfactory for a number of reasons, many of which we'll look at shortly. Instead, CSS was developed by the W3C (see *http://www.w3.org/Style/CSS/*); it comes in three parts, CSS1, CSS2, and CSS3.

## CSS1

**CSS1** became a recommendation in December 1996. It mainly provides methods of styling text – thus replacing the `<font>` tag, which was deprecated in HTML 4. Our document above could be created with an external CSS stylesheet that defined `<h1>` tags to be green and Verdana, and regular paragraph text to be blue and Verdana. In the HTML document we would need nothing more than the basic HTML tags to define a heading and a paragraph along with the attached external CSS file.

The example markup below is nothing but plain, structural XHTML and, without a stylesheet attached, will display with the default browser styles, seen below in Internet Explorer 6.

*An example of unstyled XHTML*

```
<!DOCTYPE html PUBLIC "-//W3C//DTD XHTML 1.0 Transitional//EN"
  "http://www.w3.org/TR/xhtml1/DTD/xhtml1-transitional.dtd">
<html>
<head>
  <title>Unstyled Example</title>
</head>
<body>
  <h1>hello world!</h1>
  <p>This is structural XHTML</p>
</body>
</html>
```

Attach an external stylesheet (using a `<link>` element), like so (see `ExternalStylesheet1.html` on the CD):

```
<!DOCTYPE html PUBLIC "-//W3C//DTD XHTML 1.0 Transitional//EN"
   "http://www.w3.org/TR/xhtml1/DTD/xhtml1-transitional.dtd">
<html>
<head>
   <title>CSS Example</title>
   <link href="test.css" rel="stylesheet" type="text/css" />
</head>
<body>
   <h1>hello world!</h1>
   <p>This way uses much less markup!</p>
</body>
</html>
```

We can now affect the way that the basic markup looks in a CSS supporting browser by way of the CSS rules below which would be the contents of an external file named `test.css` – we will be covering attaching external stylesheets later in this chapter.

```
h1 {
   color: #339900;
   background-color: Transparent;
   font-family: Verdana, Geneva, Arial, Helvetica, sans-serif;
}

p {
   color: #003399;
   background-color: Transparent;
   font-family: Verdana, Geneva, Arial, Helvetica, sans-serif;
}
```

The above markup consists of two rule sets, one for `h1` (text within `<h1></h1>` tags) and one for `p` (text within `<p></p>` tags).

Each of the rule sets consists of the **selector** (for example, `h1` or `p`), then a pair of curly braces (`{ }`). Within those curly braces you place the **directives**, which say how you wish this selector to be (in this case) displayed on the screen. It is worth noting that there are directives that allow you to set how you would like a specific selector to be read by the screen reader if someone is using such technology to read your page (this is why we said "in this case" above), but most of the directives you will use day to day affect the on-screen display of the elements on your page.

The directives themselves consist of property and value combinations separated by a colon (:). In English you are saying "this is what I want to change, and this is the value I want to change it to". For example:

```
color: #003399;
```

shows that I wish to change the color of the selector that opened this rule set to `#339900` (a nice shade of green). In a CSS-supporting browser the page would now render like this:

*Some simple XHTML, styled with CSS*

With CSS you only need to define how you want your tags to be styled once, so if further `<h1>` and `<p>` elements were added to the HTML document, they would also be styled by the CSS. Compare this to the first example, where you would need to write `<font>` tags for each `<h1>` and `<p>` that occurred within the HTML document!

## CSS2

**CSS2** became a recommendation in May 1998: it builds on the CSS1 specification, adding support for positioning elements (meaning images, blocks of text, or other items on your pages) and support for different 'media descriptors' in order to provide different stylesheets that will be used depending on the device that the user views the web page with (such as a separate stylesheet for print as we will cover later in this chapter, or a stylesheet specially designed for someone using a screen reader – a device that reads the page out to them).

## CSS3

**CSS3** is still in development and brings with it a new, modular, approach to CSS in order that devices that do not have the capability to support the entire specification, can support the necessary modules, and authors can understand which modules the device they are designing for will understand. Additionally, the modular approach means that certain modules of the specification can be updated in isolation from the rest of the specification, something which is necessary as the language grows in complexity.

### A Note on CSS Support

*The first browser to support any CSS at all was Microsoft Internet Explorer 3; Netscape did not add in support until Netscape 4 and used an implementation that relies on JavaScript being enabled in the browser – if JavaScript is turned off in any version of Netscape 4, CSS will never be applied either!*

*At the time of writing browser support for CSS1 (mainly dealing with the formatting of text) and much of CSS2 is excellent. The newest browsers (version 5 and 6 browsers) are relatively standards-compliant and apply CSS well. Browsers that do not support any CSS at all, for example, those that do not render visually (screen readers), and devices such as PDAs and web-enabled phones will just skip over the CSS and display documents that, if correctly marked up, are perfectly readable, but will not be styled quite as nicely (this is also know as **Degrading Gracefully** –code that degrades gracefully is code that works fine on browsers that fully support it, but will also be perfectly usable on older browsers that do not, albeit in a more basic format.)*

*The main problem that we have at the moment is browsers that support CSS in a bad way, and that crash or render pages unusable when confronted with it. Netscape 4 is the main problem in this category, however its use is diminishing and with a little forethought it is possible to use complex CSS within your sites and not cause any problems for this 5-year-old browser. We will discuss this issue in more depth at the end of this chapter.*

# Benefits of CSS

HTML was originally developed in order to allow the easy distribution of documents, and therefore does not lend itself very well to the styling and formatting of text and layouts. While it is used extensively in this manner, all use of HTML in this way could be considered a 'hack' (a use of the markup that is outside of the job it is intended for). CSS however has been conceived as a presentational language and, used correctly, can allow for powerful formatting and styling of your documents without compromising their structure in any way. Using HTML to style a document is a bit like using a wrench to hammer in a nail when you have a hammer in your toolbox!

## Separating Document Structure from Presentation

As we saw in the previous example, CSS allows you to remove the presentational markup from your documents into a separate file. This separation of structured content from presentation has many benefits in the areas of accessibility, flexibility in design, smaller file sizes, browser support, and the shortening of time taken in development and maintenance of your web site, as you'll see shortly.

First, however, it is important to understand exactly what falls into each category.

**Document structure** includes your content, marked up in a logical way by the use of tags that describe the content's meaning rather than how it should be displayed. These include paragraphs (`<p>`), heading levels (`<h1>` to `<h6>`), line breaks (`<br />`), references to image files (`<img>`), hyperlinks to other documents (`<a>`), and divs and spans (`<div>` and `<span>`).

**Presentation** means any way of describing how the document structure should be displayed. This is the whole purpose of CSS, but in HTML this includes `color` attributes, `align` attributes, `<center>` elements, and `<font>` elements.

### Shorter Development/Update Time

Once you have set up a stylesheet for the common elements across your site, adding new pages that are consistent with the rest of the site is simple, as any page that has the stylesheet linked to it will take the same styles for elements such as headings, paragraphs, and borders. Should a change be needed to the font face or colors used throughout the site, only that one stylesheet will need to be altered for the changes to be reflected consistently across the whole site.

### Accessibility

The use of CSS naturally leads to less tag misuse when marking up your document structure. By **tag misuse**, I mean the use of HTML structural elements/tags to force a visual effect. For instance, some developers may use an `<h1>` element simply because they want large text rather than because the text is a natural heading. Also, complicated nested tables are sometimes used to create a border effect, which is a bit of a misuse of tables really.

Accessibility devices use the structural HTML tags to place emphasis on different page elements. For example, a screen reader may read out the headings first in order to give the user a choice as to what they want to have read next. If tags are misused, the device will still treat the wrongly marked-up headings as important structural topics to be read out. By using CSS, you can create attractive pages that still sound correct when read out by a screen reader, since the screen reader can choose to ignore the styles you apply.

CSS also means that it is easy to change the stylesheet attached to any page, be this by the user or by the site developer. The user could specify the stylesheet that their browser uses to view pages – for example to enlarge the text size. The developer can easily create different versions of their site, with different stylesheets, changing the text size or even the color scheme in order to help those who find reading small text difficult or who have difficulties reading text that has certain color combinations. In this way it is possible to combine your design ideas with ways to make the site easy to use for as many of your visitors as is possible.

### More Flexibility in Design

As we have already discussed, HTML was not designed to do anything more than mark up text documents in order to make distribution of those documents simple. HTML provides very limited ways to create visually appealing layouts, and the methods of creating complex layouts in HTML often lead to inaccessible pages that render very badly on alternative devices such as PDAs or web-enabled cell phones.

CSS allows you to:

- Have more precise control over the spacing between letters, rows, and words

- Reduce the amount of padding that separates a heading tag or other structural element from other elements within the document

- Create effects that before would have needed an image file (such as buttons that change when the mouse rolls over them)

Additionally, CSS allows you to move away from the grid layout that is imposed by HTML tables and position items more freely on the page.

### Smaller File Sizes

CSS creates smaller file sizes in two ways:

- It allows you to specify in one stylesheet the styles that will apply to a number of different elements, only once each, rather than having to specify these styles individually for each and every element that needs them.

- The use of CSS to create complex layouts allows for smaller file sizes when compared to nested table layouts.

Additionally, if all the HTML pages on a site link to the same CSS stylesheet, then the CSS stylesheet is usually only downloaded once. When it is first downloaded from the server, the browser **caches** the file (stores it in its own memory) and then uses this cached file whenever it needs the stylesheet rather than downloading the stylesheet again. Since less content needs to be downloaded from the server, therefore the response times are a lot quicker.

# How to Write CSS

In the rest of this chapter we will be concentrating on writing CSS files by hand in a text editor, in order that you become familiar with the syntax of CSS. However, as with HTML, there are a variety of applications that can assist you in writing CSS files, from those that integrate CSS into a larger application (such as Dreamweaver MX) to standalone applications that are solely CSS editors.

# Writing CSS by Hand

Even if you decide to use a tool for creating CSS files, it will be necessary at times for you to be able to edit your CSS files by hand. It is worth gaining a rudimentary understanding of how CSS works before beginning to use a special editor, as it will enable you to use the editor more efficiently when you can understand the concepts behind what it is doing. To write a CSS file, all you basically need is a text editor such as Notepad, Simpletext, or any other editor that you use for HTML.

# Dreamweaver MX

Dreamweaver has had integrated CSS support since version 2. However, in Dreamweaver MX Macromedia took their support for CSS to a higher level again. Dreamweaver does still retain support for older ways of working (using `<font>` elements) and it is important to check that you are not mistakenly adding `<font>` elements to your document when working in design view. One way to avoid this is to use the *CSS Property Inspector*, which is a new feature of Dreamweaver MX.

A default installation of Dreamweaver MX will display the old style `<font>` tags *Property Inspector*.

To switch to the new style *CSS Property Inspector* that will give you easy access to all the styles defined in your stylesheet, simply click the little 'A' icon that you will find to the right of the '*Format*' input box and your *Property Inspector* will switch to the CSS version.

Dreamweaver MX allows you to edit your CSS files without actually going into the code via its CSS dialog, shown on the right.

While we are not going to go into a detailed description of how to create CSS files in Dreamweaver MX in this chapter, by the time you have completed it you should have enough CSS knowledge to be able to understand the Dreamweaver help files and create CSS in Dreamweaver MX, should you wish to do so. Other visual development environments, such as Adobe GoLive and Microsoft FrontPage, also have some support for CSS and, once again, with an understanding of the concepts behind CSS you should have no problem using the CSS functionality within these tools.

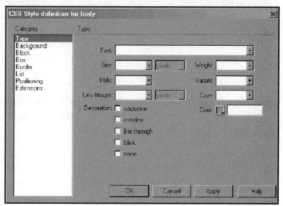

*The CSS dialog in Dreamweaver MX*

CSS: Modern Layout and Style

## Dedicated CSS Editors

There are a variety of standalone CSS editors now on the market. These editors usually allow you to create your CSS in a text editor environment, but also have wizards, code hints, color pickers, and other tools that will assist you in writing CSS. Two editors that are well worth looking at if you are writing CSS are:

- Topstyle (*http://www.bradsoft.com/*). This can act as a standalone product or can be integrated into Dreamweaver MX.

- Style Master (*http://www.westciv.com/style_master/index.html*). This is available for both the Windows and Macintosh platforms and offers a robust CSS development environment.

# Ways of Implementing CSS

In my earlier examples I showed the use of CSS in an external file. This should be seen as the optimal way of working with CSS; however, there are in total three ways in which you can use CSS: **inline**, **embedded**, and, as we saw earlier, with an **external stylesheet**. Let's look at these three different implementation methods more closely.

## Inline

Inline CSS styles are applied to one page element at a time within the flow of the document. They use a `style` attribute with a value equal to the declaration part of the rules we looked at above. The selector part of the rule isn't needed, since the rule is automatically applied to the element in question.

```
<h2 style="font-family: Verdana, Arial, Helvetica, sans-serif; color: #663366;">
   My heading
</h2>
```

This style will only affect the `<h2>` element that it is applied to; another `<h2>` element on the page would not take on this style rule. Using inline CSS is not the best way to use CSS as you lose many of the advantages that we discussed earlier, such as smaller file sizes and ease of updating your document by changing global stylesheet properties. In fact, inline styles have many of the same pitfalls as using `<font>` elements within your document.

Inline CSS is sometimes necessary for certain DHTML effects where you want to change the CSS display properties of a page element with JavaScript, and Dreamweaver uses it for its CSS positioning (known as layers within Dreamweaver). Unless you have a specific need to use inline CSS, then it is best to avoid using it.

## Embedded

An embedded stylesheet is one that is placed within a `<style>` element between the `<head>` and `</head>` tags of a document. The style rules described in it will only affect that particular document.

For example, the code opposite will style all `<h2>` tags within the page (see `EmbeddedStylesheet.html` on the CD.)

```
<!DOCTYPE html PUBLIC "-//W3C//DTD XHTML 1.0 Transitional//EN"
   "http://www.w3.org/TR/xhtml1/DTD/xhtml1-transitional.dtd">
<html>
<head>
   <title>Embedded CSS Example</title>
   <style type="text/css">

     h2 {
        font-family: Verdana, Arial, Helvetica, sans-serif;
        color: #cc99cc;
     }

   </style>
</head>
<body>
   <h2>
     Text to be styled
   </h2>
</body>
</html>
```

While this method is significantly better than using inline CSS from a file size and ease-of-updating point of view, you would need to include this code on every document within your web site. To change the color of these `<h2>` tags to green throughout your site would involve making the change on each and every page.

## External Stylesheets

Using an external stylesheet allows you to fully benefit from CSS. To create an external stylesheet you simply take the style rules and place them into a file with the extension '.css', as seen earlier. You then link to this CSS file from your documents. For example, to move your rules for `<h2>` elements into a stylesheet file, all you need to do is copy those rules into a text editor:

```
h2 {
   font-family: Verdana, Arial, Helvetica, sans-serif;
   color: #cc99cc;
}
```

Save it as `global.css`

Attach it to your document by adding the following line of code between the `<head>` and `</head>` tags of your HTML document (see `ExternalStylesheet2.html` on the CD):

```
<!DOCTYPE html PUBLIC "-//W3C//DTD XHTML 1.0 Transitional//EN"
   "http://www.w3.org/TR/xhtml1/DTD/xhtml1-transitional.dtd">
<html>
<head>
   <title>External CSS Example</title>
   <link href="global.css" rel="stylesheet" type="text/css" />
</head>
<body>
   <h2>
     Text to be styled
   </h2>
</body>
</html>
```

You can add rules for as many elements as you like in one stylesheet and you can also link to multiple stylesheets from one document. As well as global styles that you link to from every document, you may also have some styles that are only needed for certain pages (for instance for a form). By putting those additional styles in a separate stylesheet, you only need to link to it where it is needed.

## The Cascade

In the term "Cascading Style Sheets", "Cascading" refers to the fact that one stylesheet cascades over the previously applied stylesheet. What we mean by this is that the different methods of applying CSS take precedence over each other. Take the following example (CascadeExample.html), where we use all three different applications of CSS on one HTML document:

```
<!DOCTYPE html PUBLIC "-//W3C//DTD XHTML 1.0 Transitional//EN"
   "http://www.w3.org/TR/xhtml1/DTD/xhtml1-transitional.dtd">
<html>
<head>
   <title>CSS Cascade Example</title>
   <link href="global2.css" rel="stylesheet" type="text/css" />
   <style type="text/css">

      h1 {
         font-family: Verdana, Arial, Helvetica, sans-serif;
         color: #cc99cc;
      }
      h2 {
         font-family: Verdana, Arial, Helvetica, sans-serif;
         color: #cc99cc;
      }

   </style>
</head>
<body>
   <h1>
      Text to be styled
   </h2>
   <h2>
      Text to be styled
   </h2>
   <h2 style="font-family: Verdana, Arial, Helvetica, sans-serif;
              color: #663366;">
      Text to be styled
   </h2>
</body>
</html>
```

The accompanying CSS file, global2.css, looks like this:

```
h1 {
   font-family: courier, courier new, monospace;
   color: #cc99cc;
}
h2 {
   font-family: Verdana, Arial, Helvetica, sans-serif;
   color: #cc99cc;
}
```

An external stylesheet is applied to the document first; looking at the external stylesheet, you'd expect this document to be displayed with three headings. The first is to be in Courier font (monotype "typewriter" look-a-like text), and the other two are to be in the same Verdana font we saw earlier. They are all to be in a fairly light mauve color.

However, all is not how it might first seem – we have also inserted an embedded stylesheet in the `<head>` of our HTML document, which says that the top-level heading should not be in Courier font, but in Verdana instead. This stylesheet takes precedence over the external one, so Verdana it is.

Next, look at the inline style we have applied to the second `<h2>` element. This instructs the browser to display this element as Verdana, but in a darker color than the mauve we were expecting. This takes precedence over both the external and embedded stylesheets, so the darker color will be used for this element. The page ends up being displayed like this:

As a quick guide, remember this order of precedence (highest on the left):

Inline > Embedded > External

# Selectors

Earlier in this chapter we saw how applying CSS rules can change the way that structural tags are rendered, while also preserving the structure of your markup. This method provides a simple way of creating and maintaining a consistent look and feel for your site, without bloating the HTML with presentational markup. If you are working with several content authors who add content to the site, then redefining tags will mean that their content will fit in with the rest of the site, using all the formatting defined in your stylesheet.

This use of (X)HTML element names as selectors is vital in order to retain the structural integrity of your document whilst being able to create the style that you wish to see displayed in the browser.

## CSS Classes

CSS classes allow you to create a set of style rules that you can apply to any page element you want. This has further power over using HTML element names as selectors – doing that will affect every instance of that tag, whereas creating CSS classes will allow you to choose which tags take on that style.

For example, let's create a simple CSS file containing two simple classes:

```
.light {
  font-family: Verdana, Arial, Helvetica, sans-serif;
  color: #cc99cc;
}
```

```
.dark {
  font-family: Verdana, Arial, Helvetica, sans-serif;
  color: #663366;
}
```

Note that the selectors are preceded by periods. This means that each rule applies to any element within the HTML document that has a `class` attribute set to `"light"` or `"dark"`. For example, the first rule would be applied to these elements:

```
<h2 class="light">This heading is styled by class light</h2>
<p class="light">This paragraph is also styled by class light</p>
```

And the second rule would be applied to these elements:

```
<h2 class="dark">This heading is styled by class dark</h2>
<p class="dark">This paragraph is also styled by class dark</p>
```

## ID Selectors

In a similar way to class selectors, described above, you can also have ID selectors. We just use a # instead of a period in the style rule:

```
#light {
  font-family: Verdana, Arial, Helvetica, sans-serif;
  color: #cc99cc;
}
```

and use an `id` attribute rather than a `class` attribute in the HTML:

```
<h2 id="light">This heading is styled by id light</h2>
```

However, within an HTML document, the value of an `id` attribute must always be unique – we cannot have both these elements:

```
<h2 id="light">This heading is styled by id light</h2>
<p id="light">This paragraph is also styled by id light</p>
```

within the same HTML document. So, whereas you can use a `class` for rules that may be applied to multiple elements in one document, you can only use an `id` for rules that are applied just once. For example, a unique ID may be used to denote the area that will contain your navigation, or for a footer that appears at the bottom of every page. We will look at using IDs later in this chapter, when we discuss page layout with CSS.

# Text Styling with CSS

Now we've looked at the theory behind writing CSS stylesheets, we can take a further look at the different style properties available. With the above examples we have begun to touch on how to style text with CSS. However, using CSS gives us more powerful ways to style text than simply changing colors and fonts.

On the CD there are two stylesheets (`textstyles1.css` and `textstyles2.css`) that demonstrate different ways to manipulate text within your documents. By applying these stylesheets to an (X)HTML page you will be able to see the changes that they make to the text – use these example stylesheets as a base for your own experimentation.

Let's have a look at a few of the style properties available.

# font-size

This property can be used to set the size of your text. However, as well as a number, the value of this property needs to specify a unit. The most useful unit choices are pixels, points, ems, and percentages. You can group these ways of sizing text into those that style to an **absolute** size (the size remains the same even if the user changes their settings in the browser) and **relative** (the sizes scale according to the user's browser settings and the relative sizes of other text elements).

Note that earlier browser versions (version 4 browsers) have a variety of problems with font sizes and you will need to test carefully and in some cases implement an alternative stylesheet for these older browsers. We will discuss ways to cope with old browsers and their broken CSS implementations at the end of this chapter.

## Pixels

```
p {font-size: 12px;}
```

Setting the font size in pixels (a pixel is a single unit on the monitor display and therefore will scale depending on what screen resolution the user is set to) means that in many current browsers the size will remain static even if the user adjusts the font size from within their browser. Setting the font to a very small size using pixels may mean that users cannot easily read your text.

## Points

```
p {font-size: 12pt;}
```

Specifying a font size in points means specifying the size in inches. As computer screens are different sizes, the way that the browser interprets this is vague. Additionally, the Mac usually treats 1 inch as 72 pixels and Windows sets it at 96 pixels, so text that is comfortable to read on a PC running Windows may be more difficult to read on the Mac. Specifying text size in points can be very useful when creating a stylesheet for print, something that we will consider later in this chapter.

## Ems

```
p {font-size: 1em;}
```

Using ems (a scaling factor relative to the value of the current element's 'font-size' property) to size your text means that the user will be able to resize the fonts used in your document to a comfortable level if necessary, and the fonts' sizes relative to one another will remain the same. They can be a little tricky to get used to as you need to remember that the sizing is relative, however they are very useful from an accessibility standpoint.

## Percentages

```
p{font-size: 80%;}
```

Using percentages again allows you to specify your font sizes in a way that will allow the user to adjust the sizes to suit them while your various structural elements (for example, headings and paragraphs) will remain in correct proportion to one another. The percentage we are using here is a percentage of the browser's default size, which varies from browser to browser, so using percentages certainly allows you to get the different page elements nicely in proportion to each other, but your results will vary from browser to browser, so make sure you test your pages thoroughly to make sure they appear satisfactorily in multiple browsers.

# font-family

We have already seen this property in use in our earlier examples to set the font used for text. It is possible to specify a single font face in CSS by using the rule:

```
font: Arial;
```

However, this is not advisable as different users of your site will have different fonts installed on their computer – they may not have the font that you specify at which point the browser will most likely display its default font. While some basic fonts are included with the operating system installation of computers, these vary between Windows, Mac OS, and Linux-based systems, so you want to be sure that your font doesn't default to something hard to read, should the user not have the font that you chose installed. The way to do this is to specify a font family.

```
p {font-family: Verdana, Geneva, Arial, Helvetica, sans-serif;}
```

The above rule specifies the list of preferred fonts in order of priority. If one in the list isn't installed, the browser should look for the font specified next in the list. If none of these fonts are found installed on the machine, the browser uses the system's default "**sans serif**" font. By that, we mean a font without any sharp ends to the letters.

For a **serif** font (one with sharp ends to letters) you may wish to use:

```
p {font-family: "Times New Roman", Times, serif;}
```

This gives the final choice as the default serif font to be found on a user's computer. You can also see from the above that a font name that contains whitespace such as "Times New Roman" needs to have quotes around it within the rule, to indicate that the words should all be grouped together as one entity.

There is evidence that a sans serif font is more readable on the computer screen where a serif font is more readable in print, so if your site contains a lot of content for your user to read, consider a sans serif font for your body text.

# font-weight

This allows you to set the weight of a font – the effect of this is usually to render the font in bold type. Although there are varying degrees of `font-weight`, most browsers do not render the various levels. Possible values for `font-weight` include relative values such as:

`font-weight: bolder;`

This renders the weight of the font of this element bolder than its parent element, whereas:

`font-weight: 800;`

usually renders as bold and is an absolute weight – it takes no reference from other elements.

## line-height

CSS allows us to specify the **leading** (spacing between the base of one line of text and the base of the line of text above it) by setting the `line-height` property. You can set this rule as an absolute size (using pixels) or you can set it to be relative to the text size (this is necessary if you have used a text size set in ems or percentages that will allow the user to scale the text so it is comfortable for them to read.) On the CD that comes with this book, sample stylesheet `textstyles1.css` has the `line-height` specified in pixels, while `textstyles2.css` shows the `line-height` using relative units.

### Keeping It Readable

*While CSS allows us to style our text in many new ways it is important to remember that the most important thing is your content, and the user being able to read your content. Large line-spacing and tiny fonts may look attractive but, on a large block of text, may be very difficult to read. Consider your users at all times, check your pages in different browsers and, if possible, on different computers, set up in a different way to the one you use to develop your sites in. Make sure that your efforts to create a pleasing look have not rendered your content to be unreadable on some platforms.*

# Styling Hyperlinks

You have probably seen links in action on web sites that change their style depending on whether your mouse is hovering over them, or you have clicked on them. These types of effects can be created with CSS, using **pseudo-class selectors**, which are applied to page elements when they are in a certain state, rather than at all times.

## Basic Styles for Links

In order to see how pseudo-class selectors work, we will look at the common usage of creating attractive styles for your links to other documents. Hyperlinks (`<a>` tags with `href` attributes) are given a default color by most browsers, which denotes them as links. Traditionally this is blue for pages you have not visited, red when you click on the link, and purple for links to pages that you have already visited.

We could change the color of the actual link in its unclicked state by specifying a style for `<a>` tags. However this would pick up all anchors in the document, including those without `href` attributes that just mark a place in the text that can be linked to. So to change the color of unvisited links, we use the `:link` pseudo-class, like so:

```
a:link {color: #4682B4;}
```

This is all very well, but once you have clicked on the link it will revert to the default visited link color. To change the color of visited links we use:

```
a:visited {color: #483D8B;}
```

To change the color of the link in its active state (at the point it is clicked on) you can use:

```
a:active {color: #483D8B;}
```

Perhaps you would like to create an effect where, when the user hovers over a link on your page, it changes color as if to say 'Click me!' In order to do this we can use `a:hover`:

```
a:hover {color: #DA70D6;}
```

The order in which you add these definitions to your CSS file is very important. CSS-compliant browsers will not render the styles if they are not in the following order:

LINK, VISITED, HOVER, ACTIVE

What else might you want to do? Links are usually displayed with an underline – perhaps you would like to remove the underlines? You can do this by setting the following rule:

```
a:link {text-decoration: none;}
```

*A word of warning: while you can create all sorts of effects with CSS, make sure that your links do indeed look like links. Rendering them the same or very close in color to the body text and removing the underlines will make it very difficult to spot them within your text! Also, most web users are used to the standard colors and underlines for links – anything radically different may confuse them.*

## Creating Multiple Link Styles in One Document

Setting the rules we discussed above will apply the styles to every link within your document – you do not need to add anything to the basic markup for a link to cause it to use these style rules. You may, however want to have more than one set of link styles in a document. Perhaps you have areas of your page that have a dark background and therefore need light text and link colors, as well as a main body with dark text and link colors. To support this, we need to combine the class selectors we used earlier with the pseudo-class selectors that we have just discussed. The style rules opposite will style all links in the document, but display different styles to any links that have a class of 'green'.

```
a:link {
  color: #4682B4;
  background-color: transparent;
  text-decoration: none;
}

a:visited {
  color: #483D8B;
  background-color: transparent;
  text-decoration: none;
}

a:hover {
  color: #DA70D6;
  background-color: transparent;
  text-decoration: underline;
}

a:active {
  color: #483D8B;
  background-color: transparent;
  text-decoration: none;
}

a.green:link {
  color: #00B502;
  background-color: transparent;
  text-decoration: underline;
}

a.green:visited {
  color: #005701;
  background-color: transparent;
  text-decoration: underline;
}

a.green:hover {
  color: #FEFF31;
  background-color: #C0C8D0;
  text-decoration: underline overline;
}

a.green:active {
  color: #005701;
  background-color: transparent;
  text-decoration: underline;
}
```

To try this code out, see the files `anchorStyles.html` and `anchorStyles.css` on the CD that comes with the book.

The first four rules apply to every link within the document. Notice that, as well as changing colors in different states, the links will become underlined when the mouse hovers over them.

**8**

**CSS: Modern Layout and Style**

The final four rules have longer selectors – let's look at the first one in detail.

```
a.green:link
```

The selector starts by saying it applies to `<a>` elements. It then specifies that the element must have a `class` attribute with value "`green`". Finally, it says the element must be an unvisited link.

These four rules again change the colors of the links in different states. In addition note that a link that is hovered over becomes underlined and overlined, and has a different background color.

With these eight style rules defined in your stylesheet, links of the following form will be affected by the first four rules:

```
<a href="myURL.html">link</a>
```

In comparison, links with `class` attributes set to "`green`" as below, will be affected by the latter four rules:

```
<a href="myURL.html" class="green">link</a>
```

# Creating 'Button' Effects for Navigation with CSS

We can take our use of CSS for the styling of links one step further to create navigation buttons purely with CSS. In the past this is something that would have involved the creation of an image file.

Note: to try out this example, see the `buttons.html` and `buttons.css` files on the CD.

To start creating our navigation, first we need to create the basic markup for the links. In a new HTML document add the following within the `<body>` element:

```
<p class="myButton"><a href="link1.html">link one</a></p>
<p class="myButton"><a href="link2.html">link two</a></p>
<p class="myButton"><a href="link3.html">link three</a></p>
<p class="myButton"><a href="link4.html">link four</a></p>
```

*Simple HTML links*

Here we have `<p>` elements with a `class` of `myButton`, wrapped round links. In your browser this should display as a simple list of links as shown.

Now, in a new stylesheet file, we add the following style rule. It will be applied to all elements with `class` attributes set to `myButton` – all the `<p>` elements that surround the links in this case. You will recognize these style rules as being simple text-styling rules.

```
.myButton {
    font-weight: bold;
    font-family: Verdana, Geneva, Arial, Helvetica, sans-serif;
    font-size: 12px;
}
```

We attach this stylesheet to the HTML page we just created using a `<link>` tag within the head of the document, as we discussed earlier. If you refresh the page after saving it you should see that the links now appear bold.

Now we need to create a style for the links that will make them appear like buttons. We don't have any `class` attributes actually applied to the `<a>` elements themselves, but we don't necessarily want every link in the document to look like a button, so we need to use a slightly different syntax to create the selectors. What do these <a> elements all have in common? They are all contained within another element (a `<p>` element) that has a `class` attribute set to `myButton`.

So, to solve this problem we can create a selector that will only be applied to an `<a>` element inside another element with a class of `myButton`, like so:

```
.myButton a:link {
  padding: 4px;
  text-decoration: none;
  width: 130px;
  display: block;
  color: #333366;
  background-color: #CFCFCF;
}
```

`.myButton a:link` tells the browser that we want the following styles to be applied to the pseudo-class `:link` where it is contained within something that has a class of `myButton`. The rules that we have created here give some **padding** to the text (so that we have some space around the edge of the text), remove the underline (by setting the `text-decoration` to `none`), set the width of the button, and give it a background color and text color, all of which should be becoming familiar to you. `display: block;` instructs the browser to display the area of the button as a block-level element, thus making the entire button clickable (and a link to the page) rather than just the text.

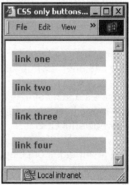

We also add a similar set of rules for the selectors `.myButton a:visited` and `.myButton a:active` (see `buttons.css`). If you view this page in the browser after adding these rules to the stylesheet, you should see something like that on the right:

To make these buttons look slightly more like buttons, we can add a border to them in order to give the effect of a 3D button. To do this we use a lighter border color on the top and left of the button to give the impression of light shining on the edge of the raised button, and a slightly darker color underneath to give the impression of a shadow. The border rules look like this:

*HTML Links, styled with CSS*

```
border-top: 2px #E9E9E9 solid;
border-left: 2px #E9E9E9 solid;
border-bottom: 2px #8E8E8E solid;
border-right: 2px #8E8E8E solid;
```

You simply need to add these lines into the rules for the buttons (remembering to add them for `:visited` and `:active` as well). You may notice that there appear to be several style values combined with one style property here and you would be correct. We could write each one out longhand:

```
border-top-width: 2px;
border-top-color: #E9E9E9;
border-top-style: solid;
```

However, that triples the amount of CSS code and so the shorthand is most convenient. You can use longhand or shorthand for many styles; many people use a combination of both. We have tended towards using the longhand styles as we explain the syntax in this chapter, but you will see both used interchangeably on the Web.

After adding the border styles, you should have something that is looking rather button-like when viewed in the browser:

We will add one more thing to our CSS buttons: create the effect of the button being pressed when you hover over it. To do this, we need to create a set of rules for `.myButton a:hover` and in those, reverse the border colors:

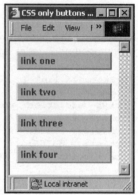

*Our final CSS-styled HTML links, with some shading added to make them look like buttons*

```
.myButton a:hover {
   padding: 4px;
   text-decoration: none;
   width: 130px;
   display: block;
   color: #333366;
   background-color: #CFCFCF;
   border-top: 2px #8E8E8E solid;
   border-left: 2px #8E8E8E solid;
   border-bottom: 2px #E9E9E9 solid;
   border-right: 2px #E9E9E9 solid;
}
```

Add this after `.myButton a:visited` and before `.myButton a:active` within the stylesheet.

This was a fairly simple demonstration of the kind of effects you can get using just CSS. You can use these basic techniques to create some beautiful navigation effects that really demonstrate just how powerful CSS is.

The advantages of using CSS for navigation rather than creating graphics for buttons are many and include quicker download speeds, and not needing to create a new graphic each time someone wants to add something onto the navigation. They are also very accessible to those using an alternative device as, to a device that does not render CSS, they will appear as simple text links, so you can still easily navigate around your site. Additionally, creating navigation in this way is vital if you are working with a database-driven site, where the navigation may be created from items held within a database: it is very difficult and time consuming to find out what each of these will be in order to create a specific image for each one.

# CSS for Forms

Another area in which CSS is very useful is to change the appearance of rather ugly looking default form fields. By using fairly simple CSS you can create attractive and easy-to-use forms.

Note that version 4 browsers, in particular Netscape 4.x, can start to behave very strangely when confronted by forms styled with CSS, and if you are to do this you would be advised to provide a separate stylesheet for version 4 browsers in order that your forms are still usable by someone using one of these old browsers. Methods of doing this are discussed in the final section of this chapter.

## A Search Form Box

In order to see how CSS can be used to create attractive looking form fields, we will create a small search box as might be used when integrating a search facility onto your site. The HTML for the search box includes a text input field and a submit button, placed inside a small table.

Note that the finished code for this example can be found on the CD that accompanies this book as `searchform.html` and `searchform.css`.

```
<form action="myScript.php">
  <table width="200">
    <tr>
      <th colspan="2">Search this site:</th>
    </tr>
    <tr>
      <td><label for="keywords">Keywords:</label></td>
      <td><input type="text" name="keywords" id="keywords" /></td>
    </tr>
    <tr>
      <td colspan="2">
        <input type="submit" value="Submit" />
      </td>
    </tr>
  </table>
</form>
```

When viewed with a browser, this will give you a basic form like the one shown to the right:

This form looks OK, but after a while it starts to get boring, having the same style for all your forms – let's add style to this form with CSS! We will start by actually styling the form elements themselves, so let's add the following style rules to a new stylesheet:

*A basic HTML form*

```
.searchtext {
  width: 100px;
  border: 1px solid #000;
  background-color: #E2E2E2;
  color: #000;
  font-size: 10px;
}
```

We will now attach the stylesheet to our HTML document using the `<link>` tag and then apply it to your text input field by adding `class="searchtext"` to it:

```
<input type="text" name="keywords" id="keywords" class="searchtext">
```

The text input field should change to a small neat gray box with a black border. There is nothing in the above CSS rule that we have not used before on other page elements. You can style the *Submit* button in the same way by the application of a class that uses the following rules:

```
.submit {
  border-top: 1px #E9E9E9 solid;
  border-left: 1px #E9E9E9 solid;
  border-bottom: 1px #8E8E8E solid;
  border-right: 1px #8E8E8E solid;
  background-color: #cccccc;
  color: #000000;
}
```

To finish off we can style the table itself by applying a class to the table to give it a neat border, and specifying rules for the fonts used within the table with the addition of the following rules:

```
.searchbox {
  border: 1px #8E8E8E solid;
}

.searchbox td{
  font-family: Verdana, Geneva, Arial, Helvetica, sans-serif;
  text-align:right;
}

.searchbox th{
  font-family: Verdana, Geneva, Arial, Helvetica, sans-serif;
  color: #5C5C5C;
  background-color: transparent;
}
```

All you need to do to your form to enable it to apply these rules, is to apply the class `searchbox` to the opening `<table>` tag.

```
<table width="200" class="searchbox">
```

Our form will now appear as shown below:

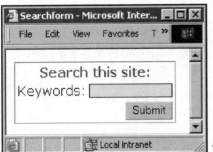

An HTML form, styled with CSS to make it look more presentable

# Page Layout with CSS

In *Chapter 6* we learned how to lay out a page using tables. While this is a common way to lay out HTML pages it is not optimal, mainly because tables were not designed to lay out pages and some of the techniques used to force these layouts can make pages slow to load, inaccessible to alternative devices, complex to code, and even worse to pick through and change at a later date. CSS gives us the power to create layouts that enable us to keep our document structure and presentation separate. As new designers, these techniques are the way of the future and by learning them now you will be giving yourself a head start over those who are still clinging to old methods.

## The Box Model

Every page element (paragraph, table, etc.) is contained within a box. When we change the margin, padding, or border on a class of a redefined HTML tag we are changing it on that element's box. Every box has content, padding, a border, and a margin, and the browser, if given no other directions, has its own defaults for what the values of the padding, border, and margin should be.

## Border

You can change the values of the entire border of a box by specifying rules that apply to border such as `border-width`, `border-style`, and `border-color`:

```
border-width: 1px;
border-style: solid;
border-color: #000000;
```

These can be combined into one line by using the shorthand property `border`, as follows:

```
border: 1px solid #000000;
```

You can also change the top, left, bottom, and right portions of the border separately. For example, the code below will only change the left-hand border:

```
border-left-width: 1px;
border-left-style: solid;
border-left-color: #000000;
```

We can combine this code into one line as follows:

```
border-left-style: 1px solid #000000;
```

On most HTML elements, the border defaults to a zero width – basically, it isn't in existence. However, images that have a link to another document applied to them usually have a default behavior of surrounding the image with a border of the same color as that which is set for styling anchor tags that link to other documents (`<a href="destination">`). The `border-style` property (which in the example above is set to solid, denoting an unbroken line around the box) can be set to a variety of styles, support for which varies between browsers:

| border-style value | Effect |
|---|---|
| none | No border, the `border-width` value will be set to 0 |
| hidden; | Same as none |
| dotted; | A series of dots |
| dashed; | A series of short dashes |
| double; | A double border (two unbroken lines) |
| solid; | An unbroken line |
| groove; | A border that looks as if it is carved into the page |
| ridge; | The opposite of groove |
| inset; | A border that looks as though it has been embedded into the page |
| outset; | The opposite of inset |

## Padding

As with border, you can specify the padding for the entire element or set individually for top, left, bottom, and right, for example:

```
padding: 4px
```

```
padding-left: 4px;
padding-right: 2px;
```

The area of padding takes on the background color of the element it is applied to and can be seen as space between the content and the border (whether you have a visible border or not).

## Margin

Similar to padding, the margin can be set for the entire element, or you can individually set top, left, bottom, and right, for example:

```
margin: 4px
```

or:

```
margin-left: 4px;
margin-right: 2px;
```

Margins are always transparent (and therefore show through the color of your page background or other element that the element is on top of) and add space outside the border of the box. You can even use negative values for margin properties (although we can't say that this would be called for very often).

# Positioning

Any element on the page may be positioned with CSS. To describe fully the different ways of positioning page elements could take up an entire book. However, by demonstrating how to build a simple page using CSS positioning I hope to introduce you to the concept and enable you to find out more about this flexible way of working.

## A Two-Column Layout

As an example of laying out a page using CSS we will create a simple two-column layout using absolute positioning.

Note that the finished code for this example can be found on the CD that accompanies this book as `csslayout.html` and `csslayout.css`.

Firstly we need to create an HTML page that contains our content and document structure. In a new HTML file we need to define two areas of the page to form our two columns. We use `<div>` tags to do this – one division called `leftnav` to place our navigation in, and one called `content` for the page content. We are going to assign `id` attributes to these, because they will be unique within the document.

```
<div id="leftnav">
   <p><a href="link1.html">link 1</a></p>
   <p><a href="link2.html">link 2</a></p>
   <p><a href="link3.html">link 3</a></p>
   <p><a href="link4.html">link 4</a></p>
</div>
<div id="content">
   <p>Lorem ipsum dolor sit amet, consectetuer adipiscing elit. Nam auctor tempor
   est. Donec neque turpis, ornare sed, congue non, congue sit amet, mauris. Ut eu
   purus. Donec orci ligula, ultricies vel, volutpat a, pretium quis, libero. Morbi
   quam nisl, accumsan sit amet, placerat sed, ornare eget, elit. Class aptent
   taciti sociosqu ad litora torquent per conubia nostra, per inceptos hymenaeos.
   Nam ut nulla quis velit tincidunt ullamcorper. Sed leo tortor, feugiat vel,
   rhoncus eu, imperdiet ut, pede. In hac habitasse platea dictumst. Sed venenatis.
   Fusce nec augue vel turpis adipiscing pharetra. In cursus enim ac erat sodales
   pretium.</p>
</div>
```

When viewed in the browser you will see that the `content` division falls underneath the `leftnav` division which is the behavior that you would expect, as the `<div>` element does not give any formatting of its own – it is simply wrapping the areas in order that we can address them separately with CSS:

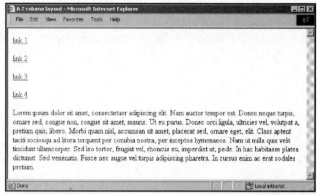

*Two basic <div> elements – one for navigation, and one for page content*

Now we will create a new stylesheet file and attach it to the page. In the new stylesheet, let's add the following two sets of rules:

```
#leftnav {
  position: absolute;
  left: 0px;
  top: 0px;
  width: 130px;
}

#content {
  position: absolute;
  left: 160px;
  top: 0px;
}
```

If you now view your page you should find that the content is now sat to the right of the navigation.

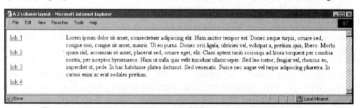

*The same two <div> elements, with CSS applied to them to achieve a
bicolumnular layout*

The rules should be fairly self-explanatory. We have set an absolute position on both divisions, setting the navigation to be 0 pixels from the left (so right against the left-hand edge of the **viewport** – the viewable area of the browser window) and set the content to start 160px away from that edge in order to make sure it clears the navigation. Absolute positioning takes the area out of the normal flow of the document and in this case we are placing the item in absolute pixel units from the top and left-hand side of the viewport. We can then add to this basic layout by adding padding and margins to both navigation and content.

The left navigation bar would be an ideal place to use the navigation buttons that we created earlier in this chapter, so the last thing we have done to our `csslayout.css` stylesheet (apart from adding a simple rule to display the contents of `<p>` in a sans-serif font) is to copy the CSS for our buttons into it.

All we then need to do is to add a `class` attribute with a value of `myButton` to each of the `<p>` elements in the division `leftnav`. Our final layout example should look as follows:

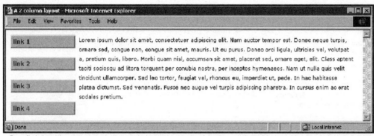

*Our finished layout example – again we see the bicolumnular layout, plus we have applied our button styling to the links as well, to give a nice page effect*

Any page of your site with this stylesheet attached and the relevant divisions marked up within the document will now display in the same fashion as this page. This makes site-wide updating of the layout far easier. If you have a 50-page site based on a layout like this and the client wants you to make the buttons ten pixels smaller and bright pink, all you need to do is make those changes once in the stylesheet. With a non-CSS layout you would need to make that change on each page of the site.

To show how easily you can change a document's layout with CSS – let's see how we can quickly move our menu over to the right-hand side of the content. To do this all we need to do is simply go into our `csslayout.css` stylesheet and edit a few lines within the rule sets for the areas `#leftnav` and `#content`, like so:

```
#leftnav {
  position: absolute;
  right: 0px;
  top: 0px;
  width: 130px;
  margin-top: 10px;
  margin-left: 10px;
  margin-right: 6px;
}

#content {
  position: absolute;
  left: 10px;
  top: 0px;
  margin-top: 10px;
  padding-right: 160px
}
```

We have now changed the absolute positioning in `#leftnav` to be 0 pixels from the right instead of the left. This will move the menu over to the right-hand side of the viewport.

We then need to make space for it, otherwise the content will flow over the menu. We could make space by setting a width on `#content`, however this would have the effect of making the width of that content area static, rather than liquid and flowing with the size of the viewport. What we do instead is apply some padding to the right-hand side of `#content` that is wide enough to clear the menu – `padding-right: 160px;` We will also want to move the content closer to the left-hand side of the viewport, because the menu is not there anymore – we will change `left` to be `10px`. If you preview your page in a browser it should look like this:

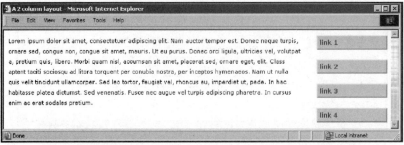

*Our layout example again, but with the navigation moved to the right-hand side*

The above examples hopefully demonstrate some of the power of CSS. By using the example pages on the CD you will be able to edit and experiment with this way of laying out pages and see how many different layouts you can make simply by altering a few rules in a stylesheet.

### CSS-P in Dreamweaver MX

As we have already discussed the CSS capabilities of Dreamweaver MX in this chapter, we would like to close this section on CSS layouts with a discussion on the methods used by Dreamweaver MX to create CSS layouts. Dreamweaver refers to divisions (`<div>` elements) positioned using absolute positioning (as we have just used in the previous example) as "layers". These should not be confused with Netscape 4's `<layer>` element, which is now deprecated and is usually only found in backwards-compatible pages.

*use of inline CSS positioning is less than optimal*

While Dreamweaver MX will open and display CSS layouts of the type we have just created, if you were to create a layout within Dreamweaver MX you would find that it creates the layout using inline CSS positioning. As we have already discussed, the use of inline CSS positioning is less than optimal as you then lose the ability to make changes site-wide by just changing one stylesheet, and you end up with far larger (and thus slower to load) documents.

# Creating a Stylesheet for Print

CSS2 brought with it "media descriptors" that will allow a developer to specify that a different stylesheet is used for different types of browsers and devices that recognize these descriptors. The descriptors that are available in CSS2 are:

| Descriptor | Description |
| --- | --- |
| aural | Intended for speech synthesizers (screen readers) |
| Braille | Intended for Braille tactile feedback devices |
| embossed | Intended for paged Braille printers |
| handheld | Intended for handheld devices (typically small screen, monochrome, limited bandwidth) |
| print | Intended for documents to be printed |
| projection | Intended for projected presentations |
| screen | Intended primarily for color computer screens |
| tty | Intended for media using a fixed-pitch character grid, such as teletypes, terminals, or portable devices with limited display capabilities. |
| tv | Intended for television |

Actually, there is only patchy support for most of these media descriptors. However, there is support for some. We are going to consider the use of one of these media descriptors, print, that can be very helpful in day-to-day web site design.

# Creating the Print Stylesheet

As web developers, we are often required to create documents for print. As you probably already realize from our discussion on CSS for text styling, what looks good on the screen does not always look good once printed. In the past we have often had to prepare separate, printable versions of our documents in order to get round this problem, but with media descriptors we have another option.

Here we will create a print stylesheet for our csslayout.html page. Anyone wanting to print the content of this page would probably not want to print the navigation. More complex pages may have logos and other graphical elements that are unnecessary once the document is printed.

As we are going to base our print stylesheet on our existing page stylesheet, the first step is to save our existing csslayout.css stylesheet as print.css – we'll alter it as necessary shortly. We need to attach this second stylesheet to our page and specify that it is to be used for print. Where we first had one line linking to a stylesheet, we now have two:

```
<link rel="stylesheet" href="csslayout.css" type="text/css" media="screen" />
<link rel="stylesheet" href="print.css" type="text/css" media="print" />
```

Now we need to edit print.css. As we are going to hide the navigation anyway, we can remove anything relating to the buttons from the stylesheet. To actually hide the navigation, go to the rule with selector #leftnav and add the declaration display: none. You can remove the other declarations for #leftnav from this print stylesheet as the leftnav division will not be displayed.

You can make as many changes as you like to the stylesheet for print – change the left margin width for the content area, specify the font size in points (which, while not suitable for the Web, are perfect to be used for print) or perhaps change to a serif font which is easier to read when printed. Your final print stylesheet should look something like this:

```
body {
  background-color: #ffffff;
  color: #000000;
}

p {
  font-family: "Times New Roman", Times, serif;
  font-size: 14pt;
  line-height: 20pt;
}

#leftnav {
  display: none;
}

#content {
  position: absolute;
  left: 40px;
  top: 0px;
  margin-top: 10px;
}
```

The screenshot below shows how it displays in *Print Preview* from IE 6.

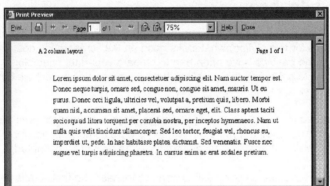

*Our example as it will appear in print,*
*thanks to our Print stylesheet*

The print stylesheet has good support amongst the modern browsers. If it is absolutely vital that your pages may be printed cleanly, then you may still need to consider the use of an alternative method of creating a page for print. However, for many sites, creating a print stylesheet simply offers an extra convenience to the visitor, so you should certainly consider providing one.

# Older Browsers

You may encounter designers and developers who are reluctant to use CSS because of browser issues. However, these issues are, for most site designs, easily avoided, and the benefits of CSS far outweigh the small amount of work needed to counter browser problems. Anyone still using a very old browser (pre Netscape version 4 or IE version 3) that has no CSS support is going to see unstyled content. However, anyone using a version 2 or 3 browser on the Web today would probably be relieved to see unstyled content after the mess they will see when trying to view many sites! So you may choose not to worry too much about browsers before version 4.

# Version 4 Browser Issues

There are still people using version 4 browsers (usually a version of Netscape 4), often not through choice, but because their place of work, school, or college refuses to upgrade. The percentage of Netscape 4 users varies depending on your target audience, but seems to be about 4% on average. The problem with Netscape 4 is that it tries to interpret CSS, and while it has few problems with the styling of text, as I have mentioned in this chapter it has many problems when you begin to style form fields, links, or images that are links, or try to position page elements. These problems may simply be that your page looks a bit strange or may be more serious – they may stop the user being able to complete your forms, or click on your navigation.

# Beating the Version 4s

This author's personal view is that we shouldn't continue to design solely in the way we designed five years ago because some people are still using an old browser. Luckily there are a few simple tricks that we can use in order to be able to create attractive designs using CSS for the standards-compliant browsers and produce something that will not break Netscape 4!

## @import

We have been attaching our stylesheets with the `<link>` tag throughout this chapter. The `<link>` tag is the most widely used method of attaching external stylesheets, as it is supported by browsers both old and new. However, there is another method of attaching a stylesheet that is not recognized by Netscape 4 browsers and we can use this lack of support to our advantage. We can create our main stylesheet and link it to our document using the following markup (which Netscape doesn't understand):

```
<style type="text/css">

  @import url("global.css");

</style>
```

New compliant browsers (such as IE 5+, Mozilla, Netscape 6+, and Konqueror) will see the stylesheet and render the pages as per the rules it contains. If you view the page in Netscape 4, however, you will see unformatted text.

For some sites, leaving Netscape 4 with unformatted text might be acceptable. If you don't expect to get many visitors using older browsers, you at least know that the odd one you do get will not encounter a broken page due to your CSS. If however, you feel that you want to provide Netscape 4 users with some styling, then you can attach another stylesheet, using the `<link>` tag that we have used throughout this chapter, before the imported stylesheet:

```
<link href="oldbrowsers.css" rel="stylesheet" type="text/css" />
<style type="text/css">
  @import url("global.css");
</style>
```

Note that the linked stylesheet must be placed before the imported one. Compliant browsers will read both stylesheets, but the values for style properties set in the first will be overridden by any values set in the second. This is an example of the cascade order that we looked at earlier on in the chapter.

A good way to create your `oldbrowsers.css` stylesheet is to take a copy of your `global.css` stylesheet (as we did with the print stylesheet), remove any styles that you know will upset Netscape 4 (such as rules to style form fields), and then make any other changes to make the way that Netscape 4 renders your page look acceptable. As long as any styles that you set within the first stylesheet are overridden in the second, these rules will not change what users of compliant browsers see.

## JavaScript

It is also possible to use client-side JavaScript in order to detect the browser and write out the correct stylesheet for the browser being used. This method relies on the user having JavaScript turned on, but can be very useful if you find that a bug in a particular browser causes a crash etc. and you need to isolate that browser and display an alternative stylesheet to it that won't break it.

We can also use JavaScript to detect whether the user is visiting with a newer, more standards-compliant browser or a pre-version 5 browser and display stylesheets accordingly. This method doesn't check for the user-agent of the browser, it simply checks for a browser that supports this W3C DOM method. As browsers before version 5 do not support the W3C DOM, this method successfully isolates those browsers. (You will be learning more about JavaScript in *Chapters 9* and *10* of this book, so this method may make more sense if you return to it after reading those chapters.)

```
<script language="javascript" type="text/javascript">
if (!document.getElementById)
{
document.write('<link rel="stylesheet" href="oldbrowsers.css" type="text/css" />');
}
else
{
document.write('<link rel="stylesheet" href="global.css" type="text/css" />');
}
</script>
```

In the above method we are not overwriting one stylesheet with the values of the other. Version 4 browsers will only see the rules in the `oldbrowsers.css` stylesheet and compliant browsers only see the rules in `global.css`.

## Server-Side Detection

If you use a server-side language on your site such as PHP, ASP, Coldfusion etc. it is possible to detect the browser's user agent and write out the stylesheets depending on which version of the browser you discover. If you are using server-side detection then you need to test very carefully to ensure that you have not mistakenly excluded any modern, compliant browser! As a Konqueror on Linux user I frequently find myself viewing a version of a site meant for older browsers as the person writing the script did not think about odd folk on Linux platforms. For server-side basics, go to *Chapter 15* of this book.

# Summary

This has been a short introduction to a language that will become very familiar to you as you move into the world of web design and development, and is an area that you are well worth putting in the effort to understand well, at an early stage in your career.

There are many opportunities for learning more about CSS. One of the best ways is by simply using the language more and more. Take the stylesheets on the CD and experiment with what happens when you change them. This will help you to understand the syntax and the effect that CSS has on your documents. Secondly, there are many resources on the Web where you can go to expand your knowledge and get answers to your questions – the online resources I have listed below are good places to start. Thirdly, there are many books available on this subject: for a practical, well-written resource on how to take your CSS knowledge to the next level, check out *Cascading Style Sheets: Separating Content from Presentation* (*Owen Briggs et al, glasshaus, ISBN: 1904151-04-3*).

# Resources

The W3C CSS Section*: http://www.w3.org/Style/CSS/*

CSS Guide by Western Civilization: *http://www.westciv.com/style_master/academy/css_tutorial/*

*C*SS layouts that you can use as a starting point – *http://glish.com/css/*

'Little boxes': more CSS layouts and how to create them: *http://www.thenoodleincident.com/tutorials/box_lesson/boxes.html*

The CSS-discuss mailing list: *http://three.pairlist.net/mailman/listinfo/css-discuss*

# 9

- JavaScript tutorial

- Storing data with JavaScript

- Decision making and control structures

**Author: Chris Ullman**

# JavaScript Basics

JavaScript is a vital addition to any web developer's toolkit. It is the most widely used programming language in the browser by quite some margin, and it was the first language to be introduced to build upon HTML's lack of interactive features. It enables web developers to respond to events, such as a mouse button being pressed or the mouse being moved, without having to hop back to the server first (thus saving data from flowing around the Internet unnecessarily). And unlike Flash, Java, or many other of the Web's more glittering technologies, it doesn't require any downloads or plugins: the three major browsers already contain all you need to write and run JavaScript programs.

Commonly, JavaScript is muddled up with its namesake Java, but it actually has little in common with this programming language. JavaScript was originally christened **LiveScript** by its creator Netscape and renamed, in part, to cash in on the popularity of Java. Its syntax resembles the programming language C, from which some of its structures are derived, so it will be familiar to many experienced programmers. It went from being a proprietary solution on Netscape to one that was governed by a set of universal standards (**ECMAScript**) and is supported by any major browser worth its salt (Internet Explorer, Netscape, and Opera).

Note that the version of ECMAScript supported by IE is actually called **JScript**. This is Microsoft's own implementation of ECMAScript, but is virtually identical to JavaScript, so we won't be treating them any differently here.

We're going to embark on a whirlwind tour of JavaScript in the next two chapters and dip into its major features and uses. To do this, it's necessary to teach some programming structures, but we'll try and keep them brief and to the point. Often, useful scripts are little more than a couple of lines long, so don't be deterred by the initial volume of information that will be heading your way, as it will just help you to determine in which situations the use of JavaScript would be most appropriate.

On the Web you will find many pre-written scripts which you can insert into your own web pages and which can be used with the minimum amount of customization. We will provide a few such scripts for you in the next chapter.

In this chapter we'll discuss:

- What client-side scripting is

- How to insert a script into your web pages

- How to get your web page to react to simple user interaction

- How you can store information from the user in your web pages

- How to take a course of action depending on a user's decision

# What Is JavaScript?

Before we go any further we need to outline what JavaScript is, especially in relation to HTML pages, and also in relation to other programming languages. Put at its most simple definition, JavaScript is a **programming language**. Programming languages allow us to create **programs** that tell the computer exactly what to do. Programs are made up of lines of instructions, which are processed sequentially by the computer. At its simplest, a program can be made up of one line. You've already seen HTML, but this isn't a true programming language; rather it's a markup language, which is used to describe the structure of a web page. In practice this means it's less complex than true programming languages and doesn't contain any of the same features or structures.

JavaScript is a particular type of a programming language known as a **scripting language**. Scripting languages are any languages that can be embedded into applications. This application doesn't necessarily have to be a browser, but in this chapter we will only be talking about JavaScript as a browser-based scripting language. In short, you type some JavaScript into your web page, along with your HTML, and the browser will do its best to run the web page. Programs in scripting languages are usually known as **scripts**.

JavaScript isn't the only scripting language found on the Web. Microsoft has its own scripting language, **VBScript**, which is common only to the Internet Explorer browser on the Windows platform. Its popularity briefly blossomed in the late 1990s, but these days it is less commonly used and even Microsoft provide JavaScript (or **JScript**) support in Internet Explorer. JavaScript, by contrast, is understood by Netscape (versions 2 onward), Internet Explorer (versions 3 onwards), and Opera (versions 5 onwards). While JavaScript is a bit "pickier" than VBScript (for instance you have to be careful about the case of the lines you type in), it's generally accepted as being slightly more powerful and faster than VBScript, and its more widespread usage makes it a better candidate for use on the Web.

# What Is Client-Side Scripting?

Recall what actually happens when you browse to a web page. You type in the URL, and the browser sends a request for that page over the Internet. This request is processed by a target machine, which holds the web page you desire. If the target machine has the page, then it returns it to you; if it hasn't got the page then it will return a relevant error message instead. The two parts to the browsing process are the browser – the **client** – and the machine that holds the web page you wish to view – the **server**.

When we say that a language is browser-based or **client-side**, we mean that the language is dealt with by the client or browser. The browsers have a component, known as a scripting engine, built in. It is this engine that does the work of translating the scripting language into something the browser can understand or display. The presence of the relevant scripting engine determines whether your browser supports JavaScript or VBScript or both. We've already mentioned which browsers support JavaScript natively, without needing any plugins or special attachments.

So to recap, when you request a web page with some associated JavaScript, that whole page is returned to you – HTML, JavaScript, and all. It's then up to the browser to take both the HTML and the JavaScript and render the viewable web page.

There are advantages and disadvantages to using client-side languages, but we need to look at an alternative option first before expounding upon them.

The flip-side of the coin is the **server-side** languages. You can actually use both JavaScript and VBScript on the server-side as well as the client-side, but the way that they operate is different. What happens is that when you request a page, the processing of the script is done on the server before the web page is returned to the browser. In fact, all that the browser gets to see is the HTML that has been created by the server-side language as opposed to a page containing script and HTML. Examples of server-side technologies are Microsoft's **Active Server Pages** (**ASP**), which can use JavaScript or VBScript, Microsoft's **ASP.NET**, Macromedia's **ColdFusion**, **JSP**, and open source **PHP**. We'll touch upon these very briefly later in the book in *Chapter 15*, but really they are beyond the scope of the book and are in the realm of the more experienced web professional.

There is a time and a place for the use of both client-side and server-side languages. Client-side languages are used when you need an immediate response to a particular action. Perhaps the user moves a mouse over a given area on the web page, or they click on a mouse button. A server-side language would have to wait for the distant server to respond, which is often not an option because it would be too slow. However, as we said, JavaScript has weaknesses. It's not particularly secure, so you shouldn't use it to process credit-card details, or interrogate databases containing sensitive information. This isn't to say don't use client-side scripting languages at all, but just consider exactly the kind of tasks you need it to perform. In fact, this chapter and the next chapter are purely concerned with the use of JavaScript as a client-side language, so as you will see there is plenty you can do with them.

## Sandboxing

Another concern of many web users when viewing pages containing JavaScript is security. Is it safe to view this page? Am I downloading viruses or code dangerous to the contents of my hard drive? What can this page do to my computer? The answers are "yes it is safe" and "the pages you download can do very little to affect the contents of your hard drive". At worst, JavaScript in web pages can crash a machine by creating an infinite loop or opening an infinite amount of new windows, but this is something easily averted by shutting down the rogue page from Task Manager in Windows, or a process list in UNIX.

Since the creation of scripting languages, a primary concern has been the prevention of scripts from affecting key functions on a computer, such as erasing files on your hard drive, enabling other users to have access to your computer, or crashing your machine at will. This is prevented because JavaScript operates in something known as a **sandbox**. This is an area where the code is prevented from getting at vital areas of your computer, such as your hard drive. This isn't to say that JavaScript can't write to your hard drive (we'll discuss how it does that when we cover cookies in the next chapter – and why they aren't such a bad idea), but the way in which it can is strictly limited and secure: it can't just delete the contents of the hard drive. The downside is that, as a result of sandboxing, you'll find that JavaScript doesn't have any great graphical or file-handling capabilities.

As a side note though, the sandbox doesn't mean that scripting is always safe and secure. It just means that the act of viewing a web page alone over HTTP can't damage your machine. If you choose to download and run a script from a web page onto your own machine outside a web page environment, it's still possible to end up with a virus. Typically VBScript has a lot of problems from viruses, as a version of this language also forms part of Outlook in the Microsoft Office suite, and e-mails sent with rogue attachments can carry VBScript scripts that activate and cause damage when the e-mail is opened up. Here we need to make a distinction though: a scripting language in this context is something that is embedded into an application – here the application is Outlook. The scripting language embedded into your web page has much less capability for this, because of sandboxing.

## Why Use JavaScript?

You may be wondering what exactly you can do with JavaScript if it's restricted from doing too much. Well, I hope to make a watertight case before you proceed any further. It is capable of a lot more than HTML can do on its own. For example, you can use it to:

- Create basic interactive features such as rollovers (images that change as a mouse moves over them) or dynamic menus (menus that only appear when a mouse moves over them).

- Take a user's details and check to see whether they've entered valid information, such as a valid e-mail address and no blank space for a required field.

- Create timers and then perform actions at specific times such as getting adverts to pop up– yes, unfortunately many of the Web's more annoying features are down to a little bit of JavaScript.

- Detect a particular type of browser and adjust your page accordingly.

- Dynamically alter the styles and setting on a web page (via CSS, which we covered in *Chapter 8*).

- Open new windows or send users to different sites.

- Do some basic customization of your site for users who've visited your site before.

- Create rudimentary games.

JavaScript's three most common uses boil down to **browser detection**, the **validation** of information contained within forms, and **simple interactivity** with the user. Without these features, the Web would be a pretty dull and lifeless place.

However, note that in all browsers that support JavaScript, the user can also disable it via the browser's menus. This means that building a web site with JavaScript always requires you to provide a non-JavaScript alternative if you want to get good "usability grades". JavaScript can serve to enhance a site, but a site relying on JavaScript totally for its functionality is not something a web designer should aim at.

I've spent enough time talking about what JavaScript is, and when and how you should use it, so it's now time to see some of its more practical applications.

# Inserting a Script into Your Page

I've already alluded to the fact that JavaScript is mixed in with HTML, but it isn't the case that you can just liberally sprinkle in an HTML tag here and a JavaScript line there. JavaScript programs, or scripts to give them their more accurate name, are commonly placed within the confines of the special HTML `<script>` tag.

## The <script> Element

The `<script>` element, like most HTML elements, comprises of an opening and closing tag. Anything contained between the tags is no longer treated as HTML, but as script. The `<script>` tag should appear within the `<head>` tags of an HTML document, or within the `<body>` tags if it relates to a particular HTML element or part of the page.

The `<script>` tag is valid with any version of HTML (from version 3.2 onwards) or XHTML, but we will be using HTML 4.01 Transitional for this chapter, partly because this is the default that Dreamweaver MX uses and also because we will be looking at frames in the next chapter, which are part of the transitional rather than strict standard.

The presence of the `<script>` tag alone is usually enough to indicate that you're using JavaScript, but to make certain you need to specify the language via the `<script>` tag's attributes.

### The type Attribute

The `type` attribute indicates which scripting language you wish to place within the `<script>` tags. Typically this will take the format shown overleaf when specifying JavaScript:

```
<script type="text/javascript">
```

or this format when specifying VBScript:

```
<script type="text/vbscript">
```

This attribute is mandatory in HTML 4.0 and onwards: valid HTML requires that you specify it. However, earlier versions of Netscape (pre-version 6) don't recognize the `type` attribute. They used the `language` attribute in place of this. The `language` attribute just takes the name of the language as its instruction:

```
<script language="javascript">
```

When inserting scripts using Dreamweaver MX, you'll see that alongside the `type` attribute, it also uses the `language` attribute:

```
<script type="text/javascript" language="javascript">
```

If you don't supply any information about the scripting language you are using, then the browser will just revert to using its default language. In most cases, this will be JavaScript, although for early versions of IE, it may well be VBScript, so it's best to specify the `type` attribute up front.

## The src Attribute

The other attribute of the `<script>` tag that is of interest is the `src` attribute. We won't be using this along with the `<script>` element in the chapters of this book, but it provides a means whereby you can separate the JavaScript out into a separate file, saved commonly with a `.js` extension. The `src` attribute is used to indicate where this JavaScript file is located. It can be used to indicate either a local file location:

```
<script type="text/javascript" src="/Program Files/scripts/example.js" />
```

or an external URL:

```
<script type="text/javascript" src="http://www.examplesite.com/scripts/example.js"
/>
```

Using a separate file for scripts in this way has many of the advantages that using a separate CSS file does, as we discussed in *Chapter 8*. These include making it easier to manage your code, only having to maintain code in one file, and making the page load faster a second time (since the file will be downloaded once to the browser cache).

## The First Example Program

Having explained where the JavaScript goes, it's now time to create a very small example program. To do this, start the web page editor of your choice. We're going to assume that you're using Dreamweaver MX, but if you aren't using this product, don't worry. It's just as easy to use any text editor, such as Notepad or Simple Text, to create the examples with. All of the code necessary has been supplied in this chapter and the next; simply cut and paste all of the code rather than just the highlighted code if you're not using Dreamweaver MX.

## Using Dreamweaver MX to Insert Scripts

First create a new blank HTML page in Dreamweaver MX. Then go to the *Scripts* tab of the *Insert* toolbar; you will find three icons. Click on the *Script* icon, which looks like this:

This will yield a dialog with three boxes.

The *Language* box can be either set to *JavaScript*, *JavaScript 1.1*, *JavaScript 1.2*, or *VBScript*. We will be using just the basic *JavaScript* option here. In Dreamweaver, this will set both the `language` and `type` attributes of our `<script>` tags.

The *Content* box is where the script itself can be added. The Dreamweaver dialog doesn't actually give you much room in which to place the script code, so we recommend for anything longer than a line or two, you revert to inserting the JavaScript via *Code View* instead.

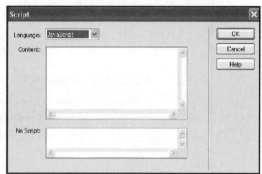

*The Dreamweaver MX Script dialog box.*

The *No Script* box allows you to specify some alternative text/HTML content, to be displayed by any browser that doesn't have JavaScript support. This may be unlikely to represent a high percentage of your audience but, as we said above, it is also possible to turn off JavaScript support in some browsers. Anything placed within this box will be placed in `<noscript>` tags, within the page. It usually contains a message explaining that the page may not work as expected, and should also provide alternative content that allows use of the page, albeit perhaps in a more restricted way.

Type the following line into the *Content* box and press *OK*. Make sure you follow the capitalization here exactly.

```
alert("You're using " + navigator.appName + " aren't you? How did I know...");
```

Click on the *Show Code View* icon in the toolbar to see how and where the code has been placed:

```
<!DOCTYPE HTML PUBLIC "-//W3C//DTD HTML 4.01 Transitional//EN">
<html>
<head>
<title>First JavaScript Example</title>
<meta http-equiv="Content-Type" content="text/html; charset=iso-8859-1">
</head>
<body>
<script language="JavaScript" type="text/JavaScript">
alert("You're using " + navigator.appName + " aren't you? How did I know...");
</script>
</body>
</html>
```

Dreamweaver has placed three lines of code inside our HTML. Two are basic HTML markup: opening and closing `<script></script>` tags. As we suggested it might, Dreamweaver has created `language` and `type` attributes for you, despite the fact that they both actually do the same thing. This is to make sure all browsers that read JavaScript can run this page.

**JavaScript Basics**

Inside is our single line of JavaScript. Before we explain what it does, let's see the script in action. To do this, save the page as `FirstExample.html` and go and view the page in the browser of your choice. It will display a message corresponding to your own browser whenever you open the page:

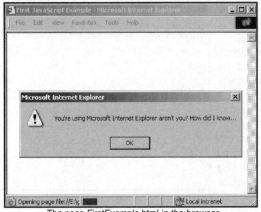

This example script just performs some very basic browser detection. When you run the script, you are greeted with this message telling you which browser you are using every time you view the page.

*The page FirstExample.html in the browser.*

If you're using Opera you will find rather distressingly it tells you that you are using Microsoft Internet Explorer or Netscape. This is because the smaller browsers tend to "spoof" the major ones. It's an early indication of browser incompatibilities and scripting, and the fact that a web page which shows something perfectly correctly on one browser might not show up as expected on another. However, we won't worry about that quite yet – we'll discuss that in the next chapter. Instead, we'll scoot over it and hurry on to explaining what the JavaScript you've written actually does.

This single line:

```
alert("You're using " + navigator.appName + " aren't you? How did I know...");
```

is an alert function. The `alert()` function produces a dialog, which requires the user to click on a button before it will disappear. This type of dialog is also called a **modal dialog**. Typically this feature is used when you want to warn the user or inform them about some action that is undoable. Inside the parentheses of the alert function is the text that the user will see displayed.

> *this feature is used when you want to warn the user or inform them about some action that is undoable*

The text is composed of three parts: two parts are text within quotation marks and the section in the middle is the `navigator.appName` expression, which retrieves information about the user's browser. `navigator` itself is actually an object which represents the browser, and `appName` is a property of this object, which gives details of the make of the browser. However, we're getting ahead of ourselves here once again. We'll consider objects again before the chapter end, but for now think of `navigator.appName` as a single expression that returns the make of the browser. So, JavaScript evaluates `navigator.appName` as *Microsoft Internet Explorer* or *Netscape Navigator* depending upon which browser you are using.

You should notice also that each code statement ends with a **semicolon**. This is common to nearly every line in JavaScript and is a way of indicating to the browser that you have completed that statement of code. Without it, the program wouldn't know where the statement has ended, although JavaScript has a facility for "guessing" where the end of the statement should end. It isn't strictly necessary to use it, but for the purposes of these two chapters we will use it to try and make the code clearer, especially when it spans two lines.

Of course, by itself this code is of little merit unless you permanently wish to irritate users every time they log on to your web page by telling them something they probably already know. However, this browser-checking code could be altered to run extra code customized to a particular browser, for example so that you could use a particular effect native to Internet Explorer (such as one of those effects that makes the text fade in Star Trek style), while in Netscape the same text is displayed in a different color. Hopefully you can start to see how this begins to make a more user-friendly and flexible environment in which to browse.

Perhaps of more immediate interest is another way of inserting JavaScript into your web page as part of an HTML tag itself. This allows you to get your page to react or display messages only in response to a certain event occurring. These are known as **intrinsic events**.

## Intrinsic Events

Without getting into a full-blown discourse on events, let's just say that events, like real-life events, happen on your computer. They usually take the form of a mouse button being clicked, or a mouse being moved, or an image being dragged and dropped. Now, as the browser is monitoring for these kind of events the whole time, it's possible in HTML to have elements on your web page, such as images or text, react when an event occurs to them. So if a mouse moves over an image, then that image can be made to generate an event. If you click over a link, then the `<a>` tag could generate an event.

> *It's possible in HTML to have elements on your web page react when an event occurs to them*

Each HTML element usually comes with its own set of events. These events are accessible as extra attributes for the tags, called **event handlers**. Overleaf is a comprehensive list of them and the elements to which they apply:

JavaScript Basics

| Event Handler | Description of Event | HTML Elements That Use It |
|---|---|---|
| onload | Generated when pretty much anything is loaded into a window | <body>, <frameset>, <img> |
| onunload | Generated when the document has been removed from a window or frame | <body>, <frameset> |
| onclick | Generated when the left mouse button is clicked and the cursor is over an element | Most elements |
| ondblclick | Generated when the left mouse button is double-clicked and the curscr is over an element | Most elements |
| onmousedown | Generated when a mouse button is first pressed and the cursor is over an element | Most elements |
| onmouseup | Generated when a mouse button is released and the cursor is over an element | Most elements |
| onmouseover | Generated when a cursor is moved onto an element | Most elements |
| onmousemove | Generated when a cursor is moved while hovering over an element | Most elements |
| onmouseout | Generated when a cursor is moved away from an element it was over | Most elements |
| onfocus | Generated when an element receives **focus** (becoming the element currently in use) by being clicked by the mouse or navigated to via a *tab* key press | <a>, <area>, <label>, <input>, <select>, <textarea>, <button> |
| onblur | Generated when an element loses focus (becoming an element that is no longer in use) | <a>, <area>, <label>, <input>, <select>, <textarea>, <button> |
| onkeypress | Generated when a key is pressed and released over an element | The elements that can receive focus |
| onkeydown | Generated when a key is pressed over an element | The elements that can receive focus |
| onkeyup | Generated when a key is released over an element | The elements that can receive focus |
| onsubmit | Generated when a form is submitted | <form> |
| onreset | Generated when a form is reset | <form> |
| onselect | Generated when the user selects some text within a form field | <input>, <select>, <textarea> |
| onchange | Generated when a field on a form loses focus and has had its value changed | <input>, <select>, <textarea> |

These event handlers are used just like extra attributes of HTML tags. For example:

```
<input type="button" value="Click Me" onclick="alert('Hello');" />
```

The only difference is that instead of supplying a normal text value to the attribute, you can supply some JavaScript instead. This JavaScript can do anything: display a message, open up a new window, move a user to a different page, or display a new set of information. In this case it would display the message "*Hello*" in a dialog box when the user clicked the button "*Click Me*".

So, by using these event handler attributes of certain HTML tags, you can insert JavaScript into your code without having to use the `<script>` tags. This way makes sure that the JavaScript is only run whenever a desired event occurs. Generally, you'd restrict the usage of JavaScript in this way to fairly simple scripts of one or two lines.

We'll now look at a quick example whereby we create an element in our own web page and get it to react to an intrinsic event.

## Intrinsic Event Example Script

In this example we're going to create a small `<div>` block and color this block blue. Whenever the user moves the mouse over the blue area, an event will be generated and a message will pop up to the user.

Dreamweaver MX makes it very easy for us to add these events. We'll start by creating a new blank HTML page. Next go to the *Layout* tab of the *Insert* panel in *Design View* and make sure *Standard View* is selected in the menu bar to add a layer to the page. Color it blue and assign it the properties *L 100px*, *T 100px*, *W 150px*, and *H 100px* (short for "offset from the left-hand edge", "offset from the top of the page", the "width", and the "height"). Make sure the `<div>` tag is selected and add the text "Whatever you do, don't move your mouse over here". Change the font text to white by clicking on the *text color* icon (which looks like an empty square with the current color inside of it):

Next right-click on the `<div>` tag in Dreamweaver and select the *Edit Tag <div>* option to bring up the *Tag Editor*. Click on *Events*, scroll down to *onMouseOver* and type the following code in the dialog (in *Design View* , just edit the tag manually):

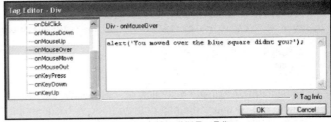

*The Dreamweaver MX Tag Editor.*

Save the page as `EventExample.html` and view the page in your browser (noting that it will not work in Netscape 4). If you move your mouse over the blue rectangle, then the following dialog appears:

Of course we're betting on the user's curiosity here to get the better of them and do exactly what they're being told not to.

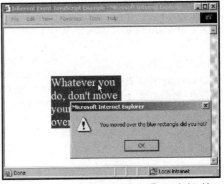

*The page EventExample.html in the browser.*

If you change to code view, you'll see the following:

```
<!DOCTYPE HTML PUBLIC "-//W3C//DTD HTML 4.01 Transitional//EN">
<html>
<head>
<title>Inherent Event JavaScript Example</title>
<meta http-equiv="Content-Type" content="text/html; charset=iso-8859-1">
<script language="JavaScript" type="text/JavaScript">
<!--
function MM_reloadPage(init) {  //reloads the window if Nav4 resized
  if (init==true) with (navigator) {if
((appName=="Netscape")&&(parseInt(appVersion)==4)) {
    document.MM_pgW=innerWidth; document.MM_pgH=innerHeight;
onresize=MM_reloadPage; }}
  else if (innerWidth!=document.MM_pgW || innerHeight!=document.MM_pgH)
location.reload();
}
MM_reloadPage(true);
//-->
</script>
</head>

<body>
<div id="Layer1" style="position:absolute; left:100px; top:100px; width:150px;
height:100px; z-index:1; background-color: #0000FF; layer-background-color:
#0000FF;" onMouseOver="alert('You moved over the blue rectangle did you
not?');"><font color="#FFFFFF" size="+2">Whatever you do, don't move your mouse
over here</font></div>
</body>
</html>
```

Immediately, you'll see a section of script within the `<head>` tags that Dreamweaver has added. Ignore this as this script has nothing to do with our script; it is just something that Dreamweaver adds automatically and is used to reload the window in Netscape 4 if the browser window is resized. If you're creating the page with another text editor, there is no need to copy this section.

However, there is one contentious point about this code: Dreamweaver has added HTML comment syntax around it (`<!--` and `-->`). Dreamweaver thinks it is being helpful here, as it means that older browsers that don't understand `<script>` tags will not attempt to render the JavaScript code as text. However, this can cause problems in the XHTML standards so you are not advised to use these comment marks around your code.

*JavaScript has a different syntax to HTML for adding comments*

As an aside, JavaScript has a different syntax to HTML for adding comments (notes to yourself or other developers that won't be interpreted as script by the browser). You can add single lines using double slashes:

```
// this is a line of comment.
```

Alternatively, to add several lines, you would start with `/*` and end with `*/`:

```
/*
these are
several lines
of comments
*/
```

Anyway, as well as taking notice of our brief digression on comments, we actually want you to note the highlighted text in the `<body>` tags where the code has been added. The code that generates the message is JavaScript once again, but here it is embedded into the `<div>` tag, via the `onmouseover` attribute.

```
<div ...
     onmouseover="alert('You moved over the blue rectangle did you not?');">
```

The value of the `onmouseover` attribute is a single alert function, which creates a dialog box with a message, just as in the last example. The only difference between the two examples is that this one only runs in response to the user moving over the blue rectangle.

Once again, on its own this code isn't overly useful. However, this might be more useful if you imagine it applied to a list of menu items. Perhaps, whenever you move over one menu item, a relevant submenu appears. This is something we're going to look at in the next chapter. Before we can look into providing an item like this, we need to look into some of the fundamental features of JavaScript in more detail.

# Storing Data in JavaScript

This has been quite a gentle grounding in JavaScript so far, so let's up the ante and introduce some programming structures. Perhaps the single most important feature of any programming language is its ability to remember information. This can take the form of remembering what values a user places in a form, storing the identity of the user and addressing them by their name further into the site, or keeping an eye on the time the user has spent on a particular page. Now, while there might be many individual ways of solving these problems, the one solution common to all when you only need to store the information for the duration of the page is to store the item of data within a variable.

## Variables

You can think of a variable as a repository or box where you wish to store important information for later use. Technically speaking, a variable is actually a **name-tag** or **handle** for where the computer can find a certain bit of information that it has stored. For example, a variable storing the number of fish left in my pond after the heron has come calling would look like this:

```
NumberOfFish = 3;
```

The computer stores the number 3 in a box labeled "`NumberOfFish`". The equals sign is known as the **assignment operator**. To the left of the equals sign you have the **variable name** or **identifier**, and to the right of it you have the information you wish to associate with that name – the **value**.

It doesn't *have* to be numerical data you store – it could equally be textual information. In this case the information would have to be given within quotation marks. So, if I wished to store the name of my favorite pizza topping I could do that too:

```
FavoritePizzaTopping = "Artichoke";
```

These variables will hold the information you tell it to for the duration of the script, or until you change it to something else. However, when naming variables, there are a set of rules and guidelines you should observe, as not just any name is suitable for a variable name.

## Naming Variables

For starters, like most programming languages, JavaScript has its own set of words that are reserved exclusively for its own use. For example, the word "case" is reserved and so the following line wouldn't be permissible:

```
case = "the affair of the missing budgerigar";
```

This is because JavaScript makes use of the word "case" in a command of its own and to use it in a variable name would confuse matters. There are too many reserved words to list here (see the CD for a full list), but if you try to follow a naming convention then you should avoid this problem.

One particular convention is where each variable is started with the first letter (or first few letters) of the data type, followed by the variable name whose first character is begun in uppercase, for example `sText` or `iNumber`. This technique is known as **Hungarian notation**. Alternatively, you can capitalize the first letters of words throughout the variable name, such as I did with `NumberOfFish` above. This technique is known as **camel casing**.

Note that in JavaScript variables are case-sensitive. This means the variable `numberoffish` is different to the variable `NumberOfFish`. The following code:

```
NumberOfFish = 4;
numberoffish = 5;
```

wouldn't update the contents of `NumberOfFish`. Instead, you would have two separate variables, one containing the number 4 and the other containing the number 5.

Also it's not possible to use particular characters which are reserved in JavaScript, namely the +, - , *, %, !, <, >, =, ?, ~, &, and / characters, because most of them are used within arithmetic operations and can be confusing for this reason. Instead, you can use the underscore character to break up names, which is perfectly legal. So, the following name would be illegal:

```
knife+fork = "cutlery";
```

but this one would be legal:

```
knife_fork = "cutlery";
```

It is also acceptable to have numbers in your variable names, as long as the variable name doesn't start with a number. So the following variable is legal:

```
variable2 = 18;
```

while this one would cause an error:

```
2variable = 18;
```

In practice, it is best to give your variables names that are as descriptive as possible. In the old days of micro-computers such as Sinclair Spectrums or Commodore 64s, you only were only allowed a couple of characters for a variable name, so names such as a, b, x, y, and z, or ab and cd predominated. This made programs very hard to follow, but to this day you'll see some programmers reluctant to give their variables meaningful or long names. However, in JavaScript there is no excuse: variable name lengths are practically unlimited. Consider the following two variables. Which is more helpful?

```
x = "16th September 2002";
todays_date = "16th September 2002";
```

Remember that most often you will be the person who has to go back and understand your scripts, and if you have over ten, or even over a hundred, variables to sort out, it is easy to lose track of what each one might be doing.

## Declaring Variables

Before you can use a variable, you have to announce to the computer that this name is going to be used to store information. This is done by the process of **declaration**. To declare a variable you place in front of it the keyword var the first time the variable is used, for example:

```
var new_variable;
```

Using variables without declaring them first won't actually cause an error, but it is still advisable to declare them since not doing so uses more memory and can cause side-effects in functions (which we will look at shortly). If we wanted to store today's date, then the correct usage would be:

```
var todays_date;
todays_date = "16th September 2002";
```

It is also possible to combine a declaration and an assignment of variable value all on one line:

```
var todays_date = "16th September 2002";
```

Once a variable has been declared, you shouldn't re-declare it. Once again, JavaScript doesn't actively prevent you from doing this, but it is unnecessary and would generate errors in other programming languages.

It's also possible to use one variable to supply the value of another one. For instance you can set up two variables as follows:

```
var todays_date;
var todays_date2;
todays_date = "16th September 2002";
todays_date2 = todays_date;
```

This is very common in JavaScript, so you need to get used to the concept. Another thing you might notice here is that we've supplied a date to the variable todays_date. Dates don't fit into either category of numerical or textual data that we've looked at. Indeed, JavaScript has more than just these categories for defining data, and the way variable data is recognized and placed into types affects what you can actually do with the information. For instance, if you've got numerical data stored, you probably want to be able to perform mathematical operations on it, while if you've got textual information, then you might just want to be able to stick two words together. If you've got two dates, you'll want them treated in a different way again.

# Data Types

We've already said above that JavaScript uses the addition of quotation marks as delimiters to differentiate between text and numbers, but there's more to it than that. JavaScript carries an implicit set of data types to help recognize and distinguish between the different types of data it can store.

Data types don't need explicit definition in JavaScript. This is because JavaScript is a **weakly typed language**, which means JavaScript works out what kind of data it's meant to be dealing with by itself. In many programming languages it is common to have to announce beforehand whether you are going to be storing numbers, text, dates, or another type of data within the variable before you use it. These are **strongly typed languages**. This isn't the case in JavaScript, but that doesn't mean data types don't exist at all. Indeed, JavaScript will categorize and manipulate data according to the data types it thinks it is dealing with.

## Numerical Data Type

In programming, there are two common numerical data types: **integers** (whole numbers with no decimals) and **floating point** (fractional) numbers. JavaScript treats every number as a floating point number. It recognizes these numbers because there are no quotation marks surrounding the data. Both of these are valid variables, therefore:

```
var a_number = 1;
var a_fractional_number = 1.345693;
```

There isn't much more to defining numerical variables, so we'll look at how JavaScript performs mathematical calculations now.

## Mathematical Operators

JavaScript supports all of the most common mathematical operators:

- Addition (+)
- Subtraction and negation (-)
- Multiplication (*)
- Division (/)

They can be used with variables to perform arithmetic. For example, to add two numbers together you could do the following:

```
var Calculation = 10 + 16;
```

So the variable Calculation holds the number 26. You could also add a number to an existing variable containing a number:

```
var Calculation2 = Calculation + 5;
```

So Calculation2 holds the number 31. Of course, you could define two separate variables and add them together:

```
var Number1 = 10;
var Number2 = 16;
var Number3 = Number1 + Number2;
```

So Number3 now contains the number 26.

It is also possible to combine several arithmetic operators to perform more complex arithmetic operations:

```
var Calculation3 = 16 + 14 - 3 * 2;
```

Calculation3 contains the number 24. Just as with basic mathematics, simple rules of precedence (parentheses, division, multiplication, addition, subtraction) are applied. So, if you want a particular part of the calculation performed before another part, say, if you wanted the above calculation to be calculated in the sequence in which it appeared (that is addition, followed by subtraction, followed by multiplication) then you would have to use parentheses:

```
var Calculation4 = ((16 + 14) - 3) * 2;
```

In this way the result 54 would be obtained and not 24 as in the previous calculation.

You also have **increment** and **decrement** operators in JavaScript. This is because a common task is to add 1 to a variable and still leave it with the same variable name:

```
Number4 = Number4 + 1;
```

9

**JavaScript Basics**

Rather than having to write this out, you can use the double `++` (increment) operator as follows to add 1:

```
Number4++;
```

Equally, to subtract 1 from the value, you can use the double `--` (decrement) operator:

```
Number4--;
```

Both the numerical data type and mathematical calculations in JavaScript are simple and inherently intuitive; as such they don't require any further discussion.

## String Data Type

Text is stored in something known as **strings** in JavaScript. We've already said that JavaScript recognizes text since it is given within quotation marks: these can either be double quotes or single quotes, with the proviso that they must both be double quotes, or both be single quotes. For example, text can be stored in a variable as follows:

```
var text_variable = "hello, I am a robot";
```

or

```
var text_variable = 'hello, I am a robot';
```

The reason for JavaScript recognizing both quotes is so that you can use one inside the other. For example, by abbreviating the following line, to encompass the apostrophe, you would need to do as follows:

```
var text_variable = "hello, I'm a robot";
```

You could not use the single quote as the string delimiter in this case as JavaScript would then not know which single quotes to treat as delimiters and which to treat as part of the text.

There is also an **escape character** (\) within JavaScript that can be used in conjunction with other characters to create **escape sequences**. These escape sequences allow you to display characters, like quotes, new lines, and form feeds. Here is a list of some of the most commonly used escape sequences.

\b backspace

\f form feed

\n new line

\r carriage return

\t tab

\' single quote

\" double quote

\\ backslash

To use any one of these special characters within text, you can replace it with the escape sequence instead. For example, to use the above line of code with single quotes as the string delimiter, you could do the following:

```
var text_variable = 'hello, I\'m a robot';
```

There are many more characters that can be represented by escape characters, but typically you won't need them, other than for very specialist applications.

## Concatenation

It is possible to add strings together in a process known as **concatenation**. In JavaScript, this is done by the + operator. Unlike with numbers, this isn't the same as performing sums; it just involves placing one string on the end of the other. You can concatenate two pieces of text:

```
var text_concatenated = "Red" + "Roses";
```

or a piece of text and a string variable:

```
var text_variable1 = "Red";
var text_concatenated = text_variable1 + "Roses";
```

or two variables:

```
var text_variable1 =   "Red";
var text_variable2 =   "Roses";
var text_concatenated = text_variable1 + text_variable2;
```

The result of all of these will be exactly the same: `text_concatenated` will contain the string `"RedRoses"`.

Note that even if your "string" is a number, so long as it is surrounded by quotes, JavaScript treats it as a string. So if you use the + operator on two numbers masquerading as strings, then they will be concatenated rather than added. For example:

```
var text_concatenated = "10" + "10";
```

This will store the string `"1010"` in the variable `text_concatenated` and not the number 20.

## Type Conversion

What happens if you try and use mathematical operators on something treated as a number and something treated as text? JavaScript will attempt to provide some implicit **type conversion**. In other words, it will look at what it is being told to operate on, and try to convert one of the data types into the other one. It does this according to a set of rules depending on the operators you are using.

For instance, if you wish to add a number to text, a string will be created. For example:

```
var Number1 = 17;
var Text1 = "Seventeen"
var Combine = Number1 + Text1;
```

`Combine` will contain the string `"17Seventeen"`. JavaScript has converted the number `17` to a string, so the resulting variable `Combine` contains a concatenated string. It will do the same even if you place a number inside the string.

```
var Number1 = 17;
var Text2 = "17";
var Combine = Number1 + Text2;
```

This time around `Combine` will contain `"1717"`.

However, if you try and perform subtraction or another mathematical operation on a number contained as a string, then it will convert the string to a number:

```
var Number1 = 17;
var Text3 = "12";
var Combine = Number1 - Text3;
```

Here `Combine` will contain the number `5`. This is because the string `"12"` will be converted to the number `12`. If you try and use these other mathematical operators with text, such as the following:

```
var Number1 = 17;
var Text4 = "Twelve";
var Combine = Number1 - Text4;
```

then `Combine` will contain the value `NaN`, which stands for **Not a Number**. JavaScript is not clever enough to be able to convert the string `"Twelve"` into a number.

Type conversions are quite a large subject area within their own right, but to ensure they don't take up too much space here, it suffices to say that given any calculation, JavaScript will try and perform the operation for you. However, you might not always get the result that you expect. If at all possible, you should only perform operations on variables of the same type. If you are not sure of the kind of data type contained within a variable, then there are two JavaScript functions that might help. The function `String()` returns a string and `Number()` returns a number. To make sure our variable really is what we think it is, we would do the following:

```
Number1 = 17;
RealNumber1 = Number(Number1);
```

`RealNumber1` would contain `17`, but if there were any doubt over whether what it contained was a number or a string, this would sort it for you.

## Boolean Data Type

There is another data type that JavaScript uses as well: **Boolean** data. Variables containing Boolean data can have one of two values: `true` or `false`. This type of data helps to enable the computer to make a decision based on whether something is true or false. Typically Boolean data is used with JavaScript's decision making structures, so we can't demonstrate the effectiveness of it at this moment, but we will do when we look at the `if` structure in a few pages' time.

To create a Boolean variable, you use exactly the same technique as the numerical variables and leave out the quotation marks:

```
var is_weather_sunny = false;
```

## Dates and Other Objects

Dates unlike numbers, text, and Boolean data do not have their own data type in JavaScript. However, you probably want to be able to treat a date as a date, as opposed to text as the following line would:

```
var todays_date = "16th September 2002";
```

or as a long division sum as the following would:

```
var todays_date = 9/16/2002;
```

Dates have something special devoted to them, the **Date object**.

### What is an object?

An object can be thought as a special kind of data type, which contains more than one piece of related information or functionality. To get at the different pieces of information, we use the **properties** of the object, and to activate the pieces of functionality of the object, we use its **methods**. An often-used analogy to an object is a car. It has methods, such as "shift gear" and "brake", and properties, such as "color" and "speed".

In fact, as you dig deeper into JavaScript, you will see that most of JavaScript is composed of objects. We've already seen one in our first example: the `navigator` object that represented the browser. This belongs to a set of objects that represent different bits and pieces within the browser; it also includes the `document` and `window` objects. There is also a completely different set of objects that JavaScript supplies itself. These objects are different as they are constructed by JavaScript and can have many individual occurrences or **instances** as they are known.

The `Date` object fits into the latter category as you can create many instances of it, and it doesn't represent a specific part of the browser. It provides a specific function which is to return the current date and time.

Like many objects, to access data held in the `Date` object, you have to create an instance of it, using a special function called a **constructor**:

```
var todays_date = new Date();
```

For all intents and purposes this is a normal variable assignment, with the `todays_date` variable being assigned a new instance of the `Date` object. However, the parentheses (`()`) next to `Date` give away that this is no ordinary variable assignment: they indicate a function call. In fact, the word Date is defined as a constructor in JavaScript.

So instead of pointing `todays_date` at a piece of data or another variable, we are actually using the `Date()` constructor function to create a new object and then pointing the variable to that object. You can pass a date within the parentheses of the `Date()` constructor, but if you don't pass anything, then JavaScript will automatically assume that you want to use the current date.

To access the information inside the object, you can append extra commands known as **methods** to the instance of the Date object within your variable. For example, to isolate just the year from the current date, you would do as follows:

```
var this_year = todays_date.getFullYear();
```

We can use the method `getFullYear()` to return the value of the year and store it in the variable `this_year`.

We'll be looking further at the `Date` object in the next chapter, where we'll also discuss many other objects, methods, and properties.

## Variable Example Script

We've just spent a lot of pages expounding upon the theory behind variables, so let's let off steam and start putting some of what we've learned into action. Variables on their own can't do much, so we're a bit limited in this example, but we'll create a few variables, assign some values, and return them to the user.

Using Dreamweaver MX (or your preferred tool), create a new HTML page, go into code view, and insert the following script, within the `<body>` element, either by hand or by using the *Insert Script* icon:

```
<script language="JavaScript" type="text/JavaScript">
var Number1 = 100;
var Number2 = 50;
var Text1 = " Red Roses";
var Text2 = "5.85";
var Result;

document.write("Adding a number to a number - ");
Result = Number1 + Number2;
document.write(Result);

document.write("<br /> Adding a number to a string containing some text - ");
Result = Number1 + Text1;
document.write(Result);

document.write("<br /> Adding a number to a string containing a number - ");
Result = Number1 + Text2;
document.write(Result);

document.write("<br /> Multiplying a number with a string containing a number - ");
Result = Number1 * Text2;
document.write(Result);
```

```
document.write("<br /> Multiplying a number with a string containing some text - ");
Result = Number1 * Text1;
document.write(Result);
</script>
```

Then view this in your browser:

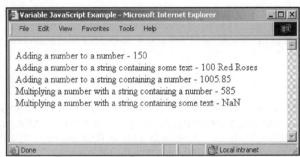

*The page VariableExample.html in the browser.*

The first thing to notice about the code is that we use the `document.write()` statement to display things in the web page. Any text (within quotation marks) given within the parentheses of this statement is written to the page and then interpreted as HTML by the browser – however, if you supply variable names (not within quotation marks), then the contents of the variable will be displayed.

So, `document.write()` is just a way of writing straight to the web page in JavaScript. We're using it in preference to the `alert()` function we saw earlier, which brings up a dialog. When to use each depends on whether you want the information displayed on the page or as part of a dialog that can be dismissed by the user.

We've already talked about everything else this script does. For example, we add a variable containing a number to a variable containing a number:

```
Result = Number1 + Number2;
```

By adding the contents of `Number1` (`100`) to `Number2` (`50`), we get the total `150`. We use the new command `document.write()` to display the answer:

```
document.write(Result);
```

Note that `document.write()` also has another important difference to the alert dialog. If you supply HTML tags as text to `document.write()` then the browser will actually render these tags. For example, the following line:

```
document.write("First Line<br>Second Line");
```

JavaScript Basics

will create text on two separate lines in the browser:

*First Line*
*Second Line*

If you supplied the same HTML tags to the `alert()` function, it would display:

*First Line<br />Second Line*

We make use of this fact in several lines of our script, to ensure that each line of text starts on a new line in the browser.

## Arrays

There is one last data structure we have to mention before we move into JavaScript's programming structures, and this is the **array**. An array isn't a separate data type; commonly it is a collection of variables of an existing data type or of several different existing data types. You would use arrays when you have groups of related information that you want to access sequentially. For instance if you wanted to store six lotto numbers, instead of storing them in six separate variables, you could store them in an array, named after the week those 6 numbers were drawn.

Like `Date`, `Array` is actually one of JavaScript's objects. To create an array you just assign your variable name to an instance of the `Array` object:

```
var array_of_numbers = new Array();
```

You can then reference each individual variable in the array with the array variable name followed by an index number in square brackets. For example, to assign three values or **elements** in the same array, you could do the following:

```
var my_cats = new Array();
my_cats[0] = "Custard";
my_cats[1] = "Jemima";
my_cats[2] = "Magic";
```

While there are three elements in this array, the index numbering starts at 0. This is because arrays are **zero-based**: the first element in the array is at index 0. So, any array that goes up to the index number 2, actually contains three elements. It's possible to specify in advance, when creating the array, a maximum index number as follows:

```
var my_cats = new Array(2);
```

This is meant to cut down the amount of memory used by the array. However even specifying the array in this way, it is still be possible to assign a value to index position 3, for example:

```
my_cats[3] = "Rhubarb";
```

JavaScript is very flexible and able to accommodate your change of plans, and would extend the array by one. It is also flexible enough to allow you to assign variables of a different data type to the same array:

```
var a_random_array = new Array();
a_random_array[0] = "A jeweled sceptre";
a_random_array[1] = 5603.23
a_random_array[2] = true
```

Why you'd want to do this might be a question open to debate! Finally, arrays don't just need to have a single set of indices. Indeed, you can make arrays that contain other arrays as elements, just by adding extra indices. To do this you need to create a variable as an array and then create each element in the array as another array, as follows:

```
var address_book = new Array();

address_book[0] = new Array();
address_book[0][0] = "Vervain Delaware";
address_book[0][1] = "42 Chelworth Gardens";
address_book[0][2] = "Vervain_Delaware@justanotheremail.com";

address_book[1] = new Array();
address_book[1][0] = "Rheingold Cabriole";
address_book[1][1] = "103 Syntactic Street";
address_book[1][2] = "Rheingold_Cabriole@justanotheremail.com";
```

This method of filling arrays with data (more commonly known as **populating arrays**) is quite tortuous though. Imagine having an array with 100 variables or more – would it require 100 lines of code to fill it all? The answer is no, but we have to delve into control structures to find a superior way of filling our array.

This concludes our discussion of variables and data storage. We've learned how to store information in different ways, and how to display it to the user either as a dialog box or straight on to the web page. This doesn't give us much of an idea how we might manipulate the data though. To do that, we need to look at how we can control the data in a way that makes our scripts truly useful.

# JavaScript Control Structures

Most common programming languages are divided up into three basic areas of control over the flow of programming. These are:

- Branching or making decisions
- Repetition or looping
- Modular structures or functions

JavaScript is no different in this respect and it is these structures that provide the powerhouse of the language. We're going to look at all of these structures in this next section.

## Making Decisions

Up until now we've described scripts as strictly sequential beasts, and that's still broadly true. After line one has been read by the computer, then it will move down to line two, and so on. However, there are often occasions where you will want to diverge from the rigidity that a strict sequential nature enforces. For instance, what happens if you have a quiz question with right and wrong answers? How will the computer decide between showing users a message telling them they're right or they're wrong? Obviously there has to be some criteria for deciding between running one part of script and another.

## The If Structure

The **if** structure is just such a decision-making structure. We earlier mentioned that Boolean data types have a major use: it is in decision-making they play a vital part. The if structure takes a condition and tests whether it evaluates to `true` or `false` (that is, a Boolean value); it must be one or the other.

Let's look at a real-world example. Someone looks outside and sees if it is raining. If it's raining, they'll take their umbrella, but if it's not, then they won't. Based on what they can see, the condition is either true or false.

JavaScript does the same thing: it tests the condition. If it's `true`, then one section of the program is run, and if not, then it isn't. Just as there are distinct courses of action that can be followed if it is raining, there are distinct sections of code that can be run if the condition is `true`, and that's exactly how JavaScript plays it.

The if structure takes the keyword `if`, followed by the condition in parentheses, and then the course of action that should be followed in curly braces.

```
if (condition)
{
   course of action
}
```

Our real-world example above can be expressed in JavaScript as follows:

```
var take_umbrella = false;

if (weather == "raining")
{
   take_umbrella = true;
}

document.write(take_umbrella);
```

We define a variable `take_umbrella` that represents whether we take an umbrella as being `false`. We then test a variable called `weather` (which we assume to have been defined and set to an appropriate value earlier in the script) to see if it is raining.

Here the test for equivalence is denoted with the double equals sign "`==`" or **equality operator**, one of the many comparison operators. If it does equal `"raining"`, then the code inside the curly braces will be run, and this will change the value of `take_umbrella` to `true`. Otherwise, it won't run. Clearly the condition (`weather == "raining"`) can only return one of two values, either `true` or `false`. There is no gray area in computing: either it is absolutely true, or it is absolutely false. The code inside the braces will only ever be run if the condition is true.

There is also a shorthand for the above statement: you don't explicitly need the condition to be a comparison of two items. If you already had a Boolean variable `is_raining`, then you could write it as follows:

```
var take_umbrella = false;

if (is_raining)
{
   take_umbrella = true;
}

document.write(take_umbrella);
```

What if `is_raining` wasn't a Boolean value? In this case, JavaScript tries to turn whatever is between the parentheses into a Boolean value, much as we saw it try to turn strings into numbers and numbers into strings earlier in this chapter. However, as we also mentioned there, the intricacies of how JavaScript converts data types to other data types is beyond the short introduction to JavaScript in this book.

## Comparison Operators

The equality operator that we saw above isn't the only operator in JavaScript you can use to compare two sets of data. There are also the following:

- `A < B`   Less than operator, tests to see if A is smaller than B.
- `A > B`   Greater than operator, tests to see if A is larger than B.
- `A <= B`   Less than or equal to operator, tests to see if A is smaller or the same as B.
- `A >= B`   Greater than or equal to operator, tests to see if A is larger or the same as B.
- `A != B`   Not equals operator, tests to see if A is not the same value as B.

The operators are all used in the same way as the equality operator. For instance, if we wanted to see whether the temperature was greater than 25, we could test it as follows:

```
if (temperature > 25)
{
   document.write("My, it's hot today!");
}
```

You can also use these to compare text. In this context, the greater than and less than operators are now used to test the order in which the strings appear in the alphabet. The following would be used to conclude that `"aardvark"` comes before `"crocodile"` in alphabetical order.

```
text1 = "aardvark";
text2 = "crocodile";
if (text1 < text2)
{
alert(text1 + " comes before " + text2 + " in the alphabet");
}
if (text2 < text1)
{
alert(text2 + " comes before " + text1 " in the alphabet");
}
```

Of course, things get more complicated if you want to test for more than one condition at a time. This involves the use of logical operators.

# Logical Operators

There are several logical operators in JavaScript, but we're going concentrate on the most common three: **AND**, **OR**, and **NOT**. The first two can be used to combine the outcomes of conditions, while NOT can be used to reverse the outcome of a condition. Ultimately, the final result must always evaluate to either `true` or `false`, but there are rules as to how logical operators combine.

All three operators, when used within the if structure, are largely intuitive, since the way they work in JavaScript is the same way that they work in the real world. We'll start with the AND operator.

### The AND Operator

The AND operator in JavaScript is `&&`. Going back to our real world example of the weather, we could say that we will take a coat if the weather is both raining and cold. This can be written in JavaScript as such:

```
var take_coat = false;

if ((weather == "raining") && (temperature < 15))
{
   take_coat = true;
}

document.write(take_coat);
```

Here both conditions (`weather == "raining"` and `temperature < 15`) have to evaluate to `true` for the course of action to be taken. If it isn't raining, then the first condition evaluates to `false`. In this case the combined condition will always evaluate to `false`, no matter what the second condition evaluates to. Similarly if the temperature is over 15 degrees then it isn't cold, so the second condition will evaluate to `false`, meaning that the combined condition is also `false`. The only circumstance under which the course of action in curly braces will be taken is if both conditions are `true`. This can be summed up as in the opposite table.

| AND Condition 1 | AND Condition 2 | Combined Condition |
|---|---|---|
| true | true | true |
| true | false | false |
| false | true | false |
| false | false | false |

JavaScript evaluates the conditions in the order it encounters them, left-most first. When it encounters one that evaluates to `false`, then it stops checking, since no matter what the other condition evaluates to, the combined result will always be `false`. Note that it is possible to combine as many conditions as you want with AND.

## The OR Operator

The OR Operator in JavaScript is `||`. It says that, given two conditions, if one or the other is `true`, then the combined result is `true` and the specified course of action will be taken. Back to our real-world example of the weather again, we could say that if it is hot or it is sunny, then we will take our sunhat.

```javascript
var take_sunhat = false;

if ((weather == "sunny") || (temperature > 25))
{
   take_sunhat = true;
}

document.write(take_sunhat);
```

Here the only time we won't take our sunhat with us is if both conditions evaluate to `false`, that is the weather isn't sunny and the temperature is equal to or less than 25.

| OR Condition 1 | OR Condition 2 | Resulting Condition |
|---|---|---|
| true | true | true |
| true | false | true |
| false | true | true |
| false | false | false |

Like the AND operator, there is also a quick route out for JavaScript this time: if any of the conditions evaluate to `true`, then JavaScript can stop checking as the combined result will be `true`. Once again you can combine a whole series of OR operators together, and even mix them in with AND operators, using parentheses to group conditions as necessary.

## The NOT Operator

The NOT operator simply reverses the result of any condition. It only takes one condition as an input; if the condition is `true` it turns it `false` and if the condition is `false` it makes it `true`. The NOT operator in JavaScript is represented by an exclamation mark (`!`). Back one more time to our real-world example: if it isn't thundering then, whatever the weather, I will go for a walk. This can be portrayed in JavaScript as:

```javascript
var go_for_a_walk = false;

if (!(weather == "thunder"))
{
```

```
   go_for_a_walk = true;
}

document.write(go_for_a_walk);
```

You could also write the same condition using the "not equals" comparison operator as follows:

```
var go_for_a_walk = false;

if (weather != "thunder")
{
   go_for_a_walk = true;
}

document.write(go_for_a_walk);
```

Note that parentheses can be used to group a set of conditions that you want to negate by placing the NOT operator outside; in this way, AND, OR, and NOT operators can be combined together.

## The If Else Structure

So far we've only looked at very simple branching where we either take one course of action, or don't take that course of action. However, situations in computing demand more flexibility than this, because in the event of one condition not being `true`, then you might want to pursue a different course of action. JavaScript handles this with an additional keyword: **else**.

```
if (condition)
{
   one course of action ...
}
else
{
   alternative course of action ...
}
```

Here all we are saying is that if the condition is `true` we take one course of action, or if it is `false` then we take an alternative course of action. In our real-world example, we could say that if it is raining we'll take our umbrella, but if it's not raining we'll take our bike instead (it's pretty hard to cycle with an umbrella). JavaScript would represent it like this:

```
var take_object = "nothing";

if (weather == "raining")
{
   take_object = "umbrella";
}
else
{
   take_object = "bike";
}

document.write(take_object);
```

If we look at this short section of script, we can see that while `take_object` contains `"nothing"` when we first create it, by the end of the script it must contain either one of `"umbrella"` or `"bike"` depending on what the condition (`weather == "raining"`) returns. If it returns `true` then it will contain `"umbrella"`; if it returns `false`, it will contain `"bike"`.

## If Else Structure Example Script

We've done enough hypothetical usage of the if construct, so let's see the structure in action. In this example, we'll get a user to make a selection from a page and then we'll customize a reply depending on the user's choice.

In Dreamweaver MX, create a new HTML page, add a form, and insert the following highlighted code:

```
<!DOCTYPE HTML PUBLIC "-//W3C//DTD HTML 4.01 Transitional//EN">
<html>
<head>
<title>If structure JavaScript Example</title>
<meta http-equiv="Content-Type" content="text/html; charset=iso-8859-1">
</head>

<body>
Which do you prefer?
<form name="form1">
   Cats<input type="radio" name="choice" value="cat" Checked>
   Dogs<input type="radio" name="choice" value="dog">
   <br>
   <br>
   <input type="button" value="Submit choice"
     onclick="if(this.form.choice[0].checked)
                {alert('A suave and sophisticated choice');}
              else
                {alert('A noble and authoritative choice');}">
</form>
</body>
</html>
```

Save the page as `IfElseExample.html`. If you view this in the browser you will see the following:

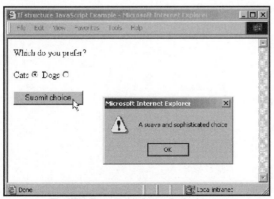

*The IfElseExample.html page in the browser.*

This example just detects which choice you have made and displays the message associated with that choice. We've added the JavaScript as an attribute of the `<input>` tag.

```
<input type="button" value="Submit choice"
    onclick="if(this.form.choice[0].checked)
                {alert('A suave and sophisticated choice');}
            else
                {alert('A noble and authoritative choice');}">
```

As you can see, it's a fairly straightforward `if else` structure. The two courses of action just display a dialog box using the `alert()` function. Take another look at the condition, which might cause some confusion. The condition is:

```
this.form.choice[0].checked
```

The words `this` and `form` are used to refer to the current form. The word `choice` refers to the name of the radio buttons in the web page; if you check the code you will see that `choice` is the value of the `name` attribute that the `<input>` tags have. The 0 in square brackets after the word `choice` is rather like the array index we saw earlier. Each radio button that shares the same name is allocated an index number in the array. Cats, being the first radio button, is given index 0, while Dogs is given index 1. The `checked` word is a property that returns `true` if a form element has been selected.

So, in this condition we are checking to see whether the `choice[0]` or Cats radio button has been selected. If it has been selected, the condition will return `true`, so we run the first part of the script. If it hasn't been selected, then we can assume that the second radio button must have been selected (one of the two buttons is selected by default), and so we display the second message.

We will look in more depth at how JavaScript can access the contents of elements in a web page, like this, in the next chapter.

## Switch Case Structure

There are times where instead of one or two courses of action, you might have a whole list of possible outcomes. Imagine a grading system at a school where pupils who score an A have a distinction, a B a merit, a C a good pass, a D an adequate pass, an E a borderline pass, and below that a fail. It is possible in JavaScript to represent this as a series of `if` structures as follows:

```
var grade;

if (mark == "A")
{
   grade = "Distinction";
}
else if (mark =="B")
{
   grade = "Merit";
}
else if (mark == "C")
{
```

```
   grade = "Good Pass";
}
else if (mark == "D")
{
   grade = "Adequate Pass";
}
else if (mark == "E")
{
   grade = "Borderline Pass";
}
else
{
   grade = "Fail";
}

document.write(grade);
```

Here each new if structure is preceded by the keyword else, to link them all together. However, there is an alternative structure called a **switch** structure, which makes it much easier to do. Instead of having to list the variable and each case every time, switch works as follows:

```
switch (variable to be tested)
{
   case possible_value_1:
      // code here
      break;
   case possible_value_2:
      // code here
      break;
   default:
      // code here
      break;
}
```

For each possible value or set of values your variable has, you create a new case. The last "catch-all" case is set as default at the end. case effectively becomes the variable you are testing against. The break keyword means that if a case has been matched, then no further cases are tested. Without it, switch would carry on testing all of the other cases. It's reminiscent of the if structure in this way.

A grading system using a switch structure goes like this:

```
var grade;

switch (mark)
{
   case "A":
      grade = "Distinction";
      break;
   case "B":
      grade = "Merit";
      break;
   case "C":
```

JavaScript Basics

```
      grade = "Good Pass";
      break;
   case "D":
      grade = "Adequate Pass";
      break;
   case "E":
      grade = "Borderline Pass";
      break;
   default:
      grade = "Fail";
      break;
}

document.write (grade);
```

With less code, it's much easier to follow, and if any case is matched in the structure, the `break` statement in each case means that JavaScript drops out of the `switch` structure entirely and moves to the first line after it.

# Loops

The introduction of computers into all walks of life has particular advantages for those involved in repetitive tasks, as the automation of repetitive tasks is one area where computers excel. In fact, nearly all programming languages have structures for repeating sections of code over and over again. JavaScript is no exception and has two distinct types of loop for dealing with repetitions.

## The for Loop

The first of the two we'll look at is the **for** loop, where you specify in advance how many repetitions of the loop you wish to make.

```
for (Loop Variable = Loop Start Value;
     Condition Loop Variable must fulfill;
     Change in Loop Variable Value on each loop)
{
   // Code here
}
```

The code in between the curly braces is then repeated as many times as specified by the three parameters. An example of a simple loop would look like this:

```
for (loop_count = 1; loop_count <= 9; loop_count++)
{
   document.write(loop_count);
}
```

This would yield the result of the numbers 1 to 9 being printed to the page (*123456789*), with a number being printed for each iteration of the loop. Let's walk through this more slowly to see how we arrive at this result.

On the first pass of the loop, the variable `loop_count` is set to 1. Then, `loop_count` is tested to see if it is less than 9. As 1 is less than 9, we execute the loop, which writes the contents of `loop_count` to the screen (in this case the number 1). The third parameter, `loop_count++`, means that 1 is then added to the `loop_count` variable.

We go around the loop again. This time `loop_count` is equal to 2. We test it to see if it is smaller than 9; it is so we execute the code in the loop. This writes the number 2 to the page. Finally, we add one to the `loop_count` variable.

The loop repeats again seven further times. Only when `loop_count` gets to a value of 10 does the loop stop, meaning that the code isn't executed. This is because the condition specified in the second parameter (`loop_count <=9`) fails. Instead, the next line after the closing curly brace will be run.

You can use the loop to count down instead of up, for example if you substitute the decremental operator for the incremental one as follows:

```
for (loop_count = 9; loop_count < 1; loop_count--)
{
  document.write(loop_count);
}
```

This would yield the result *987654321*, as the loop starts at 9, checks to see if it is below 1 each time, and subtracts 1 from the total, if it is not.

One of the most useful things about loops is that you can use them to fill your arrays with data. For example, if we'd created an array of ten elements and wanted each element to hold a value that is ten times the loop counter value, we could do the following.

```
var our_array = new Array(10);

for (loop_count = 0; loop_count<=9; loop_count++)
{
  our_array[loop_count] = loop_count * 10;
}
```

Here, `our_array[0]` would hold the value `0`, `our_array[1]` would hold `10`, and so on up to `our_array[9]` which would hold `90`. Rather than requiring ten separate variable definitions, we've filled the array using just one definition, repeated ten times over.

One important point to take note of is that we have "hard-coded" the number 9 into our loop test. What happens if you don't know the length of the array in advance? The measurement of the array's length harks back to objects again. `Array` is a constructor function, just as `Date` is. It is used to create objects. An `Array` object has several properties, one of which is `length`, which returns the length of the object.

```
var our_array = new Array(10);

for (loop_count = 0; loop_count<=our_array.length; loop_count++)
{
  our_array[loop_count] = loop_count * 10;
}
```

JavaScript Basics

This code is almost identical to the code that precedes it, but it has more flexibility built in. If the array length was increased from 10 to 15 (by changing the number between the parentheses in the first line that defines the array), then the loop would iterate 15 times.

## Conditional Loops

The second type of loop is used in situations where you don't know exactly how many repetitions of the loop are needed. In fact, often that number isn't certain when you begin the loop (it may be changed as you continue around the loop): you just need the loop to continue while a given condition holds true.

There are two versions of this type of loop, which for all intents and purposes are identical apart from the point where the condition is checked. They are the **while** and **do while** loops.

### The while Loop

The `while` loop puts the condition to check at the head of the loop, tests it first, then repeats the loop while the condition is `true`. If the condition is found to be `false` immediately, then the contents of the loop won't be run at all.

```
while (condition)
{
   //do code here
}
```

An example of its use could be collecting shopping list items from the user and adding them to an array. In this example, we'll make use of the `prompt()` function, which is similar to `alert()` that we've used before. This again pulls up a dialog box, but this time asks the user for some input. The first parameter of the function gives the text for the dialog box, and the second parameter gives the default text to appear in the textbox.

```
var user_value;
var shopping_list = new Array();
var index = 0;

while (user_value != "done")
{
   user_value = prompt("Enter an item, or type 'done'.", "done");
   if (user_value != "done")
   {
      shopping_list[index] = user_value;
      index++;
   }
}
```

The loop will iterate all the while `user_value` is not equal to `"done"`. Within the loop, `user_value` is set to the value input by the user, via the `prompt()` function. So long as this does not equal `"done"`, the value is added as the next element in the array `shopping_list`. As soon as the user enters the value `"done"`, the value is not added to the `shopping_list` array, and the loop is not run again.

### The do while Loop

The **do while** loop is identical to the `while` loop except that the condition is placed at the end of the loop rather than at the start. In other words, this loop must always be executed at least once before the condition is checked.

```
do
{
   //do code here
}
while (condition)
```

### Infinite Loops

One thing to be aware of, particularly with conditional loops, is **infinite looping**. If you have a situation where the loop counter is altered during the loop in such a way that it will always meet the condition that tells the loop to run again, then you will create an infinite loop. This undesirable state of affairs is quite capable of crashing the browser of any who view your web page.

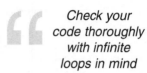

*Check your code thoroughly with infinite loops in mind*

By and large, infinite loops are easy enough to avoid, but they will stop the browser responding if you get into one, so it is wise to check your code thoroughly with them in mind.

## Loop Example Script

We're going to run off a quick example now where the user supplies a number of invoice copies that they need and the program displays that many copies. Open up a new page and insert the following code:

```
<!DOCTYPE HTML PUBLIC "-//W3C//DTD HTML 4.01 Transitional//EN">
<html>
<head>
<title>Looping JavaScript Example</title>
<meta http-equiv="Content-Type" content="text/html; charset=iso-8859-1">
</head>

<body>
How many invoice copies do you want?
<form name="form1">
<select name="invoice">
   <option>1</option>
   <option>2</option>
   <option>3</option>
   <option>4</option>
   <option>5</option>
</select>
<br>
<br>
<input value="Submit choice" type="button"
       onclick="for (var loop_count=1;
                  loop_count <= this.form.invoice.selectedIndex+1;
                    loop_count++)
                {
```

```
                        alert('Printing Invoice copy ' + loop_count);
                }">
</form>
</body>
</html>
```

Save this as `LoopingExample.html` and view it in your browser. Choose a number from the drop-down listbox and the dialog will appear the same number of times as your selected number:

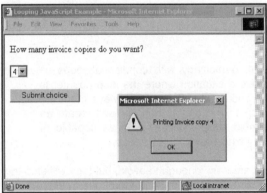

*The LoopingExample.html page in the browser.*

The JavaScript `for` loop that performs this functionality has three parameters:

```
for (var loop_count=1; loop_count<=this.form.invoice.selectedIndex+1;
loop_count++)
{
   alert('Printing Invoice copy ' + loop_count);
}
```

The first parameter starts the `loop_count` at the value 1.

The second parameter interrogates the `<select>` tag, which we named `invoice`. It finds the value of its `selectedIndex` property (the index of the option that the user has selected in the drop-down listbox on the form). Note that these indices start at zero in the same way as array indices, so a `selectedIndex` of 0 actually corresponds to the user choosing "1". To get the value that the user chose, we add 1 to the `selectedIndex` value.

The third parameter of our loop increases our `loop_count` by 1.

So, the loop runs an iteration and displays the appropriate message, until the `loop_count` is less than or equal to the value the user selected.

# Functions

Functions are commands in JavaScript that do something for us. They may take some input from us (a parameter) and they may return a value as a result, but they don't have to.

Functions split into two distinct categories in JavaScript. There are built-in functions that JavaScript provides us with; we can just call these functions and JavaScript will understand what to do. However, JavaScript also has the capacity to allow you to write your own functions.

## JavaScript Built-in Functions

We're not going to spend too long on JavaScript built-in functions, as there are far too many to do justice to. One function that might be of interest and demonstrates aptly how JavaScript functions work is the `isNaN()` function. In the section on data type conversion we suggested that some text could be converted to numbers and some couldn't. It would be a lot easier if you could test this up front, rather than try and perform a calculation and return the value `NaN` (Not A Number) if it didn't work.

For example, you may ask a user for a salary value that you need to be a number (for instance to calculate a tax value from it). However, there is no guarantee that they would actually provide a number: they may input `"thirty thousand dollars"` or `"none of your business"`. Before you accept the value, you could check it using the `isNaN()` function to see that it is indeed a number. The following JavaScript code would do the trick:

```
var user_value;

if (isNaN(user_value))
{
   alert("Try again, and this time supply a number!");
}
else
{
   var tax_value = (user_value / 100) * 24 ;
}
```

The `isNaN()` function returns either `true` or `false` depending on whether the `user_value` was a number or not. It is also capable of converting a number supplied as a string, to a number. So the following:

```
isNaN("432")
```

would return `true`.

However, not all JavaScript functions return Booleans: other functions, such as the math functions, might return numbers. For instance, the `sqrt()` function works out the square root of a number:

```
var total = Math.sqrt(9);
```

Actually, although this works just like a function, `sqrt()` is a method of the built-in `Math` object. The `Math` object has many other methods you can use in your code, such as `abs()` which returns the absolute value of the parameter it is passed, and `random()` which returns a random number between 0 and 1.

## Writing Your Own Functions

The advantages to writing your own functions are numerous, but most importantly it saves the bother of having to repeatedly type out the same code. When writing functions there are two parts to think about: the definition of the function itself and how you call the function.

A function definition takes the following format:

```
function function_name(parameter)
{
    //function code here
    return value;
}
```

A function can take any name, within the same constraints that apply to naming variables. Within the body of the function itself there can be a `return` line, which is where the value calculated inside the function is passed back to where the function was called from, if you want to return a value.

The function call can be part of either a variable definition:

```
var variable_name = function_name(parameter);
```

or an `if` condition:

```
if (function_name(parameter)
{
    //do code
}
```

It isn't restricted to just these places either; you can simply write:

```
function_name(parameter)
```

or have some complex expression in which you call the function.

A quick example in JavaScript might be our tax rate calculator.

```
function TaxRate(SalaryBeforeTax)
{
    var SalaryAfterTax = SalaryBeforeTax - ((SalaryBeforeTax/100) * 24);
    return SalaryAfterTax;
}
```

You could call this function as follows:

```
SalaryAfterTax = TaxRate(user_salary);
```

Notice that when calling the function, we've supplied a variable user_salary that is passed to the function. (This variable would be defined elsewhere in the code, and would have a value supplied by the user.) This variable is called SalaryBeforeTax within the function definition. We use this value as a basis on which to calculate the new figure, and return this as SalaryAfterTax.

Now let's put this example into the context of a working example.

## Custom-Built Function Example Script

For this last example, we're going to demonstrate a better way of using event handlers. Rather than stuffing all the code in an event handler attribute, we'll place it in a function instead. We'll get the user to input their salary figure and then calculate what their salary is after tax at a 24% tax rate.

Open Dreamweaver MX and insert the following code:

```
<!DOCTYPE HTML PUBLIC "-//W3C//DTD HTML 4.01 Transitional//EN">
<html>
<head>
<title>Function JavaScript Example</title>
<meta http-equiv="Content-Type" content="text/html; charset=iso-8859-1">
<script language="JavaScript" type="text/JavaScript">
function TaxRate(SalaryBeforeTax)
{
  var SalaryAfterTax = SalaryBeforeTax - ((SalaryBeforeTax/100)*24);
  alert("Your tax adjusted salary is $" + SalaryAfterTax);
  return SalaryAfterTax;
}
</script>
</head>

<body>
What is your current salary?
<form name="form1">
  <input type="text" name="user_salary">
  <br>
  <br>
  <input value="Submit choice" type="button"
onclick="TaxRate(user_salary.value)">
</form>
</body>
</html>
```

Save this as `FunctionExample.html`. If you run this in the browser and supply the value 20000, you will see the following:

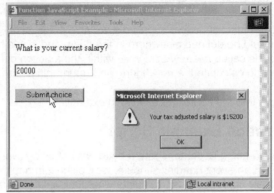

*The FunctionExample.html page in the browser.*

Here we've directed the browser to call a function defined in a script at the top of the page whenever the user clicks on the *Submit choice* button:

```
<input value="Submit choice" type="button" onclick="TaxRate(user_salary.value)">
```

We've passed it the contents of the textbox using the name of the `<input>` tag, `user_salary`, and the `value` property. We'll be looking at forms and the passing of values in greater depth in the next chapter, but in the meantime just think of it as a direct link to whatever the user has put in the textbox. The `onclick` event handler now calls the function `TaxRate()` with the value that we submitted, which was 20000.

The script starts off by passing 20000 as the `SalaryBeforeTax` value:

```
function TaxRate(SalaryBeforeTax)
{
  var SalaryAfterTax = SalaryBeforeTax - ((SalaryBeforeTax/100)*24);
  alert("Your tax adjusted salary is $" + SalaryAfterTax);
  return SalaryAfterTax;
}
```

This means that we create the variable `SalaryAfterTax`, based on a `SalaryBeforeTax` value of 20000. This value is then displayed within a dialog box. The `SalaryAfterTax` value is returned, although strictly speaking it doesn't need to be, as we don't make use of it outside the function.

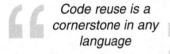

*Code reuse is a cornerstone in any language*

Here we can see functions already make it easier to separate our script from our HTML, and this is something you should always try to do. By putting more of your code into reusable sections, it means there is less code to maintain, less code to debug, it's easier to follow, and it's more efficient. Code reuse is a cornerstone in any language; in the next chapter we will look at building some scripts to handle some common problems and situations, which you can insert into your web pages and reuse.

# Summary

In this chapter you've been given a very swift introduction to JavaScript. It's been a bit short on practical applications and examples, but this is because you need to be familiar with the basic building blocks of the language before you can start using it in useful ways – this we will be doing in the next chapter.

We started in this chapter by placing JavaScript in its context to HTML and to other client-side languages. We explained what advantages it offers over server-side languages, and why and when you should use it. We moved on to two different ways of inserting JavaScript into your web page using Dreamweaver before launching into a full-blown discussion of how to use JavaScript itself.

The sections on using JavaScript focused on two areas: storing data in variables and the control structures of the language. Both sections are essential to programming in JavaScript – without them you wouldn't be able to do very much at all. With data storage, we looked at how JavaScript identifies and handles data, and the different types of data that can be stored. With control structures we looked at three major features: decision-making `if` and `case` structures, repetition-inducing `for` and `while` loop structures, and modularizing functions, both JavaScript's built-in ones and home-made ones.

Believe it or not, while there are other bits and pieces to learn, these are basically all you need to make some practical and useful JavaScript scripts.

**9**

**JavaScript Basics**

# 10

- Validating forms and using cookies
- Image rollovers and dynamic menus
- Frames, windows, and timing the user

**Author: Chris Ullman**

# Applying JavaScript in Your Pages

If the last chapter was all about getting to know JavaScript, then this chapter is about applying our practical knowledge in a useful way. We're going to make use of the basic syntax and control structures learned in the last chapter and really stretch them as we delve into some useful scripts and common applications of JavaScript. The idea is to provide some practical bits of codes that you can adapt and place in your own web pages.

We'll divide this chapter into some of the main areas of interest to the web developer that JavaScript can deal with. These are:

- Getting information from the user through forms

- Storing information about the user and remembering details about them, using cookies

- Making sure your web page works in all browsers

- Getting new windows or pop-ups to appear

- Timing the user while they are on a particular page or performing a specific task

As we could fill a whole book with these subjects alone, we'll be necessarily brief, but the aim will be to provide working scripts for you to embed and adapt throughout. Before we launch into this, we need to add one last piece to our JavaScript jigsaw, something that we briefly came across in the last chapter, but only touched upon, namely **objects**.

# Objects

In JavaScript nearly everything can be represented as an object. The web page the user is viewing, the separate frames on the web page, the elements within the HTML that you write, and even the browser itself.

As we already said in the last chapter, you can manipulate objects by using their:

- **properties** – Items of information about the specific object
- **methods** – Things that the object can do
- **events** – Things that the object can react to (this is the way objects let us know something has happened to them)

JavaScript has a strict hierarchy of objects. This means that in order to use one object, you might have to reference another different object. This hierarchy is known as an **object model**.

A very simplified view of part of the object model JavaScript uses looks like this:

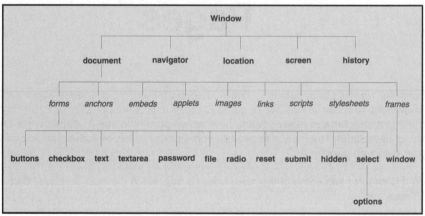

*In this diagram, the words in bold represent actual objects, and the words in italics represent collections of objects, all of the same type.*

At the top level of the object model we have the `window` object, which represents absolutely everything in the browser.

Underneath that we have objects that represent different parts of the browser: the `navigator`, `location`, `screen`, and `history` objects are all concerned with specific non-web page parts of the browser. (Recall that we made use of the `navigator` object in the first example of *Chapter 9*.) The other object under `window` is `document`, which represents the entire web page.

Underneath the `document` object, we see that the objects are broken down into specific HTML elements. Some of these elements are represented by their own objects, but some of them are represented by **collections**. Collections are like the arrays we met in the last chapter (in fact, you'll note that we refer to them as arrays later in this chapter). They can be used with an index number to access a specific element on the web page.

This tree structure is important to understand, since JavaScript has to navigate it to get to the item it wants. For example, to get to a button on a form, strictly speaking you would use something like:

```
window.document.form.button
```

Note that we start at the top of the tree, and work down to the object we want, using periods in between the object names. However, more often than not, you can omit a level or two from this hierarchy, as long as there remains enough information for JavaScript to uniquely identify the item you are talking about. Typically you can just mention the `document` object to reference the item you want:

```
document.form.button
```

Actually, the individual form and button within the form need to be identified properly so that there can be no confusion between forms and buttons within the same page. Elements can be identified in one of two ways. First, you can use the value given to the `name` attribute of each element:

```
document.myform.mybutton
```

Secondly, you can use their position in the web page via an index to the collection of objects:

```
document.forms[0].mybutton
```

This will immediately point to the first form on the page and the button with the name `"mybutton"` within that form.

If the above explanation is not clear to you yet, don't worry. We'll be using these constructs in the examples throughout this chapter, and will explain them in context then.

# Scripting for Browser Compatibility

In the last chapter we touched upon a sticky subject in client-side scripting when we saw that our simple browser testing code worked fine for IE and Netscape, but not in Opera. This is only the tip of a very large iceberg in browser-incompatibility, and you have to drill back into a little history to see what has been going on.

Originally Netscape introduced JavaScript as a proprietary add-on that could access various parts of your web page. Web developers soon demanded scripting access to all parts of the web page, from images and form elements, right down to the text itself. Before version 4 of both IE and Netscape, accessing these bits and pieces on the page was only possible in a limited way. If you wanted to manipulate the text ... well, that was out of the question. However, version 4 of both browsers saw the introduction of **Dynamic HTML**, which allowed dynamic manipulation of more areas of the web page. "Dynamic HTML" refers to the ability of JavaScript (and other technologies) to control HTML elements on the web page.

The Internet was only loosely regulated by a few standards back in the mid 1990s and, as such, the browser vendors were breaking new ground and creating solutions to the dynamic manipulation of the page themselves. In their implementation of Dynamic HTML, Microsoft offered common sets of scripting properties and methods for manipulating text, while Netscape used the proprietary `<layer>` tag. Neither solution would work on the other browser. To howls of derision from the general developer base, it was realized that the next dramatic step in the evolution of browsers and web pages would require two completely different sets of coding to make it work.

Eventually, in stepped the W3C. They introduced a standard for manipulating the page that relied on objects, properties, and methods, and was called the **Document Object Model** or **DOM**. This standard is not identical to either browser manufacturer's solution, but most closely resembles the solution of Microsoft. These objects that represent the different elements on the page are, in theory, common to both browsers. The majority of the time, they are. However as we will see, to make sure our JavaScript works in both major browser latest versions, we do some tinkering from time to time.

We've now given you a quick introduction to objects, but the best way to understand them is to get to use them, and they will be cropping up throughout the chapter. So let's start looking at some examples of common applications of JavaScript within your web page.

# Getting Information from the User

We start with the subject of how to get feedback from the user of your web page. As discussed in *Chapter 4*, HTML forms are the markup syntax used to gain the feedback; they are used to group together similar HTML elements that capture data supplied by the user. Typically forms are used to get information such as names, addresses, e-mails, phone numbers, passwords, and, on secure servers, details such as credit card numbers and expiry dates. The data can be entered either as text, or by selecting checkboxes or radiobuttons associated with a particular line of text, or even choosing from drop-down listboxes that supply a selection of options.

A common belief held by people only familiar with HTML is the idea that to capture information from the user, all you need is HTML. However, while the different elements within a form do store data, there is no way of getting at this information without either a client-side scripting language (such as JavaScript) or a server-side technology.

Before we launch into a description of how JavaScript allows you access to this information, we need to look at the `<form>` element itself.

## Forms

As you know, the `<form>` element is used to create a form. All elements that create the textboxes, radiobuttons, and the like must be enclosed between the opening and closing `<form>` tags:

```
<form name="form1" id = "form">
  <!-- body of form goes here -->
</form>
```

*It's good practice to set identical* name *and* id *attributes, as* id *attributes are the way that most other HTML elements are uniquely identified.*

The `<form>` element's name attribute allows the form to be uniquely identified within the JavaScript code.

As we mentioned earlier in our brief foray into objects, JavaScript identifies forms on the page by the means of a form object. The form object allows access to the contents of the HTML form in JavaScript, either as part of the document object as shown oppposite:

```
document.form1
```

(where `form1` is the value given to the `name` of the form) or via the `document.forms` array or collection. Each form we create on the web page is automatically placed in a new index number in this array, starting with zero, so if the above form is the first form on the page, it can be accessed through:

```
document.forms[0]
```

On their own, neither of these techniques allows you to get directly at the information contained within the form, but they provide a pathway to this information. It's the form control elements themselves that are responsible for holding the information. Let's take a quick review of the most common form control elements:

| HTML Form Control | Appearance | Description | Implementation |
|---|---|---|---|
| Textboxes | text here... | Single line boxes for typing text into | `<input type="text">` |
| Password fields | ▓▓▓▓▓▓▓▓ | Textboxes with one important difference: anything you type into them is disguised on screen, usually by an asterisk | `<input type="password">` |
| Textareas | Several lines of text... | Multiple line boxes for typing text into | `<textarea rows="3">`<br>`   <!-- content -->`<br>`</textarea>` |
| Radio buttons | ◉ ○ | Multiple choice buttons that occur in groups: only one out of each group can be selected | `<input type="radio">` |
| Check boxes | ☑ ☐ | Single and multiple choice buttons that allow several independent answers | `<input type="checkbox">` |
| Listboxes | A B C | Multiple line textboxes from which you're allowed to select one or more options | `<select size="3">`<br>`   <option>`<br>`   <option>`<br>`   <option>`<br>`</select>` |
| Drop-down listboxes | A ▾ / A B C | Textboxes with a button that reveals a drop-down menu, from which you're allowed to select one or more options | `<select size="1">`<br>`   <option>`<br>`   <option>`<br>`</select>` |

*Table continued on following page*

| HTML Form Control | Appearance | Description | Implementation |
|---|---|---|---|
| Buttons | Click here | Button to which the developer can attach various actions | `<input type="button">` |
| Submit buttons | Submit Query | Button with built-in functionality to submit HTML forms to the web server | `<input type="submit">` |
| Reset buttons | Reset | Button with built-in functionality to clear the contents of an HTML form that hasn't already been submitted | `<input type="reset">` |

These form control elements are accessed in JavaScript as properties of the form object. For example, consider the textbox created by the following lines:

```
<form name="form1">
  <input type="text" name="textbox1" />
</form>
```

The value that the user types into this textbox can be accessed via the following:

```
document.form1.textbox1.value
```

In this string, `document` refers to the web page, `form1` refers uniquely to our form, and `textbox1` is the identifier for our textbox (given as the `name` attribute of our `<input>` element). The `value` property is how we access the contents of any textbox, textarea, or password box.

However, before you start trying to access the contents of the textbox, you have to have some way of indicating to JavaScript that the user has finished typing in their information. For this reason, you will find that most HTML forms include a button of some sort. When the user wants to submit the information, they press the button. We can code JavaScript that listens for this event, and when it occurs does something else (such as access the textbox's contents).

To do this, you will typically link the button to a function using the `onclick` event handler, as discussed in *Chapter 9*.

```
<input type="button" name="button" value="Click here"
        onclick="button_click()" />
```

Here we've placed a function call to a function `button_click()` within the `onclick` event handler. Once this button has been pressed, the function will be run.

Let's take a look at a quick example, which takes the name and address from a user and returns the properties they supply to the web page.

## Accessing Textboxes

Open up Dreamweaver MX and create a new HTML page with a form, called `form1`. Add two textboxes, named `username` and `useraddress`, to the form and a button, called `submitbutton`. Add an `onclick` event handler attribute to the button and connect it to the `submitbutton_onclick()` function. You also need to add the script given below in the head of the page, which contains the function.

*As with Chapter 9, if you are using a text editor such as Notepad or Simple Text instead of Dreamweaver MX, then you can just type in the script as a whole (or access the file on the CD).*

```
<!DOCTYPE HTML PUBLIC "-//W3C//DTD HTML 4.01 Transitional//EN">
<html>
<head>
  <title>Textbox example</title>
  <meta http-equiv="Content-Type" content="text/html; charset=iso-8859-1">
  <script language="JavaScript" type="text/JavaScript">
    function submitbutton_onclick()
    {
      document.write ("Hello " + document.form1.username.value +
                      ", I see you live at " + document.form1.useraddress.value);
      document.close();
    }
  </script>
</head>

<body>
  <form name="form1" action="" method="get">
    Please type in your name:
    <input name="username" type="text" /><br />
    Please type in your address:
    <input name="useraddress" type="text" /><br />
    <input name="submitbutton" onclick="submitbutton_onclick()"
           type="button" value="Click Me" />
  </form>
</body>
</html>
```

Save the page as `TextboxExample.html`. When you run this script you will see a form asking you to supply a name and address. Do so, and click on the button:

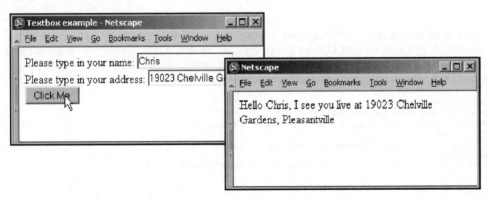

10

Our function only contains two lines:

```
function submitbutton_onclick()
{
    document.write ("Hello " + document.form1.username.value +
                    ", I see you live at " + document.form1.useraddress.value);
    document.close();
}
```

When the user clicks on the button, our function is run. It displays a message, using the `document.write()` method. This uses the contents of both of our textboxes. The first textbox, `username`, returns the value `'Chris'`, while the second textbox, `useraddress`, returns the value `'19023 Chelville Gardens, Pleasantville'`. In both cases we use the `value` property to return information to the user. Once again, we use the same pedantic (but necessary) way of identifying the values of these textboxes:

*document.form_name.form_control_name.value*.

Note that this time the use of `document.write()` differs to previous uses since the page has already completely loaded when the function is run. For this reason, the message overwrites the form that was previously displayed in the page.

The second line of the function (`document.close()`) is needed to inform the browser that we've stopped writing to the page. Without it, this page won't work in some older browsers.

You should note that the `value` property doesn't always contain the information in a format that the web developer can make direct use of. For instance, if you have a checkbox or a radiobutton, then to get the information back, you will have to use a slightly different methodology.

## Accessing Radiobuttons and Checkboxes

Radiobuttons and checkboxes are different to textboxes in a number of ways. First, the user's input is making a choice from specific options rather than making arbitrary input of their own. Second, rather than just returning information from one element, you'll be returning information from a group of elements.

For example, we may have a page with a quiz question that has three possible answers, given using radio buttons:

What is the capital of Albania?
○ Tirana
○ Valetta
○ Vaduz

We want to be able to check which answer the user selected, rather than having to check each radiobutton individually. As radiobuttons are rarely used as single items, whenever there is more than one radiobutton, they are grouped in arrays, which are accessed in a similar way to our textboxes, but with an extra level of detail. The code for our example is:

```
<form name="form1">
    What is the capital of Albania? <br />
    <input type="radio" name="radiogroup1" value="Tirana" />
    Tirana<br />
    <input type="radio" name="radiogroup1" value="Valetta" />
    Valetta<br />
    <input type="radio" name="radiogroup1" value="Vaduz" />
    Vaduz<br />
</form>
```

You can access the value of the first radiobutton as follows:

```
document.form1.radiogroup1[0].value
```

This would return the value from the first radiobutton, `"Tirana"`, regardless of which of the options had been picked by the user. Increasing the value in the array from `0` to `1` would return `"Valetta"`. This is all very well, but not much use given that it is the actual choice that the user made that you are after.

The property that tells you what the user selected is the `checked` property. It will return `true` for the radiobutton that has been checked and `false` for those that haven't. So, the following:

```
document.form1.radiogroup1[0].checked
```

would be `true`, only if the user had selected option `"Tirana"`.

To check through all of the radio buttons, you need to cycle through the whole array. But how big is the array? As we saw in *Chapter 9*, arrays have a `length` property, which returns the number of elements in the array. In the case of the `radiogroup1` array, it returns the number of radiobuttons in the group. This would be accessed as follows:

```
document.form1.radiogroup1.length
```

To check each item in the group, you would then create a loop, supplying the above `length` property as the number of times you wish to go around the loop:

```
for(var controlIndex = 0; controlIndex < document.form1.radiogroup1.length;
    controlIndex++)
{
  if (document.form1.radiogroup1[controlIndex].checked)
  {
    var user_selection = document.form1.radiogroup1[controlIndex].value;
  }
}
```

This loop checks each element in the array in turn to see whether it was chosen by the user. If it was, then we store the value of the selected radiobutton in a variable called `user_selection`.

Let's put this all together in a short example. Open up Dreamweaver MX and create a new page with a form containing three radio buttons and a button, as in our example above for a quiz question. Then add the script as shown in the head of the code below:

```
<!DOCTYPE HTML PUBLIC "-//W3C//DTD HTML 4.01 Transitional//EN">
<html>
<head>
  <title>Radio Button Example</title>
  <meta http-equiv="Content-Type" content="text/html; charset=iso-8859-1">
  <script language="JavaScript" type="text/JavaScript">
  function button_onclick()
  {
    var answer="Tirana";
```

```
        for (var controlIndex = 0; controlIndex < document.form1.radiogroup1.length;
            controlIndex++)
        {
          if (document.form1.radiogroup1[controlIndex].checked)
          {
            if(answer ==  document.form1.radiogroup1[controlIndex].value)
            {
              alert("Well done, you knew Tirana was the capital");
            }
            else
            {
              alert("Unfortunately you selected the capital of a small European "
                    + "principality, the correct answer is Tirana");
            }
          }
        }
      }
    </script>
  </head>

  <body>
    <form name="form1">
      What is the capital of Albania? <br />
      <input type="radio" name="radiogroup1" value="Tirana" />
      Tirana<br />
      <input type="radio" name="radiogroup1" value="Valetta" />
      Valetta<br />
      <input type="radio" name="radiogroup1" value="Vaduz" />
      Vaduz<br />
      <br />
      <input name="button" type="button" value="Click Me" onclick="button_onclick()" />
    </form>
  </body>
</html>
```

Save the page as `RadioButtonExample.html` and run the example in your browser. Choose one of the radiobuttons, and click on the button:

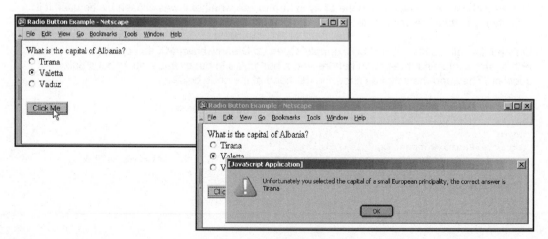

Our function `button_onclick()` works by setting a variable containing the correct answer 'Tirana':

```
var answer="Tirana";
```

We then start a loop to go through the contents of the radiobuttons, using the `length` property to determine how many there are:

```
for (var controlIndex = 0; controlIndex < document.form1.radiogroup1.length;
     controlIndex++)
{
```

We then check each radiobutton's `checked` property in turn to see whether it's `true`:

```
if (document.form1.radiogroup1[controlIndex].checked)
{
```

Inside this `if` statement, we perform another check. We know this section of code is only run when we find the radiobutton that the user has checked. In this situation, we need to compare the value of this radiobutton (that is, the user's answer) with the contents of our variable `answer`:

```
if(answer ==  document.form1.radiogroup1[controlIndex].value)
{
   alert("Well done, you knew Tirana was the capital");
}
else
{
   alert("Unfortunately you selected the capital of a small European "
         + "principality, the correct answer is Tirana");
}
```

Depending on which response we get, we display a dialog informing the user of their correct or incorrect answer.

## Accessing Listboxes

Listboxes and drop-down listboxes are different beasts again. Not only are they created using the `<select>` and `<option>` tags, but, like radiobuttons and checkboxes, we need to find the selected value rather than the input value.

For example, a drop-down listbox containing potential holiday destinations might look like this:

```
<select name="holidaydest" size="1">
   <option>Barcelona - Cultural and lively Catalan capital</option>
   <option>Prague - Literary and Gothic heart of Europe</option>
   <option>Paris - Bustling and Gourmands Paradise in the Seine Basin</option>
   <option>Lisbon - Charming and Architectural Gateway to Europe</option>
   <option>Munich - Beer Drinkers Nirvana situated at the foot of the
        Alps</option>
</select>
```

To get a particular option, you must use the `options` array as follows:

```
document.form1.holidaydest.options[0].text
```

This would access the text for the first option on the list, that is `"Barcelona - Cultural and lively Catalan capital"`. Notice that we use the `text` property here, rather than the `value` property we have used earlier. The `value` property would access any text supplied in the `value` attribute of each `<option>` tag.

To find out the actual option the user has selected, we must use the `selected` property of the `option` object, which once again holds `true` if a particular item has been selected and `false` if it has not.

```
document.form1.holidaydest.options[0].selected
```

To determine how many options there are in the listbox, you use the `length` property as before. So to discover which option a user has selected, you must loop through the entire `options` array, checking each `selected` value:

```
for (var controlIndex = 0; controlIndex < document.form1.holidaydest.length;
     controlIndex++)
{
  if (document.form1.holidaydest.options[controlIndex].selected)
  {
    var user_selection =document.form1.holidaydest.options[controlIndex].text;
  }
}
```

As this is very similar to the way that radiobuttons and checkboxes work, let's go one step further in our full example: we'll change the drop-down listbox to a normal listbox (by changing the `size` attribute of `<select>` to 5 – this does not mean a change to our script) and allow the user to select several items at once. The listbox as given above can only have one option selected at once, but by adding the attribute `multiple="multiple"` to the `<select>` tag, multiple option selections can be allowed. The function will then not work as planned. Why? Because for each selected option, the variable `user_selection` will be re-declared and overwritten with the text for that option.

Open up Dreamweaver MX and create a new page with a listbox and a button contained within a form, and the script as given in the head of the page below:

```
<!DOCTYPE HTML PUBLIC "-//W3C//DTD HTML 4.01 Transitional//EN">
<html>
<head>
<title>Listbox example</title>
  <meta http-equiv="Content-Type" content="text/html; charset=iso-8859-1">
  <script language="JavaScript" type="text/JavaScript">
  function button_onclick()
  {
    var details=" ";
    for (var controlIndex = 0; controlIndex < document.form1.holidaydest.length;
         controlIndex++)
    {
```

```
        if (document.form1.holidaydest.options[controlIndex].selected)
        {
            details += "<br />" +
document.form1.holidaydest.options[controlIndex].text;
        }
    }
    document.write("We'll send you brochures for: " + details);
    document.close();
  }
  </script>
</head>

<body>
  Choose destinations you want to receive brochures on:<br />
  <form name="form1">
    <select name="holidaydest" size="5" multiple="multiple">
      <option>Barcelona - Cultural and lively Catalan capital</option>
      <option>Prague - Literary and Gothic heart of Europe</option>
      <option>Paris - Bustling and Gourmands Paradise in the Seine
Basin</option>
      <option>Lisbon - Charming and Architectural Gateway to Europe</option>
      <option>Munich - Beer Drinkers Nirvana situated at the foot of the
Alps</option>
    </select>
    <br /><br />
    <input name="button" type="button" value="Click Me"
onclick="button_onclick()" />
  </form>
</body>
</html>
```

Save the page as ListboxExample.html, and open it in your browser.

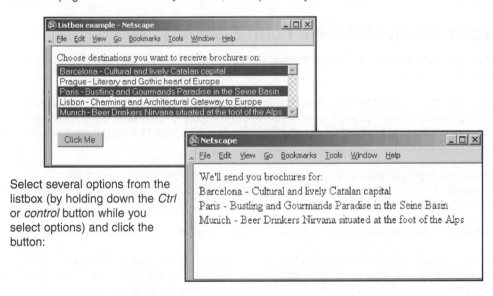

Select several options from the listbox (by holding down the *Ctrl* or *control* button while you select options) and click the button:

The function that does this has only changed by the addition of a few extra lines compared to the function we discussed earlier. We start it by declaring a variable, `details`, and with a loop, to loop around all of the contents of the `options` array:

```
var details=" ";
for (var controlIndex = 0; controlIndex < document.form1.holidaydest.length;
     controlIndex++)
{
```

Inside there is the check to see if we've found the item the user selected in the list:

```
if (document.form1.holidaydest.options[controlIndex].selected)
{
```

If this check is `true` then we add the text of the chosen option to our `details` variable. We also add a `<br />` tag to it, so that when we display each selection it is shown on a different line.

```
details += "<br />" +
document.form1.holidaydest.options[controlIndex].text;
```

Finally, after the `for` loop has completed looping through the options, we display the selections as a whole with the `document.write()` statement:

```
document.write("We'll send you brochures for: " + details);
document.close();
```

The `<select>` element makes it easy to select multiple items and pass their values straight to JavaScript.

This brings us to our next topic in forms: when should we use each form element?

## When to Use the Different Form Elements?

The answer to when should you use the different form control elements is normally down to your own discretion.

Textboxes should be favored for any kind of text input. The password box is not a secure way of passing passwords, unless you're on a secure server, and should only be used if the information being passed is not being checked via the JavaScript code, which might be viewed via the *View Code* or *View Source* option on a browser.

Radio buttons are generally used when there are a set of related options that a user can choose from. However, if they select one button, then all other selections are removed. In other words, one choice is mutually exclusive of all others.

Checkboxes are used when you need to get a yes/no-type answer to one or more questions.

Drop-down listboxes are favored when you have more options than can sensibly be displayed directly in the page, such as a list of all possible states in the US or countries in the world. They can be used to pack in a lot of information without messing up the layout of the page.

Finally, there are three types of button, but we've only looked at one so far (the plain button). One of the others, the reset button, isn't that commonly used as it simply removes all that a user has already typed in and resets all of the form fields back to the default values. Given that it is quite likely to be used accidentally in place of the submit button by the user, it should be used carefully. We didn't talk about submit buttons either, as this is something that is mainly used with server-side languages to submit the contents of a form to a web server. (For more on server-side technologies, see *Chapter 15*.)

# Form Validation

You've now got a good idea of how forms and the different elements work in JavaScript, but we've avoided talking about perhaps JavaScript's most common application with regard to forms. This is the ability to check whether a user has supplied the correct information within a form. For instance, have they supplied a correct e-mail address? Have they supplied a realistic age (that is, between 1 and 130)? Have they left any fields in the form blank? JavaScript can check these kinds of problems, even before the user has submitted the form in some cases. This has an advantage over checking the data is valid once it is sent to the server, as otherwise you have to submit the form to the server and wait for a reply. With JavaScript, it can be as instant as the moment the user types an incorrect key.

The best way to describe form validation is to see an example of it in action. Open up Dreamweaver MX and create a form with four textboxes, one for a name, one for e-mail, one for a password, and one for the age of the user. Add the script given below too:

```
<!DOCTYPE HTML PUBLIC "-//W3C//DTD HTML 4.01 Transitional//EN">
<html>
<head>
  <title>Form Validation Example</title>
  <meta http-equiv="Content-Type" content="text/html; charset=iso-8859-1">
  <script language="JavaScript" type="text/JavaScript">
  function check()
  {
    var details_accepted = true;
    var check_strudel = false;

    if (document.form1.name.value == "" || document.form1.age.value == "" ||
        document.form1.email.value == "" || document.form1.password.value == "")
    {
      details_accepted = false;
      alert("One of the required fields is empty");
    }

    if (document.form1.password.value.length < 4 ||
        document.form1.password.value.length > 8)
    {
      details_accepted = false;
      alert("Password is too short or too long");
    }

    if (document.form1.email.value.indexOf("@") != -1 &&
        document.form1.email.value.indexOf(".") != -1 )
    {
```

```
            check_strudel = true;
        }

        if (check_strudel == false)
        {
          alert("You have not supplied a valid e-mail address");
          details_accepted = false;
        }

        if (details_accepted == true)
        {
          alert("All details appear to be correct, your submission has been
                logged.");
          return true;
        }
        else
        {
          return false;
        }
      }

    function check_number()
    {
      var last_number = document.form1.age.value.length-1;
      last_key = document.form1.age.value.substr(last_number, 1)
      var check_digit = false;
      if ("0123456789".indexOf(last_key) != -1)
      {
        check_digit=true;
      }

      if (check_digit == false)
      {
        document.form1.age.value="";
      }
    }
    </script>
</head>

<body>
  Please enter the following details:<br />
  <form name="form1" onsubmit="return check()">
    Name:<br />
    <input name="name" type="text"
            onChange="javascript:while(''+this.value.charAt(0)==' ')
                        this.value=this.value.substring(1,this.value.length);" />
    <br />
    Age: <br />
    <input name="age" type="text" size="3" maxlength="3" onkeyup="check_number()"
            onChange="javascript:while(''+this.value.charAt(0)==' ')
                        this.value=this.value.substring(1,this.value.length);" />
    <br />
    Email:<br />
    <input name="email" type="text"
            onChange="javascript:while(''+this.value.charAt(0)==' ')
```

```
                    this.value=this.value.substring(1,this.value.length);" />
    <br />
    A password between 4 to 8 characters:<br />
    <input name="password" type="password" size="8" maxlength="8"
            onChange="javascript:while(''+this.value.charAt(0)==' ')
                    this.value=this.value.substring(1,this.value.length);" />
    <br /><br />
    <input name="submitbutton" type="submit" value="Click To Submit Details" />
    </form>
</body>
</html>
```

Save the page as `FormValidationExample.html`. If you run this code in your browser, it will perform four checks for you. It will check to see that:

- You have entered text or numbers in all of the fields.

- The e-mail has "@" and "." characters in it – we're not going to mail it separately to find out whether it's truly valid, which is what would be required to test its validity properly.

- The password field has between four and eight characters.

- Nothing other than numbers have been put into the age field.

Try and put erroneous data in and see what happens:

Of course, this example isn't perfect, and there are ways of fooling it (such as holding a letter key and pressing a number and then releasing the letter, followed by the number, within the age field), but then there's no guarantee that the user is telling the truth about their age either! Form validation can't make it impossible for a user to enter incorrect details: you could still enter the following:

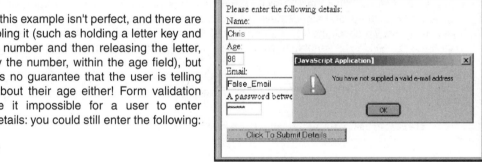

*Name: abc*
*Age: 300*
*Email: False@false.email.com*
*Password: password*

There's no sensible way to weed out such deliberate misinformation, but the hope is that, by forcing the user to provide certain details, they will provide correct details. It should make it harder for the user to just send blank details too. Let's look at the code now.

We do the form validation within two functions. The first function, `check()`, is run when you actually submit the details, via the `onsubmit` event handler attached to the form. Within this function, we first set two variables that will hold Boolean values that indicate whether the details are accepted and whether we have found an @ symbol (which we'll call a strudel) within the e-mail address.

```
var details_accepted = true;
  var check_strudel = false;
```

The first check is to see whether anything has been entered into the fields. We check all four form fields and if any of them is empty, we change the details_accepted variable to false and post an alert dialog up to the user:

```
if (document.form1.name.value == "" || document.form1.age.value == "" ||
    document.form1.email.value == "" || document.form1.password.value == "")
{
   details_accepted = false;
   alert("One of the required fields is empty");
}
```

Now this might look a fairly perfunctory check. What is to stop the user just adding a few blank spaces? To deal with this we've added some code in the textboxes themselves, which trims any leading spaces and effectively empties the box if all the user has entered is leading spaces. This code placed in the onchange event handler is:

```
javascript:while(''+this.value.charAt(0)==' ')
            this.value=this.value.substring(1,this.value.length);
```

This code just checks for space characters at the beginning of the input data and removes them if they are there.

The second check within the check() function is for the password length. The value of the password is a string, and strings have a length property that tells us the number of characters in the string. So, we check the length property of the value of this field and, if it is under 4 or over 8, the details_accepted variable is set to false and the alert dialog informs the user:

```
if (document.form1.password.value.length < 4 ||
    document.form1.password.value.length > 8)
{
   details_accepted = false;
   alert("Password is too short or too long");
}
```

The third and final check in this function uses the indexOf() function to check the data input into the mail address for a strudel and a period. Both checks take the same format, so consider the check for a strudel (@). If one is found, the indexOf() function returns a number that specifies how far into the string the strudel was found. If no strudel is found, the function returns -1. So if we find an strudel and a period (that is, if both the indexOf() functions do not return -1), we change the check_strudel variable to true.

```
if (document.form1.email.value.indexOf("@") != -1 &&
    document.form1.email.value.indexOf(".") != -1 )
{
   check_strudel = true;
}
```

Next we check the variable check_strudel. If it is false (that is we didn't find both a strudel and a period) then we change the details_accepted variable to false and alert the user once more.

```
if (check_strudel == false)
{
   alert("You have not supplied a valid e-mail address");
   details_accepted = false;
}
```

If none of the details have tripped the `details_accepted` variable over to `false`, then we assume everything is OK, as far as we can verify, and let the user know the details have been accepted. We return `true` to the function call in our `onsubmit` event handler. This allows the form to be submitted to the server, though we won't cover the intricacies of that here. If the function returns `false`, then form details are not submitted.

```
if (details_accepted == true)
{
   alert("All details appear to be correct, your submission has been logged.");
   return true;
}
else
{
   return false;
}
```

This still doesn't explain our second function. Our second function, `check_number()` actively prevents the user from adding any non-numerical characters to the form's `age` textbox. This foregoes the need for checking after the user has filled in the form. We isolate the last character that the user supplied by attaching an `onkeyup` event handler attribute to the relevant `<input>` tag and associating it with the `check_number()` function. When a key is pressed and released, this event is generated and calls the function.

The `check_number()` function starts by measuring the current length of the string typed into the `age` textbox, taking one away from this, and storing this in the variable `last_number`.

```
var last_number = document.form1.age.value.length-1;
```

We then use this variable, with the `substr()` function which chops out a section of a string, to cut the last character out of the string and store it in the `last_key` variable.

```
last_key = document.form1.age.value.substr(last_number, 1);
```

We create a flag (a **flag** is another name for a Boolean variable) to see whether we have found a letter or not. Initially we set this to `false`.

```
var check_digit = false;
```

Then we use our old friend `indexOf()` to check to see whether the last key typed was a number or a letter. If it was a number we set `check_digit` to `true`.

```
if ("0123456789".indexOf(last_key) != -1)
{
   check_digit=true;
}
```

At the end we check our flag, and if it is `false`, in other words if the last character in the data string was not a number, then we simply blank the whole `age` textbox.

```
if (check_digit == false)
{
   document.form1.age.value="";
}
```

In this way we have provided four simple validation checks to make sure the data supplied by the form is useful to us. You can provide many more checks yourself, but these are examples of some of the most common. Now the user has supplied their data, what happens when they next come to the web site?

# Remembering a User

More frequently on large corporate web sites, if you've visited the site more than once, the site will do something to acknowledge that you have been there before. Whether it is just to remember your name, or to store a unique ID which can be used to link to a whole profile of details (such as name, address, purchasing details, and previous orders), the bottom line is that they all depend on cookies.

## What Is a Cookie?

A cookie is a small string of text stored on the user's computer, with a maximum size per cookie of 4096 bytes. The cookie usually contains information in the form of a unique user identifier, some information (usually in the form of Boolean or numeric values) that can only be made sense of by the site you visited, the date that the cookie was created, and when it should expire. All cookies have an expiry date, whether it's within 24 hours of visiting the site or 24 years – after that date the cookie will be automatically removed, if it hasn't been already.

The Internet Explorer and Netscape browsers store cookies in different places. You can view cookies in Internet Explorer via the *Tools > Internet Options* dialog. Click the *Settings* and then *View Files* buttons. This will show all of your temporary Internet files. If you don't delete temporary files very often and have been using your machine a little while, then the list could be very long. To find the cookies, sort the files by type and look up the files of type '*Text Document*':

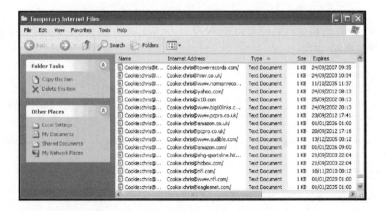

In Netscape versions 6 upwards, cookies can similarly be viewed (and deleted) via the *Tools > Cookie Manager > Manage Stored Cookies* dialog.

If you open a cookie up from either browser with a text editor, you'll see there's nothing much to write home about. Here, I've opened my cookie for the *Microsoft.com* site:

So what's all the fuss about?

# The "Controversial" Nature of Cookies?

The very idea that a web site can store information on your computer is anathema to some users. It seems at the very least an invasion of privacy and at the most downright dangerous and insecure. However, cookies aren't anywhere near as controversial as their reputation might have you believe:

First of all, all they can do is store text. No matter what information you place in a text file, it isn't possible to place a virus or malicious code within it (although beware of opening any strange text files with something that might convert HTML tags into their viewable controls – in which case text could potentially be dangerous).

Secondly, the amount that a cookie can store (4096 bytes) isn't going to be taking up too much space on anybody's hard drive. Your average graphic file is a lot bigger.

It's possible to set both Internet Explorer and Netscape to turn off cookies and delete all existing ones via the dialogs we detailed above for viewing them. However, you might find the Web a pretty barren place without them and end up having to supply registration information and user details to every site you go to, every time you visit them.

So, despite a lot of noise made about them initially, most people accept cookies as necessary. Combined with JavaScript, they're a very powerful tool given the lack of any other facilities for storing "session" information and persisting a user's profile or identity.

## How to Store and Retrieve Information from Cookies

In JavaScript, the cookie is a property of our old friend the `document` object. There are six items of information you can store in a cookie with JavaScript, which are:

- name – This is an identifier for a cookie.

- value – This is a compulsory value storing numerical or text data that JavaScript can access and make sense of.

- expires – This is the date at which the cookie will cease to exist.

- domain – Cookies are only available to pages in the domain they were set in, such as microsoft.com. You can specify extra sub-domains with this property.

- path – Cookies can not only be set as specific to a particular domain, but also to specific paths within this domain. Using this option, you can specify the paths needed.

- security – This is a Boolean value denoting whether a cookie should be sent to the server if the web server isn't using a secure channel.

Most of the time when using cookies, you only actually need the first three options: name, value, and expires. At its very simplest, a cookie only needs a name and value. It could be set like this:

```
document.cookie = "userid=ChrisU01;";
```

where `userid` is the name and `ChrisU01` is the value. Since no expires date is set, by default, this cookie will be deleted when the user **session** expires – that is when the user closes the browser. Such cookies are known as **transient cookies**. If you want the cookie to persist for longer than one visit, then you need to set the expiry date as follows:

```
document.cookie = "userid = ChrisU01;expires=Thu, 3 Oct 2003 00:00:00;"
```

Note that each new item in the cookie string is separated by a semicolon. The time at which a cookie expires is written in the form `hours:minutes:seconds`. The complete date format has to be in a certain form, so unless you are familiar with date formats, it would be a good idea to use the Date object to supply the correct format. We look at the Date object at the end of this chapter.

## An Example of a Cookie at Work

The best way to showcase the effectiveness of cookies is with a quick example. We'll ask the user for their name. Then, when they come back to the site for a second time, we will greet the user with their name and show them some alternative information that we didn't use the first time.

Open Dreamweaver MX, create a new page and insert scripts as follows:

```
<!DOCTYPE HTML PUBLIC "-//W3C//DTD HTML 4.01 Transitional//EN">
<html>
<head>
  <title>Cookie Example</title>
  <meta http-equiv="Content-Type" content="text/html; charset=iso-8859-1">
  <script language="JavaScript" type="text/JavaScript">
  function retrieve_Cookie()
  {
    var get_cookie = document.cookie;
    var cookie_index = get_cookie.indexOf('ghuserid=');
    if (cookie_index == -1)
    {
      document.write('Welcome to our site for the first time stranger. To make '
      + 'things a little more friendly, please enter your name:'
      + '<br /><form name="form1">Name:<br /> <input name="name" type="text" />'
      + '<br /><br /><br /><input name="button" type="button" '
```

```
                + 'value="Click To Submit Details" onclick="button_onclick()" /></form>');
      }
      else
      {
        var cookieStart = get_cookie.indexOf("=",cookie_index)+1;
        var cookieEnd = get_cookie.indexOf(";", cookieStart);
        if (cookieEnd == -1)
        {
          cookieEnd=get_cookie.length
        }
        var get_user_name = unescape(get_cookie.substring(cookieStart,cookieEnd));
        document.write("Welcome back " + get_user_name);
      }
    }

    function button_onclick()
    {
      var dateToday = new Date();
      dateToday.setMonth(dateToday.getMonth() + 1);
      var dateExpires = dateToday.toGMTString();
      document.cookie =
                "ghuserid="+document.form1.name.value+";expires="+dateExpires+";";
      document.write("Thank you, your details have been recorded.");
    }
    </script>
</head>
<body>
  <script language="JavaScript" type="text/JavaScript">
    retrieve_Cookie();
  </script>
</body>
</html>
```

Save the page as `CookieExample.html`. When you run the code for the first time in your browser you will see the following form. Enter your name:

Then when you click on *Click to Submit Details*, it tells you that your details have been recorded.

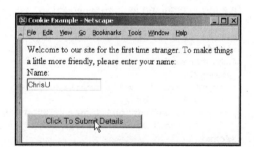

When you go back and rerun the page after closing the browser (and for every subsequent time, up to one month after you last opened the page), you'll get a different front page, stating your first name:

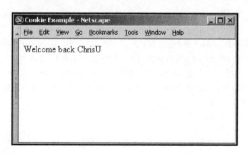

This is all down to the cookie that is stored the first time you visit the page. The page has two functions, `retrieve_Cookie()` and `button_onclick()`. When you open the page, `retrieve_Cookie()` is automatically called. This function starts by storing the contents of `document.cookie` in a variable `get_cookie`:

```
function retrieve_Cookie()
{
  var get_cookie = document.cookie;
```

It then stores the index of the text "`ghuserid=`" within the string in the variable `cookie_index`. The cookie we set is called `ghuserid`, so this will hold a number specifying how far into the cookie string our particular cookie is, or the value `-1` if our cookie is not already held within the string.

```
  var cookie_index = get_cookie.indexOf('ghuserid=');
```

We use this in our next `if` statement, which checks whether this is the first time the user has opened the page:

```
  if (cookie_index == -1)
  {
```

If it is, we dynamically write a form to the page. We use the `document.write()` method, but in the text that is written we place HTML tags creating a form.

```
    document.write('Welcome to our site for the first time stranger. To make '
    + 'things a little more friendly, please enter your name:'
    + '<br /><form name="form1">Name:<br /> <input name="name" type="text" />'
    + '<br /><br /><br /><input name="button" type="button" '
    + 'value="Click To Submit Details" onclick="button_onclick()" /></form>');
  }
```

This form contained in `document.write()` is actually the following HTML:

```
Welcome to our site for the first time stranger. To make things a little more
friendly, please enter your name:<br />
<form name="form1">
  Name:<br />
  <input name="name" type="text" />
  <br /><br /><br />
  <input name="button" type="button" value="Click To Submit Details"
         onclick="button_onclick()" />
</form>
```

This form will be displayed, just as though it had always been in place in the page.

However, if our `ghuserid` cookie is already present, then we have to extract the user name from the cookie information. To do this, we find the first occurrence of the `=` equals operator in the cookie string after the occurrence of our cookie name `ghuserid`. This is done via the `indexOf()` method which returns to our variable `cookieStart` the position in the string where the equals sign is found.

```
  else
  {
    var cookieStart = get_cookie.indexOf("=",cookie_index)+1;
```

We then need to find the end of our cookie value. As long as our `ghuserid` cookie is not held at the end of the cookie string, it will be followed by a semicolon. So, we first find the index of the first semicolon in the cookie string after the position of the equals sign stored in `cookieStart`.

```
var cookieEnd = get_cookie.indexOf(";", cookieStart);
```

However, if our cookie was found at the end of the cookie string, this semicolon won't appear. Our `cookieEnd` variable will hold the value -1, since the semicolon was not found. In this case, we reset `cookieEnd` to the whole length of the cookie string, which will be the index position of the end of our `ghuserid` cookie.

```
if (cookieEnd == -1)
{
  cookieEnd=get_cookie.length
}
```

Now we have the index positions of the start and end of our cookie value, we use the `substring()` method to extract the part of the cookie we want, which is the name the user entered in the form, and store it in the variable `get_user_name`:

```
var get_user_name = unescape(get_cookie.substring(cookieStart,cookieEnd));
```

We then display this as part of the message to the user.

```
document.write("Welcome back " + get_user_name);
  }
```

Our second function, `button_onclick()`, is the one that creates the cookie. It is run whenever someone clicks the button that we wrote to the page using the `retrieveCookie()` function we discussed above. It starts by creating a new Date object (more on this later).

```
function button_onclick()
{
  var dateToday = new Date();
```

Then we add one month from the current date by calling the `setMonth()` method of Date and using it add one to the value that the method `getMonth()` returns for today's date.

```
dateToday.setMonth(dateToday.getMonth() + 1);
```

Next we have to translate this to a string, before we can read it into the cookie information, as the cookie expires value only accepts strings:

```
var dateExpires = dateToday.toGMTString();
```

Then we store this information within `document.cookie`, along with the name the user supplied to the textbox called `name`.

```
document.cookie =
            "ghuserid="+document.form1.name.value+";expires="+dateExpires+";";
  document.write("Thank you, your details have been recorded.");
}
```

In this way the cookie is able to present two different sides of the same page, one with generic details for a new user, and one containing information customized to a particular user. As cookies are unique to the browser that created them, they are able to add personalization features to each individual. This example has only scratched at the surface: typically, you'd then use a server-side technology to integrate with JavaScript and pull up the details or a relevant profile. This is beyond the scope of this book, but hopefully we've given you enough to be able to start working on creating and storing your own cookies.

# Rollovers

Rollovers are one of the most popular and common features on web pages. They are images that change or "roll over" when a user moves their mouse pointer over them. They rely on the `document.images` object to work and are one of the simplest demonstrations of JavaScript's capabilities.

## Creating Rollover Buttons

A very common example use of rollovers is where they are used to seemingly "highlight" text, so we're going show you how to do exactly that in this example. We'll create a rollover for three images surrounded by links (commonly called **buttons**): a mailing list button, a comments button, and a database button. To create a rollover button, you already need to have two versions of the image that you intend to "rollover". We'll assume that you've already created your own images

mailinglistnormal.jpg     commentnormal.jpg     databasenormal.jpg

mailinglisthigh.jpg     commenthigh.jpg     databasehigh.jpg

(which should be of the same size), or are using the images supplied on the CD.
Assuming that the image is being used as a link to another page, the JavaScript is placed within the anchor `<a>` tag linked via the `onmouseover` and `onmouseout` event handlers. This JavaScript is then responsible for loading the images when the mouse pointer is over or not over the button.

Rollover images can have their associated JavaScript auto-generated in Dreamweaver. However, the coding supplied by Dreamweaver involves hard coding your image names and links into your JavaScript code. One golden rule of programming is to avoid putting anything in the code that might need changing, as otherwise when you come to update it, you create yourself a lot of extra work: you find yourself changing both the HTML and the JavaScript.

Instead we're going to use some of the features of the most up-to-date browsers (IE 5+ and Netscape 6+) to create a piece of JavaScript that will roll over any amount of buttons you wish to put on the page, as long as you adhere to some simple rules when placing the anchors and image tags. The rules are that:

- The anchor <a> element must contain the <img> element

- The images used must take the form of `namenormal.jpg` and `namehigh.jpg`, where name is assigned in the id attribute of the element

A typical image and link should look like this:

```
<a href="name.htm" onMouseOver="rolloverImages(event, 'imagehighlight')"
                   onMouseOut="rolloverImages(event, 'imagenormal')">
  <img id="name" src="namenormal.jpg" width=110 height=32 border=0 /></a>
```

As long as you insert images in this format into the <body> of your page, the example will be able to identify each image and change the image correctly.

Now let's create a working page that can do this. In Dreamweaver create a new HTML page and add the following markup and script:

*Note that the closing* </a> *needs to be placed straight after the* <img> *element with no gap. Otherwise, a superfluous underline mark appears in the browser.*

```
<!DOCTYPE HTML PUBLIC "-//W3C//DTD HTML 4.01 Transitional//EN">
<html>
<head>
  <title>Rollover Example</title>
  <meta http-equiv="Content-Type" content="text/html; charset=iso-8859-1">
  <script language="JavaScript" type="text/JavaScript">
    imagehighlight = new Image();
    imagenormal = new Image();
    function rolloverImages(e)
    {
      if (document.images)
      {
        if (window.event)
        {
          elem = event.srcElement;
          if (!elem.id)
          {
            if(elem.firstChild)
            {
              elem = elem.firstChild;
            }
          }
        }
        else if(e)
        {
          elem = e.target;
        }
        imagehighlight.src = elem.id+"high.jpg";
        imagenormal.src = elem.id+"normal.jpg";
        elem.src  = eval(rolloverImages.arguments[1] + ".src")
      }
    }
  </script>
</head>
```

```
<body>
   <a href="mailinglist.htm" onMouseOver="rolloverImages(event, 'imagehighlight')"
                          onMouseOut="rolloverImages(event, 'imagenormal')">
     <img id="mailinglist" src="mailinglistnormal.jpg" width=110 height=32
        border=0 /></a>
   <a href="comment.htm" onMouseOver="rolloverImages(event, 'imagehighlight')"
                       onMouseOut="rolloverImages(event, 'imagenormal')">
     <img id="comment" src="commentnormal.jpg" width=100 height=32 border=0 /></a>
   <a href="database.htm" onMouseOver="rolloverImages(event, 'imagehighlight')"
                        onMouseOut="rolloverImages(event, 'imagenormal')">
     <img id="database" src="databasenormal.jpg" width=100 height=32 border=0
        /></a>
</body>
</html>
```

Save this as RolloverExample.html.

In the main body of the JavaScript code, we create two variables containing new instances of image objects. These variables are used to store the names of the highlighted and normal versions of the image.

```
imagehighlight = new Image();
imagenormal = new Image();
```

The second piece of code is the function rolloverImages() and this performs the rollover transformation. First the function checks to see if there is an object present in the document.images collection.

```
function rolloverImages(e)
{
   if (document.images)
   {
```

If there is an object present, then the variable elem will be set to reference the HTML <img> element that generated the event. We have to use the DOM-specific e.target to obtain this for Netscape and the IE-specific event.srcElement to obtain this for IE. The code that does this (shown below) is a little complex due to differences between the browsers, but it basically has this effect.

```
      if (window.event)
      {
        elem = event.srcElement;
        if (!elem.id)
        {
          if(elem.firstChild)
          {
            elem = elem.firstChild;
          }
        }
      }
      else if(e)
      {
        elem = e.target;
      }
```

Next we create `src` properties for the image objects we created earlier (`src` being the location of where the image can be found). As within `elem.id` we have the `id` attribute of our image, we set `imagehighlight.src` to equal the `id` attribute plus the suffix "`high.jpg`" and `imagenormal.src` to equal the `id` attribute plus the suffix "`normal.jpg`". This creates a full image name.

```
imagehighlight.src = elem.id+"high.jpg";
imagenormal.src = elem.id+"normal.jpg";
```

Finally, we takes the `src` property of our image (held in variable `elem`) and set it to whatever the image wasn't before. How do we know what it wasn't before? We make use of the second argument passed to the `rollover_button()` function within the `onmouseover` and `onmouseout` event handlers of the `<a>` elements. So if the image was highlighted, it sets it to normal, and if it was normal, it sets it to highlighted.

```
elem.src  = eval(rolloverImages.arguments[1] + ".src")
    }
}
```

If you run this code and view it in the browser, the image will be highlighted when you move over it and deselected when you move off it.

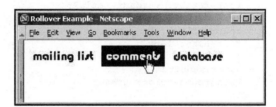

# Menus

Dynamic menus are perhaps a less common application of JavaScript, mainly because people choose to use either Flash or server-side technologies to provide this kind of functionality. However, if you don't have access to these technologies, they are still a popular alternative on many web sites.

We're going to create a simple drop-down menu which highlights the menu item that the user is currently hovering over. This goes one step further than the previous example using rollovers as it allows us to display and hide a whole menu system. It does this by moving the menu off the screen when it is not required and moving it back on when it is. Note that this script will only work in the more recent versions of the major browsers, such as IE 5.5 onwards and Netscape 6 onwards.

There are four main things we need to worry about in the code:

- Displaying the menu
- Hiding the menu
- Highlighting a menu item
- Deselecting a menu item

We're going to create three functions to look after the first two of these tasks, and the last two we are going to deal with using CSS stylesheets.

# Basic JavaScript and CSS Menu

Don't be put off by the length of this code. It is rather daunting, but is also quite repetitive, and some features of it should be familiar to you from the last example. Note that it uses CSS, which we have already come across in *Chapter 8*.

```
<!DOCTYPE HTML PUBLIC "-//W3C//DTD HTML 4.01 Transitional//EN">
<html>
<head>
  <title>Menu Example</title>
  <meta http-equiv="Content-Type" content="text/html; charset=iso-8859-1">
  <style type="text/css">
  span {
    font-family: verdana, arial;
    text-decoration: none;
    font-size: 16px
    }
  a:link.menuItem {
    font-family: verdana, arial;
    text-decoration: none;
    color: blue;
    font-size: 16px
    }
  a:hover.menuItem {
    background-color: green;
    }
  span.menubar {
    position: absolute;
    top:10px;
    background: silver
    }
  span.options {
    position: relative;
    top: 28px;
    visibility: hidden
    }
  </style>
  <script>
    menuVis = false;

    function menuShow(e)
    {
      if (menuVis != true)
      {
        if (window.event)
        {
          var elem = event.srcElement;
        }
        else if (e)
        {
          var elem = e.target;
        }
        if (elem.nodeType == 3)
        {
          elem = elem.parentNode;
```

```
        }
        var sub_menu = "title" + elem.id.substr(5,5);
        var elemnew = document.getElementById(sub_menu);
        elemnew.style.visibility = "visible";
        menuVis=true;
      }
    }

    function hideOnMouseLeave (element, evt)
    {
      if (element.id.substr(0,5)=='popup')
      {
        element = element.nextSibling;
        if (element.nodeType == "3")
        {
          element = element.nextSibling;
        }
      }
      if (element.contains && evt.toElement)
      {
        if (!element.contains(evt.toElement))
        {
          element.style.visibility = 'hidden';
          menuVis=false;
        }
      }
      else if (evt.relatedTarget)
      {
        if (!contains(element, evt.relatedTarget))
        {
          element.style.visibility = 'hidden';
          menuVis=false;
        }
      }
    }

    function contains (container, containee)
    {
      do
      {
        if (container == containee)
        {
          return true;
        }
        containee = containee.parentNode;
      }
      while (containee);
      return false;
    }
  </script>
</head>

<body>
  <span class="menubar" id="popup1" onmouseover="return menuShow(event)"
        onmouseout="hideOnMouseLeave(this,event)">
    Companies
```

```
    </span>
    <span class="options" onmouseout="hideOnMouseLeave(this, event);"
        style="position: absolute; background: beige" id="title1">
    <a class="menuItem" href="company1.htm">Corduroy Enterprises</a><br />
    <a class="menuItem" href="company2.htm">Denim Advocates</a><br />
    <a class="menuItem" href="company3.htm">Viceroy Industries</a><br />
    <a class="menuItem" href="company4.htm">Trojan Investments</a><br />
    <a class="menuItem" href="company5.htm">Argentan Ltd</a>
    </span>
</body>
</html>
```

Save the page as `MenuExample.html`. If you run this code in the browser, you will have a single tab. If you move over the tab, the drop-down menu appears. If you move over a particular menu item, it is highlighted and the link comes up in the browser's status bar:

When you move the cursor completely away from the menu item, the menu will disappear completely again.

This example works in both IE and Netscape browsers as we've been careful to put in code that is standard to them, and where it hasn't been possible, we've used decision-making branch statements to execute a couple of lines of code native to Internet Explorer. The code is quite lengthy and we don't expect it to be understood in depth; its main aim is to be reusable in other examples. However we will run through quickly what each function does.

The first function, `menuShow()`, checks to see if the menu is already visible by checking the `menuVis` variable. This is set to `false` before any of the functions are run, as the menu shouldn't be immediately visible. The function starts by getting a handle on the object/element that generated the event that caused the function to run. If `window.event` has been generated, then we know it's IE, and so we use `event.srcElement`. If it's `e`, then when know it's Netscape and we use `e.target`. We've left a final else branch open (that is, not present): this is for the case where you know that an older browser is going to be viewing the menu. You can insert a break here and some alternative static menu text for users of older browsers.

```
    if (menuVis != true)
    {
      if (window.event)
      {
        var elem = event.srcElement;
      }
      else if (e)
      {
        var elem = e.target;
      }
```

The function then checks to see which node generated the event. If the node that generated it is text (`nodeType 3`), then we need to move one up the tree structure to the parent node, as we aren't interested in changing the properties of the text. To move one up a tree, we just set the current HTML element to whatever its parent is.

254

```
if (elem.nodeType == 3)
{
    elem = elem.parentNode;
}
```

The next section of code identifies the specific element that generated the event by `id`. This isn't strictly necessary for this example, but if there were more than one menu it would be essential. This is what makes our code extensible. However, we are making some assumptions: if you create more than one menu, each menu tab `<span>` must have an `id` of the form `popup1`, `popup2`, and so on. Also, each menu `<span>` for that tab must correspondingly be called `title1` for `popup1`, `title2` for `popup2`, and so on. You would also have to have separate stylesheets for each new menu.

We start by setting `sub_menu` to `"title"` plus the number that appears on the end of the `popup` ID (in other words, the number in the `id` attribute of the `<span>` tag which forms the tab). We use the `substr()` function to extract this number.

```
var sub_menu = "title" + elem.id.substr(5,5);
```

Once we have a reference to the `<span>` element that contains the menu (stored in `sub_menu`), we can identify which menu is using the `document.getElementById()` method. We then make the menu visible by changing its style to visible:

```
var elemnew = document.getElementById(sub_menu);
elemnew.style.visibility = "visible";
```

Lastly we change the `menuVis` variable to demonstrate the menu is now visible.

```
menuVis = true;
```

So all this function is doing is identifying the menu we want to move, and then using the `style.visibility` property to make it visible.

The second function, `hideOnMouseLeave()`, provides the direct reverse functionality of the first function and just makes the menu invisible. However, it actually has to do things in a different way, and calls up a second function in the middle to help.

Once again a lot of the function's code is taken up by checking which browser is being used and setting up the variable to reflect the event that has been generated. We start by creating a variable test, which checks to see how the event was generated. It could be generated in one of two ways, either by the mouse moving off the menu tab or off the menu itself. This is important because if it has come off the menu tab, then we need to make some adjustments to the code before we make the element invisible.

The test involves getting hold of the element that generated the event. If the menu tab generated it, then it will have the identifying prefix "`popup`":

```
if (element.id.substr(0,5)=='popup')
{
```

If this is so, then we need to move down the tree to the next sibling from `popup`, which will be the menu itself:

```
element = element.nextSibling;
```

**10**

Netscape adds another problem in that the next sibling along from the `popup` tab, is the text it contains rather than the menu tab. Therefore we have to move two siblings along in Netscape to get to the menu. We check for Netscape by checking to see if it has returned a text node, rather than an element node.

```
if (element.nodeType == "3")
{
   element = element.nextSibling;
}
}
```

Now the `element` variable contains a reference to the menu that we want to make invisible. Here we must differentiate between the two browsers again. The end result is the same; all we want to do is change the `style` setting of our menu to `hidden`. However the problem is getting at the `style` setting. To get at this `style` setting, we have to identify the element that the mouse has just moved away from. In IE you use `event.toElement`, while in Netscape you use `evt.relatedTarget`.

```
if (element.contains && evt.toElement)
{
   if (!element.contains(evt.toElement))
   {
      element.style.visibility = 'hidden';
      menuVis=false;
   }
}
else if (evt.relatedTarget)
{
   if (!contains(element, evt.relatedTarget))
   {
      element.style.visibility = 'hidden';
      menuVis=false;
   }
}
```

In IE, to get at the `toElement` setting, it may be necessary to move up to the element that contains our menu item. If it is, then we call the third function `contains()`. The third function simply allows us to move up through our document until we get to the tag that created the menu:

```
function contains(container, containee)
{
   do
   {
      if (container == containee)
      {
         return true;
      }
      containee = containee.parentNode;
   }
   while (containee);
   return false;
}
```

We know we've reached this tag if our containing tag matches the tag it contains. Once it does, the `contains()` function returns `true`, allowing the `hideOnMouseLeave()` function to successfully hide the menu.

The last bit of our program, the bit that highlights the menu choices, isn't done in JavaScript at all. Instead, we used the following CSS properties:

```
a:link.menuItem {
  font-family: verdana, arial;
  text-decoration: none;
  color: blue;
  font-size: 16px
  }
a:hover.menuItem {
  background-color: green;
  }
```

These change the color of the background of our link, depending on whether a mouse is hovering over it or not. We saw this in detail in *Chapter 8*.

# Frames and Windows

JavaScript on the Web is often synonymous with the pop-up advert or a new window opening. Here we'll look at how this works in practice, but first we'll take another look at a related topic: frames.

## What Is a Frame?

As discussed in *Chapter 6*, frames are sections within your browser window into which different web pages can be loaded. They are generally discouraged by many senior developers, since they can cause navigation problems, but you may well need to use them if you are developing an existing site that has made use of them.

## How to Identify a Frame?

The reason we have bracketed frames in with windows in this part of the chapter is that they are both identified in the same way by JavaScript, using the `window` object. Whereas the `document` object identifies everything within the window, the `window` object deals with the particulars of the window itself, such as its size and positioning.

Some of the most commonly used properties of the `window` object governing this are:

- `parent` – a reference to the parent window of the current window (this could either be the window that opened the current window, or a frameset window that contains the current window as a frame)

- `self` – a reference to the current window

- `top` – a reference to the topmost window (this is the window that is finally reached by repeatedly accessing the parent property)

- `name` – the name of the window

- `screenLeft` (IE) /`screenX` (Netscape) – position of the left-hand side of the window on the screen in pixels

- `screenTop` (IE) /`screenY` (Netscape) – position of the top of the window on the screen in pixels

- `location.href` – a property of the location object (an object that is also a property of the window object), which contains information about the window's URL

Let's look at an example page containing three frames.

```
<!DOCTYPE HTML PUBLIC "-//W3C//DTD HTML 4.01 Frameset//EN"
    "http://www.w3.org/TR/html4/frameset.dtd">
<html>
<head>
  <title>Frameset Example</title>
  <meta http-equiv="Content-Type" content="text/html; charset=iso-8859-1">
</head>

<frameset cols="20%, *" id="Window1">
  <frame name="menu" src="menu.html">
  <frameset rows="25%,*" id="Window2">
    <frame name="content1" src="content1.html">
    <frame name="content2" src="content2.html">
  </frameset>
</frameset>

<noframes><body></body></noframes>
</html>
```

Save this as `FramesetExample.html`. Assuming you created suitable pages for `menu.html`, `content1.html`, and `content2.html`, this would produce the following:

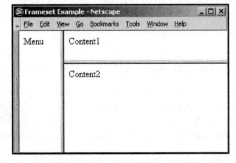

Each of these frames can be accessed from one another via the `window` object properties. For example, to get a reference to the topmost window (the whole browser window) from the menu frame window, you could create a variable and set it as follows:

```
var topWindow = window.parent;
```

As a more elaborate example, if you wanted to get a reference to one of the frames holding content from the menu frame window, you would first need to go from the menu window to the main (whole) window and then move to the content frame window by using its name:

```
var topWindow = window.parent;
var content1Window = topWindow.content1;
```

Let's see how we can use these properties to affect the contents of different frames. Open up Dreamweaver MX and place the following form (to create three radio buttons) and script in `menu.html`:

```
<!DOCTYPE HTML PUBLIC "-//W3C//DTD HTML 4.01 Transitional//EN">
<html>
<head>
  <title>Frame Example</title>
  <meta http-equiv="Content-Type" content="text/html; charset=iso-8859-1">
  <script language="JavaScript" type="text/JavaScript">
  function button_onclick()
  {
    for (var indexCounter=0; indexCounter<document.form1.choice1.length;
         indexCounter++)
    {
      if (document.form1.choice1[indexCounter].checked == true)
      {
        var which_choice = document.form1.choice1[indexCounter].value
      }
    }
    if (which_choice == "top")
    {
      var topWindow = window.parent;
      var content1Window = topWindow.content1;
      window.location.href = content1Window.location.href;
    }
    if (which_choice == "bottom")
    {
      var topWindow = window.parent;
      var content2Window = topWindow.content2;
      window.location.href = content2Window.location.href;
    }
    if (which_choice == "whole")
    {
      topWindow = window.top;
      window.location.href = topWindow.location.href;
    }
  }
  </script>
</head>

<body>
  <form name="form1">
    <p>
      <input type="radio" name="choice1" value="top" />
      Top Frame
      <br />
      <input type="radio" name="choice1" value="bottom" />
      Bottom Frame
      <br />
      <input type="radio" name="choice1" value="whole" />
      New Page
      <br />
    </p>
    <input name="button" type="button" value="Click to load page"
           onclick="button_onclick()" />
  </form>
</body>
</html>
```

When you select a radio button and click the button in the left-hand frame, the contents of the selected frame is loaded into the menu frame. Yes, it is rather a frivolous example!

When the button is clicked, the `button_onclick()` function is called. The first bit of this function just ascertains which of the radio buttons has been selected and assigns it a corresponding value of `top`, `bottom`, or `whole`.

```
for (var indexCounter=0; indexCounter<document.form1.choice1.length;
     indexCounter++)
{
   if (document.form1.choice1[indexCounter].checked == true)
   {
     var which_choice = document.form1.choice1[indexCounter].value
   }
}
```

If the top button has been selected, we create a variable that lets us access the parent window of the menu frame (in other words the top window), and then we get a reference to the `content1` frame, by referencing the frame by name. Finally, to load this window into the current window, we change the `location.href` property (the URL) of the current window to be the URL of the reference to the `content1` window.

```
if (which_choice == "top")
{
   var topWindow = window.parent;
   var content1Window = topWindow.content1;
   window.location.href = content1Window.location.href;
}
```

We do a very similar thing with the bottom frame, except we set our window reference to point to the contents of the bottom frame (`content2`) rather than the top frame.

The last choice is slightly different, as we only need a reference to the topmost frame. Then we set the URL of the menu frame to point to that:

```
if (which_choice == "whole")
{
   topWindow = window.top;
   window.location.href = topWindow.location.href;
}
```

In this way we can use JavaScript to affect the contents of individual frames.

It is also possible to use the `window` object to create entirely new browser instances, as we'll see next.

## Opening Up Browser Windows (Pop-Ups)

To open up a new browser window, all you need to do is supply some details to the `window.open()` method. The `window.open()` method takes three parameters:

- The URL of the new page

- The name of the new page

- A feature string (which allows you to alter dimensions, scrollbars, location, and status of the new page)

These parameters are all supplied within quotation marks. For example, to open up a window containing the document page1.html with diameters 100 by 100, we need:

```
window.open("page1.html", "MyNewage", "width=100,height=100");
```

Here we'll create a quick example that opens up a new browser window when the user clicks on a button. Open Dreamweaver MX and create two pages. The first should contain a form with a single button and the following script code:

```
<!DOCTYPE HTML PUBLIC "-//W3C//DTD HTML 4.01 Transitional//EN">
<html>
<head>
  <title>Pop-up Example Page</title>
  <meta http-equiv="Content-Type" content="text/html; charset=iso-8859-1">
  <script language="JavaScript" type="text/JavaScript">
  var newWindow;
  function button_onclick()
  {
    newWindow = window.open("page1.html", "MyNewPage", "width=150,height=100");
    newWindow.focus();
  }
  </script>
</head>

<body>
  <form name="form1">
    <input name="button" type="button" onclick="button_onclick()"
           value="Press here for endless riches" />
  </form>
</body>
</html>
```

Save this as PopupExample.html. The second page called page1.html is the popup window:

```
<!DOCTYPE HTML PUBLIC "-//W3C//DTD HTML 4.01 Transitional//EN">
<html>
<head>
  <title>Pop-up Example New Page</title>
  <meta http-equiv="Content-Type" content="text/html; charset=iso-8859-1">
</head>
<body>
  Ha, Ha ... fooled you, just another annoying popup!
</body>
</html>
```

Open `PopupExample.html` in your browser. The pop-up window appears when the `onclick` event handler of the button is activated:

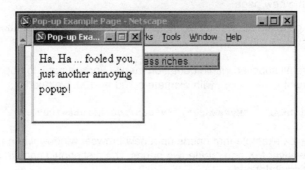

As usual, the function `button_onclick()` is called whenever the button is pressed. The first line of this function creates the new pop-up window with diameters 100 by 150 pixels, while the second one gives this new window focus:

```
newWindow = window.open("page1.html", "MyNewPage", "width=150,height=100");
newWindow.focus();
```

Actually, the `window.open()` method is more versatile than this example implies. In the first parameter to this method, we supplied the URL, but this doesn't have to take a URL. You can leave it blank, like this:

```
var newWindow = window.open("", "MyNewPage", "width=150,height=100");
```

Then you can supply your own HTML. You do this by accessing the `document` object of the new window you created, and using our earlier trick of `document.write()` to write the HTML tags. You need to open and close the `document` object as well.

```
newWindow.document.open();

newWindow.document.write('<!DOCTYPE HTML PUBLIC "-//W3C//DTD HTML 4.01 '
   + 'Transitional//EN"><html><head><title>New popup</title></head>'
   + '<body>Ha Ha…fooled you, just another annoying popup!</body></html>');

newWindow.document.close();
```

If you changed the code in function `button_onclick()` to the six lines of code above, the example would function in exactly the same way, but not require you to actively load a new page.

In our example you might also notice that the new window appears in the top left-hand corner of the screen. That's because we haven't specified at what location the window should appear. By using the third parameter of `window.open()`, it is possible to specify a lot more than just the height and width of the window. You can also specify where the window is positioned, via the top and left positions, whether the window has scrollbars, menu bars, a toolbar, or a status bar, or even if the window is resizable or not. The properties for doing this are:

- `top` – specifies the distance from the top of the screen in pixels

- `left` – specifies the distance from the left of the screen in pixels

- `menubar` – shows the menu bar

- `resizable` – allows the window to be resized by the user

- `scrollbars` – shows the scrollbars

- `status` – shows the status bar

- `toolbar` – shows the toolbar

There are more besides this, but these give you an idea of the control JavaScript gives you. You just place any of these within the third parameter. For example, to make our window have scrollbars, be resizable, and appear further across the screen, you could specify the following:

```
window.open("page1.html", "MyNewPage",
            "height=100,width=150,top=200,left=200,scrollbars,resizable);
```

## Moving and Resizing Windows

There are also methods that enable you to move and resize any window. These are the `resizeTo()` and `moveTo()` methods. They both take two parameters:

- `resizeTo(height, width)`

- `moveTo(top, left)`

Moving and resizing our window once we've created it can be done as follows.

```
newWindow.resizeTo(200,250);
newWindow.moveTo(300,300);
```

It doesn't just stop there: you can also let the window respond to different events.

## Getting the Window to React to Events

The following event handlers are all recognized by windows:

- `onblur` – occurs when the window loses focus

- `onfocus` – occurs when the window gains focus

- `onresize` – occurs when the window is resized

- `onscroll` – occurs when the window's scrollbars are used (only supported by IE 4 onwards and Netscape 7 onwards)

- `onerror` – occurs when an error arises either loading a document, image, or object

- `onload` – occurs when the contents of the window are fully loaded

- `onunload` – occurs when the contents of the window are unloaded

You simply create functions that run when these events occur. For example, you could assign a function to the `onblur` event handler. The following line script would run the `window_onblur()` function every time the window is about to lose focus.

```
newWindow.onblur = window_onblur;
```

Note that parentheses aren't included after the function call. This is the function that the event called:

```
function window_onblur()
{
  newWindow.resizeTo(200,200);
  newWindow.moveTo(300,300);
  newWindow.focus();
}
```

This would have the very annoying effect of bringing the window back into focus and to the forefront, every time you tried to move back to the browser.

## Disabling These Features

One commonly asked question is, "How can I stop windows popping up the whole time?" Well, it is possible, but not via a feature in Internet Explorer. It is possible in Netscape 7 under *Edit > Preferences* in the *Advanced* section under *Scripts/Plugins*. With IE, you'd have to use other software or write a routine (in a language other than JavaScript) that detects whenever a new window is opened and closes it immediately on opening.

# Timing a User's Actions

In the last chapter we discussed the different data types and how date information wasn't actually stored as a data type but as a separate object. We've already seen in the example that uses cookies how we could perform temporal arithmetic – namely add one to a month, to get the next month – but the Date object provides a lot more functionality besides. Also, JavaScript has access to an accurate timing mechanism. However, before we can do that, we need to talk a little about the Date object itself.

## The Date Object

To create an instance of a Date object and assign it to a new variable, you just need:

```
var todaysDate = new Date();
```

If you were to view the contents of the variable you have created, you would get back today's date and time.

```
document.write(todaysDate);
```

When you return the contents of the Date object in this way, you get something like:

*Thu Oct 3 17:18:42 UTC+0100 2002*

This gives you the current date, the time down to seconds, the UTC (universal coordinated time) adjustment, and the year.

You can also set a specific date when creating an instance of the Date object as follows:

```
var yesterdays_date = new Date(2002, 9, 7);

var date_string = new Date("October 10, 2002");
```

This is all well and good, but what happens if you want to separate out a single portion of the date, such as the month, or the year? The Date object provides properties and methods that allow you to access this:

- `getMilliseconds()` - gets the milliseconds only
- `getSeconds()` – gets the seconds only
- `getMinutes()` – gets the minutes only
- `getMonth()` – gets the month only (this is returned as a number between 0 and 11, 0 for January and 11 for December)
- `getHours()` – gets the hours only
- `getDate()` – gets the day only
- `getFullYear()` – gets the four-digit year only

There are more, but you get the point. To return the month, you would need to use this as a method of your Date object as follows:

```
var todaysDate = new Date();
alert(todaysDate.getMonth());
```

As noted above, this returns a numerical value. To perform temporal arithmetic, you can now just add or subtract to the numerical value returned by the method. For example:

```
todaysMonthplusOne = todaysDate.getMonth() + 1;
```

If you wished to set a Date object's time or date, there are an equivalent set of methods for setting the particulars of the time.

- `setMilliseconds()` – sets the milliseconds only
- `setSeconds()` – sets the seconds only
- `setMinutes()` – sets the minutes only
- `setMonth()` – sets the month only
- `setHours()` – sets the hours only
- `setDate()` – sets the day only
- `setFullYear()` – sets the four-digit year only

Of course time and date are not universal across the globe, so you can specify the UTC times and offsets from UTC time as well. (There is an equivalent set of set and get methods for the UTC time.) You can retrieve the UTC setting and return it as a string via the following method:

```
todaysDate.toUTCString();
```

To convert it to the locale string you can then set it as follows:

```
todaysDate.toLocaleString();
```

or to get the difference between the UTC time and the locale, you can use the `getTimezoneOffset()` method which returns the offset in minutes between the local time and the UTC time:

```
todaysDate.getTimezoneOffset();
```

Try these out in your own pages to see the time zone differences.

## Getting Your Script to Delay First Before It Runs

Separate to the Date object, JavaScript has a `setTimeout()` function for causing a delay of a specified amount of time before some script is run. The `setTimeout()` function takes two parameters, the first is the JavaScript you wish to run (usually a function name) and the second is the amount of milliseconds by which you wish to delay the function:

```
setTimeout(function, amount_of_time)
```

One way in which this could be used is to display a scrolling message on the screen. The principle of displaying a scrolling message is that you display a different subsection of the message after each short period of time, seemingly moving it across by adding a character to the end of the subsection and taking one from the beginning.

To create this last example, open Dreamweaver MX and create a form with a single textbox that you cannot access, add an `onload` event handler to the `<body>` tag, and add the following script as well:

```
<!DOCTYPE HTML PUBLIC "-//W3C//DTD HTML 4.01 Transitional//EN">
<html>
  <head>
  <title>Scrolling Message Example</title>
  <meta http-equiv="Content-Type" content="text/html; charset=iso-8859-1">
  <script language="JavaScript" type="text/JavaScript">
  var message = " *** This is our super scrolling message which is too long to be"
    + " comfortably displayed within the narrow confines of your browser. *** ";

  function scroll_message()
  {
```

```
       message = message.substring(1,message.length) + message.substring(0,1);
       document.form1.textbox.value = message;
setTimeout("scroll_message()",180);
   }
   </script>
</head>

<body onload="scroll_message()">
   <form name="form1">
     <input name="textbox" type="text" size="30" readonly="readonly" />
   </form>
</body>
</html>
```

Save the page as `ScrollExample.html`, and try it out in your browser. The message appears to scroll inside the textbox, but in fact all it is doing is calling the function every 180 milliseconds to display an ever-changing section of the message and give the impression of movement.

We start our script by defining the variable `message` for the message itself.

```
var message = " *** This is our super scrolling message which is too long to be"
    + " comfortably displayed within the narrow confines of your browser. *** ";
```

The function `scroll_message()` then redefines the variable `message` by removing the first character at the beginning of the message and adding it back to the end of the message. The `message` variable is then assigned as the contents of the textbox.

```
function scroll_message()
{
   message = message.substring(1,message.length) + message.substring(0,1);
   document.form1.textbox.value = message;
```

Then the clever bit: at the end of the function, we set the function to be re-called every 180 milliseconds using the `setTimeout()` function. Our message will scroll until we exit the page.

```
   setTimeout("scroll_message()",180);
}
```

This last example is a good place to stop as we have covered an awful lot in this chapter.

# Summary

This chapter is not meant to be an in-depth treatment of the major areas in which you can use JavaScript. There hasn't been time or space to give any of the subjects the detail they deserve. What it has been is a brief glance at the kind of methods employed by developers to:

- get information from the user

- retain this information between page visits

- make sure the web pages are compatible to both browsers

- perform operations such as moving between windows, opening new windows, and creating timers

These disparate techniques are all ways in which JavaScript can be used to embellish your web pages and give them extra interactive features. JavaScript's role as a programming language in its own right is probably becoming less important with the introduction of many other technologies. However, as a quick-fix toolbox to give your pages extra bits of functionality without having to develop full-blown applications, it is invaluable.

# Resources

In order to further your knowledge of JavaScript, try the many books available, including *Practical JavaScript for the Usable Web* (glasshaus, 2002, ISBN 1904151051).

There are also many sites that you can use for reference or to learn more techniques, including:

- Microsoft's JScript page: Go to *http://msdn.microsoft.com/* and search for JScript

- Netscape's JavaScript reference: Go to *http://devedge.netscape.com/* and look for JavaScript manuals in the Library

- A JavaScript resource site: *http://www.javascript.com/*

- The JavaScript Source: http://javascript.internet.com

- JavaScript Kit: *http://www.javascriptkit.com/*

**10**

# 11

- Introduction to usability

- Knowing the site audience

- Usability testing

- Accessibility

**Author: Crystal Waters**

# An Introduction to Usability

By this point in the book, you will have learned a lot about the Web, from the background behind it all, through the technologies used to build it, to the design principles that, when followed, make the Web an exciting, useful, fun, informative place to be! The combination of good design and good coding is what makes a web site successful, that is, easy to use, pleasing to look at, and able to provide the services and functionality the user needs.

But what do we call the factoring that determines whether a site is good or not? The term you will hear bandied around is **usability**, a term that refers to the overall worth of a site in terms of the measures we mention above.

To get the idea, have a look at some of your favorite web sites, and some others besides. Are these sites easy to use? Do they give you the services you require, and can they be found easily? Are they visually appealing? Are they a pleasure to use (or are they frustrating, requiring a lot of thought to get to where you want to go)? If you can answer "yes" to some of these questions, the site you are looking at is probably pretty usable.

In this book, even though you may not have thought about it much, we have already seen a lot of usable teachings, for example using standards (such as XHTML and CSS) to build your site, designing a good page layout, making sure your site is easily and intuitively navigable, optimizing your images so they look great and load fast etc. These are all examples of things that will contribute to making your site more **usable**.

So what is the point of this chapter? Well, here we aim to provide you with some useful information on why usability is important to consider, and how to go about identifying what needs to be done to enhance the usability of your site in a manner that works. We will look at:

● Knowing your target audience: It is easier to build a site when you know a little about your site users – what their needs and preferences are, and what technology they have to access the site.

- Finding out about your audience: So we want to know about our target audience, but how do we gather the information? This section looks at the methods available to do so.

- Accessibility: A subset of usability that refers to how usable a site is by people with disabilities, such as visual impairment, or cognitive disabilities. As well as being the right thing to do, there is legislation to ensure that people with disabilities are not discriminated against due to web sites being inaccessible to them. How do we make sure that our web sites are accessible?

When applying the term and practice of "usability" to a project, the goal is to focus on the end user of a site. The most simple rule of thumb when trying to apply usability principles to a web site is that you, the designer, are not the user, and if you're designing for a client, they are not the user either. Both you and your client are integral to determining design, content, and site structure, but only the resulting site visitors are the people that determine whether a site is successfully usable. You and the client don't have the distance to be objective.

# Knowing Your Target Audience

A well-designed site can influence the way a person uses it, but as its creator, you are responsible for also creating an experience that balances good design with assisting your site visitors in getting what they want (or where they want) when they want, along with making the client happy by driving visitors to purchase products, read articles, or whatever else the site goal may be.

Think about your favorite web sites for a second, and ask yourself what kind of audience they attract. Your average web site is not aimed at everyone on the planet, from kindergarten pupils to nuclear physicists. Instead, we need to work out what the primary (and secondary) target audience of the site is, so we can develop it to suit. Once the target market is narrowed down to a somewhat common denominator, the denominator should determine how the site functions, its content, and its overall layout and design.

For example, at the most basic level, kindergarten pupils may need a site with one-syllable words and primary colors, large menu buttons with immediate visual and audible feedback, and simple music and directives. For a scientist intent on finding up-to-the-minute papers and images showing say, research techniques or cell growth patterns, any gratuitous or extraneous content only gets in the way. The look, feel, presentation, and development of these sites are totally different, but your goal remains the same in developing them.

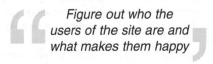
*Figure out who the users of the site are and what makes them happy*

How do you create a site for people you've never met and make your clients happy with a site that its users have never used before? If possible, the first step is trying to figure out who the users of the site are and what makes them happy, and then translating that into a site that also makes the client happy.

# Who Are These "Users"?

According to Nielsen/NetRatings (*http://www.nielsen-netratings.com*), overall there are about 450 million people estimated to be online in the world, spending an average of about 10 hours per month browsing, breaking down to about 45 seconds per page and a total amount of time per session running just a touch over 32 minutes. eMarketer (*http://www.emarketer.com*) has an even higher estimate of global users for 2002: 529 million, with an estimate that nearly 200 million more will go online by 2004.

According to Global Reach (*http://glreach.com/* – a consultancy in San Francisco that specializes in driving web traffic from other countries to those in the US), 228 million people who access the web speak English, and 339 million speak languages other than English (some of whom overlap because people browse the Web in two or more languages).

But we know that our audience is more than just a number counted in millions. Each member of our site audience is unique perhaps falling into a demographic category, but still seeking out information or products specific to their needs. Knowing who these people are, and how they are grouped together into various target audiences is only part of the usability puzzle.

## Defining a Site's Audience

You and your clients probably have some idea of who the preferred audience for a site would be: if your client sells female shoes, then it is probable that the majority of visitors to their site will be women. If the site specializes in sports bras for nursing mothers, then the audience estimate could be even more definite – women of child-bearing age who have very young children, and also play sports. The better defined the site topic, the better we can estimate the audience. But while we might know, or at least be able to guestimate, whether our audience will be male or female, and perhaps how old they are, we still have to find answers to other key questions.

There's no way that we can know everything about every single person that uses our sites, and it may be close to impossible to ever determine exactly what an 'average' user is. The hardest element of the successful web site equation is the people for whom we design. Each one has different preferences, abilities, technical knowledge, and experience levels.

Since there are around 500 million people online, with access to a lot of web sites, it can be difficult to nail down a demographic. Luckily (at least in the amount-of-work respect) not one of us can claim that all 500 million of those people are coming to our site.

If your clients have experience with their market already – for example, they've owned a chain of stores for 25 years, and are now moving sales to the Web – then they are your most important asset when it comes to determining the people who will use the site. The more experience the client has with serving their existing audience, the more they can assist you in helping to profile the potential web audience. If they are good at what they do for their audience, then it is fair to assume that they have nailed down the formula for satisfying their customers fairly well. This is an ideal starting point.

11

The process of finding out about your target audience is often termed **Audience profiling**. For more information on this, refer to *Chapter 3*. In this chapter we drill further down into two main areas to consider when looking at your target audience:

- The technology the users use to access the Web, including hardware, software, and connection speed.
- The level of technical expertise of the users themselves.

## The User's Available Technology

It is important to take a look at how your prospective audience accesses the Web, and with what kind of equipment and software, as there are many browsers and devices to choose from with which to surf the Web, from traditional desktop PCs, to mobile phones and PDAs.

### Different Browsing Methods

These days, the majority of web users tend to adopt the newer available browsers (version 5+ browsers) fairly quickly, so browser support is much less of a problem than it used to be. However, there are still people out there using older versions of browsers, for various reasons such as:

- They are stubbornly refusing to "download now!" when told they need a new browser, or they are constrained to using an older browser by company policy.
- They figure they don't spend enough time online to warrant spending the time or money on a new version.
- Their computer system can't support the system requirements of a newer browser.
- They don't know how to install new software.

Others have grown used to the quirks and buttons and functions of an older browser, and don't want to face a new learning curve. Of course, this is not the only problem. As we mentioned above, as well as the high-end graphical browsers, there are more people using alternative devices to surf the Web, as well as people using text browsers, and web users with disabilities using browsing aids such as voice browsers and screen readers.

No matter what the reason, there are still people using versions of web browsers that may not be what we want to design for (maybe we want to use CSS for layout, but that browser doesn't support the CSS properties we want to use). But it is obviously good business to support as much of your target audience as possible. It may sound like madness to do lots of extra work to support, say, an older version of Netscape, because 0.2% of our audience uses it, but if you are working on a big, well-established site with, say, 10 million users, that's 40,000 users you are talking about! It suddenly doesn't seem quite so insignificant.

And a lot of the time, it isn't a huge issue anyway, so long as you are aware of the facts. Take screen readers for example. As you will see in the *Accessibility* section later on in this chapter, supporting screen readers does not require you to learn any complicated new technologies; it is merely a matter of coding your sites with standards-compliant, intelligently written (X)HTML.

## Connection Speeds

Considering the connection speed of your target audience is important. While those in urban areas have fast DSL and cable modem possibilities, those in less urban areas simply don't have these options made available to them. While prices are becoming more comparable to regular dial-up accounts, those that might have the availability may not be able or willing to afford the extra cost that high-speed suppliers demand.

What that leaves us with are people who are using phone lines to get online, and compared to what many of us have as designers, that's significantly slower. If we have, say, a cable modem, our perception of how a site loads and presents itself will be much different to that of a home user with 56k dial-up modem access.

If we demand that they download a plugin or a new browser to access our site, then that is putting a significant limitation on their access to your site. You should generally be careful not to bloat your web pages with huge graphics and animations, but in the case of users using dial-up access, this becomes much more of an issue. A user who is confronted with incredibly slow-loading pages will soon get frustrated and go elsewhere. If you feel that you have to include such things on your web pages, at least give users the option to skip past intro animations, and possibly provide a lower-spec version of the site.

> *A user who is confronted with incredibly slow-loading pages will soon get frustrated and go elsewhere*

## User Hardware Technology

Another key factor to profiling your audience is finding out what kind of hardware gets them online. Unlike the development community, the average consumer doesn't run out and buy the fastest computers, and the biggest monitors. The bells and whistles that we take for granted may be out of the user's reach or interest.

No matter how refined your demographics, your users will have a variety of hardware setups at home and in the office. They'll have different processors, and amounts of RAM and hard drive storage space. Those with newer consumer-oriented systems will have tons of RAM and hard drive space that comes standard with their machines, but those with older systems, at home, at school, or at work, may have more of a challenge processing what we might demand of their browsers and systems. This could be because of financial limitations, lack of interest in new equipment (computers may be a hobby or convenience rather than a way of life, like for others of us!). A school might lack funding for new equipment every time a new product comes to market, and even the biggest corporations have to watch their bottom line rather than purchase every recommended upgrade.

**Monitor bit depth and screen size** obviously will influence how a site is viewed. Huge variations in bit depth (which basically refers to the quality of on-screen images) isn't as serious an issue as the "old days" when the majority of monitors only displayed 256 colors.

The actual physical size of a page, however, remains a variable. From teeny PDA screens up to high-definition 23-inch active-matrix liquid crystal displays that support a 1,920 by 1,200-pixel resolution, web-viewing options run the gamut.

Viewing devices such as small Palm screens (see *http://www.palm.com*) and the 23-inch Apple Cinema HD Display (see *http://www.apple.com*) are, at least for now, far from being the standard viewing tool for the Web. Still, these are the kinds of advancements and technologies that web designers have to keep an eye on. Not so long ago, 14- or 15-inch monitors that only displayed 256 colors were the norm. Now most people have monitors with higher bit depth and more physical screen space.

Why is window size so important? Think about a site you might have visited recently that forced you to open your web window bigger in order to view the entire page. Then, you might have gone to another page, only to have to resize your window again. Or perhaps the design was too wide for your screen, so you found that you had to horizontally-scroll to view the bit of the page that interested you. It's a bit annoying, isn't it?

For example, the screenshot below shows *CDNow.com* displayed full-screen (in IE 6) on a monitor set to show 640 by 480 pixels. The whole navigation and main content aren't viewable unless we use the horizontal scroll bar on the bottom of the screen.

*CDNow.com in 640 x 480 resolution*

Next, let's look at *CDNow.com* displayed full-screen on a monitor set to show 800 x 600 pixels (see below). Notice that the horizontal scroll bar has almost disappeared, and we can now view all of the main navigation – we are now viewing the window at the size for which it was designed.

CDNow.com in 800 x 600 resolution

Finally, in the next screenshot we can see *CDNow.com* displayed full-screen on a monitor set to show 1024 x 768. The design has "spread out" to fill the screen width-wise. Those with monitors set at this bit depth only benefit in seeing more information vertically, since the site seems to have been designed for optimum viewing at 800 x 600.

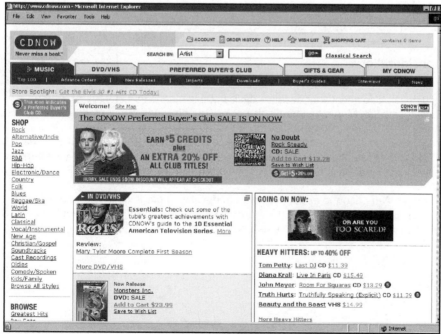

CDNow.com in 1024 x 768 resolution

If part of your site is cut off on a user's monitor – especially a navigational cue or other content that is important for users to view – then you might want to reconsider your design. Knowing what settings your audience uses will give you the lowest common denominator for which to design. It isn't the kind of information that is the easiest to collect, so you might want to send some questionnaires round, for example to your friends and colleagues (see more about methods of collecting information later in this chapter).

It is useful to get a package that allows you to test your site in development at different resolutions. For example, in Dreamweaver, any document window can be set with pre-set pixel measurements. Dreamweaver (see below) comes with a number of standard screen size settings, and you can choose from them by clicking on the *Window Size* button, which brings up the drop-down menu.

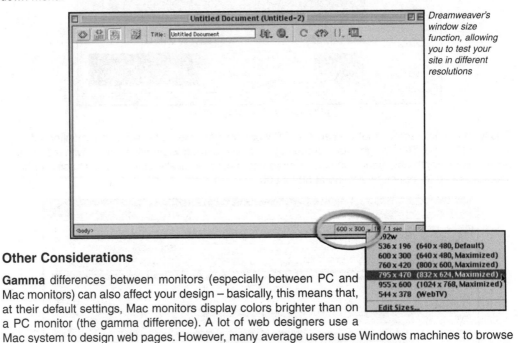

*Dreamweaver's window size function, allowing you to test your site in different resolutions*

## Other Considerations

**Gamma** differences between monitors (especially between PC and Mac monitors) can also affect your design – basically, this means that, at their default settings, Mac monitors display colors brighter than on a PC monitor (the gamma difference). A lot of web designers use a Mac system to design web pages. However, many average users use Windows machines to browse the Web. The simplest solution to this potential problem is to make sure you test your pages on both Windows machines and Macs before your pages go live on the Web.

Fireworks MX has an option to assist designers in optimizing graphics for viewing on other systems (for example, a designer using a Mac, who wants to know if their site looks OK on a PC). Opposite is an image in its original state, opened in Fireworks on a Mac.

If we go to the *View* menu and select the *Windows Gamma* option (this option will now be checked), the image will now appear in Fireworks as it would in default Window settings. From here, you can change or optimize the image to look its best if this is what the majority of your site users will be seeing.

While gamma may not make or break your site design, it can significantly change the appearance of your design as seen by your audience. Take the time to test your site on the platforms your audience use the most.

Other equipment variations that can affect how you would design your site include:

- User processor speed: Can they handle Flash or new browsers? QuickTime Movie downloads?

- Sound abilities: Does your design feature sound? What if your users don't have speakers or a sound card? It is generally recommended that you don't feature sound unnecessarily (for example, background soundtracks), but certain sites, such as a record company's web site, may feature downloadable sound clips.

## User Technical Knowledge

You also need to think about how familiar your target audience is with technology in general and how often or how much they want to use the Web. If a site demands a certain level of web experience, such as being able to download plugins or install new browser versions, then either the audience should be expected to know how to do this, instructions should be made easily available and easy to understand, or the site concept and design should be rethought (although often it's a simple matter of pressing *OK* a few times). What may be obvious to us – how to fill out a form, how to tell if a page is secure, even how to scroll to see more information – may be a new experience for some markets.

Let's look at a good example of providing sufficient help to a site's users. *Cooking.com* puts its *Help* option in clear view at the top-right of every screen. The *Help* page gives assistance in both using the site (Shopping Process/Check Out, Search Tips, Order Tracking, and so on), and in explaining various content areas (Wedding Registry, Gift Ideas, and Recipes).

*What may be obvious to us ... may be a new experience for some markets*

If it is known that the target audience has significant web experience, web-specific help may not be necessary, at least on the top level (although the *Cooking.com* site *Help* icon is noticeable, but still inconspicuous enough not to hamper the experience of those who don't need to use it).

*Cooking.com provides an easily accessible help page for its users*

Including links to sites that give significant help to web novices may suffice. If you think that a part of your audience will be web novices, include a link to an established web-instructional site, such as the BBC's WebWise (*http://www.bbc.co.uk/webwise/*):

*The BBC's Webwise site – providing technical help for Internet novices*

# How Do We Find Out About Site Users?

So, we know that the user experience is important and we need to find out who our users are and what they want if we are to improve it. But *how* do we find out about it, before and after the site is launched? The next few sections show us how.

## Ask!

There's no more straightforward way to get answers than asking questions. Questions can be as simple as "do you like our site?", but to get the most out of it, find out more specific information about your users, such as the things we looked at above. Another good question to ask is "what kind of services are they interested in?" – this will help you to customize a site's content and advertising pursuits.

One good way of collecting such results is using online surveys. For example, when entering the Yahoo! Maps area, users were asked to take a survey via a pop-up window (see right). The incentive of the possibility of winning cash is one option, the other is to choose *close window*, skip the survey and go on about our business.

*The pop-up window that takes you into the Yahoo! survey*

If the user accepts taking the survey, they are presented with:

1. A thank you for choosing the survey and what they might get for completing it.

2. Information about the survey, including privacy information and why this survey is being taken.

3. Feedback about where they are in the survey process.

4. Easy-to-decipher multiple-choice questions.

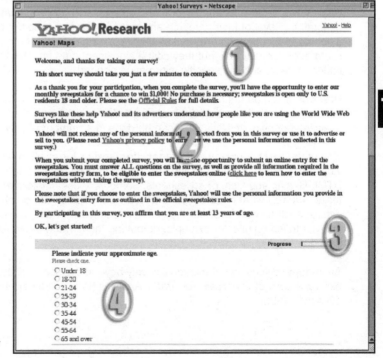

*A typical online survey*

At the end of the survey, the user fills out their personal information and enters the survey sweepstakes (see below). Yahoo! also includes an opt-in box for users to state that they'd like to participate in future studies.

You could easily put up a simple survey on your own web site by way of a simple form page, which e-mails the results to you, or even just some contact details and a request for feedback.

# Web Statistics

In general, statistics that are made available for public consumption are specific to the web market at large, rather than that of your target market. Sites such as Nielsen NetRatings (*http://www.nielsen-netratings.com*) and eMarketer (*http://www.emarketer.com*) post the most general, top level of their research and statistics for free, and then often charge significant amounts of money for more market-specific information. Research firms can also compile information for your use, but they cost a significant amount. This is a choice that depends on your budget, needs, and the specific information needed.

However, if you do not have the kind of capital available to invest in such statistics, and want to harvest some statistics that are more particular to your own site, you can always collect and analyze your own statistics. This can be done in a number of ways.

One of the most popular ways is **analyzing server logs**: when you are running a web site, your web server keeps log files, which detail all of the files requested from the server, whether they are HTML files, image files, or stylesheets. Some very useful information can be disseminated from these, such as what parts of your site are most popular, the demand for pages over time, and user details, such as what browser they used to access your site. You can use custom software to analyze these results, for example, outputting them into a database, and then representing the data graphically.

An in-depth discussion of this topic is way beyond the scope of this book – for more information, pick up a copy of *Practical Web Traffic Analysis* (Peter Fletcher et al, glasshaus 2002, ISBN: 1904151-18-3).

# Usability Testing

User testing ideally puts objective eyes on your project and either confirms that your design and structure works, or that it needs improvement. Objective site users can also give feedback and perspective that you and your client (or others that have been close to the site during its development or redesign) simply are unable to experience in any other way. Whether formal or informal, user testing can give improvement ideas, spur on new developments, help to improve navigation, or confirm that your design is right on the money. It all depends on what you want to find out. Testing methods fit into three different basic categories:

> User testing ideally puts objective eyes on your project.

**Diagnostic testing** works to identify problems in a site. Through diagnostic usability testing, ideally you find out what works, what doesn't, what needs simple improvements or changes, and what needs to be thrown out and redesigned from scratch. This type of testing is done during site development – earlier is generally better, because this gives you more time to fix any problems that are uncovered.

If you want to see how you measure up to your competition, **comparative testing** is what you're looking for. In this kind of testing, your site might be compared with one or more competitor's sites. Is there anything on their sites that you are lacking? Testers might also be presented with two or more design versions of the site to pick the best from. This is also obviously better done during the development of your site – if you decide that your site needs to be changed to measure up to your competition, the earlier you make this decision the better.

When the site is finished or almost finished, **verification testing** checks to see if the site is meeting the goals of the project and the client's satisfaction.

The specific pieces of information you should look for can be any of the following:

- Can someone easily purchase products from your site?

- When help or contacts details are required, are they readily available on your site?

- Is your site faster than your competitors' sites? Is their site easier to use?

- What kind of emotional reaction does your site's color scheme, icons, and layout give its users? Is it the kind of reaction you expected/wanted?

- Is your site accessible to those with visual impairments/cognitive disabilities? (This is very important, as we shall see in the section on Accessibility.)

- Do people enjoy using your site?

- Does your site give users the services they desire/were expecting?

Of course, there are a huge number of questions you could try to answer with regard to your web site – but the ones above are the sort of things you should be getting at.

There are all kinds of levels of user testing. You can start with asking people in your office, or even your friends and family, to check out a site and tell you what they like and dislike. Posting a note to a web-design mailing list asking for a site critique will often draw some very dramatic opinions, and very constructive feedback.

Some good mailing lists to go to for this kind of feedback are the **evolt.org** mailing list (see *http://evolt.org*), and the **WebDesign-L** mailing list (see *http://www.webdesign-l.com*). Both of these lists are well established, with large communities, who are made up of Web Developers, Web Designers, Information Architects, Usability Consultants, Database Developers, and web professionals from a number of other disciplines too. These community members are generally very enthusiastic, knowledgeable, and willing to help out. However, you should observe simple mailing list etiquette rules. For more details, see *Chapter 16*.

On the opposite end of the spectrum, more elaborate user testing can take place in facilities that are built specifically for that use, and include such setups as one-way mirrors, cameras that focus on the user's facial expressions and hand movements, video cameras from every angle, and experts to analyze all the various kinds of information gathered from this high-level interrogation method. This type of testing, of course, costs a lot of money, and you need to think about what you are prepared to pay for your usability testing, and what your budget will stretch to.

In between the very simple and very elaborate testing options are many other options. First of all, you can familiarize yourself with sites and newsletters published by professional usability firms, authors, practitioners, and pundits (see sidebar for some examples). This will give you a better idea of what you are looking for, and what kinds of questions to ask and tests to perform to find it.

**Creative Good** (*http://www.creativegood.com*), founded by Mark Hurst in 1997, was among the first usability firms specializing in web experiences. His e-mailed newsletter is free, and can be subscribed to at *http://www.creativegood.com/newsletter.html*.

The **Nielsen/Norman Group** (*http://www.nngroup.com*), founded by Donald Norman and Jakob Nielsen, does custom usability studies, as well as selling usability reports as varied as Web Usability for Senior Citizens to How to Conduct Usability Evaluations for Accessibility.

Those interested in communing with experienced usability experts and learning more about methodology as it applies to the Web can check out Jared Spool's **User Interface Conference**s (*http://www.uiconf.com*).

The talented team at **Adaptive Path** (*http://www.adaptivepath.com/*) travels around the US to bring usability workshops to developers.

**Usable Web**, maintained by Keith Instone (*http://www.usableweb.com*), is a popular source of information and a portal for usability and user-testing resources.

Let's take a look at proven methods of user testing – what the big usability boys do when they're testing users, what you want to learn from the testing, and determining whether or not it is crucial for you to hire an outside firm. Whether formal or informal, expensive or just the cost of a couple of pizzas, usability testing is definitely recommended.

## Types of Usability Testing

You will probably hear about many different trademarked names and consultancy-branded terms for different kinds of usability tests. However, basically what you need to know are the kinds of tests that can be useful to you in your web site development. Here are a few of the more popular methods:

**Coaching method:** This method involves face-to-face (or side-by-side) interaction between the person being tested and the site developer. The expert "coach," or the developer or person familiar with the site, answers tester's questions, and gives them pointers as they use the site. This is a lot like teaching a class about a site, and is a method most often used with users new to the web. The goal is to find out what kinds of direction these novices might need in relating to a site.

**Focus groups:** Focus groups are usually a group of about 5 to 10 chosen testers who are guided by an objective moderator to go through the testing process. The group discusses their opinions and experience with a site, and the moderator keeps them on topic, guides the discussion to various parts of the site, but otherwise lets them have freeform discussion. Typically, focus groups are held in rooms with one-way mirrors and microphones, so that you can listen in and watch the discussion without them being disturbed by your presence. It is important to ensure that the testers are at ease, and in as natural an environment as is possible in this situation.

**Thinking aloud:** The thinking aloud method encourages the person being tested to think out loud as they use a product, explaining their movements, and voicing their concerns and opinions.

**Performance measurement:** Performance measurement is a quantitative testing method, which gathers data about how test participants executed various tasks. For example, the test may have a number of users try to access a certain area of a site, time how long it takes them to get there, and count how many clicks it took to find. It can be used to test sites against one another, or to test the usability benchmarks of one site. This is one of the more formal testing methods, and is often used in conjunction with interviews and questionnaires, below.

**Question-asking:** This method is a lot like the thinking aloud test, but the persons giving the test ask direct questions about the site and the user answers questions out loud. This, in theory, helps the user verbalize their thoughts more clearly and thoroughly.

**Co-discovery learning, or constructive interaction:** This test puts two testers together, encouraging them to help each other and solve problems together. It's another thinking-aloud method that is believed will be more helpful than a question-asked or thinking aloud method, since researchers believe that people will be more direct with one another about problems and solutions when they are working together, rather than talking to someone related to the project.

**Questionnaires and interviews:** This method is the best one for remote testing, since questions can be e-mailed or mailed to testers, or they can be talked to over the phone, or questions can be posted online.

To choose what types of tests to employ, look at the resources you have available to allocate to the testing process. If you have a large cash budget at your disposal, then it is well worth employing a usability professional to carry out some tests for you, including focus groups and coaching, and performance measurement. This method usually benefits from thinking aloud or question asking.

If you haven't got very much money to spend on your testing, a much cheaper method to employ would be to direct some users to a test site and/or ask them to fill in a questionnaire, either offering them, say, an Amazon voucher, or hoping that they will contribute out of the goodness of their hearts.

You should also consider the amount of time you have to do the tests. If you are severely constrained by time, then it might be more worth your while getting some quick questionnaire feedback, rather than organizing a large, complicated focus group session.

## Types of Results

There are quite a few other formal ways of testing users, but there are only a limited number of results categories, all of which are beneficial to site development:

**Behavior:** Behavior results are the results of watching or recording a person's interaction and behavior with a web site. Watching people's behavior points out what parts of a site or page are difficult to use, fun, or don't get discovered at all.

**Opinion:** Opinions might be the hardest to deal with, but they are the criticisms and reflections that testers have about their experience with the site and thoughts about it in general. This can range from "I like the color scheme!" to "I don't understand these menu choices, they are confusing".

**Subjective:** Subjective results are influenced by emotion. As a site's designer, for example, you can't be objective about a site because it's your baby: you've invested time, effort, passion, and if it's your own, perhaps money into it, so it's impossible for you to be completely objective. Or you might love the site, but hate the client, or the other way around. Either way, the result is biased. Subjective results can be interesting, but aren't a true indicator of what the audience's reaction would be.

**Objective:** Objective results are the opposite of subjective results: they aren't affected by outside emotional influences. These results aren't biased and are more helpful to you as a developer.

**Qualitative:** Qualitative results are those that are based on opinion and experience, and can't be measured against one another.

**Quantitative:** Quantitative results can be counted and measured against one another: for example, you might keep track of how long it takes a number of different people to find a particular product on your site, or how many clicks it takes to make a purchase.

## Finding People to Test

Where do you find all these people to test, whether informal or formal, in person or online?

The first place to start is with your client's databases and mailing lists. If they have a customer newsletter, request that they include a notice that you are looking for users to test the client's new site. If they have an existing site and you've worked on a redesign, put out a notice on the current site for potential users. These people would be helpful in comparing the old and new sites, if they've had experience with it before.

Ask your client for the name of five or six employees from various parts of the company, such as one from marketing, one from sales, one from content, one long-term employee, one new hire, and so on, that haven't seen the new site yet. This will give you interesting insider information and a perspective that you or your client may have missed.

If these two options aren't available, placing advertisements in newspapers, online, or in flyers on college bulletin boards may find you a selection of people willing to put your site to the test. Be prepared to offer some sort of incentive – some research firms pay by the hour, some offer pizza and a beverage, some a T-shirt or other goodie. Try to keep it fair: if you're setting up a test that may take hours, it's asking a lot for a couple slices of pizza. A hungry tester may not be able to keep their objectivity.

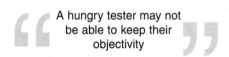

A hungry tester may not be able to keep their objectivity

Some companies even keep testing crews on their books, taken from the general public, so all the hard work finding the people is done for you. This is a useful type of service, although it often costs you a nominal fee to use.

## Scenarios

Before testing begins, spend some time with your client to come up with sample scenarios that you want testers to try. For example, if the site is a product catalog, the scenario you might want to set up is to direct testers to find a particular product, buy it, and check on their order. Give them a discount code, ask them to make an exchange or return, make them find out how much shipping will be to their house before they make a purchase. Give them a URL in the "middle" of the site, and ask them to find their way to the homepage. Ask them to give you their perspective of how big the site is, how many people work for the company, how reliable the business is. Figure out what you want to learn, and ask testers to try it.

# Accessibility

Last, but certainly not least, we will now look at the topic of Accessibility. Accessibility is a subset of usability, which refers to making web sites usable by those with disabilities, such as vision impairment or cognitive disabilities. It is of utmost importance that you make your sites as accessible as possible – your site's target audience will include some users with disabilities, and you want to appeal to as much of your target audience as possible. In addition, most accessibility measures will have an added bonus of improving the general usability of the site too.

Another thing to consider is that making sites accessible is not only the right thing to do – there also exists legislation that makes it illegal to discriminate against people with disabilities by making inaccessible sites, for example Section 508 in the US (see the section below), which requires that all electronic and information technology (including web sites) are accessible to people with disabilities.

There is not really much of an excuse to produce inaccessible sites these days. As you will see when you look at the guidelines referenced shortly, none of the techniques for making sites accessible are particularly difficult to implement, and as long as you write sites in well thought-out, standards-compliant markup, your sites should be largely accessible anyway.

Next we will look at a little history of the accessibility movement, and then go on to look at the guidelines available to help us make our sites accessible. We will also look at the software available to help test your sites for accessibility, and make it clear what you need to do to achieve accessibility.

This section is not a complete look at accessibility by any means, as an in-depth discussion would be beyond the scope of this book. It provides enough information to make you aware of the importance of these issues, able to make your sites accessible, and ready to go and find out more. For a complete look at the world of accessibility, pick up a copy of *Accessible Web Sites* (Jim Thatcher, Cynthia Waddell et al, glasshaus 2002, ISBN: 19041510-00-0).

## History

The web accessibility story started back in 1995, when technical accessibility issues were being uncovered with reference to online content. The issues arose partially because web technology was changing – the simple pure text environment was being shifted towards a more complicated, multimedia environment.

To address these issues, Cynthia Waddell wrote the first accessible web design standard for the local governing body of San Jose, California, in 1996. This standard was soon noticed from further afield, and similar practices were adopted by the whole US government. Accessibility standards are now being looked into by governments throughout the world.

As well as this legislation, there are other bodies that have taken an interest in promoting and teaching accessibility. For example, the W3C formed the Web Accessibility initiative (see *http://www.w3.org/WAI/*), which is dedicated to promoting accessibility among web developers, and authors of web authoring tools.

## Making Sites Accessible

As mentioned above, making sites accessible really isn't a difficult process. It usually involves nothing more than making sure that your sites are coded with well thought-out, standards-compliant markup. We won't include an exhaustive discussion of the specific coding techniques that need to be employed, as they can be found within the guidelines at the URLs included shortly. Let's have a look at the tools employed by users with disabilities, and then go over the guidelines you should follow to make sure your sites are accessible.

## Accessibility Tools

The most common tools you will come across are special browsers and applications that "speak" the contents of the web page, to enable them to be used by users who are visually impaired. These are called **voice browsers** and **screen readers**. Good examples of these programs are:

- JAWS for Windows: see http://www.freedomscientific.com/fs_products/software_jaws.asp.

- Window-Eyes: see http://www.gwmicro.com/windoweyes/windoweyes.htm.

- IBM's Home Page Reader: http://www-3.ibm.com/able/hpr.html.

Since these browsers read out the text on a web page for the user, you can run into problems if you start to use lots of pictures on your web site. Remember the complicated sliced page layouts we met in *Chapter 6*? These are not very accessible, as a screen reader cannot read out textual content if it is contained within an image, and will instead read out something like "image", every time it encounters one. It is wise to represent important textual information as text, not images. If you must use multiple images, then make sure each `<img>` element has got meaningful information contained within its `alt` attribute.

Another disadvantage of having textual content as images on a site is that if, say, a user who is partially sighted attempts to use a text-resizing function in a normal web browser (such as Internet Explorer) to make the text larger, and therefore easier for them to read, the text won't resize.

Table layouts can also cause problems – as we have already learned in *Chapter 6*, screen readers generally read out table cells from left to right, taking each column in turn. This will cause your web site to not make sense if you have employed an unusual table layout.

Also, it is important to use structural HTML elements, rather than the old-fashioned presentational ones. This is because screen readers will interpret structural elements such as `<em>`, `<h1>`, and `<strong>` appropriately, for example, raising the tone of the voice used to indicate emphasis.

These are only a few examples of how proper, valid markup aids accessibility. For more details, check out the following URLs.

## The Web Accessibility Initiative

The **Web Accessibility Initiative** (see *http://www.w3.org/WAI/*) was launched by the W3C in 1997, to "promote and achieve web functionality for people with disabilities." The most significant W3C Recommendation they have produced, in terms of relevance to web developers, is the **Web Content Accessibility Guidelines** (WCAG), released in 1999, which can be found at *http://www.w3.org/TR/WCAG10*. This is where you can find pretty much all you need to make your web site accessible.

For quick reference, you can find a full list of all the points you need to be aware of to make a web site accessible (called **checkpoints**) at *http://www.w3.org/TR/1999/WAI-WEBCONTENT-19990505/full-checklist*.

Basically, these checkpoints are organized into three priority levels, based on their impact on the accessibility of a site. These priorities are as follows (quotation taken from the above URL):

- "[Priority 1]: A web content developer must satisfy this checkpoint. Otherwise, one or more groups will find it impossible to access information in the document. Satisfying this checkpoint is a basic requirement for some groups to be able to use web documents."

- "[Priority 2] A web content developer should satisfy this checkpoint. Otherwise, one or more groups will find it difficult to access information in the document. Satisfying this checkpoint will remove significant barriers to accessing web documents."

- "[Priority 3] A web content developer may address this checkpoint. Otherwise, one or more groups will find it somewhat difficult to access information in the document. Satisfying this checkpoint will improve access to web documents. "

## Section 508

The US Access Board published a specification called the **Electronic and Information Technology Accessibility Standards** in late 2000, pursuant to the US rulemaking process as required by **Section 508 of the Rehabilitation Act Amendments** of 1998 (or simply Section 508). (The Section 508 guidelines are based on the WCAG.)

The particular bits of Section 508 that really relate to software and web developers are **Software Applications** (Section 508 Subpart B CFR 1194.21) and **Web-based intranet and Internet Information and Applications** (Section 508 Subpart B CFR 1194.22). These can be found at *http://www.access-board.gov/sec508/guide/index.htm* – see the second and third links on the page.

# Accessibility Testing

As with all aspects of web site development, testing is one of the most important things you can do. You'll be pleased to hear that there are many software packages available that are dedicated to testing sites to see if they are accessible. These programs are mostly fairly simple – when given a URL to go to or a web page to look at, they will trawl through the web material given to them, and return a report detailing exactly what needs to be done to a web page/site to make it accessible, including any checkpoints it had violated, and the fixes required. Two of the more popular accessibility testing tools are as follows:

- **Bobby**: Available at *http://bobby.watchfire.com/bobby/html/en/index.jsp*, there is a downloadable version of Bobby available that can be bought (follow the link on the above page), but there is also an online version available at the above URL – it requires you to enter a URL of a web page you wish to test, and then choose to validate it against either the Section 508, or the WCAG guidelines. When you submit the URL, it will return a report to you, detailing what needs to be done to make the web page accessible. The online version can only test single pages at a time, whereas you can get the downloadable version to test batches.

- **Lift**: This is available from *http://www.usablenet.com*, and is reasonably costly, but worthwhile. It produces similar reports to Bobby, but has some useful extra features, such as a validation function that checks to see if it thinks that the alt attribute content you have provided for your <img> tags adequately describes the image. There is also a version of Lift that can be integrated with Dreamweaver: it is rather usefully integrated with the Dreamweaver IDE.

There are other tools out there, but these are two of the better ones available.

# Summary

Concentrating on making a site usable takes more effort than you'd first think, even after you've chosen the right technologies to code it in, and you've got a good design for it (which you should be able to do very well, if you've read the rest of the book up to here). It's not just making a good site that matters – you also need to deliver a site that's right for your target audience. This chapter should have given you a good idea of how to work out who that audience are, and how to best cater for their needs, even if they include people with disabilities.

Testing is particularly important, both during development and afterwards, as a constant companion to site maintenance. Often site developers conduct usability testing a number of times during the site's development, rather than waiting until the entire project is over and ready to launch. Catching problems along the way gives you the opportunity to fix things along the way, too.

After the site launches, it's invaluable to have a mechanism with which site users can continue to offer feedback. Even if it's only a feedback e-mail address, make sure you give them a way to contact you, and invite them to send you ideas and criticisms. There is only one sure agreement among everyone who advocates user testing: just do it. And use it to make your site better.

11

# 12

- What are the standards and why are they important?

- HTML and XHTML DOCTYPES

- Validation of your site

**Author: Rachel Andrew**

# Standards Compliance

The importance of complying with standards cannot be over-emphasized. In this chapter I will explain why validating your web pages against the standards for HTML, XHTML, and CSS is so vital. I will also give you some advice on how to go about working to the official recommendations.

## What Are These "Standards" Anyway?

Standards are rules that specify how markup languages, such as HTML, and stylesheets, such as CSS, should be written. Most are **open standards**, meaning they are freely available to be viewed and used by anyone.

Open standards allow the Web to be a fully accessible medium. Any manufacturer of a piece of software (be that a traditional browser, a PDA, or software to be used by screen readers or Braille readers) can view the standards and know exactly what its software will need to be able to do.

What would happen if the standards weren't available? HTML and JavaScript have evolved due to input from competing browser manufacturers who have added to and changed the basic markup. While these additions were made in order to allow people to create more interesting and visually pleasing effects, those made for one browser often do not work in another, and do not take into account future devices that may need to access the Web.

Open standards offer a consistent, non-proprietary feature set, for the language they define. Device manufacturers can then build to this, to ensure that their device will be able to display or read documents in the way that the document's authors intended. Ideally, open standards should also mean that web professionals can be sure that if their pages are built to the standards they will display correctly in any device that supports those standards.

While this probably sounds like common sense, in reality today's Web is a mish-mash of web pages built using different proprietary types of markup or with non-valid use of markup. Furthermore, browsers do not always display standards-compliant code correctly. This may be because they don't actually implement the standards properly, or it may be that different browser manufacturers have interpreted the standards slightly differently; each of which may be regarded as a "correct" interpretation.

One reason for the problem is the way that the Web has developed and evolved. Browser manufacturers have led the way, adding new extensions to the basic HTML, which was originally designed to mark up very simple documents. Different browser manufacturers added different extensions, and this reached a head several years ago, with developers having to create two completely different web sites, and direct their visitors to the correct one for the browser that they were using to view the site (Internet Explorer or Netscape). Additionally, some web browsers were complex enough to work out sloppy markup and still display it as the author intended, even though they shouldn't have. This meant that for many designers, checking that the site worked in the two main browsers became all that mattered, and the validity of the markup as a whole was not deemed important by them.

With the rise of alternative browsing devices, however, and a growing need to create sites that are accessible to all web users, the issues surrounding web standards have become more important. Building one site for Netscape and one for Internet Explorer might have been no big deal, but building a different site for every possible browsing device is impossible – there are new devices appearing all the time.

## The W3C

In various chapters of this book, we have mentioned the W3C in association with the HTML, XHTML, and CSS standards.

The W3C was created in 1994. To quote its own web site (*http://www.w3.org/Consortium/Points/*) the aim was to "lead the World Wide Web to its full potential by developing common protocols that promote its evolution and ensure its interoperability". In other words, to ensure that the technologies being created for the Web used open standards that could work together. The W3C is where many of these standards are created, and it is where you can find out what those standards actually are, how to use them, and even how to check whether your site validates against them.

The W3C does not just arbitrarily pass down recommendations from on high, however. It consults with, and has on its membership, browser manufacturers, large companies, and those who work in the web business, to help shape the future of web standards. The full list of members can be found on the W3C web site at *http://www.w3.org/Consortium/Member/List*.

The W3C divides the areas it is working on into what it calls **Activities**. To get a snapshot of what the W3C is doing at any given time, you can visit the list of their Activities at *http://www.w3.org/Consortium/Activities*. The groups working on each activity produce various documents, which are made publicly available. Firstly, there are **Notes**, which are simply dated reports from the group working on an Activity. **Working Drafts** represent work in progress on defining a technology, and demonstrate the W3C's commitment to working in this area. **Candidate Recommendations** have had extensive community feedback, and constitute a call for comments from those outside of the W3C. These then become **Proposed Recommendations**, indicating that the group working on the Activity has reached consensus. Finally, they become **Recommendations**, which are the documents that the W3C wishes to see used for widespread adoption.

The specifications that you will find on the W3C web site, and which I shall refer to throughout this chapter, aren't always the easiest things to read. They are written as technical specifications, rather than as user manuals. However, after you've worked with the languages for a while, they become easier to follow, and luckily there are many resource web sites available where people have studied the standards and written helpful tutorials on how to use them. I have ended this chapter with a list of such resources that will help you to get started.

# Standards for the Web

There are a variety of languages used on the Web that the W3C develops open standards for. These include structural languages, such as HTML, XHTML, and XML (which we looked at in *Chapter 4*), presentational languages, such as CSS (see *Chapter 8*), and scripting standards such as Document Object Models. JavaScript, which we covered in *Chapters 9* and *10*, isn't a standard of the W3C. Instead, it is based on **ECMAScript**, a standard developed by the **European Computer Manufacturers Association** (*http://www.ecma.ch*).

## Structural Languages

Structural languages for the Web include HTML, XHTML, and XML. These are the languages used to define the structure of web documents. As we discussed within *Chapter 8*, when talking about the separation of content and document structure from presentation, structural languages should not be primarily used to define how the content appears. That said, browsers have built-in defaults that render this structure in a clear and consistent manner, making headings larger and bolder, for instance, displaying paragraph breaks, and creating bulleted lists, etc. These defaults are, in the main, taken from the W3C recommendations, but their interpretation is not the same across all browsers – especially in the case of the older browsers. The situation is improving as manufacturers seek to work to the same recommendations, however.

### HTML

HTML is the original markup language created for the Web. It is based on an older standard called **SGML (Standard Generalized Markup Language)**, which is a far more complex language. The current version of HTML is 4.01, but on the W3C web site you can discover standards for the previous versions, as follows:

- 4.0 (*http://www.w3.org/TR/1998/REC-html40-19980424/*)
- 3.2 (*http://www.w3.org/TR/REC-html32*)
- 2.0 (*http://www.w3.org/MarkUp/html-spec/*)

HTML 4.01 will be the last version of HTML. It is recommended that web authors create new documents to an XHTML DTD, rather than HTML. In practice this means that most authors will be working to the XHTML 1.0 DTD.

### XML

Extensible Markup Language (XML) is a subset of SGML. Like SGML, it is a set of rules that other languages should follow. Because, like SGML, it defines a "grammar" rather than the actual "words" of a language, the tags are not predefined. A markup language that follows the rules set in XML is known as an **XML vocabulary**. You can create a DOCTYPE of your own to describe an XML vocabulary. This DOCTYPE will define the tags that you use within your document.

For example, you could have an XML application whose documents described your shopping list – like this:

```
<shopping>
  <food>
    <item>eggs</item>
    <item>bread</item>
  </food>
  <drink>
    <item>beer</item>
  </drink>
</shopping>
```

XML vocabularies allow the easy transfer of data between software applications, as long as the applications understand what to do with any language that follows the XML rules. Your first experience of XML is, however, likely to be through XHTML.

For more information on XML, see *Chapter 4*, or try *Practical XML for the Web* (glasshaus, 2002, 194151086) for a detailed look.

### XHTML

XHTML 1.0 is a reformulation of HTML 4.0 to follow the rules of XML 1.0. As there will be no further versions of HTML, it is best to create new documents in XHTML rather than HTML. While HTML is not going to disappear any time soon, XHTML is very close in syntax and (in its transitional form) is backwards-compatible, if you follow the basic rules explained in *Chapter 4*. It does not require a great learning curve, either, so there is little to be gained by remaining with HTML markup at this point.

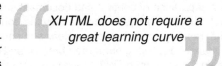

*XHTML does not require a great learning curve*

## Presentational Languages

CSS is the main presentational language of the Web. As discussed in *Chapter 8*, there are currently three levels of CSS recommended by the W3C.

### CSS Level 1

CSS Level 1 deals mainly with the styling of text elements on the page. It includes rules to define the fonts, sizes of lettering, and colors of the text used in your documents. It has wide and relatively consistent support in browsers from version 4 upwards. You can read the specification on the W3C web site (*http://www.w3.org/TR/REC-CSS1*).

### CSS Level 2

The CSS Level 2 recommendation is built on CSS Level 1 and has added support for positioning elements, media descriptors, and other more advanced features – many of which we discussed in *Chapter 8*. The support for CSS level 2 is relatively good across the newer browsers (IE 5 and upwards, Netscape 6 and upwards, Mozilla, Konqueror, and Opera). However, if you are using CSS Level 2 you will need to ensure that you are testing your site in a range of different browsers, since the implementations vary slightly, and you may well need to work around some browser bugs. You can find the specification on the W3C web site (*http://www.w3.org/TR/REC-CSS2/*).

### CSS Level 3

The CSS Level 3 recommendations are part of the W3C's current work on CSS. More details can be found at *http://www.w3.org/Style/CSS/current-work*, and we discussed some of the changes that are to be implemented in *Chapter 8*. Browsers do not yet support this level as it is currently being developed. Future browsers can be expected to, as it becomes a recommendation.

## Object Models

The Document Object Model being worked on by the W3C is often known as the 'W3C DOM'. We will not go into great detail here, but it is an application programming interface (API) for manipulating the appearance and contents of a document by way of scripts. **DHTML** uses the DOM in order to create drop-down menus and other dynamic client-side effects.

Until the W3C produced their DOM recommendations, both Internet Explorer and Netscape had their own different proprietary DOMs, which caused much confusion and extra work for web developers. In the case of Netscape 6 and upwards, this proprietary DOM has been completely replaced by the W3C version, while in Internet Explorer it has been added to the existing DOM. Therefore we are moving towards a time where you will no longer need to write code twice in order to cope with both Netscape and Internet Explorer. A script that uses the W3C DOM should behave identically in any browser. More information about the W3C DOM can be found at *http://www.w3.org/DOM/DOMTR*.

## ECMAScript

ECMAScript is a standard scripting language, which is mainly based on Netscape's JavaScript. It was developed in order to enable more consistency between the implementations of JavaScript in the various web browsers.

## Other Languages

The W3C also works on recommendations for many other languages, such as:

● Scalable Vector Graphics (SVG): *http://www.w3.org/Graphics/SVG/*

● Mathematical Markup Language (MathML): *http://www.w3.org/Math/*

If you are interested in the direction that the Web is going in, keep an eye on the W3C web site.

# Why Is Complying with the Standards Important?

If sloppy, non-valid markup displays correctly in the majority of mainstream browsers, you might wonder why it is still important to write documents that comply with the standards. However, there are a whole host of reasons why you should take the time to ensure that your documents do validate.

**12**

# Future Proofing

The latest generation of web browsers is the most standards-compliant ever: browser manufacturers have finally realized that standards are a good idea.

When Netscape brought out their version 6 browser, they dropped backwards-compatibility for many of the hacks and proprietary code that had been developed for their earlier version 4 browsers. Instead, they developed a browser that complied with the W3C recommendations. A phasing out of support for invalid markup like this could easily happen again, as mainstream browsers continue down the path of compliance with the W3C recommendations. So if you write non-standard markup, it may not even be readable in future browsers!

Additionally, many of the presentational tricks that are in common use today, are exploitations of browser behaviors. There is nothing to say that a newer version of the browser will behave in the same way. Validating your document will give you the peace of mind that your web site won't break in the latest and greatest version of Internet Explorer, Netscape, or some other browser.

# Accessibility

As you have seen in *Chapter 11*, accessibility is becoming a legal requirement in many countries. Even where it isn't, ensuring that everyone can use your site is an excellent aim. Should laws be applied to the area in which you are creating your site in the future, you will not need to begin rebuilding in order to comply with them.

Meeting the terms of the web standards will assist in ensuring that your web site is accessible to those with disabilities. Although it is still possible to create an inaccessible site, when you do stick to the standards, one thing that is certain, is that if you don't stick to them, your site is very unlikely to be accessible. Using standards gives a greater chance that devices such as screen readers and Braille readers can interpret the markup you present them with. With a solid base of valid markup, you will be on a surer footing towards ensuring that your site is accessible to all.

# Browser Independence

Writing markup to the standards means that the greatest possible number of browsers will be able to access your content. The way that these standards are created means that older browsers will still be able to understand the structure of your document and (while they may not get all the effects that you have created for the newer browsers) the content will still be legible.

PDAs and other devices that are limited in their rendering capabilities often do not have the processing power to work out what to do with presentational hacks and non-standard code, and can only correctly display content marked up to the standards. Standard markup is also easier to convert into other formats, which enables you to easily move your content between media.

# Ease of Debugging

If you are working to standards, then you can validate against those standards. We will cover validation in more detail later in this chapter but, in short, **validation** means that you run your code through a process to check whether your markup adheres to the standard, and obtain a list of any errors that you need to fix. Often, by just validating and fixing the errors that are flagged up, you can isolate and correct a display problem that you are having.

If you post to design and development related mailing lists with a problem, you are likely to get a much better response if you can demonstrate that you have validated your markup and that this has not corrected the problem. It also makes it easier for someone to look over your code in order to give help and advice. In all, you are more likely to receive helpful replies to your queries.

## Working as a Team

Working to the standards also makes it easier for other people working on your project (or taking it over after you), to pick up where you left off. Many designers create HTML pages that will be used as templates for a Content Management System or other dynamic site. By creating templates that validate against a DOCTYPE (which we'll deal with next) you will make it far easier for those who then need to incorporate that design into the final web site. You'll also look more like a professional who knows what they are doing – neat, valid markup looks far more impressive than a tangled mess of incorrectly nested tags, and proprietary code.

# DOCTYPES

Recall that we defined DOCTYPES in *Chapters 2* and *4*, and showed them in use in Dreamweaver MX. In order to create a standards-compliant XHTML document, you must first include a DOCTYPE at the very top of your document, before the `<html>` tag, that will tell the browser what standard the document adheres to. It must also be included for you to be able to validate your document, since it tells the validator which version of XHTML you are validating against. Therefore you must select the correct DOCTYPE for your document.

In this section we will discuss which DOCTYPEs you should use. Also, on the CD, you will find a selection of template pages that are a basic starting point for standards-compliant documents with correct DOCTYPEs.

## Which DOCTYPE Should I Use on My Site?

Your first choice is whether you are to work in HTML (of which the latest version that I shall assume use of is 4.01) or XHTML. Remember that if you select an XHTML DOCTYPE, but then write HTML markup, or an HTML DOCTYPE and then write XHTML markup, you will find that your page does not validate, even though it may validate against another DOCTYPE.

### HTML 4.01

You have three choices of HTML 4.01 DOCTYPE – **Strict**, **Transitional**, or **Frameset**.

### HTML 4.01 Strict

If you wish to code to, and validate against, HTML 4.01 Strict, the DOCTYPE that should start your documents looks like this:

```
<!DOCTYPE HTML PUBLIC "-//W3C//DTD HTML 4.01//EN"
    "http://www.w3.org/TR/html4/strict.dtd">
```

Coding to HTML 4.01 Strict, means that you cannot include in your document any elements that are deprecated in the HTML 4.01 recommendation, which can be found at *http://www.w3.org/TR/html401/*. These deprecated elements, which we discussed in *Chapter 4*, include `<font>` and other presentational tags; so if you are coding to the Strict DOCTYPE it is assumed you will be making use of CSS in order to style your document. You also may not use frames when using this DTD. Your document should be well-structured and easily accessible to different browsing devices.

### HTML 4.01 Transitional

The DOCTYPE for use with HTML 4.01 Transitional is as follows:

```
<!DOCTYPE HTML PUBLIC "-//W3C//DTD HTML 4.01 Transitional//EN"
   "http://www.w3.org/TR/html4/loose.dtd">
```

This DOCTYPE still follows the HTML 4.01 recommendation, but allows the use of the deprecated presentational elements and attributes that would not validate against a Strict DOCTYPE.

### HTML 4.01 Frameset

If you are creating a document that uses frames, then you should validate against the HTML 4.01 Frameset DOCTYPE:

```
<!DOCTYPE HTML PUBLIC "-//W3C//DTD HTML 4.01 Frameset//EN"
   "http://www.w3.org/TR/html4/frameset.dtd">
```

This is a variant of HTML 4.01 Transitional that allows for the use of frames (which are, themselves, deprecated).

## XHTML 1.0

As with HTML 4.01, XHTML 1.0 has three versions – **Strict**, **Transitional**, and **Frameset**.

### XHTML 1.0 Strict

The DOCTYPE for XHTML 1.0 Strict is shown here:

```
<!DOCTYPE html PUBLIC "-//W3C//DTD XHTML 1.0 Strict//EN"
   "http://www.w3.org/TR/xhtml1/DTD/xhtml1-strict.dtd">
```

As with HTML 4.01, you will only be able to validate against the Strict DOCTYPE if you ensure that you have not included any deprecated elements within your markup. These deprecated elements again include the presentational elements deprecated in HTML 4.01 but also includes the `name` attribute used in identifying form fields, images and frames. You should use the `id` attribute instead – see *http://www.w3.org/TR/xhtml1/diffs.html#h-4.10*

### XHTML 1.0 Transitional

The DOCTYPE for XHTML 1.0 Transitional is:

```
<!DOCTYPE html PUBLIC "-//W3C//DTD XHTML 1.0 Transitional//EN"
   "http://www.w3.org/TR/xhtml1/DTD/xhtml1-transitional.dtd">
```

The transitional DOCTYPE will allow the use of the deprecated elements that aren't allowed by the XHTML Strict DOCTYPE. For most people, this will be the XHTML DOCTYPE that they will validate against, since, for the sake of backwards-compatibility,there are a variety of deprecated elements that are necessary use of the now deprecated `name` attribute is still necessary for forms. Validating against a Transitional DOCTYPE for the sake of backwards-compatibility means that you can make the move to XHTML without cutting out those who are using older browsers. As the number of older browsers diminishes to a level where you feel it is acceptable to move to the Strict DOCTYPE, simply changing the DOCTYPE and running it through the validator will flag up those elements that will need to be removed or changed, to allow you to validate as Strict.

### XHTML 1.0 Frameset

The DOCTYPE for XHTML 1.0 Frameset is:

```
<!DOCTYPE html PUBLIC "-//W3C//DTD XHTML 1.0 Frameset//EN"
    "http://www.w3.org/TR/xhtml1/DTD/xhtml1-frameset.dtd">
```

As with the HTML 4.01 Frameset DOCTYPE, this is a version of the Transitional DOCTYPE that allows for the use of frames.

## XHTML 1.1

After XHTML version 1.0, the W3C developed the concept of **XHTML Modularization**. This is a way of separating the markup elements into various modules or groups. Browsers can then choose whether or not to implement various modules of elements, to enable code written using elements from those modules to be displayed.

**XHTML 1.1** is a set of these modules that most nearly corresponds to the markup elements within XHTML 1.0. However, it moves away from the legacy of HTML and the deprecated elements that were carried forward into XHTML 1.0 Transitional. It also does not include any elements needed for frames. The average web professional is not using XHTML 1.1 at this time, due to concerns about lack of backwards-compatibility. If you wanted to experiment with validating against an XHTML 1.1 DOCTYPE, however, there is only one DOCTYPE and it is:

```
<!DOCTYPE html PUBLIC "-//W3C//DTD XHTML 1.1//EN"
    "http://www.w3.org/TR/xhtml11/DTD/xhtml11.dtd">
```

## XHTML Basic

One other version of XHTML is **XHTML Basic**. This, like XHTML 1.1, is a set of modules, but it only includes the fewest number of modules needed to display very simple documents. This version of XHTML is suitable for use on low-power browsers such as those used on cell phones or PDAs.

## That DOCTYPE Broke My Layout!

In my initial discussion on the importance of web standards, I mentioned that browsers were beginning to work towards full support for web standards. In many cases, this has meant that they lose backwards-compatibility with older versions of the same browser.

**12**

Mozilla, Netscape 6, and Internet Explorer 6 attempt to assist developers by enabling their browsers to switch between ways of rendering documents. If your document has a complete DOCTYPE (like those listed above, and in the sample documents), then the browser will attempt to render your page in standards-compliant mode, displaying CSS and XHTML in the manner that the recommendations lay out. However, if you use an incomplete DOCTYPE such as:

```
<!DOCTYPE HTML PUBLIC "-//W3C//DTD HTML 4.01 Transitional//EN">
```

…or no DOCTYPE at all, then the browser will switch into its **"quirks mode"**, rendering your pages as they might have appeared in Internet Explorer 4 or Netscape 4.

If you are building a brand new web site, then this behavior should not concern you at all. If you start out with the full DOCTYPE, then you will be testing your pages in browsers that are rendering in a standards-compliant manner. Where you may find problems, is where you add a DOCTYPE to a page that previously had no DOCTYPE, and therefore was created and tested in older browsers, or in newer browsers that were running in "quirks mode".

Having an incomplete DOCTYPE is better than none at all, however. Should you need to add a DOCTYPE in order to validate an existing page and find that the addition of the full DOCTYPE breaks the layout, adding the DOCTYPE without the URL is an option. An important point to bear in mind, however, is that since we do not know whether future browsers will incorporate this kind of DOCTYPE switching, it is advisable to test with and use the correct and full DOCTYPE on all new web sites that you build.

# Web Standards and Visual Authoring Environments

Visual Authoring Environments, such as Macromedia Dreamweaver and Microsoft FrontPage, tend to get a bad press, when it comes to their ability to write good, standards-compliant XHTML. The problem with any program that generates XHTML for you, is that much of its output relies on the competence of the person who is using the tool. There can be good and bad pages created with exactly the same tool because of the user's skill (or lack of it).

> *first learn how to hand-code the markup yourself*

If you are new to XHTML, then my advice would be to first learn how to hand-code the markup yourself. In doing so, you will get an understanding of how to use the language. Even if you then move on to using an authoring tool, you will have enough knowledge to be able to go into the code and fix any errors that the tool may introduce which might prevent your pages validating. Authoring tools can save you a huge amount of time and can be very useful if you learn how to use the tool well, and understand the markup it creates.

Visual authoring environments tend to be very feature-rich and include a whole host of different ways to add to your web pages. Many of these ways will use good, standards-compliant HTML but others will not. You should be careful of the temptation to use these tools as if they are word processors. Always keep in mind the underlying code that you are creating. Most tools give you an option to view the XHTML either while you are writing it, or by launching a code view window, so that you can see what the tool is adding to your document.

## Macromedia Dreamweaver MX

The latest version of Macromedia Dreamweaver has addressed many problems with the creation of standards-compliant code found in previous versions of the product. Dreamweaver MX now inserts a DOCTYPE by default and, as shown in *Chapter 4*, you can choose whether to work in HTML or XHTML.

The markup added by Dreamweaver when working in *Design View* validates against the HTML 4.01 or XHTML DOCTYPEs. With careful use, it is possible to create pages that will validate without ever going into the sourcecode. To further assist the designer who wishes to create valid markup, Dreamweaver MX includes a built-in validator for HTML and XHTML, which will assist in flagging up any errors early on without having to make the page live.

While this latest version of Dreamweaver is the most standards-compliant ever, Dreamweaver has always tended to create solid, standards-based HTML, even in previous versions. The code it adds does not contain any proprietary, browser-specific markup, bar a few specific instances where it does so to ensure backward-compatibility for certain DHTML effects in browsers with proprietary DOMs, such as Netscape 4.

## Microsoft FrontPage

Microsoft FrontPage is another common authoring environment. Unfortunately it has very little support for standards, at present. The tool has made some moves to help those who need to create sites that are accessible, but running the average FrontPage-generated web site through the W3C's validator (which we discuss in detail soon), not only flags up incorrect usage of standard HTML tags, but also often shows up several proprietary Microsoft tags that do not exist in the specification at all.

You will probably find that you need to do a great deal of work on the site in a text editor before it will validate without errors, if you develop in FrontPage.

## Adobe GoLive

Adobe GoLive 6.0 has also added more support to its previous versions, for those working to web standards. It includes a syntax checker, which will allow you to check your document against the DOCTYPE you are using from within the environment itself. It also allows you to code in both HTML and XHTML, and use CSS extensively on your web site.

In a similar fashion to Macromedia with Dreamweaver MX, Adobe seems to have begun to really embrace web standards with their latest release. Along with the far better standards support in modern browsers, this is a clear indication of the direction that the Web is moving in. "Web standards" is becoming a selling point, both for software and developers, which is another reason to get with the program!

# Validation

I have talked about validation in general terms throughout this chapter, so here we'll find out how to actually do it. Validating your markup gives it a rubber stamp of approval as being correctly marked up to the requirements of the DOCTYPE you have used at the top of your document.

**12**

# Validating HTML and XHTML

You can validate your markup at the W3C web site, at various other online validation services, and also by using offline validators, including those incorporated into authoring environments such as Dreamweaver MX.

## The W3C Web Site Online Document Validator

To validate your XHTML syntax at the W3C web site, visit the validator at: *http://validator.w3.org/*.

The simplest way to validate a page is to upload the page to your web server and type the address of the page into the *Address* box on the W3C Validator web site, under the "*Validate by URI*" heading. You can leave the *Character encoding* and *Document type* boxes set at *detect automatically* unless you have not specified either of these in the document, or wish to see if the document will validate to a different DTD than the one on the page. The other checkboxes on this page can be helpful in debugging your document. *Show Source* will show you the entire source code for the document with line numbers, which can help you spot the line with the problem the validator has flagged up. *View outline* shows your document as defined by the heading levels which can help you to see how well-structured your page is. The other two checkboxes show you the tree structure as parsed by the validator and you probably don't need to worry about them. If you want to see what they do, just check them and run the validator.

With the address of the page in the *Address* box, click on the *Validate this Page* button. The validator will run through your document and produce a detailed report of any errors it finds. Should it find no errors, it will inform you of that fact and give you details of how to place a small button on your site declaring that your site is valid HTML or XHTML.

Of course, you do not *need* to use these buttons, but if validating your site has been a personal triumph, you might feel that you would like to show that you have made the grade! Many personal web sites display these buttons as much to show support for validating to the W3C standards as for any personal acclaim. Of course, you may also validate anyone else's web site by simply typing the URL into the validator.

If your documents are not online and you wish to check them with the validator, it is possible to validate by uploading your document to the W3C site. To do so, visit *http://validator.w3.org/file-upload.html* and follow the instructions there.

## Offline Validators

There are a variety of offline validators that you can use to check your site while you are working on it. I mentioned earlier in this chapter that Dreamweaver MX has its own built-in validator and this is a powerful and easy-to-use tool should you be already working with Dreamweaver MX. We walked through this tool for a sample document in *Chapter 4*. Personally, I always validate just before going live with a page using the W3C validator, to get a final stamp of approval, but offline tools are useful when developing a site, to check you're not introducing problems as you go along.

There are also standalone HTML validators and clean-up tools available such as:

- The CSE HTML validator, available from http://htmlvalidator.com/ for Windows

- A Real Validator available from http://arealvalidator.com/ also available for Windows

- HTML Tidy available for a wide variety of platforms at http://tidy.sourceforge.net/

## Validating CSS

The W3C also has a validator for CSS, and, just as with your HTML and XHTML markup, you should always run your CSS through this validator in order to ensure its conformance with the recommendations. To do this, visit *http://jigsaw.w3.org/css-validator/*. There you will find three ways in which to check your CSS file.

The simplest way is to upload your CSS file to your server and validate it by entering the URI of the CSS file or of an XHTML file that has embedded or inline CSS into the *Address* box, as we did for the HTML Validator, above.

Alternatively, you may upload your stylesheet to the site, or choose the *Validate your cascading style sheet with a text area* option, to copy and paste your CSS into a form (*http://jigsaw.w3.org/css-validator/validator-text.html*).

However you submit your stylesheet, the Validator will return with either a list of the errors and warnings that it has found or a congratulatory message and details of the little button you might want to display alongside your XHTML button on your web site.

CSS tools, such as Bradsoft's Topstyle (a version of which comes with Dreamweaver MX), also offer CSS validation right from the interface. If you are using such a tool, you will find that validating your CSS can become part of your workflow whenever you create a stylesheet.

## Validating Dynamic Pages

Dynamic pages (those where some or all of the data within them is pulled from a database, and those pages that are made up of server-side includes), can be tricky to validate since the page may be displayed in a number of different configurations depending on the parameters sent to it. Often, dynamic sites are based on a template

*make test validations of as many pages or states that the site can be rendered in as possible*

system whereby there is a base design that content is pulled into. A good starting point is to validate that base design before beginning to add dynamic content (or passing it over to your developer if you are working in a team). Once the site is created, make test validations of as many pages or states that the site can be rendered in as possible, to reassure yourself that the site still validates. Pages that contain server-side code will need to be uploaded to the Web in order to validate them, as the validator parses them after they have been through the web server and turned any server-side scripting into XHTML.

## Interpreting Validator Error Messages

The messages that the validator produces when it finds something that it doesn't like can seem strange. The best tactic is to take the messages one at a time. Often, you'll find that fixing one error will seem to fix a multitude of other error messages further down the page, because the validator can then parse the document correctly. For instance, the validator may report an unclosed tag, but because it has no way of knowing where you meant to close the tag, it may well report the error message further down the page than where the error actually occurs. Working through each error and then revalidating will help you to isolate where your real problems are. Most errors are very easy to fix once you spot where they have occurred.

## Common Errors and Warnings

### Closing Tag for "X" Omitted

The most common mistake to make in XHTML pages is to forget to close your elements. If an error such as that shown above is given, then it is fairly easy to work out what is wrong. However, this type of mistake can also throw errors such as "*Element X not allowed here*". This is because, by missing out the closing tag for an element, the validator thinks that the following elements are supposed to appear inside the unclosed element. There are particular rules about which elements can appear within other elements, so if these rules are broken, this latter error will be thrown.

### You Have No Background-Color with Your Color

This error, found when validating a stylesheet, points to the fact that you need a background-color for all elements that have been given a color. If you do not want any color other than the background of the parent element to show through, then set this to

```
background-color: transparent;
```

### Use of Non-Standard Properties in CSS

If you have used any non-standard style properties in your CSS, then the file will not validate. A common example of this would be the IE properties that allow you to change the color of the browser scrollbars. If you, or the client, insist on using some property that is browser-specific, there is still no reason for you not to validate the stylesheet or document, ignoring errors generated by the browser-specific code. At least you are then aware of what causes the file to not validate, and can make a decision as to whether to include the offending item.

# Summary

As someone just coming into this industry, you have the chance to start out with a strong focus on best practices, and a commitment to creating solid, valid web sites, that look good, and don't cut out vast chunks of your audience through a reliance upon old, non-standard markup. While those of us who have been around for a while have had to relearn many of our techniques in order to fully embrace web standards, newcomers to the industry can start out by learning the best ways to do things, which in many ways gives you an advantage.

As someone who has been working in this industry for several years, this author can see how the momentum for change and the move towards standards compliance has picked up through the efforts of the W3C, browser makers, authoring tool manufacturers, and ordinary developers, often spurred on by grassroots organizations such as The Web Standards Project (*http://www.webstandards.org*).

Web standards matter, valid structured markup matters, and as the case for standards becomes higher profile, it won't be too long before clients are requiring standards. In this chapter we have given a guide to what the standards are, how to work to the standards, and why you might want to do so. The resources section below should give you some further places where you can explore and learn more about standards compliance, and keep up-to-date with the latest issues and thinking on the subject.

## Resources

The following list of resources is by no means exhaustive, but hopefully will provide a way into the wealth of information that is available to assist you in creating valid markup.

- The W3C web site (*http://www.w3.org*), where you can find all the specifications, validators, and latest news.

- The Web Standards Project – *http://www.webstandards.org/*.
  "Founded in 1998, The Web Standards Project (WaSP) fights for standards that reduce the cost and complexity of development, while increasing the accessibility and long-term viability of any site published on the Web. We work with browser companies, authoring tool makers, and our peers to deliver the true power of standards to this medium."

- The NYPL Online Style Guide (*http://www.nypl.org/styleguide/*). A style guide written for the New York Public Library, but a useful resource for anyone who is starting to design and develop with web standards in mind.

- XHTML 1.0: Marking up a new dawn (*http://www-106.ibm.com/developerworks/library/w-xhtml.html*). An excellent article on XHTML by Molly Holzschlag for IBM developerWorks.

- From Web Hacks to Web Standards (*http://www.alistapart.com/stories/journey/*) an excellent article on A List Apart (*http://www.alistapart.com/*). A List Apart publishes excellent articles by professionals working in many different areas of web design and development, they have a bias toward standards-compliance. Exploring the past articles should give you some excellent information.

- My Web site is standard, and yours? (*http://www.w3.org/QA/2002/04/Web-Quality*).

- Buy standards compliant web sites (*http://www.w3.org/QA/2002/07/WebAgency-Requirements*).

- Articles from W3C Quality Assurance Interest Group (*http://www.w3.org/QA/IG/*).

- The QA Toolbox (*http://www.w3.org/QA/Tools/*): a current list of all tests and tools maintained on the W3C web site.

## Further Reading

- Cascading Style Sheets: Separating Content from Presentation (Briggs et al, glasshaus, ISBN 1904151043)

- Constructing Accessible Web Sites (Thatcher et al, glasshaus, ISBN 1904151000)

- Practical XML for the Web (Shiell et al, glasshaus, ISBN 1904151086)

# 13

- Overview of web hosting
- Choosing a domain
- Putting your site up on the Web

**Author: Rachel Andrew**

# Getting Your Site onto the Web

Whilst viewing your site on your own computer system may at times feel like the only way you will be able to ensure it looks the way you want it to, the ultimate purpose of building a site is to make it live.

There are various choices available – a free hosting account, or the web space that comes along with your **ISP** (**Internet Service Provider**) account may be suitable for a personal site, but if you are working with a more serious web application, you may need something more scalable and robust.

In this chapter we will look at the standard services offered by hosting companies and find out how to compare them, so that you don't end up paying for things you will never use, or become tied into an unsuitable account.

Also in this chapter we will look at domain names – how to register them and how transferring a domain works. We will discuss configuring basic CGI scripts of the type that often come preinstalled with hosting accounts.

## Web Hosting

When you upload your web site to a hosting company, you are simply transferring it to the hard disk of another computer. That computer is running a web server and is thus able to serve pages to a web browser when they are requested via HTTP. The range of options offered by hosting companies and the jargon used to explain those options can seem quite bewildering at first.

# Your Options for Hosting

First of all you need to decide on what your real needs are. Is this a personal web site, somewhere to just try out your ideas, or a site for a client who will pay for their own hosting? You don't always need to run out and pay for hosting for your own testing space. However, you should make sure your live environment is fast and robust enough for your needs. After all, you don't want to risk your reputation through your client's web site suffering long downtime or being slow, but you still want to give them a good deal.

*Deciding on what you need in terms of speed and reliability should help you make your first decisions on where to host your web sites.*

## Free Hosting

There are many companies that will host a web site for 'free'. These companies pay for the hosting in a variety of ways: sometimes they put banner ads of their own on your web site, or make you upload via a web tool instead of FTP (during which time you are exposed to their advertising). Sometimes they just run it as a loss leader in the hope that you will eventually upgrade to a paid version of their service with more space and functionality.

The saying "you get what you pay for" generally rings true when it comes to hosting. If your hosting is free, then you cannot expect fast responses to support requests, or a guarantee of uptime, and if you complain, you may well find that your only option is to upgrade to a paid hosting plan where they do offer such guarantees.

However, free hosting is an excellent choice for a site to test your skills on, or to use in order that you may upload problematic pages so that you can demonstrate any difficulties you are having to the members of a mailing list. This is good practice when asking for help – we will cover this more fully in *Chapter 16*. However, it is not a good solution for a site that is important, and which would cause you any kind of loss, should it be unavailable at any point.

## Hosting with Your Dial-Up Provider

Many ISPs offer a certain amount of web space along with your dial-up or cable connection. This hosting is often more reliable than free hosting as it is technically part of the package being offered to you. You therefore have some comeback, since you are paying for the service. However, the problem with this type of hosting is that it is often very limited in the services you get, and is not very scalable.

You may find that if your site is busy you can go over your bandwidth allowance. You will probably also find that you cannot use a server-side scripting language or install CGI scripts and that there is no option to upgrade your package to allow for the things you need to do. In addition, depending on the contract you've got, you might not be allowed to host a business site at all.

As with free hosting, for your own, personal site, or for testing (or for a client with very limited needs who is on a low budget), this may well be a good option. However, in situations where you need scalable hosting for a busy, large, or complex site, this is probably not the option to choose.

## Paid Shared Hosting

Both of the above options are examples of shared hosting, where your site is one of many others, hosted on the same physical computer. You also have the option of paying for shared hosting and it is this option that most professional web sites choose. Paid hosting accounts vary from a few dollars per month to a few hundred dollars per month, depending on the facilities that are made available and what guarantees are made about service levels and the amount of support that is included.

We will discuss the different services that hosting companies offer on shared accounts later in this chapter. Many sites do not need a very expensive hosting account when they get started and a good hosting company will have an upgrade path that you can choose, should your site become very busy, use up a lot of disk space, or need additional functionality, such as a database or the use of server-side scripting.

## Dedicated Hosting and Co-Location

Sometimes shared hosting is not an option. Perhaps you need to install custom programs for your site to work, or you require a large amount of hosting for lots of different sites, or the site you are working on uses more disk space than even the most expensive shared hosting packages will give you.

At this point you might consider a dedicated server for your site. This means that you have your own physical computer running your web site, based in someone else's data center. There are two options here – **Dedicated Hosting** or **Co-Location**. The difference between the two is that a dedicated server belongs to the hosting company and you are simply paying for the use of it. A co-located server is your own hardware, and in addition to paying for the hardware, you also pay a fee for it to be held within someone else's data center and for the bandwidth it uses. With these deals you usually get full access to the server and can install any software you want on it.

The hosting cost of a dedicated server will usually include the cost of keeping the software up to date with security patches and critical updates. However, should the hardware on a dedicated server fail, it will be replaced, whereas a co-located server is generally maintained at your own expense – although you will usually be able to pay for someone in the data center to fix urgent problems or run routine maintenance on it.

Having a dedicated server is a good option because it gives you the freedom to do more or less what you want with respect to what you install on it. Dedicated hosting is a great way to have your own machine without needing to know a lot about security issues. Furthermore, there should be someone on hand in the data center to reboot the thing in the middle of the night when it all goes horribly wrong!

If you go for co-location, however, you are likely to need a reasonable amount of technical expertise, and you will need to provide your own hardware, thus driving up costs. This is probably not an option you would choose initially, unless you are developing a site for a large company or have a lot of clients that you could host on your own server (and who would thus pay for that hosting).

**13**

## Hosting In-House

Larger companies often operate their own in-house servers. If you happen to be working for such a company, you may find yourself in such a position. For the average designer, however, in-house hosting is more hassle than it is worth. You would need to have a computer permanently connected to the Internet via a high-speed connection, and this would mean that you would need to be very aware of security issues and how to configure a firewall that can control remote access to your server, since that machine would be very attractive to malicious users scanning for vulnerabilities.

*A **firewall** is a combination of software and hardware that protects the server, particularly from malicious attacks*

# How to Decide on the Type of Hosting You Need

Now we've looked at what type of hosting you might need, let's go on to look at some of the options that might be available to you for your hosting.

## The Hosting Environment

As I mentioned earlier in this chapter, when you upload your web site you are moving it to another computer. That computer needs to be running an operating system and have web server software installed. In *Chapter 15* we will be looking at what you need to be able to run a web server on your own computer for testing purposes. Just about any computer can run as a small web server in such circumstances.

## Server Operating System

The operating system of the server you are using is the first decision you may need to make. Shared hosting tends to be one of two things – Windows or Unix.

Windows hosting, as you would expect, is hosting on a machine running a server version of Microsoft Windows: this could be an NT4 Server, Windows 2000 Server, or the new upcoming .NET Server.

Unix hosting could be one of a variety of operating systems: many companies offer hosting on Linux, but you may also find hosting on a commercial Unix system, such as Solaris, or another free Unix variant such as FreeBSD. To the web designer, any of these operating systems fall into the Unix category and can all be treated in the same manner. Where free or budget hosting is concerned, you usually find this on Unix hosting running a Linux operating system, as there are no license fees to pay.

### Web Server Software

When you have got your operating system installed, you now need to decide on a web server program to use. The most common software you will find is **Apache** (*www.apache.org*), which is an open source web server. While it can be installed on most operating systems, in a live environment you will tend to find it used most frequently on Unix operating systems. The second most common alternative is **Internet Information Services (IIS)** which is Microsoft's own dedicated Windows web server.

The following graph demonstrates the relative popularity of these and a few other web servers, around the Web. (Source: Netcraft Web Server Survey, *http:www.netcraft.com/survey/.*)

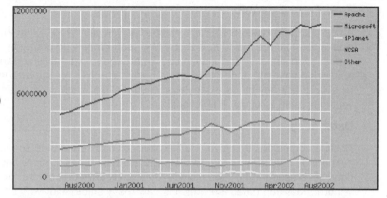

There are a variety of other servers, such as Zeus (*www.zeus.com*) and iPlanet (*www.iplanet.com*), and you may also hear mention of various application servers, which work with a web server to serve dynamic (often database-driven) content. We will discuss these application servers more in *Chapter 15*.

For a static HTML-based web site, the type of server you are hosting on may make little difference, but if you intend to incorporate server-side scripting, it may be a decision you need to consider carefully in the first instance.

## Different Services Offered by Hosting Companies

Hosting companies tend to offer a whole range of services that you may or may not need. Here I will explain the technology behind the jargon in order that you can come to your own decisions about what you need in a hosting package.

### cgi-bin

You may see phrases like "...ability to install custom CGI scripts..." listed on the services page of a hosting company. **CGI** (**Common Gateway Interface**) scripts are widely used for server-side processing, such as sending forms, guestbook pages, poll scripts, and other functionality. We will look at configuring a simple CGI script later in this chapter and you can often download various CGI scripts (usually written in Perl) from resource sites on the Web (and, with a minimum of modification, use them to incorporate some dynamic functionality into your site).

While many developers now prefer to work in a server-side language such as PHP or ASP, CGI scripts are still widely in use and, if you are taking up an account with no other server-side scripting capability, you would be well advised to have access to install your own CGI scripts, in order to add some interesting functionality.

### Ability to Use Server-Side Scripting Languages

These languages will depend on the operating system and web server of the company you have chosen, but could include PHP, ASP, JSP, and ColdFusion. If you are a Dreamweaver MX user, even if you do not intend to do a great deal of server-side work, you may be wise to choose a hosting company that will allow you to script in one of the languages that Dreamweaver MX supports, as you will then be able to use it to easily add dynamic functionality to your pages.

**13**

### FrontPage Extensions

A host that advertises FrontPage extensions will allow you to use the proprietary scripting extensions that are included with the Microsoft FrontPage authoring tool in order to add basic dynamic functionality, and also to use FrontPage's own publishing wizard. You can use FrontPage to develop your site and upload it to a host that does not support these extensions, but you will not be able to use any of the extensions on your site in such circumstances, and will need to transfer your site using a regular FTP client.

### Databases

Hosting companies that give you the ability to use server-side scripting often also allow you to use a database on your web site (we will discuss databases in more depth in *Chapter 15*). Common databases used for the Web include MySQL (usually on servers running Unix), MS Access (the Windows desktop database, which is only really suitable for very small applications), and MS SQL Server (Microsoft's database server for Windows, which is usually available on more expensive hosting accounts and is only necessary if you have a very large and busy or complex database-driven web site).

### Amount of Bandwidth Transfer Allowed

Every time a file – a page, image, or script, for instance – is requested from your site, the data transfer involved uses up a certain quantity of resources. The amount of bandwidth you use reflects the number of files transferred to visitors of your site. For web-hosting purposes, this is usually calculated on a month-by-month basis, and most hosts (particularly free or low-cost accounts) limit your use of bandwidth in any one month.

> *The amount of bandwidth you use reflects the number of files transferred to visitors of your site.*

However, these bandwidth allowances tend to be fairly generous. Unless you are having a vast amount of traffic to your site, or are offering large files to download (such as music or video files), you should have no problem in staying under the bandwidth allowances. Hosting companies usually have an option for you to upgrade or pay for more bandwidth in blocks if you go over; on the other hand, free hosting or hosting supplied by your ISP may not feature such an option, and your site may even be cut off if you frequently go over your allowance.

To reduce the amount of bandwidth that you are using, you should ensure that your file sizes are kept small by optimizing your images well and writing clean XHTML. Tools such as Dreamweaver MX offer built-in functionality for cleaning up your markup and these can be helpful in reducing your file sizes (and in writing better markup of course).

### Storage Space Offered

Your files take up space on the hosting company's server just as they take up space on your hard drive at home. Hosting companies offer a certain amount of "web space" for your files. More expensive accounts offer more space, but even the relatively small amount of space offered in an average low-cost or free account is usually more than enough for most simple sites. If you are offering downloads, or have a lot of big images then you may find you need to upgrade to an account with more space, but with a paid shared hosting account this is usually not a problem.

## Shell Access

Some accounts offer "shell access", that is, access to your account via either **Telnet** or, more usually, **SSH** (**Secure SHell**). There are a variety of tools that will allow you to SSH: a common tool is **PuTTy**, available from *http://www.chiark.greenend.org.uk/~sgtatham/putty/*.

Access via Telnet or SSH can be useful if you are writing and installing your own CGI scripts, but if you don't plan to use it, you won't need it!

## Pre-Installed Scripts

Some hosting companies offer pre-installed scripts for use in form processing (and other such typical web functionality). You may find that a hosting company does not offer you the ability to install your own scripts, but has a useful selection of scripts that can be easily used to do most of the tasks you would need a script for. Hosts that do offer a "cgi bin" often have certain, common scripts installed as a service to their customers.

## Statistics

Web servers can be configured to log details of their visitors. They do this by writing to a text file. Below is a line from the log files of one of my own sites, running on a Windows 2000 Server. There will be a line such as this for every data transfer that occurs between your site and each visitor, although yours may look slightly different, as there are a variety of log file formats. Every image file, page, and include is logged.

```
http://www.edgeofmyseat.com/developers/tutorials.asp
2002-01-10 11:56:30 195.184.114.199 - CHIWEBSOLIVIA 64.27.162.112 80 GET
/tutorials/tutorial1.asp - 200 0 0 471 78 HTTP/1.1 www.edgeofmyseat.com
Mozilla/4.0+(compatible;+MSIE+5.5;+Windows+NT+5.0)
```

Looking at the raw log file, it is possible to disseminate some useful information. For example, I can see the time of the request, the file that was requested, and the operating system and browser of the person who made the request. If a hosting company offers "raw log files" then they give you access to these raw files so that you can download them and process them via one of the many applications that are available. One of the most popular is Analog (*www.analog.cx*), which is free to download and use.

Some companies do not give you access to the files, but provide "web site statistics" that may be updated frequently, or even appear live. Some of the programs used by hosting companies for displaying statistics will tell you details about the people who are on your site at that very moment. The screenshot shown next is an example of one such package – Media House LiveStats.

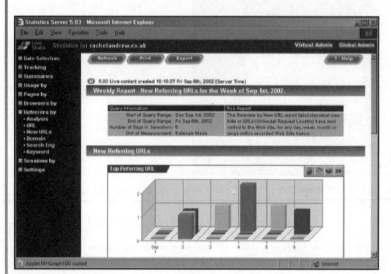

For a personal site, having some basic statistics on your visitors may be very interesting, but for a commercial site they can be vital. Statistics processed from the log files can tell you where on the Web the visitor came from and the time of their visit. If they used a search engine to find you, the logs can give you the keywords or phrase that the person typed into the engine before clicking through to your site. They can provide information about the browser and operating system used by visitors, the length of time they spent on your site, any errors returned (such as 404 pages), and much more.

Statistics are useful and important to ascertain how well the site is doing, and to give you feedback such as what parts of the site are most popular, and what bits perhaps aren't very popular (and might want revamping). It is worth seeing what your hosting company offers.

## E-mail

Most hosting companies offer e-mail along with your package. While you may already have e-mail through your ISP or dial-up provider, using the e-mail provided by your hosting company has advantages in that if you change dial-up provider, for whatever reason, you do not need to change your webmaster's contact e-mail address. Furthermore, if you had your own domain name as well, you could move hosting company without needing to inform people of the new e-mail addresses.

If you do wish to keep your e-mail with your dial-up provider, then hosting companies usually also offer mail forwarding, so that if people send e-mail to your web site address, the mail is forwarded to your own personal e-mail address. This can be helpful if you have several domains but only use one address to collect mail from.

In addition, some companies offer a webmail system that you can log in to via a web browser and check your mail wherever you are. Others offer unlimited mailboxes, forwarders, and mailing lists. If you are going to use the web host's e-mail, make sure you have all that you require.

# Domains

All machines that connect to the Internet have a unique numeric identifier known as their IP address. They generally look something like this: 212.159.6.74. Even if you are on a dial-up connection to the Internet, your ISP will assign you a temporary IP address from a list that it keeps: this will identify your computer for the duration of your connection.

Although IP addresses make perfect sense in terms of identifying specific machines within a network, they are not very easy for human users to remember or understand. For this reason most machines that are permanently connected to the network are assigned a **domain name**, to act as a more user-friendly alias to their IP address.

This is just as true of the machine that hosts your web site, of course, and the domain name of this machine forms the first and most fundamental portion of your web site's address: the bit after the *http://* and before the next forward slash (for example *glasshaus.com*). When you set up an account with your hosting company they may simply assign you a subdomain of their own domain – for example *mysite.hostingcompany.com*. This will identify the machine that your site runs on. Although this the easiest way to obtain a domain name, it has the disadvantage that if you move your site to a different hosting company your domain name will have to change and thus so will your web site's address.

You can, however, buy a domain name of your own. If you own a domain name, you are free to take it with you if you move your site to a new hosting company. The company can ensure that your domain name now identifies the new machine they are hosting your web site on. Your customers need never know that you have changed hosting companies.

## How to Buy a Domain

Your hosting company may help you in purchasing a domain, and this is probably the simplest way to get one. If you go down this route, however, make sure that the domain name is registered in your name, and that you are free to move it away from the hosting company if you change company. For instance, many hosting companies have offers whereby you can get a "free" domain. It is worth making sure that you read the terms and conditions attached, as you may find that you have problems in trying to move it away from the company later, or that a charge is made for moving it that would be greater than the cost of buying the domain name in the first place.

### Types of Domain Name

You are probably already aware that there are various types of domain name (with domains ending in *.com*, *.co.uk*, *.info*, *.gov* etc.) and these fall into various categories. Some names are available for anyone to register and others impose certain requirements, as we shall see in the next couple of sections.

## Country Codes

There are specific domain names available for most countries in the world, such as:

- .uk – United Kingdom

- .us – USA

- .ru – Russian Federation

- .za – South Africa

A full list of these country-specific top-level domains can be found on the **Internet Assigned Numbers Authority (IANA)** web site at *http://www.iana.org/cctld/cctld-whois.htm*.

## Generic Top-Level Domains

The most popular generic domain name is *.com*, and finding a good *.com* domain is becoming increasingly difficult, with many good domain names being held by "cybersquatters" – people who buy up domain names and then try to sell them for a large profit. There are a variety of other generic names, as shown in the table below, many of which have criteria for eligibility to register.

| Domain | Criteria | Operated by |
|--------|----------|-------------|
| .aero | Members of the air transport industry | SITA: *http://www.nic.aero* |
| .biz | Must be a business | NeuLevel Inc: *http://www.neulevel.biz/* |
| .com | None | VeriSign: *http://www.verisign-grs.com/* |
| .coop | Cooperative associations | Dot Cooperation LLC: *http://www.cooperative.org/* |
| .info | None | Afilias: *http://www.afilias.info* |
| .museum | Museums and members of the museum professions | Museum Domain Management Association: *http://musedoma.museum/* |
| .name | Individuals | Global Name Registry: *http://www.gnr.name* |
| .net | Officially for networks, but anyone can register | VeriSign: *http://www.verisign.com/* |
| .org | Officially for non-profit organizations such as charities, but anyone can register | VeriSign: *http://www.verisign.com/* |
| .pro | Still being established, for professional individuals | RegistryPro: *http://www.registrypro.com/* |
| .gov | US government only | US General Services Administration |
| .edu | Degree-granting US educational institutions | Educause: *http://www.educause.edu/* |
| .mil | US Military | US DoD Network |
| .int | Organizations established by international treaties between governments | IANA *.int* Domain Registry |

As well as the generic top-level domains, there are second-level domains. For example, the second-level domains of the *.uk* domain include *.co.uk*, *.me.uk*, *.ltd.uk*, and *.org.uk*. Second level domains are controlled by the registrar for that top-level domain. In the UK for example, this is Nominet (*http://www.nic.uk*).

### Is the Domain Available?

Having chosen a good domain name for yourself or your client, you need then to go and see if it is available. When working out a good domain name for a client, it is a good idea to sit with them at a computer and test availability of possible domain names as you go. Non-Internet savvy clients may get their heart set on a name that they will never be able to have!

> *clients may get their heart set on a name that they will never be able to have!*

Companies that register domain names usually have a domain name look-up system on their web site, where you can type in a name you are interested in and it will tell you if it is available. You can also do a "whois" on a domain name (to find out who has the domain name if it is taken) at **InterNIC** (*http://www.internic.net/whois.html*) for top-level generic domains or **Uwhois** (*http://www.uwhois.com/domains.html*), which allows you to search over a wide range of top- and second-level country domains as well as the generic names.

You can also search for lapsed domain names through sites such as **The Whois Report** (*http://www.whoisreport.com*): you may be able to find a distinctive name that someone has decided not to use any more.

Having found a domain that you like and checked its availability, you can then register it. You will be asked for some contact details, and (unless you are registering through your hosting provider) will need to provide particulars about where the domain is to be hosted. The information you will need to give may vary, depending on the type of domain you are purchasing.

Typically you will need to provide the billing address and the name of someone who will act as a technical contact. You will then need to provide information on the **nameservers** involved (the machines that store information about which machine IP addresses belong to which domain). You will have to say which nameserver the domain needs to point to, as well as the nameservers of your hosting company. If you are registering a domain via a method other than through your hosting company, find out what these nameservers are before proceeding. Top-level, country-specific domains may have slightly different procedures, but the registrar for that top-level domain should have all the information you need to register and configure the domain pointing.

## Transferring Domains

If you change hosting, you will need to change the entry for the nameservers on your domain and, if your domain is registered through your hosting company, you may need to change the registry of the domain either to an independent domain registrar or to your new hosting company, if they are a registrar themselves. First, upload your web site to your new hosting company: you will be given an IP address or subdomain when you need to sign up so that you can check that your site is functioning correctly.

### Changing the Registrar

If your domain is already hosted at an independent registrar, then you can skip this step. Your old hosting company may have registered the domain through another registrar, or may be a registrar themselves. Contact your hosting company to find out the situation. Ask how they prefer domain name registrations to be moved, or find an independent registrar such as directNIC (*http://www.directnic.com.*)

The new registrar will need to put in a request to the old registrar that the domain be moved. At this point an e-mail will be sent to the administrative contact, technical contact, and billing contact for the domain, all of whom need to reply, to confirm that the domain can be moved. If any of these contacts is not yourself (say, someone at your hosting company) you will need to contact that person to request that when the transfer request comes through, they reply in the affirmative.

### Changing the Nameservers

Once your domain registry has been moved (or if you were already using an independent registry), all you need to do is change the nameservers on the domain to those of your new hosting company and let the hosting company know that the domain should be picked up and pointed to your hosting account. The transfer process can take a few days, and during this time you will find that some people see your site on the old server and some on the new server.

Even more disconcertingly, if you get your e-mail through your hosting company, you will find that half of your e-mail ends up at one hosting company and half at the other during this transitional time. After a few days, however, your domain will be updated to point at the new nameservers and you can happily close your old hosting account. By keeping both accounts up and running during the transfer process, your visitors should experience no interruption in service.

It is very important that you remember to renew your domain names and keep your details up to date on the registration so that the company who is hosting the domain for you can contact you when it is time to renew the domain. If a domain name is not renewed it becomes available for registration again and you could find that someone else buys it. As that 'someone else' may wish to run a site that you would not want your name associated with, this can cause a great deal of problems.

# Making Your Site Live

Once you have your hosting organized, you will be able to upload your pages to the server and make your new web site "live". This need not be a complicated process – we will discuss how to do it now.

## FTP

**File Transfer Protocol** (**FTP**) is the most common way to move files from your computer to the server. You can use FTP from the command-line, but most of us use an **FTP client**, a program that allows you to see your files and the files on the remote computer in order to be able to transfer the correct files that make up your site.

Visual Development environments such as Dreamweaver and FrontPage also have their own ways of publishing your sites – Dreamweaver has a built-in FTP client, while FrontPage's site publishing wizard allows you to perform the same task, but requires that the FrontPage extensions are loaded onto the server.

## Available Software

There are a variety of FTP clients around and many are freeware or cost little. The FTP client I use is **WS-FTP**, and a free version of this product, WS_FTP LE, is available from *http://www.ftpplanet.com/download.htm*. The license allows it to be downloaded and installed free of charge by non-commercial and private users. More specifically:

> "WS_FTP LE is the limited edition version of WS_FTP Pro, allowing only multiple file transfers and the auto re-get or resuming feature. WS_FTP LE is shareware, available for free to educational users, government employees (US local, state, federal, and military) or to non-business home users only." (http://www.ftpplanet.com/download.htm)"

Try it out – after downloading WS_FTP LE and installing it on your computer (a simple matter of double clicking on the installer and following the prompts, and there is also a wealth of help information available on the site), start the application.

The first thing you will need to do is to enter the details that your hosting company gave you to connect to your web site. You should have an address that you wish to transfer files to, a username, and a password. You will need to enter these details into the *Session Properties* dialog:

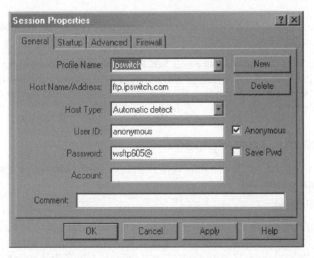

Now click *OK* and the program will attempt to make a connection with your server. If it succeeds you should see the files and folders in the remote location in the right-hand side of the application, and in the left-hand panel you can now navigate to your web site files (this is fairly typical of an FTP program).

Check with your hosting company where you need to transfer your web site files to. Some hosts will expect your index page to be in the root of the site; others (as in the example below) have a directory, perhaps called "*web*" or "*htdocs*" where you need to put the homepage of your site.

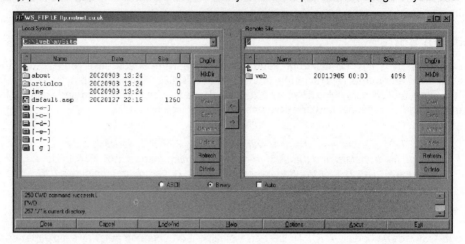

To transfer files from your local computer (the left-hand side) to the remote computer (the right-hand side) all you need to do is select them on the left, click the -> arrow, and the files will transfer over. You will then be able to see them on the right-hand side and should be able to view them at your web site address.

Some things to note are as follows:

- Make sure you have got the right file location selected on your server before you start transferring the files over.

- There are two FTP modes – Binary and ASCII. ASCII should be used for HTML files (and other markup/scripting files), whereas Binary should be used for picture files (and other similar files). However, most modern FTP programs have an auto-detect option, so you don't need to worry about this kind of thing.

## Common Problems After Upload

Uploading to your web space should be relatively straightforward. However, there are some things that occasionally catch people out.

### No Default Page Found

After upload, you should be able to view your pages on the Web by typing in your domain name, IP address, or the address that your hosting company told you to use. If you go to that address and you still see the default page of your domain you need to check that you uploaded the page that the server will use as a homepage. This is usually called something like index.html, default.html, or default.asp (this last one is an example that you would possibly use if dealing with an ASP-driven site).

If you definitely have a correctly named default page uploaded and you are not seeing it, check that you have uploaded the files into the correct directory of the web site. For instance, if the hosting company requires that your files are uploaded to */web* and you have uploaded them to / then you won't see them. If, after checking all this, you still have a problem, contact your hosting company for assistance, or read through any help files they have on their site.

### Broken Images and Files Not Found

Make sure that the paths to the images on your site are correct when uploaded. A common mistake is to have used a visual editor to create your pages and "browsed" for the images on your hard drive. The images then end up referenced as they would be on your hard drive and not as they would be on the server. Another common reason for broken images or file not found errors is if you have uploaded to a UNIX server from a Windows machine and have not accounted for the fact that UNIX is case-sensitive.

Under UNIX, `index.html` is not the same as `Index.html` or `INDEX.HTML`. Check the case of links to other pages and of image sources. Another common mistake is to use \ as opposed to / when defining paths for your images and other files, so do check all of these things if you are finding things mysteriously absent.

# Configuring a Basic CGI Script

When we talked about the services offered by hosting companies, we discussed hosts that allowed you to install your own CGI scripts and hosting that had pre-installed scripts available for your use. Here we will look at the process of configuring such as a script and what you need to do to get it working with your pages.

## Using a Standard formmail Script to Send E-mail

A standard script available on UNIX hosting accounts is a **formmail script**, which accepts contents sent to it from an HTML form on a web site, and builds them into an e-mail, which is posted to the site administrator. Getting this script working on your site consists of two tasks – creating the HTML form, and editing the script.

### Creating the Form

For this task we are going to presume that you need visitors to your site to be able to complete a form with their name, e-mail address, and comments. Here is an example page, `CommentForm.html`, with a form that posts to this script:

```
<?xml version="1.0" encoding="iso-8859-1"?>
<!DOCTYPE html PUBLIC "-//W3C//DTD XHTML 1.0 Transitional//EN"
    "http://www.w3.org/TR/xhtml1/DTD/xhtml1-transitional.dtd">
<html xmlns="http://www.w3.org/1999/xhtml">
<head>
<title>Send me your comments</title>
<meta http-equiv="Content-Type" content="text/html; charset=iso-8859-1" />
</head>

<body>
<p>Complete my form to let me know what you think of this web site.</p>
<form method="post" action="/cgi-bin/formmail.pl">
```

```
<p>Your name:<br />
  <input name="realname" type="text" id="realname" size="40" />
</p>
<p>Your Email Address:<br />
  <input name="email" type="text" id="email" size="40" />
</p>
<p>Your comments:<br />
  <textarea name="comments" cols="40" rows="6" id="comments"></textarea>
</p>
<p>
  <input type="hidden" name="subject" value="Comments Form" />
  <input type="hidden" name="redirect"
         value="http://www.mysite.com/thankyou.html" />
  <input type="submit" name="Submit" value="Submit" />
</p>
</form>

</body>
</html>
```

Let's go through the important parts of this document, and see what they do:

- The line `<form method="post" action="/cgi-bin/formmail.pl">` specifies the action of the form, which points to the location of the script on your server. Your hosting company will be able to tell you where CGI scripts need to be uploaded to in order for them to run. This will often be a directory called something like "*cgi-bin*" or "*cgi*". Make sure that this line points to the script and that the case is correct – if the script is called `FormMail.pl`, then `formmail.pl` will not work on any UNIX system.

- The line `<input name="realname" type="text" id="realname" size="40" />` creates a textbox where the user can input their name. The script is written so that a field called `"realname"` will create the name field before the e-mail address when the e-mail is sent to you.

- `<input name="email" type="text" id="email" size="40" />` is a textbox with the name `"email"` – the script will use this e-mail address as the reply-to address when sending the e-mail to you, so you will be able to reply to the actual sender of the comments from your e-mail program.

- The field `<textarea name="comments" cols="40" rows="6" id="comments"></textarea>` is where the user can enter their comments: you can call the field names anything you like as long as they are not required for the script to run, but for a complex form with many fields you are advised to name them logically so you can understand which field is which when the e-mail comes through.

- The hidden field `<input type="hidden" name="subject" value="Comments Form" />` sets the subject line of the e-mail that will come through.

- The hidden field `<input type="hidden" name="redirect" value="http://www.mysite.com/thankyou.html" />` specifies a page that the script will send the user to after the e-mail has been sent, so you can create a "thank you" page to thank the user for filing in your form.

## The Script

The script we are using is commonly installed in hosting accounts and can also be downloaded from the Web for you to install yourself from *http://nms-cgi.sourceforge.net/scripts.shtml* (select the *Formmail* script). You need to download the .zip file if you are using a Windows setup, or the .tar.gz file if you are using a Unix/Linux setup. You should find some documentation, and a formmail.pl script file contained within.

Open up the formmail.pl script in a text editor – the script might look a little scary at first but there are only a few changes you will need to make. The following is an extract from the script file, near the top of the script.

```
# USER CONFIGURATION SECTION
# ─────────────────
# Modify these to your own settings. You might have to
# contact your system administrator if you do not run
# your own web server. If the purpose of these
# parameters seems unclear, please see the README file.
#
BEGIN
{
    $DEBUGGING          = 1;
    $emulate_matts_code= 0;
    $secure             = 1;
    $allow_empty_ref    = 1;
    $max_recipients     = 5;
    $mailprog           = '/usr/lib/sendmail -oi -t';
    @referers           = qw(dave.org.uk 209.207.222.64 localhost);
    @allow_mail_to      = qw(you@your.domain some.one.else@your.domain localhost);
    @recipients         = ();
    %recipient_alias    = ();
    @valid_ENV          = qw(REMOTE_HOST REMOTE_ADDR REMOTE_USER HTTP_USER_AGENT);
    $locale             = '';
    $charset            = 'iso-8859-1';
    $date_fmt           = '%A, %B %d, %Y at %H:%M:%S';
    $style              = '/css/nms.css';
    $no_content         = 0;
    $wrap_text          = 0;
    $wrap_style         = 1;
    @config_include     = qw();
    $send_confirmation_mail = 0;
    $confirmation_text = <<'END_OF_CONFIRMATION';
From: you@your.com
Subject: form submission

Thank you for your form submission.

END_OF_CONFIRMATION
#
# USER CONFIGURATION << END >>
# ─────────────────
# (no user serviceable parts beyond here)
```

We need to do the following:

- First, set the variable `$DEBUGGING` to `0` (change `$DEBUGGING = 1;` to `$DEBUGGING = 0;`) – this will stop the debugging command from printing out lots of errors to the screen. You do not need this in ordinary use.

- The variable `$max_recipients` should be set to the number of people who will receive the form. If the form is just being sent to you, set this to `$max_recipients = 1;`. This will stop someone using your script to send out huge numbers of spam e-mails appearing to come from your server.

- `$mail_prog` needs to be set to the location of the mail program (usually sendmail, qmail, or similar) on your server – your hosting company should be able to tell you what and where it is.

- `@referers` needs to be set to the IP address and domain of the server that you are sending the script from – this stops someone else from linking to your script from another server and sending mail through it. If your domain name is `www.mydomain.com` and the subdomain of the server your site is hosted on (the address you had before you got your own domain name) is `mysite.myhosting.com`, then the referrers list would look something like `@referers = qw(mydomain.com, mysite.myhosting.com localhost);`.

- @allow_mail_to is where you put the e-mail addresses that the script is allowed to send mail to: again this is for security purposes. You will need to put your e-mail address in here.

These are the basic settings that you will need in order to get the script working – there are other options that you can change, and reading the files included with the script will help you to find out whether they will be any use to you.

After making the changes to your script, upload it to your web server. It is very important that you upload the page as ASCII and not as binary (set the FTP mode to ASCII, as explained earlier).

After uploading your script, there is one more thing you will need to do before you can test your form, and that is to change the file permissions on the script.

## UNIX File Permissions

On a UNIX server, every file you upload has a set of permissions assigned to it which says who is allowed to do what with the file. Every file also has an **Owner** and **Group** associated with it: if you created (uploaded) the file then you will be set as its Owner. The people who can use or modify files on a UNIX system are then broken down into three groups:

- Owner: the owner of the file, referred to as U.

- Group: anyone in the group that the file belongs to, referred to as G.

- Others: everyone else, including the users of your web site. These are referred to as O.

Just as there are three groups that can manage a file, there are three different things that can be done to a file:

- Read: read the file or the contents of the folder.
- Write: write to the file or create/delete files within a folder.
- Execute: execute or run the program or script.

Each of these can be turned on or off from within the system.

The on/off state of all three tasks (read, write, or execute) is represented by a three-digit binary number; each digit representing read, write, and execute, respectively. Don't worry if binary notation is foreign to you: you can skip over this next part if you want. However, if you have come across binary notation before, you will realize that, by using three binary digits, equivalent decimal values of between 0 and 7 can be represented. With this in mind, it follows that a value of 7 (equal to a 111 in binary) means "grant all permissions", while 0 (equivalent to 000 in binary) means "grant no permissions".

Each of the groups of people mentioned above has an associated permission level. An Owner would normally have all permissions (111 in binary, decimal value 7), while Group and Other normally only have Read (100 in binary, decimal 4). We represent this complete set of permissions in decimal as 744. This is a good situation for regular HTML files that are simply read, but scripts also need to be executed, so the permissions need to be changed to 755 to allow for this.

An alternative to this notation for permissions is given by a set of ten characters: drwxrwxrwx. The first rwx in this string represents the Owner, the second set of rwx represents the Group, and the third set of rwx represents other. Any permission that is not granted is represented by a hyphen, so a permission of 755 translates to drwxr-xr-x.

As the owner of a script, you can change the file permissions on it. This can be done using your FTP client. After uploading your `formmail.pl` script with WS_FTP LE, right-click on the file and select the menu option *chmod(UNIX)*. The following box will appear, containing checkboxes in which you can set the file permissions for Owner, Group, and Other. Select the appropriate checkboxes (as seen below) and click *OK*. The file permissions will be set for you.

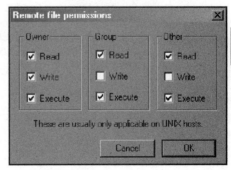

If you wish to view the permissions on each file in the directory, click the button *DirInfo* on the right-hand side of the application window and you should see all the files in the directory listed including your `formmail.pl`, which should look something like this:

```
-rwxr-xr-x   1 1267      webusers    2324 Sep  4  2002 formmail.pl
```

If you are using another FTP client then check the help files for how to "*Set UNIX file permissions*" or "*chmod*", and you should find a similar method that you can use.

All being well, you should now be able to *Submit* your form to your script and receive an e-mail back. If it doesn't work first time, check in the `ReadMe` of the script and make sure that all your settings are correct.

## Where to Find Scripts

There are many scripts available to download and use on your site. The site that the `formmail` script we have been using came from has a great number of useful scripts that will help you add a large amount of functionality to your web site. Configuring each script is usually simply a matter of looking at the `ReadMe` file provided and following the instructions.

Searching the Web for "*Free CGI Scripts*" or "*Free Perl Scripts*" will no doubt find you some other scripts too. Most come with some help files to get you started in installing and configuring them.

Make sure that, if you are using a "free" script, you stick to the copyright notice included with the script. Most authors just request that you keep their ownership notice on the script, and that, if you distribute the scripts to anyone else, you pass on all the attached files as well.

# Summary

In this chapter we have discussed how to choose a hosting environment and how to get your site live. We have also discussed how you can obtain your own domain name so that moving your hosting doesn't mean having to reprint all your stationary and business cards! Additionally we have covered how to get a CGI script installed and configured on a UNIX hosting account.

I hope that this chapter has helped to clarify your options when it comes to hosting. Web hosting is a competitive market and there are many different packages out there for you to choose from. Spending a little time considering your options at this point will help you in the future. It will enable you to talk confidently about hosting options with clients and employers, and to know whether the hosting a client has already got will support what they need to do with their web site in the future.

# 14

- Maintaining your site

- Blogging and CMS

- Third-party utilities

**Author: Rachel Andrew**

# Techniques for Site Maintenance and Administration

A web site is never really "finished". Unless you have built something that you are handing over to a client to take care of, you will need to maintain your projects: keeping them fresh, keeping links to other sites up to date, and removing old information. The simplest way to do this is to make changes on your local copy then upload it to the live web site. However, there is also an array of ways of adding to your site without needing to transfer the modifications via FTP each time. The easier your site is to update, the more likely it is that you will update it regularly. It also means that those without technical knowledge are able to make changes themselves, without having to ask you to do it for them all the time.

In this chapter we will look at ways of managing your site, from updating it in its simplest form, to ways of keeping the look and feel consistent. We will also cover third-party solutions for adding sections to your site that are easy to update, as well as other commercial and non-commercial vendor applications that can add another dimension to your web site without you needing to have specific capabilities on your own server.

## Maintaining Your Site

In it's most basic form, all you need to do to update your web site is keep a copy of your files on your hard drive and, when you want to change some content, edit the copy on your computer and then transfer it to the site using FTP in just the same way as you did when you first published the site (see *Chapter 13* for more on FTP). This method will work very well in most cases. If you are using this method and uploading entire pages to your site bear the following points in mind:

- Ensure that if you make any changes to any common page elements (such as the height of a banner) you apply this modification to all pages of the site, and upload all the modified pages.

- If you are simply making changes to and uploading a single page, such as adding something to your resume, make sure that you haven't accidentally moved any of the page structure around.

- Make sure that you remain consistent. CSS makes this easier, but it is still possible to start using a slightly different style of text formatting with a site that you haven't updated in a while, and this can make the site look messy and incoherent.

- It is a good idea to keep a page as a "template", which contains all your navigation and the rest of the design features that go around the content. You can then base new pages upon this template page, ensuring that new pages are consistent with the rest of the site.

- Make sure you check all the links in your pages, so that users do not stumble upon error messages when surfing your site.

- If you are working with a team of people this method can become very difficult as it would be easy for two of you to be working on the same page accidentally and overwrite each other's work as you upload. Dreamweaver contains built-in features to help in this situation called check-in and check-out, and there are many other solutions such as the open source CVS (Concurrent Versions System) – see *http://www.cvshome.org/* for more information.

## Keeping Your Information Up to Date

Updating your site is vital if people are going to want to return to it time after time. Even personal sites can receive relatively high numbers of visitors, if their content is fresh and interesting – people love to read other people's stories. A personal web site can also become a good "shop window" for your skills. If you are hoping to get into college or to gain employment in this industry, then displaying your abilities on your own site – where you are free to express yourself in your own way – can be an excellent way for your prospective employer to get to know a bit about you. Keeping your site up-to-date shows that you are building something that you care about.

### Checking Links

As well as checking that your internal links on your web site work and visitors can move easily from page to page, you should periodically ensure that links to external sites are still valid. Some sites (in particular news sites) move their content around or remove content regularly, so if you have external links to them it is a good idea to spend time when you're doing an update clicking on those links, and checking that they still lead to the content you were expecting.

There are a variety of third-party products that will assist you in this, and which can become useful if you have a large site with many external links. A good place to read up on such products is in the Link Management category of the Open Directory Project, which provides links to many different products. For more information, see *http://dmoz.org/Computers/Software/Internet/Site_Management/Link_Management/*.

# Keeping the Look and Feel Consistent

One of the difficulties in adding to a site over time is consistency. CSS can be a great help here (see *Chapter 8* for more on using CSS) – with all your styling information already set out in one file, it is far harder to inadvertently create page inconsistencies. However, unless you are using external CSS for the structure/layout of your pages as well as the styling, it is still easy to end up in situations where, for instance, your menu appears to move slightly as you go from page to page, because you have changed the size of a table cell, or added a new menu item on one page and forgotten to add it to another one.

Additionally, as your site begins to grow larger, making changes such as adding an item to a menu can become very time consuming, because you need to go around each page of your site copying and pasting the new menu item into each one.

There are ways to simplify the process of working with an existing site. Many visual development environments include templates as a way of locking down some areas of the page so that they can't usually be changed. Those areas are then automatically updated when the global template page itself is changed.

The template feature in Dreamweaver MX is an excellent example of this, and we shall explore how you can use this to make updating and maintaining your site simpler in the next section. If you can use a server-side language (such as ASP, PHP etc.) or **Server Side Includes** (**SSI**) on your web site (see the section later on in the chapter for more on SSI), you can build your site up using one or more shared files that reside centrally and which govern the major issues over how the site looks.

## Templates in Dreamweaver MX

Templates are one of the most powerful features of Dreamweaver MX. The theory behind a template is that you create a basic site layout containing all the universal features that you want to feature on all pages, and some placeholder content (or just a gap) where you want your content to go. You then tell Dreamweaver MX which areas you would like **editable**, so that on each page generated from the template you will be able to add unique content in this area. Other areas can be **locked**, so that, on any page generated from the template, it will be impossible to change this area from within Dreamweaver MX.

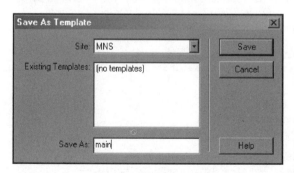

To see how templates work, you can open an existing page in Dreamweaver, and select *File > Save As Template*. A dialog box will appear (see left) that will ask you to name the template. Give it a logical name that will avoid confusion, and identify it easily throughout your site.

*Some sites may be entirely based on one template; others may have several templates – perhaps one for each main section of the site. If you will have several templates then naming them logically will help you to distinguish which template to use when creating a new page for a given section.*

**14**

Having created your template you need to create editable regions within that template, where you will be able to add your page content. For example, we have created a template from this page:

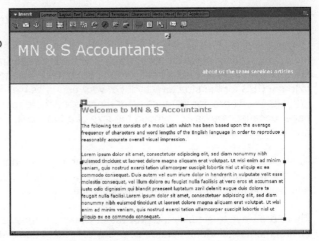

We have selected our main content area, which happens to be a positioned `<div>` (or "layer" in Dreamweaver-speak). This works equally well with a table-based layout – just select the table cell that will contain your main content.

What we are aiming to achieve here is to create a template that will allow us to produce new pages that have the top banner and navigation already in place when we first create them (these will be locked, so we can't change them in any way).

The `<div>` will play the role of main content area on the page – this will be the place where we can add material. This will automatically be the same width on each page we create from the template, to maintain consistency. To do this, we need to make the selected area editable by clicking *New Editable Region*, which is the third button along on the *Templates* tab of the *Insert* toolbar:

You will then be presented with a dialog box, into which you enter a name for this editable region. Name it something that will remind you what this region is for – remember that you can have many editable regions within one template. Giving them appropriate names will help you when you come back to the site at a later date. If you flip into *Code View*, you can see the comment tags that Dreamweaver inserts into the document to identify the different areas:

```
<!DOCTYPE html PUBLIC "-//W3C//DTD XHTML 1.0 Transitional//EN"
   "http://www.w3.org/TR/xhtml1/DTD/xhtml1-transitional.dtd">

<html>
<head>
  <!-- TemplateBeginEditable name="doctitle" -->
  <title>MN & S Accountants</title>
  <!-- TemplateEndEditable -->
  <link rel="stylesheet" href="../global.css" type="text/css" />
  <!-- TemplateBeginEditable name="head" --><!-- TemplateEndEditable -->
</head>

<body>
```

```
<div id="banner">
   <span class="tag">MN &amp; S Accountants</span>
   <p class="navlinks">
     <a href="#">about us</a>
     <a href="#">the team</a>
     <a href="#">services</a>
     <a href="#">articles</a>
   </p>
</div>

<!-- TemplateBeginEditable name="content" -->
<div id="content">
   <h1>Heading</h1>
   <p>content</p>
</div>
<!-- TemplateEndEditable -->
</body>
</html>
```

If you are editing a template – or a page generated by a template – outside of Dreamweaver MX, then ensure that you do not remove or edit these comments. If you do, Dreamweaver MX will not be able to associate the template with the page any more.

### Creating a New Page from Your Template

Once you have your template, you can create new pages from it. Select *File > New* and, when the *New File* dialog launches, select the *Template* tab at the top of the dialog (see right). In the first column you should see all of your defined sites listed. If you select the current site that you are working on you should see your new template. Select it and you will see it in the *Preview* pane on the right-hand side. Make sure that *Update Page When Template Changes* is checked and click *Create*.

Save your new page and try to click on the banner area of the page – it won't allow you to select or edit anything within that area. If you go into *Code View* you will see that the code is grayed out, and the only place where you may make an edit is between the comment tags for the editable regions.

If you have many articles that you need to copy into HTML pages, templates can really speed up and simplify the whole process. Simply create a new page from the template and then paste your new content into the editable body area. All you then need to worry about is making sure the text is formatted well; something that good use of CSS will make easy.

However, that is not all templates are good for – the real power of templates becomes even more apparent when you need to make a change to that locked region.

**14**

### Editing and Updating Using a Template

Once you have created a whole bunch of pages from your template, you may realize that you need to add another menu item to the navigation. If you had not used templates you would probably have to resign yourself to opening lots of HTML files, and copying and pasting the new HTML into the correct place in the menu. Dreamweaver MX templates can do this dull job for you. To edit all the pages that are attached to a template, open up the template itself and make your edit in the locked region of the template.

> Note: you can only update changes made to the locked region of the template across all pages – obviously Dreamweaver does not overwrite the content of the editable region as that is different for each page.

After you have added your new menu item, you then save the template in the usual way. As this is a template, Dreamweaver MX will ask you if you would like to update files attached to this template. Click *Yes*.

Dreamweaver will then display a dialog as it updates all the pages on your site that are linked to this template. The length of time it needs to do this depends on the number of files it will need to change, but once it is done it will show you a report (in the *Status* box). If there have been any problems updating any pages, it will indicate this in the line which reads *files which could not be updated*. Should Dreamweaver MX be unable to update a file, check that the comment tags for the template are intact and that the file is not set as read-only.

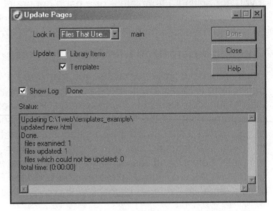

Click *Close* to get rid of this dialog and open one of the pages created from the template. It should now contain the new menu item. If you have made a change that has affected all of the files attached to a template, remember that you must then upload all these files to your hosting company.

This demonstration shows just one way of using a tool such as Dreamweaver MX to assist you in managing your site content. Using Dreamweaver MX in this way requires no additional facilities on the hosting server.

## Server-Side Includes

As we have discovered, uploading pure HTML pages, with or without the assistance of a tool such as Dreamweaver templates, may be a perfectly acceptable way of getting your updates to your site, but it does have its drawbacks when ensuring the consistency of your look and feel is considered. Having to upload and then check every page of your site for consistency is very time consuming. A way to get round this problem is to use includes.

Includes are simply parts of the HTML code for your site that are kept in a separate file, and then included in the document before it is returned to the browser (it is referenced in a similar way to how CSS files are referenced in pages – the syntax and purpose are different, but the idea is pretty much the same). This means that you can keep a part of your code that is identical across many pages in a single file.

At the appropriate point in the document flow, you just tell the server that you wish to place the contents of that file there, continuing with your page as normal afterwards. Not only does this mean that items such as navigation only need to be created once, and edited once if a change needs to be made to them, it also makes working on your pages easier, as you don't have so much code to scroll through when editing them.

You need to have the capability on your server to use includes – if you have the ability to use a server-side scripting language such as ASP, PHP, ColdFusion etc. on your account then you will be able to use includes; if not, you will need to check with your hosting company to see if you are able to use SSI on your account.

## Building a Page with Includes

Designing using includes is no different to your usual design workflow, apart from one additional step. Before you start to create content pages for your site, you want to create your include. Create your design as usual, build your HTML layout and tweak it until you are happy with how it looks. Select the part of the document that you wish to be stored in the external file and copy and paste it into another document. For example, here we are selecting the navigation from our last example for turning into an include:

```
<!DOCTYPE html PUBLIC "-//W3C//DTD XHTML 1.0 Transitional//EN"
    "http://www.w3.org/TR/xhtml1/DTD/xhtml1-transitional.dtd">

<html>
<head>
<title>MN & S Accountants</title>
<link rel="stylesheet" href="global.css" type="text/css" />
</head>

<body>
<div id="banner">
<span class="tag">MN &amp; S Accountants</span>
<p class="navlinks"><a href="#">about us</a> <a href="#">the team</a> <a
href="#">services</a> <a href="#">articles</a></p>
</div>

<div id="content">

<h1>Welcome to MN & S Accountants</h1>
<p>The following text consists of a mock Latin which has been based upon the average
frequency of characters and word lengths of the English language in order to reproduce a
reasonably accurate overall visual impression.</p>

<p>Lorem ipsum dolor sit amet, consectetuer adipiscing elit, sed diam nonummy nibh
euismod tincidunt ut laoreet dolore magna aliquam erat volutpat. Ut wisi enim ad minim
veniam, quis nostrud exerci tation ullamcorper suscipit lobortis nisl ut aliquip ex ea
commodo consequat. Duis autem vel eum iriure dolor in hendrerit in vulputate velit esse
```
includes.html

Save the include document with the code in it with a `.html` extension, if it is plain HTML. (Alternatively, if you are using a server-side technology, use the relevant extension, such as `.php` or `.asp`.)

Go back to your original document and delete the code that you just exported. In its place we need to put in a line that tells the server where to find the file that must be included here. This will look like so (if you decide to save all your includes in an `includes` directory):

`<!--#include virtual="/includes/navigation.html" -->`

*You may also see includes with the extension `.inc` – this is sometimes used because it is an easy extension to remember as being an include, but it is a bad idea, as it can create a security risk. These files could be easily downloaded, and their contents used by unscrupulous hackers. We would generally advise you not to use `.inc`.*

14

Save your original document. If you are working with SSI (and not a server-side technology) you may well need to save any pages that contain includes with a `.shtml` extension – your hosting company should be able to tell you if this is necessary. You can have as many includes as you like within a document. I often use a top include (being anything that is above the main content area) and a bottom include (everything underneath the content). Once you have created all of the includes that you need, and added the lines to put in the includes, you can use the document as a template and use '*save as*' to create new pages based on this layout. Our previous example would now look like this:

```
<!DOCTYPE html PUBLIC "-//W3C//DTD XHTML 1.0 Transitional//EN"
   "http://www.w3.org/TR/xhtml1/DTD/xhtml1-transitional.dtd">

<html>
<head>
   <title>MN & S Accountants</title>
   <link rel="stylesheet" href="global.css" type="text/css" />
</head>

<body>
   <!--#include virtual="/includes/navigation.html" -->
   <h1>Page Heading Here</h1>
   <p>Content Here!</p>

</body>
</html>
```

Each page created with this layout will use the same `navigation.html` include file, so if you need to add another item to the navigation you simply add it to that file. You now only need to upload that one file in order to change how all of your pages will look. When the page is displayed in the browser, it will not be apparent that the page has been constructed with includes: the server will have assembled the page before sending it to the browser.

Using includes helps cut down on the time you need to spend maintaining the site, and also reduces the chances of inadvertent changes creeping in over time. A combination of includes and external CSS should keep your site looking clean and professional.

# Other Solutions for Managing Your Site

Keeping your site updated, even with the use of includes to streamline the process, may not be your only challenge. Perhaps you have other people working with you on the site, or you would like to be able to update the site from other locations, not just from the computer on which your site's master files reside.

There are a variety of solutions available for you to add content dynamically to your web site using tools other than your trusty HTML editor and FTP client. These tools range from those designed for "blogs" to full Content Management Systems. (For more on Content Management Systems, or CMS, check out *Content Management Systems*, glasshaus, Dave Addey et al, ISBN 190415106X.) We shall look at some of the available tools now, and show how you can incorporate these into your site.

# "Blog" Tools – Not Just For Blogs

**Blogs**, or weblogs, have become a common form of personal publishing in the last few years. A blog is a kind of online journal, usually with a high percentage of links to other sites that the author finds interesting. Many blogs are simply the author's journal, but others have a theme, such as web development, or similar subject, that the owner of the site is interested in. Good examples of sites that use a blog format are *http://www.zeldman.com*, and *http://www.linux.org.uk/diary/*.

There is a variety of software available to help create and maintain blogs. The whole idea behind blogging is that you add to your journal frequently, perhaps from work as well as home, or from an Internet café while you are away from home. You might not have your web site files and FTP client to hand in order to update the site. Third-party blogging software allows you to add to your blog from anywhere with an Internet connection and a web browser. You simply log in with a username and password and add your new content via an HTML form.

Using these tools it is possible to create a dynamic page on your site – a place to add articles, or a news section – as well as just a typical online diary. We will look at two different third-party solutions, in order to see how they are installed and implemented, and how you can change the way that they are laid out, so that you can use them in different ways on your site.

## What Is Available?

We are going to look at two different blog tools. One is **Blogger** (see *http://www.blogger.com*), which requires no special facilities on your web host, since the updating is done on the main blogger web site and the application there transfers your changes to your own web site via FTP.

The other tool we are going to look at is **Movable Type** (see *http://www.movabletype.org/*), which needs to be installed on your own web server (for which you need to have the ability to install your own CGI scripts, and the use of some form of database storage).

## Blogger

To start using Blogger all you need is to sign up for an account on the Blogger web site (*http://www.blogger.com*). There are two versions of Blogger available, a free version and a paid-for one. We'll be looking at the free version in this chapter. However, if you enjoy using Blogger on your site there are more features available if you decide to upgrade to the paid version. These include a spell checker, title fields for your posts, image posting, changing times on your posts, creating drafts, and more (for a more detailed account of these features, go to the Blogger Pro web site – *http://pro.blogger.com*).

Once you are signed in, you can click on the *Create a new blog* option at the right-hand side of the screen. We're going to use Blogger to create a news page for our web site, so on the next page (*page 1 of 4*), give it a name that will allow you to distinguish it from other blogs you may set up in the future, as well as a description. Since this is not to be a traditional blog, you will probably want to switch the setting for *Public Blog* to *No*.

If you were creating a regular blog you would generally want other people to come and read it, so allowing it to be added to Blogger's recently updated list would be beneficial. If the Blog is added to the recently updated list, it will show up in the 'Fresh Blogs' section on the homepage of *www.blogger.com*, as long as your site is one of the last ten blogs to be updated via Blogger.

Blogger have an arrangement with a hosting company to host blogs, but for our purposes we will want the entries to be transferred to our own server. Therefore, on the second page (*page 2 of 4*) check the second option.

Now you need to complete your FTP details (*page 3 of 4*) – just as you did in order to transfer via FTP using WS-FTP or a similar FTP client (see *Chapter 13* for more details).

You will also need to enter the directory in which you wish to publish your dynamic page, and the URL of the page. For example, if your news page was to go in a directory called /about and the page was to be called news.html, you would need to enter the following settings:

- FTP Server: *www.mysite.com*
- FTP path: /about/
- Blog Filename: news.html
- Blog URL: *http://www.mysite.com/about/news.html*

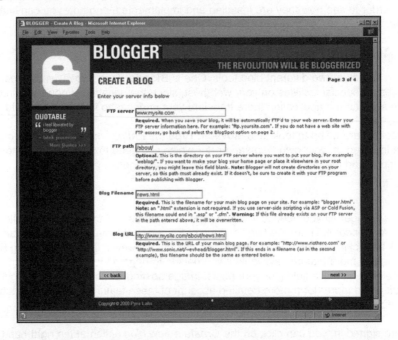

**Important**: *If the page you are going to use as your 'blog' page already exists on your site, it will be overwritten by Blogger when it transfers the file via FTP to your hosting machine, so if you eventually want to use a Blogger-generated page to substitute a page that is already in existence, create it on a new test page first until you are happy that you have edited your template so that it matches the look and feel of your site.*

The next page (*page 4 of 4*) will ask you to choose a template – we'll be modifying this template later on so pick a simple looking one. I chose Eric Costello's "Techniqz" – see opposite:

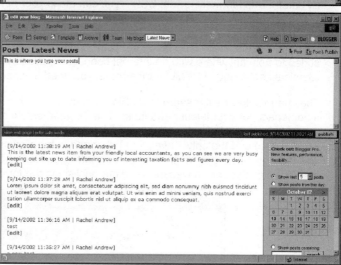

Once you have chosen an initial template, you will be asked to wait while your blog is created. Next, you will be taken to the application that allows you to make your entries and edit your blog. Blogger works by allowing you to create a page on the Blogger server, add entries to it, and then transfer the file via FTP to your own web site – just as you would if you had created the page on your own computer. The advantage of using Blogger is that you can add to this page from anywhere in the world, provided you have a browser to hand!

The options that you have once you are in the Blogger application are as follows:

- **Posts**: here you can add, edit, and delete posts, and read past posts
- **Settings**: here you can change the settings for your blog (most are self-explanatory). You will need to add your FTP Username and FTP Password in the first section. In the second section, *Formatting*, change the value of *Show* to read '*3*' and '*Latest Posts*'. You can also change the time zone here to your local time zone. In Archiving, select *No Archive* – as this is a news page, we don't really need an archive, for obvious reasons (a traditional blog page would want an archive, especially if you set it up to display just one article at a time).
- **Template**: selecting this button allows you to create a template for your page. Within the box you will see the generic template that you selected, which you can replace with your own page template. Read the notes at the bottom of this page before pasting your template into this box. Once you have done so, you need to place the Blogger tags in the places that you want the content to end up.

14

## Tips for Creating a Template

You can use anything that is already on your server in the template – remember the file is simply transferred to your server by FTP, so images, CSS files, and JavaScript can all be used. Even SSI can be used, as long as you add the correct paths to the includes. In *Settings*, you will need to give the file the correct file extension, be it *.shtml*, *.asp*, *.php*, etc. A good way to create your template is to generate it first, then upload it to your server to make sure that it works, and finally copy and paste the code into the Blogger template box.

You do not need to use all of the Blogger tags on your page. For our news page, we may just choose to display the news item and the date and time it was added. So in the content area of your page you would simply need to add the following:

```
<Blogger>
  <$BlogItemBody$>
<p><$BlogItemDateTime$></p>
</Blogger>
```

By careful when formatting with CSS – you can make your news items or articles look less like a 'blog' and more like part of your page (this is OK, of course, if this is what you want). If you simply use the `<$BlogItemBody$>` tag in the main content area of your page, no-one need even know that the page was updated using Blogger – yet you still have an easily updateable web page that can be added to from anywhere with an Internet connection, even by someone who does not have technical knowledge of HTML. Furthermore, you need no special requirements on your own server!

The image below demonstrates how Blogger can be used to add a simple yet updateable area to a homepage for your latest news items. The Blogger template and CSS file for this layout is available in the code for this chapter which appears on the CD (as `blogger.html` and `global.css`) and the only setting that I changed in the *Settings* screen of the Blogger application was to format the date (which is in the *Formatting* section of *Settings*). You would need to upload the CSS file to your own webspace before publishing the template into Blogger.

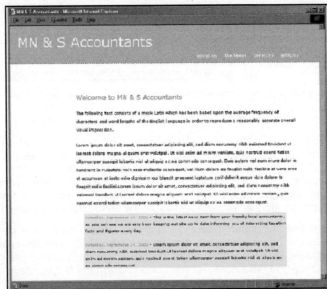

## Movable Type

To install Movable Type, you need to ensure that you have the required facilities available on your hosting account. You will need:

- To be able to install custom CGI scripts

- Perl, version 5.004_04 or greater, on the web server

- Support for the `DB_File` Perl module **or** MySQL & *DBD::mysql*

If you are not sure about any of these things, then get in contact with your hosting company to find out. The Movable Type web site has a page detailing these requirements, and a sample letter to send to your hosting company (to help set them up) at *http://www.movabletype.org/requirements.shtml*.

### Installation

Having ascertained that you have the ability to use Movable Type on your server, you need to download the `.zip` file from the Movable Type web site at *http://www.movabletype.org/download.shtml*. Extract this file, and you should find yourself with a folder including all the files you need to install Movable Type.

The file *index.html* from this folder contains some very comprehensive and easy to follow installation instructions, so is a good place to start. The installation procedure requires you to make some decisions about where the files should be located. Edit the script files to the correct location of Perl on your server (your web hosting company may be able to tell you this, if you haven't installed Perl on the machine yourself) and then make changes to the config file in order to tell the scripts where you have uploaded the various parts of the system to.

*Note: When you need to open the files to make changes to them, do so in a text editor such as Notepad or similar, which will not change the formation of the scripts. Perl is not like HTML, and if you introduce additional line breaks etc. you will find that you have errors after installation.*

I would not recommend using Movable Type if you have never installed a CGI script before, but if you have a basic understanding of how to install scripts, and understand where you can put things on your web server, then you should be able to get up and running with this fairly quickly.

The support forums on the Movable Type web site (see *http://www.movabletype.org/cgi-bin/ikonboard/ikonboard.cgi*) are informative and friendly, and if you run into difficulties during installation then do visit them - someone may already have posted a similar problem, and the answers could be just what you need to continue your installation.

### Using Movable Type for Displaying Articles

As with Blogger, Movable Type is designed as a tool to run a blog. However, as it is installed on your own server, there are more possibilities for customizing how it displays your content, for example if you want to use Movable Type to display articles on your site. First you need to create a new blog within Movable Type.

*Note: When creating a new 'blog', ensure that the directory where the pages will be located has read, write, and execute rights for everyone – CHMOD 777.*

**14**

In the *Core Setup*, set your local site path and the archive paths to be the same directory when you create this blog, and name it *Articles*.

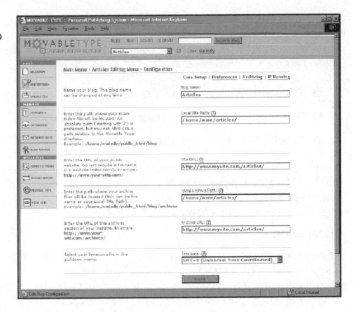

In *Preferences* set the *number of days displayed* to *1*, and in *Archiving* set the *Archive Type* to *Individual*:

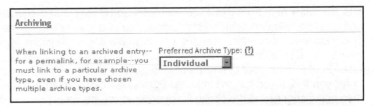

After creating your new *Articles* blog, you should be able to view the page on your site at the URL you specified. Unless you have already set up a template, it will be using the default Movable Type template, as seen here:

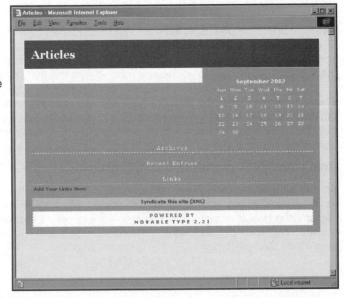

To edit this template, in order to display our articles, choose the *Templates* option in the Movable Type administration area. Click to edit the *Main Index* template and you will be taken to a page with the contents of the template displayed within a form textarea:

Within this template there are many tags that are important to the application. The Movable Type tags look like this:

```
<$MTBlogDescription$>
```

They should not be edited or removed unless you do not want that item to be displayed on your page. For our *Articles* page you will need to edit three templates – *Main Index*, *Stylesheet*, and *Individual Entry Archive* (the templates that I used for each of these are available on the CD, as `mt_mainindex.html`, `mt_stylesheet.css`, and `mt_individualarchive.html`.)

The easiest way to create a template is to design your page (or take an existing page from your site) and put placeholder text where the dynamic text will go, until you are happy with the look of it. Then replace the placeholder text with the Movable Type tags.

The Movable Type tags that I have used are as follows:

- `<$MTBlogName$>`: prints the name that you gave your blog onto the page

- `<link rel="stylesheet" href="<$MTBlogURL$>/styles-site.css" type="text/css" />`: links the style sheet correctly to the location of this page

- `<MTEntries lastn="1">`: MTEntries denotes the start of the entries, `lastn="1"` tells the application to only print one entry onto each page (as these are articles rather than blog entries)

- `<$MTEntryTitle$>`: the title of this entry/article

- `<$MTEntryBody$>`: the text of this article

- `</MTEntries>`: closes the area in which entries may be posted

- `<MTArchiveList archive_type="Individual">`: opens the archive list and shows that we want Individual entries on archive pages

14

- `<$MTArchiveLink$>`: the URL of the archive page

- `<$MTArchiveTitle$>`: the title of the archived article

- `</MTArchiveList>`: closes the area within which archives may be published

As an example, my *Main Index* template contains the following markup:

```
<!DOCTYPE html PUBLIC "-//W3C//DTD XHTML 1.0 Transitional//EN"
  "http://www.w3.org/TR/xhtml1/DTD/xhtml1-transitional.dtd">

<html>
<head>
  <title>MN & S Accountants - <$MTBlogName$></title>
  <link rel="stylesheet" href="<$MTBlogURL$>/styles-site.css" type="text/css" />
</head>

<body>
  <div id="banner">
    <span class="tag">MN &amp; S Accountants</span>
    <p class="navlinks">
      <a href="#">about us</a>
      <a href="#">the team</a>
      <a   href="#">services</a>
      <a href="#">articles</a>
    </p>
  </div>

  <div id="content">
    <MTEntries lastn="1">
      <h1><$MTBlogName$> - <$MTEntryTitle$></h1>
      <$MTEntryBody$>
    </MTEntries>
    <hr />
    <h2>Previous Articles</h2>
    <p>
      <MTArchiveList archive_type="Individual">
      <a href="<$MTArchiveLink$>"><$MTArchiveTitle$></a><br />
      </MTArchiveList>
    </p>
  </div>

</body>
</html>
```

There are many different tags and ways of configuring Movable Type. The full list of tags available and the ways to use them can be found at: *http://www.movabletype.org/docs/mtmanual_tags.html*.

The *Articles* page that is created by way of the templates available on the CD (see screenshot below) is a simple concept, displaying the most recently posted articles on the main *Articles* page, and a list of previous articles below it to allow people to easily browse older content. This concept could be taken further within the design of your site, and it does not immediately look as if you have used blog software to accomplish the *Articles* pages.

As is the case with Blogger, as your site grows and you take on more personnel, you could allow a content editor to access the blog application in order to add new articles, and they would not need to understand HTML or even how to transfer via FTP in order to add their content.

# CMS Tools

**Content Management Systems** (**CMS**) range from open source products such as PHP-Nuke and PostNuke, to large, expensive software packages created by major manufacturers. What they have in common is the ability to manage and post content without the need for direct editing of the HTML files. Whilst the big, commercial CMSs are out of reach for most of us, the open source products can be downloaded and used by anyone who has the correct server environment, and can prove very useful if you have the need to create a community site.

## What Is Available

The tools listed below are free to download and install on your server, and all do similar things. They allow for the adding, editing, and deleting of content in a variety of formats, and also allow for discussion and collaboration, with optional extras that can be configured into the base system to add all sorts of other functionality – voting systems, for instance.

When choosing a CMS:

- Check out the web site for that system (which will usually be running on the code they offer anyway, so it's a great way to see it in action). Have a look around at what is available. The web site for the software will usually be using the latest version of the code, so you will be able to see which features it includes.

- Try to find some other sites that are using this code as their CMS (often the product site will have links to some examples). By looking at other implementations of the same basic code, you can get a feel for how customizable the product is and what things people are doing with it.

- Find out what help is available during and after installation – does the help file look easy to follow? Is there a forum where users offer support to each other?

- Ask yourself the question "Do you have the necessary requirements on your server to be able to run the system?".

The following CMS tools are examples of open source tools that can be downloaded and implemented free of charge. There are many other such tools, and searching the web will turn up a variety of solutions for you to consider. The ones listed here are some of the best, in our opinion.

### PHP-Nuke

PHP-Nuke (*http://phpnuke.org*) describes itself as a "news automated system specially designed to be used in intranets and Internet. The Administrator has total control of his web site and registered users, and he will have in his hand a powerful assembly of tools to maintain an active and 100% interactive web site using databases."

To install and run PHP-Nuke, you will need a hosting account with MySQL, Apache, and PHP4.x, which is a fairly standard set-up for a UNIX-based hosting account.

### PostNuke

PostNuke (*http://www.postnuke.com*) is a weblog/content management system. The base code is fully customizable, and in addition, the tool is extendible through additional modules and blocks written by members of the community.

PostNuke needs PHP4.01 pl2 / MySQL 3.23 as a minimum server environment in order to install and run.

### Slash

Slash (*http://www.slashcode.com*) is a database-driven news and message board, using Perl, Apache, and MySQL. The install is slightly more complicated and less user-friendly than some other products, but the end result is highly customizable. Slash is the base code that *http://slashdot.org* (a very busy community web site) is run on.

You will need Apache, MySQL and Perl installed on your server in order to install Slash.

# Other Third-Party Utilities

As well as turning your whole site over to a CMS or adding updateable features by way of using blog software, there are a whole host of third-party utilities available for little or no cost that can help in keeping your site fresh and useful, so that your visitors will return for more.

*They range from online polls, guest books, and forum software, to search engines*

These facilities are typically hosted on the server of the company providing the service, and range from online polls, guest books, and forum software, to search engines. The advantage of using a service that is remotely hosted is that you need no special functionality on your own server, although you should be aware that you are then relying on a third party to keep the service up and running. In addition, you are working within your budget, so having a contingency plan in case the service vanishes or becomes prohibitively expensive is a good idea.

Let's examine one of the most popular available site utilities in more detail – the **Search Facility**.

# Adding a Search Facility

A search facility is a useful addition to any web site – especially as your content grows (although in most circumstances, it should never be relied on exclusively as site navigation – see *Chapter 7* of this book for more discussion on usage of search functions). However, writing and implementing even a simple search facility for your site is a relatively complex task.

You can find various open source scripts that you can install in order to give you search functionality, or you can look to a third party to fill this need. There are a variety of third-party, hosted search solutions, but a popular choice is Atomz (*http://www.atomz.com*) who offer a free search solution for your site as long as it consists of less than 500 pages. Larger sites have the option to upgrade to the Atomz paid search, but many sites are unlikely to exceed this limit. The Atomz search not only provides your visitors with an easy way to search your site, but it is also fully customizable.

You can upload your own template to make the search result appear within a page layout that resembles your own site. This means that unless your visitors are paying attention to the URL in the address bar, they will not realize they have left your site, even though the results are actually displayed on the Atomz site.

## Adding a Remotely Hosted Search Facility

To add the free Atomz search to your site, go to the Atomz web site at *http://www.atomz.com/* and click on the *Atomz Search* link. Once in the search section, you will need to register for a trial account (follow the *trial account* link in the left-hand navigation, then follow the on-screen prompts). The trial account gives you access to the Atomz *Express Search:* the free, cut-down version of their commercial search services, with a 500 page maximum limit.

Once you have your trial account, you will be able to log into Atomz and create your Express Search account. You can implement searches on multiple sites using your Atomz login, and the first thing you will need to do is create an account with the basic details of your site (this process is also very simple to follow).

Once you have created a Search account on Atomz you can select the *Templates* option in the left-hand menu. There are ready-to-use templates available, but we are interested in making the Atomz search look just like our own web site. Select *Templates > Template Editor* in order to get started.

In the template editor you will be presented with the HTML code that makes up the generic template in a large textarea. If you have been following this chapter you can probably already guess how this works: special tags are used within regular HTML. The Atomz tags all begin with the word SEARCH and look something like this:

```
<SEARCH-IF-RESULTS>
```

**14**

To edit the template you need to insert your own design around the necessary tags for the Atomz search to display correctly.

*If you have any images, stylesheets, or external JavaScript files they will need to be referenced with their full URL back on your own server, as the Atomz application will just load them from there. For example: http://www.mysite.com/global.css.*

While in the editor, you can test your template by clicking the *Test* tab at the top (see the previous screenshot). This does not publish the new template to the site, but will allow you to run a search using it in order that you can see whether there are any errors and if it looks correct. Any errors that do occur are usually caused by you accidentally deleting or editing one of the Atomz tags. Your aim is to get the search results to look as if they are being displayed within your own web site, as we can see with our example site, below:

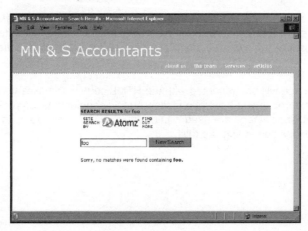

Once you are happy with the way that the template looks, click *Publish Changes* and you will be able to make this template live, so that anyone searching from your site will use it.

You now need to add a search form to your own web site that will send the keywords that the user has entered to Atomz, which will then display the results of the search within your template. Atomz have given you some help in constructing your search form by providing some examples. To find them, select *HTML* from the left-hand menu.

You can add a standard search form – which is simply a text input box and search button, suitable to go on every page of your site:

Alternatively, you can choose to include a more advanced search form, which you would probably place on a page of its own with some instructions on how to get the best out of a search. The advanced search form HTML, as provided by Atomz, looks like this when displayed in a browser:

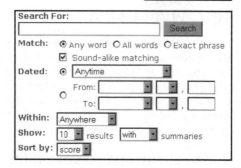

Whichever form you select, the process is the same. Copy the HTML given to you from the Atomz web site and paste it into the page on which you want the search to display.

```
<!-- Atomz Search HTML for MN &amp; S Accountants -->
<form method="get" action="http://search.atomz.com/search/">
   <input size=15 name="sp-q"><br>
   <input type=submit value="Search">
   <input type=hidden name="sp-a" value="sp100239ab">
   <input type=hidden name="sp-f" value="ISO-8859-1">
</form>
```

You can edit this HTML, add classes to style the form fields, change it into XHTML, or edit the layout of the form. Just make sure that you do not edit any of the values or names of the fields, as it is these values that the Atomz search engine will be using to return the results to you. Below, you can see that I have edited the above code in order to make it fit in with the style of my site – and also to make it XHTML-compliant:

```
<!-- Atomz Search HTML for MN &amp; S Accountants -->
<form method="get" action="http://search.atomz.com/search/">
   <input name="sp-q" class="text"><br />
   <input type="submit" value="Search" class="submit" />
   <input type="hidden" name="sp-a" value="sp100239ab" />
   <input type="hidden" name="sp-f" value="ISO-8859-1" />
</form>
```

14

The search form will look something like this:

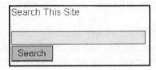

You can now test your search form – as you are linking out to a third-party application, you don't even need to upload the form to test it. Once you are happy that both form and template are correct, you can upload it to your site with your new search facility ready to go!

# Tips When Using Third-Party Software or Services

Third party utilities and software can be an excellent way to add functionality to your web site without needing to become a scripting guru first, particularly in the case of more complicated software, such as Movable Type or PHP-Nuke. They can also help you in learning web application concepts, such as the interaction between code and databases, which will stand you in good stead should you wish to explore server-side scripting or database-driven web sites in the future. There are, however, a few points that you should be aware of if you are using these services and software. We will look at these now.

## Code Validity and Accessibility

While you may be coding to web standards yourself, and ensuring that your code is accessible, the creators of the third-party software may not. In the Atomz example above I could, to an extent, convert the scripts into XHTML and remove font tags etc. However, in some applications, customizing is not possible or at least very difficult to achieve. When choosing a third-party solution, it is a good plan to find out whether you can fully customize the output or whether they are coding in support of standards before you become tied into something that will cause your pages not to validate.

## Reliability

If you are relying on a third-party solution hosted on another server, then you need to know whether it is reliable, whether you are still going to be able to edit your site, and that everything works. Consider the implications of this before using third-party software and plan for what you would do in the event that your third-party solution stops working, goes out of business, or switches to a paid business model that you can't afford.

If you are concerned about the reliability of the solution you can search Google groups (*http://groups.google.com*) to see what other users are saying about it. Don't be put off by the odd moan, but if there is a constant theme of dissatisfaction, then you may wish to seek an alternative!

## Security and Updates

If you are using a solution that you install on your own server, check for any security updates and alerts associated with them. Products such as PHP-Nuke are constantly being updated – both in response to new requests from the community and to ensure that any security issue that is uncovered (or other bug) is fixed, and a patch made available for users. Check the product's home sites regularly for updates.

# Summary

In this chapter we have looked at ways to manage your site, from simple updates using your HTML editor and an FTP client, to using blog software or open source CMS applications. This has been a whistle-stop tour of the various solutions available to you. Some of these solutions can be an excellent learning experience in themselves, and can add a whole new dimension to even a simple web site.

When looking for a solution for yourself or for a client, always check around to see what is available before deciding that you need to build something from scratch or hire a programmer. If you have a need for something, it is likely that someone else has already had that need and has created software to fill that need! While many of the solutions may seem complex and difficult to install at first glance, most do not use anything much greater than the skills we have already employed on simpler projects.

Furthermore, many of the products have a community of users built up around them, who are usually happy to help out with questions about installation or customization.

14

# 15

- Server-side scripting overview

- Databases: what are they and why are they useful?

- Getting started with server-side development

**Author: Rachel Andrew**

# Server-Side Scripting

A few years ago, all that most people wanted for a web site was a few static pages giving some information about their company and a way to contact them. This is what we would call a 'Brochure Site' as it is really nothing more than an online brochure for the company. Today, most companies want something rather different, they want to have interactive features, they understand the value of being able to keep their content fresh easily, and want to sell products, run surveys, allow discussion, and a whole host of other functionality.

This functionality can't be achieved by client-side technologies alone. XHTML and JavaScript can be used to manipulate the way pages appear in the browser (and this is what we mean by client-side) but for much interactive functionality something needs to take place on the server – be that storing of posts to a forum, or serving up of content based on a search. For these dynamic pages we need to use **server-side scripting**. There are many different types of server-side scripting, but the technologies we will explore in this chapter are:

- Active Server Pages (ASP)
- ASP.NET
- PHP Hypertext Preprocessor (PHP)
- ColdFusion
- JavaServer Pages (JSP)

Note that we will be covering a lot of ground in this chapter, and broaching quite a few subjects that may appear rather complicated and daunting to you at this present time. We therefore ask you to view this material as a valuable view into your future, to be mastered gradually as you further your skills, rather than something you'll be expected to grasp immediately. Believe us, we didn't! Look to the *Resources* section at the end of the chapter for further reading beyond this chapter.

# What Is Server-Side Scripting?

> ...code that is processed on the server prior to the output being sent to the browser.

Server-side scripting refers to code that is processed on the server prior to the output being sent to the browser. With the static pages we have seen so far, the browser requests the HTML page, which is then simply served back to the browser. With a page containing server-side script, the script is first **parsed**, or interpreted, by the server, creating the HTML that is then sent back to the browser. If you view the source of a page that contains server-side scripting from within your browser, all you will see is the output HTML.

For example, if you were using ASP you might have a page that looked like this:

```
<%Option Explicit%>
<%Dim strHello
strHello = "Hello, World" %>
<!DOCTYPE html PUBLIC "-//W3C//DTD XHTML 1.0 Transitional//EN"
   "http://www.w3.org/TR/xhtml1/DTD/xhtml1-transitional.dtd">

<html>
<head>
<title>Hello</title>
</head>

<body>
<h1><% Response.Write(strHello) %></h1>
<p>This page has a .asp extension and therefore will be parsed by the server
before the output is returned to the browser.</p>

</body>
</html>
```

When this page is requested from a server that supports ASP, the browser returns the following page:

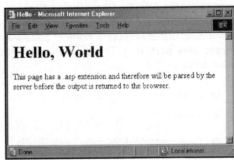

Viewing the source on this page through the browser shows only the output HTML markup.

```
<!DOCTYPE html PUBLIC "-//W3C//DTD XHTML 1.0 Transitional//EN"
   "http://www.w3.org/TR/xhtml1/DTD/xhtml1-transitional.dtd">

<html>
<head>
<title>Hello</title>
```

```
</head>

<body>
<h1>Hello, World</h1>
<p>This page has a .asp extension and therefore will be parsed by the server
before the output is returned to the browser.</p>

</body>
</html>
```

As you can see from the example above, you can treat pages that contain server-side script in exactly the same way you treat an HTML page – you simply need to give them the correct file extension, so that the server knows it must handle them slightly differently to plain HTML files.

In the example above, I assigned the words *"Hello, World"* to a text variable (known as a **string**) at the top of the script. That string could just as easily have come from a database or from input the user had put into a form that posted to this script. The end result is the same: the server puts the page together and places the contents of the variable strHello between the <h1></h1> tags.

# How Does It Work?

There are several links in the chain of events that allow server-side scripts to work. Let's look at an example.

Say we have an online club, where people can register and discuss their interests with fellow enthusiasts. Members visit the site via their home PCs, or similar devices. A server computer handles these requests and uses a database to store or retrieve the information about members and their discussions.

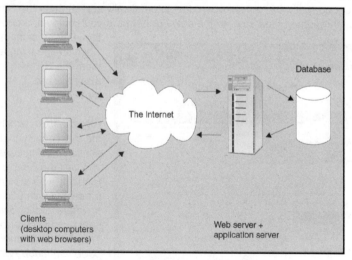

## The Browser

The users visit a web page containing a form that allows them to search a database of members' interests. One user types in *'flower arranging'* and hits the *Submit* button.

## The Web Application Server

A web server in general serves up static HTML, managing the delivery of the page to each site visitor using HTTP (Hyper Text Transfer Protocol).

A **Web Application Server**, on the other hand, is the part of the web server that processes server-side code (be that ASP, PHP, ColdFusion, or any other such technology) and passes the resulting HTML back to the main web server, which in turn passes it to the site visitor.

In the example above, when the search form submits its input to a page with a `.asp` extension, the application server runs the script in the ASP page and comes to a point at which a query has to be sent to the database. A **query** is a special instruction for retrieving, updating, or modifying the data in a database. The application server connects to the database and passes it the query, which in our example would instruct the database to look for members who have an interest in flower arranging.

## The Database

On being passed the query, the database performs a search on members' interests and finds all the members who have an interest in flower arranging. It passes this information back to the application server, which can then process the rest of the ASP script, including this information and serving the results back to the browser as HTML.

## Why Use Server-Side Code?

Server-side code brings with it many benefits. There is no other way to add advanced functionality to your sites, and even in small ways, using server-side code allows you to change what the user sees according to a variety of different conditions. Perhaps when a user first comes to your site, they are asked whether they would prefer to view the site in English or Spanish. They choose Spanish and, rather than writing an entire Spanish version of the site and making sure all the internal links work correctly, the server-side code automatically serves them the Spanish content from a database throughout their time on the site. Furthermore you could set a cookie to identify this user as someone who is Spanish speaking and then show them the Spanish text straight away the next time they arrive at the site.

Amazon is an excellent example of the functionality that can be achieved using server-side code. If you visit the Amazon homepage regularly, you are immediately presented with books that you may be interested in, based on your past purchases or browsing habits. They have a feature called '*The page you made*', which gives you recommendations based on your previous clicks around the site.

I have frequently bought books based on the recommendations made to me by Amazon, and in this way they increase their potential sales by alerting customers to other titles that may be of interest – perhaps titles they might miss when simply searching the site themselves.

Server-side code can enhance the user's experience of a site by giving them the content that they want.

# What Options Are Available?

There are a wide variety of server-side languages available to you, and you may find that one language suits your needs better than another. However, you may be tied to using certain operating systems or server software, which restricts the choices available. Once you become proficient in using one language, however, you will find that learning a second language is far easier – the fundamental concepts are the hard part to grasp, and they are common to all languages. At the end of the day you can look up syntax in a book if you need to: it's knowing the general approach to solving a given problem that you need.

If you are not tied to any language but want to get started in server-side development, then you should have a brief look at all the languages in question. The resources at the end of this chapter will help you in doing this. There are plenty of tutorial web sites where you can have a quick go with a language, to see if you can understand it. Other factors in your choice will be what you eventually hope to do in your web design and development career – a designer who has even a rudimentary knowledge of server-side scripting can be an asset in the workplace. However, if you want to move into web development, then you may be wise to pick one language and really learn it well.

When reading up on languages, you will no doubt encounter people who are out to prove that their language of choice is better, faster, prettier, and sexier than the others. As with many things to do with computers, people tend to group themselves into opposing clans in order to throw stones at each other. There is usually some truth in the issues raised during these altercations but, as someone new to the server-side arena, it is far better to ignore the hype and start with a language you are comfortable with, get your head around the concepts, and worry about ideological purity or code optimization later on.

## ASP

Active Server Pages (ASP) is a technology rather than a language. You can actually use a variety of scripting languages to write ASP (including VBScript, JScript – Microsoft's version of JavaScript, PerlScript, and Python). VBScript is by far the most common language used to write ASP, however. The *'Hello, World'* example above is an example of ASP written using VBScript.

### Which Platforms and Servers Support This?

ASP is a Microsoft technology, and most ASP developers will go on to host their applications on servers running Windows with **IIS (Internet Information Services)** as their web server.

- Windows 2000 Server ships with IIS5, which uses ASP3.0.

- IIS5.0 can also be used on Windows XP Professional.

- Windows NT4 Server comes with IIS4 in the NT option pack. This uses ASP2.0.

- A simplified version of the IIS server, for users of Windows 95/98/ME, also exists, called PWS (Personal Web Server). It can run all the code IIS4 can, but hasn't the delivery capacity to be used as a live server and is only intended for code testing.

However, a Microsoft server is not the only option. Companies such as Sun, with their **Sun ONE Active Server Pages** (*wwws.sun.com/software/chilisoft/*), and Styron with **iASP** (*www.stryon.com/products.asp?s=1*) have their own implementations of ASP, which will run on Linux and other UNIX operating systems. These can be excellent choices if you would like to develop in ASP but wish to use a UNIX operating system on your server.

### Why Code in ASP?

ASP with VBScript is relatively easy to learn if you have not learned a scripting language before. There is also a great deal of support for ASP within Dreamweaver MX, so if you want to use Dreamweaver as you learn the technology, then ASP is a good place to start.

*Note: You cannot install IIS or PWS on Windows XP Home. If you are upgrading to XP, and intend to do ASP development, you are advised to upgrade to XP Professional.*

For small-scale applications, ASP is fine. Hosting on Windows servers with support for ASP is easy to find, inexpensive to obtain, and you can develop functionality fairly rapidly with this technology. You can easily install IIS or PWS (depending on your operating system), so development and testing of your applications will be relatively simple, on your desktop computer.

ASP can be limited, and for some projects a more robust solution may be required. While you can port ASP applications to UNIX running Sun ONE Active Server Pages or iASP, ASP is probably not your choice if you wish to develop an application that can be moved from Windows to Unix with a minimum of fuss.

## ASP.NET

ASP.NET is a technology that forms part of the **Microsoft .NET framework** (*http://www.asp.net*). As with ASP, it is a technology rather than a language, but where ASP only allows development with scripting languages, ASP.NET enables the use of full programming languages, which work faster and are more flexible. The most commonly used languages are **VB.NET** and **C#** (pronounced "see sharp"), but development is possible in a multitude of other languages.

The previous example page can be translated into an ASP.NET page (with a `.aspx` extension) that looks something like this:

```
<%@Page Language="VB"%>
<script language="VB" runat=server>

    Sub helloWorld()
        Response.Write ("Hello World!")
    End Sub

</script>
<!DOCTYPE html PUBLIC "-//W3C//DTD XHTML 1.0 Transitional//EN"
   "http://www.w3.org/TR/xhtml1/DTD/xhtml1-transitional.dtd">

<html>
<head>
<title>Hello</title>
```

```
</head>

<body>

<h1><%helloWorld()%></h1>

<p>This page has a .aspx extension and will need to be uploaded to a server that
has the .NET Framework installed.</p>

</body>
</html>
```

### Which Platforms and Servers Support This?

ASP.NET is obviously a Microsoft technology and can only be run on servers that have the .NET framework installed. Many hosting companies that offer classic ASP accounts are now beginning to offer ASP.NET hosting too. As with all of these options, you will need to check whether your host will allow this.

Meanwhile, other companies are currently developing solutions that allow the deployment of ASP.NET applications on other server operating systems.

### Why Code in ASP.NET?

ASP.NET is a very new technology, and more robust than classic ASP. It is better suited to high-end environments, but it is a more complex technology to learn than classic ASP. However, if you are intending to move into web development, as opposed to design, it may be worthwhile for you to start work in ASP.NET. It is a new technology, which means that you will not be up against people with six years experience when applying for jobs.

The relative newness of this technology can also be a downside though, since there are fewer online tutorials and help sites in existence. This situation is likely to change as more people embrace the technology and move from classic ASP. You can also develop in ASP.NET using Dreamweaver MX.

## PHP

The abbreviation PHP (*www.php.net*) is what is known as a **self-referencing acronym**: an obscure form of programming joke. It stands for **PHP: Hypertext Preprocessor** (and so, by implication, is an abbreviation for itself!).

PHP is an open source scripting language that is especially suited to web development and can be embedded into HTML. Its syntax is similar to JavaScript.

*What is open source?*

*You will come across the term 'open source' frequently, particularly if you choose to work in PHP and MySQL. Open source software is created by collaboration; it is free to download and use, and the sourcecode (the code that makes the software work) is freely available for people to examine, change, fix bugs in, or release in a different format. The Linux operating system is an example of open source software – while companies can charge for support, CDs and manuals, or other software they include in the box they sell it in, the actual software itself remains free (which is why you can buy a glossy box of most Linux distributions, but may also download the distribution yourself freely from the Web). For more information see: http://www.opensource.org/.*

Again, here's our example translated into PHP, with a `.php` extension:

```php
<?php
$varHello = "Hello World" ?>
<!DOCTYPE html PUBLIC "-//W3C//DTD XHTML 1.0 Transitional//EN"
  "http://www.w3.org/TR/xhtml1/DTD/xhtml1-transitional.dtd">

<html>
<head>
<title>Hello</title>
</head>

<body>
<h1><? Ech=$varHello $></h1>
<p>This page has a .php extension and therefore will be parsed by a server
running PHP before the output is returned to the browser.</p>

</body>
</html>
```

### Which Platforms and Servers Support This?

PHP is available for almost all operating systems and servers. As it is an open source technology, you will often find it available on lower cost hosting packages running on the Linux operating system. You can also download a version of PHP to run on your local computer in order that you may test your sites.

### Why Code in PHP?

PHP is a good choice for the beginner. It is relatively easy to learn – particularly if you have already had some experience of a scripting language like JavaScript. It is available on a large number of low-cost hosting accounts and can be installed locally for testing without incurring any costs. There is also a large community of PHP developers who write tutorials and try to help people get started using PHP for their application development. Additionally you can often find pre-built applications written in PHP and released as open source, so with a small amount of PHP knowledge you can begin customizing these applications for your own use instead of needing to write something from scratch.

## ColdFusion

ColdFusion is a tag-based server scripting language (**ColdFusion Mark-up Language** or **CFML**) and is owned and developed by Macromedia (*http://www.macromedia.com/software/coldfusion/*). It's a natural choice for many designers and developers who have a good knowledge of HTML. The language can be extended with **Custom Tags** as well as user-defined functions. ColdFusion applications can integrate with the major industry standards, such as COM, CORBA, or Enterprise JavaBeans (EJB).

Here's our example in ColdFusion, with a `.cfm` extension:

```
<!DOCTYPE html PUBLIC "-//W3C//DTD XHTML 1.0 Transitional//EN"
  "http://www.w3.org/TR/xhtml1/DTD/xhtml1-transitional.dtd">

<html>
<head>
```

```
<title>Hello</title>
</head>

<body>
<cfset varHello = "Hello World">
<h1><cfoutput>#varHello#</cfoutput></h1>
<p>This page has a .cfm extension and therefore will be parsed by a server
running ColdFusion before the output is returned to the browser.</p>

</body>
</html>
```

### Which Platforms and Servers Support This?

In order to run your ColdFusion applications, your host needs to be running ColdFusion Server, which is a Macromedia product. ColdFusion Server can be installed on a variety of operating systems, including Windows and Linux, and so is a good choice for applications that require cross-platform compatibility on the server. There are a small number of tags that are only available on one platform or another, so it is wise to check the documentation if you are building something on a local Windows development server, for example, and then intending to deploy it on a server running Linux.

### Why Code in ColdFusion?

As ColdFusion is a Macromedia product, there is excellent support for it across the product line, including a great deal of functionality available to link Flash with ColdFusion applications. So, should you be working in Macromedia Flash, you may find that ColdFusion is a natural choice. ColdFusion is tag-based, like HTML, which can make the transition into a server-side scripting language easier if you only know HTML at the moment.

ColdFusion is, however, a proprietary solution and hosting can be relatively expensive to find, since the hosting company not only needs to pay for the operating system software (if they are not running on open source software, such as Linux) but also needs to pay for ColdFusion server licenses.

## JSP

JavaServer Pages (*java.sun.com/products/jsp/*) is part of the Java family developed by Sun and is an extension of the **Java Servlet Technology**. JSP uses tags and "scriptlets" written in Java in a comparable way to ASP. Much of the power of JSP is the fact that it can be combined with other parts of the Java family to create robust, cross-platform, large-scale, and secure web applications. However, this power comes at the cost of being a relatively complex language to learn.

Our example translated to JSP looks like this:

```
<!DOCTYPE html PUBLIC "-//W3C//DTD XHTML 1.0 Transitional//EN"
  "http://www.w3.org/TR/xhtml1/DTD/xhtml1-transitional.dtd">

<html>
<% String strHello = "hello, World"; %>
<head>
<title>Hello</title>
</head>
```

```
<body>
```

**`<h1><%=strHello%></h1>`**
```
<p>This page has a .jsp extension and therefore will be parsed by a server
running an application server that supports JSP before the output is returned to
the browser.</p>

</body>
</html>
```

### Which Platforms and Servers Support This?

The Java technology is cross-platform, the idea being that you can "write once and run anywhere". There are a variety of application servers available which allow you to run JSP across the spectrum of operating system environments. There are commercial servers such as Macromedia Jrun, IBM WebSphere, and BEA Weblogic, and open source servers such as Tomcat, which you can also download to install on your own machine in order to test your pages.

### Why Code in JSP?

JSP is probably not the language of choice for the web designer who just needs to have an understanding of server-side code in order to be able to incorporate a small amount of functionality into their sites. As it is part of a larger and more powerful group of technologies, it can be harder to work with. You can produce JSP applications using Dreamweaver MX, but this factor is yet to be widely adopted by web professionals. The help and support available within the general JSP community tends to presume a certain level of understanding, rather than being geared towards the true beginner.

That said, if you are keen to get into large-scale application development, then JSP is a good direction to be working in. Learning the relatively small part of Java that forms JSP will stand you in good stead for beginning to work with other aspects of the Java Technology, such as **EJBs (Enterprise Javabeans)**.

# Databases

One of the main reasons we use server-side scripting is in order to be able to retrieve information from a database. A database is simply information that has been stored in a way that is easily searchable and retrievable. You may already be familiar with a desktop database, such as Microsoft Access, and the way that information is stored in tables that can be linked to each other.

Each **table** in a database consists of **records** (horizontal rows of data) and **fields** (vertical columns), rather like a spreadsheet.

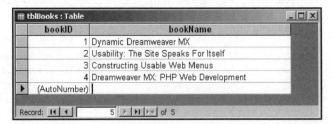

As we saw briefly earlier on, any action on the database – such as inserting, updating, or deleting a record, or in any way manipulating the data – is done via a **Query**.

# Why Use a Database on the Web?

A database is a very efficient method of storing and retrieving data. Of course, it is possible to store information by writing and reading from text files and, for small applications (for instance a guest book), this method can be sufficient. However, if you need to manipulate the data in any way, such an application can become slow and resource-intensive, especially if multiple users try to alter the same data at once. Moving the searching and sorting of the data into a purpose-built database means that your applications will run faster.

> " *Moving the searching and sorting of the data into a purpose-built database means that your applications will run faster.* "

# How Web Pages Interact with a Database

Basic interactions between a web page and a database include:

- Inserting data, such as adding names and e-mail addresses to a list of web site visitors who would like to receive an e-mail newsletter.

- Displaying data that is held in the database, for instance allowing the administrator to view all the names and e-mail addresses on a web page.

- Deleting information from the database.

- Using the data. For example, in the process of sending an e-mail to all the people who wish to receive it.

In order to 'talk' to your database, you need to use a language that it understands. That language is called **Structured Query Language** or **SQL**. Any database that you come across is likely to understand SQL. Although many databases have their own proprietary extensions to the SQL language, these tend to be used for more complex queries within the database itself, and the basic language remains the same.

For example, to retrieve all records from a database table called `tblBooks` you would need to pass the following command to the database:

```
SELECT * FROM tblBooks
```

If I were to run this command on the table illustrated in the earlier screenshot, I would receive the following data:

| 1 | Dynamic Dreamweaver MX |
|---|---|
| 2 | Usability: The Site Speaks for Itself |
| 3 | Constructing Usable Web Menus |
| 4 | Dreamweaver MX: PHP Web Development |

To create a page that retrieves this information from a database you need to use your server-side language of choice to create a connection to the database and then send the database the SQL query so that it can return the required information. In ASP with VBScript, it would look something like the code overleaf:

```
<%Option Explicit

Dim conn, rs, strSQL
Set conn = Server.CreateObject("ADODB.Connection")
conn.ConnectionString = "dsn=DSN;uid=USERNAME;pwd=PASSWORD"
conn.Open

Set rs = Server.CreateObject("ADODB.Recordset")
strSQL = "SELECT * FROM tblBooks"
rs.Open strSQL, conn
%>
<!DOCTYPE html PUBLIC "-//W3C//DTD XHTML 1.0 Transitional//EN"
   "http://www.w3.org/TR/xhtml1/DTD/xhtml1-transitional.dtd">

<html>
<head>
<title>Books I have read</title>
</head>
<body>
<h1>Books I have read</h1>
<ul>
<%Do While Not rs.EOF%>
<li><%=rs("bookName")%></li>
<%rs.MoveNext()
loop%>
</ul>

</body>
</html>
<%
rs.Close
Set rs = Nothing
conn.Close
Set conn = Nothing%>
```

The code above the DOCTYPE is simply opening a connection to the database and then creating a **recordset**. A recordset can be thought of as the table of information that you have retrieved from the database stored in memory ready for you to use. On this page, we used this information to print out a list of the books held in the table. The part of the script that prints out the data is between the <ul></ul> tags as I wanted to create one list item (<li>) for each entry.

```
<li><%=rs("bookName")%></li>
```

In VBScript, as in PHP4 and JSP, we can use = to show that we want to print something out to the screen. If you look at the previous example, you will see that each block of ASP is placed within <% %> tags. This lets the server know that there is something to be parsed or interpreted here. When it encounters the opening <%, the web server hands the processing of the document over to the ASP web application server, which then processes the script, interpreting it and handing the HTML output back to the web server for sending back to the client's browser. When the closing %> is met, the web application server stops processing and hands the job of sending the page back to the main web server. You will find similar tags in other languages; for example, in PHP you would use <? ?>.

So, here we are asking it to print out the current row of the recordset called `rs` and print the field named `bookName`, which is the name of the field in the database. The code that encloses this statement:

```
<%Do While Not rs.EOF%>
statement here
<%rs.MoveNext()
loop%>
```

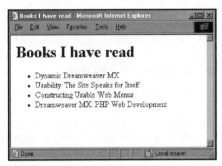

simply tells the recordset to loop through each record it has retrieved until it gets to the end. The resulting page looks like the image shown on the right:

At the end of the page, we have some code that reads:

```
<%
rs.Close
Set rs = Nothing
conn.Close
Set conn = Nothing%>
```

This simply shuts down the connection to the database and frees up the memory that the recordset was using. If we didn't do that, we'd run out of memory pretty fast!

While this brief example used ASP with VBScript, the logic is the same for whichever language/technology you are using:

- Connect to the database

- Retrieve a recordset of data by passing an SQL Query to the database

- Do something with that data

- Close your recordset connection (to reclaim memory usage)

- Close your connection to the database

# What Types of Database Are There?

There are many databases available for you to use on your site. However, the ones that you are most likely to come across in a shared hosting environment are MySQL, Microsoft Access, and Microsoft SQL Server. Other names you might hear discussed include Oracle, PostgreSQL, mSQL, and FoxPro. These databases can be roughly split into two groups: **File-based databases** and **Database servers**.

## File-based Databases

Microsoft Access and FoxPro are file-based databases. With a file-based database you create your database file locally and then can transfer it via FTP to your server in the same manner as you would any other files for your web site. If you are using a file-based database, then you should ensure that the location to which you will upload it is outside of the web-enabled directories of your web site, otherwise a malicious user would be able to retrieve it by just typing, say *http://www.mysite.com/mydatabase.mdb* in their browser and downloading the database.

For example, folders in a shared hosting account with support for file-based databases may include *database*, *ftp*, *logs*, and *www*. The site files go into the *www* folder and the database would be uploaded into the *database* folder where it cannot be accessed with a web browser.

Using a file-based database, such as Access, is a good way to learn the principles of designing and connecting to a database, as it has a user-friendly and simple interface and you can create your database on your own computer before uploading it. Microsoft Access is available on many low-cost Windows hosting accounts. It is limited in the number of users that it can support simultaneously, but for a personal or small business site, with a relatively low amount of traffic, such a database will serve you well. Access is, however, a Microsoft application and as such can only be deployed on a server running the Windows operating system.

### Database Servers

Database servers, which include MySQL, postgreSQL, Microsoft SQL Server, and Oracle, are a more robust way of implementing a database on your site. When you develop on a database server, you do not create a file on your own computer. Instead, you need to create your database directly within the server (although you could install a server on your own computer and then transfer your data from your local server to the live server).

Database servers tend to offer a higher level of functionality than the file-based databases. They are designed for a multi-user environment and are therefore more suitable for a high-traffic web site or one where many people could potentially be altering the data at the same time. The higher-end commercial database servers, such as Microsoft SQL Server or Oracle, are very expensive. While they can be found on shared hosting accounts, they do come at an additional cost. Open source database servers, such as MySQL and postgreSQL, can be found on low-cost hosting. MySQL is usually the choice for those hosting companies that offer PHP and a database. If you are developing for the UNIX environment, then MySQL is likely to be your database of choice.

# Getting Started with Server-Side Development

In order to be able to develop and test server-side code you will need to be able to run that code on your own computer, in the same way that the web server does when you upload it to your live site. This means that you will need to install a web server on your computer. Doing so can open you up to potential security issues, particularly if you have a permanent (DSL, Cable, or ISDN) connection and a static IP address. There are tools that scan networks looking for open ports, which malicious users can employ to compromise your system.

If you are installing a server:

- Ensure that you keep your security patches up to date
- Use a firewall (many routers act as a firewall so if you have a router to share your connection between several computers, check the manual to ensure it is blocking attempts to access your network)
- Turn your web server off when you are not using it, if you are unsure as to how secure you are

# What You Will Need

The exact software that you will need to install on your computer will depend on the language or technology you have chosen.

| Technology | OS | Web Server | Application Server |
|---|---|---|---|
| ASP | Windows | IIS | n/a |
| ASP.NET | Windows | IIS | .NET Framework |
| ColdFusion | Windows | IIS / Apache | ColdFusion Server |
| ColdFusion | Linux/Unix | Apache | ColdFusion Server |
| JSP | Windows | Apache / IIS | Tomcat |
| JSP | Linux / Unix | Apache | Tomcat |
| PHP | Windows | Apache / IIS | PHP |
| PHP | Linux / Unix | Apache | PHP |
| PHP | Mac OS X | Apache | PHP |

In the above table I have outlined the most likely choices for your own development environment. If you decide that web development is more your thing than design, then you may begin to look at other options for web and application servers. However, the options above are the most documented and used; as a rough estimate these would cover around 95% of server technology in use today, so as a start you should probably select one or other of these combinations.

You will also probably want to use a database. If you are working on Windows, then you may use Access – it is also a simple process to upgrade an Access database to Microsoft SQL Server if you do not have a copy of SQL Server running locally. You can also download and install MySQL on Windows, Linux, Unix, and Mac OS X. The resources at the end of this chapter include URLs that will assist you in setting up a local database server.

## Setting Up a Local Server

Once you have a local web server installed on your computer, you will be able to launch a browser and type one of:

*http://localhost/*
*http://computer_name/*

to view the pages in your web server's root web directory. These are run through the web server just as they would be on a live server. If you have an Access database or MySQL installed and running, you will be able to connect to the database and retrieve information from it to test your pages just as they will act on the server of your hosting company.

### IIS/PWS Web Server

If you are running Windows 2000 or XP Professional, then you can install IIS from the CD. To install IIS go to *Settings > Control Panel > Add/Remove programs* in the Windows *Start* menu. Then select *Add/Remove Windows Components* and check the *Internet Information Services* checkbox. You will need to insert the Windows 2000 / XP CD and it will install IIS for you.

For Windows 98, you will need to run the PWS `setup.exe` program on your Windows 98 CD. It can be found in the `addons\pws` folder on the CD.

To check your server is running properly type:

*http://localhost*

into a web browser. You should get a default homepage, which shows that your server is now configured to serve pages:

This is all that you need to do in order to be able to serve classic ASP on your own computer. If you want to test ASP.NET applications, then you will also need to download the .NET framework from Microsoft. It is available from *http://www.asp.net/download.aspx* and comes in two versions: **.NET Framework Redistributable** and **.NET Framework Software Development Kit**. Both downloads will allow you to run ASP.NET applications, but unless you are on a very fast connection you will most likely go for the first option as it is a much smaller download. The Software Development Kit comes with a large number of examples and thorough documentation, however, so if you have a fast enough connection, you may find the latter worth the time spent getting it. You will also probably need the latest MDAC (Microsoft Data Access Components) also downloadable from Microsoft

> *Note: You cannot run ASP.NET on Windows NT4, Windows 98, Windows ME, or Windows XP Home.*

(*http://www.microsoft.com/data/*).
The ASP.NET Framework is installed by way of a simple wizard when you run the downloaded file, and after installation you should be able to run both classic ASP and ASP.NET applications.

### Apache Web Server

You can install Apache on many operating systems including most versions of Windows, Mac OS X, Linux, and other Unix-based systems. The site (*http://httpd.apache.org*) has versions for most systems, so find a suitable version and download it. If you are planning to install Apache for Windows, you will need to download a Win32 installation program and also read the detailed and easy-to-follow instructions found at: (*http://httpd.apache.org/docs/windows.html*).

It is wise to consider the application server that you wish to use with Apache for your dynamic pages before continuing with the installation. Apache itself is not an application server: you need to install PHP, ColdFusion Server, or a JSP server such as Tomcat, before you can serve your pages. The order in which you install these things can be important, so it is a good idea to gather the downloads that you need before starting. Since a step-by-step guide to installing these systems is outside the scope of this chapter, I have included the URLs of a number of sites that should help you get started with installing and configuring Apache plus application servers on Windows, Linux, and Mac OS X in the *Resources* section.

## Home Directories

You can just place all your files in the default web server directory of your server. However, it is easier to create a directory that will hold all of your different sites and use that as your home directory.

Make a new directory on your computer, where you will store your site files. This can be anywhere you like – I call mine `1web` and underneath that are separate directories for each site.

### Using IIS

Select *Start > Settings > Control Panel* from the Windows *Start* Menu, and open *Administrative Tools*. Open *Internet Services Manager*.

You should see your computer name. Expand the + next to it and you will see a second level of options:

Right-click on *Default Web Site* and select *'Properties'*. Then choose the *Home Directory* tab and you will be able to browse for the directory that you created.

Click *OK*.

## Using Personal Web Manager

Again, select *Start > Settings > Control Panel* from the Windows *Start* Menu, and open *Administrative Tools*. Open *Personal Web Manager*, and click the *'Advanced'* button. Right-click on the *<Home>* at the top of the Tree view, select *Properties*, and browse for your new home directory.

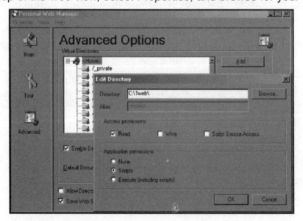

## Using Apache

If you wish to change your home directory, you will need to edit a file called `httpd.conf`, which stores the configuration for the web server. It is just a text file, so it will open in a simple text editor, like Notepad (or similar, for non-Windows platforms). The exact location of this file will depend on exactly where your Apache server is installed on your computer, but is usually found inside a folder called *conf*, inside the root of the main *apache* folder.

This file can look rather intimidating at first glance, but it is fairly logical if you work your way through it. The line in the file that points to your home directory will vary between platforms and (in the case of Linux) between distributions. If you wish to change the home directory of the server, just search for the line that begins `DocumentRoot` and modify the directory path that follows it to the path to your own preferred directory. Unless you are using a customized copy of `httpd.conf`, it is very likely that there will be accompanying comments in the file itself, instructing you on how to make this change.

# Finding Hosting for Your Site

As you will realize by now, once you start working with server-side code, you will need specific things available on your hosting account. As well as having the functionality to run the server-side script, you would also be wise to find out other details of the account, and how they operate. Some hosting companies offer a better service than others. Many hosting companies offer a 'Control Panel' that will allow you to easily configure such things as secured directories, your databases, and make other changes to the environment. These can be very useful when working with server-side script.

## Working with Database Servers

As we have mentioned, working with a file-based database such as Access is simply a case of creating your database using your local copy of Access on your own machine, uploading it to the web host, and then connecting to it with your pages. Database servers however are different, in that you do not have a file to transfer. Hosting companies that offer database servers will inform you as to how to connect to and use your database.

### MySQL and PHPMyAdmin

If you have a hosting account that includes MySQL, you should be given information about how to create and work with your database by the hosting company. This may be via a web front-end, or you may need to use SSH or TELNET into the hosting company and connect to the database using the command line. You may also be able to connect to the database using a graphical front-end to MySQL, such as phpMyAdmin (*www.phpmyadmin.net*).

phpmyAdmin is a product used by many hosting companies in order to give people a simple way to administer their MySQL databases from the Web. On low-cost hosting companies, this is often the only way you will be able to administer your database and, while it can be a little slow going, in comparison with working at the command line, it is a helpful tool if you are not confident with SQL.

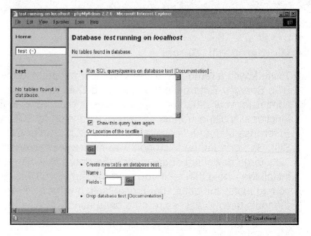

The phpMyAdmin initial page will normally take you into your database, since the hosting company will usually have created your database for you. When you log in, you will be able to go straight to that database. You can then create the tables directly in the interface. If you have created a script file either from the MySQL command line or with the graphical tool you are using on your desktop, you can upload the file, and your database will be created. phpMyAdmin allows you to either use form fields to create tables and columns, or enables you to simply paste the SQL query directly into a form box and it will run the command for you.

### The Command Line

Unless you have become comfortable working at the command line on your local system, you will probably wish to avoid using a hosting company that will only give you command-line access to MySQL. While this is a very quick and powerful way to work, you need to have a good working knowledge of the SQL required to create, edit, and delete databases. If you intend to go on to do more web development, this is very useful knowledge to have, but for the beginner, or the designer who simply needs to get a small database online, learning SQL in depth may not be top of your list of priorities!

The screen capture below shows the MySQL command line being used to create and insert data into a table.

If you can use the command line to connect to your database, you may also be able to use a third-party tool that you run on your own computer and point to your live MySQL database. There are a variety of these tools available and many offer other functionality such as the ability to convert databases from MS Access format to MySQL. I have listed some such applications in the *Resources* section at the end of this chapter.

### Microsoft SQL Server

To work with a remote SQL Server, most people use the tools available from Microsoft as part of SQL Server – Enterprise Manager and Query Analyzer. These tools give you a visual way to administer your database, upsize Access databases to SQL Server, and create more advanced functionality using Transact-SQL (an extension to SQL) within the database server itself. Enterprise Manager is available on the SQL Server CD or by downloading the 120-day trial of SQL Server from the Microsoft web site (*www.microsoft.com/sql/downloads/default.asp*). This is a fairly large download and includes the entire SQL Server database. However, you don't need to install the whole thing – if you start the install you will get an option to simply install the tools. If you do install the actual database itself, it will stop functioning after the time period is up. However, the tools used to access remote databases will still function. If you are on a dial-up connection and would have difficulty in downloading the software, then it is possible to order the CD from the Microsoft web site.

# Working with Dreamweaver MX

One way to ease yourself gently into database-driven application development is to use Dreamweaver MX, which has the capability to write code visually using ASP, ASP.NET, PHP, JSP, and ColdFusion server models. You will need to have a web server up and running in order to use this built-in functionality of Dreamweaver MX fully, but it is an excellent way to start learning the concepts of server-side site development and for much simple functionality you won't need to hand-code at all.

Using a visual environment like Dreamweaver MX is often a good way to get started with server-side code, particularly for designers who are used to thinking in a visual way (especially if you are already comfortable using that environment for design work). The concepts behind developing web applications are the most difficult thing to grasp. Using a visual environment can help you get a grasp of those concepts. If you keep one eye on the code that is being created and think about what it is you are actually doing as you interact with the database, you will quickly become more comfortable with the code itself, and have less trouble working from tutorials, or figuring out how to edit the code yourself.

# Hand-Coding

Visual tools are all very well, but you actually need nothing more than a text editor to create dynamic pages. Some text editors offer syntax highlighting, and this is very useful in helping to differentiate between XHTML, JavaScript, and server-side code. Syntax highlighting also often helps show you where you have forgotten to close a tag or quotation mark, for instance.

Other useful features in a good text editor include the ability to store useful pieces of code in a manner that allows you to drop them into a page later on, so that you can reuse them easily. After a while you can build up quite a library of such pieces of code and this can save a lot of time doing repetitive tasks. An editor with such capability is Dreamweaver MX with its *Snippets* tab (found on the *Code* panel). Not only does this provide a wide selection of pre-built code snippets, you can add your own. The next screenshot shows a page in Dreamweaver MX with syntax coloring and the *Snippets* panel open to the right of the document.

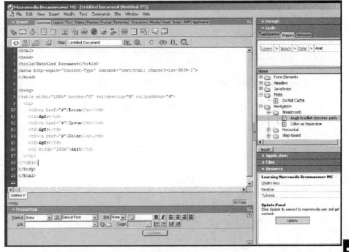

Dreamweaver MX is available for both Windows and Mac OS X. There are other excellent editors also available for Mac OS, Linux, and Windows. I have included URLs for a variety of them in the *Resources* section at the end of this chapter.

# Summary

In this chapter we have been on a lightning tour of server-side web development. It is outside the scope of this book to delve further into these issues, as each technology can and does take entire books to write about – even on a basic level. What I do hope to have achieved, is to give you a basic understanding of what server-side development is and the various options that you have available to you, so that you can do your own research on the subject.

The Web today is becoming an increasingly dynamic medium. Even if you outsource the actual development of server-side code to someone else, I would still advise you to get a good understanding of the underlying concepts, as outlined in this chapter, so that you can understand the bigger picture and talk knowledgeably about the subject with clients and fellow workers.

# Resources

The Web is full of resources that can help you in learning a server-side language, and to research which language you feel is best for the work you are doing.

## Languages and Technologies

### ASP

Introduction to ASP – *http://hotwired.lycos.com/webmonkey/98/39/index2a.html?tw=programming*
ASP Beginners FAQ – *http://www.4guysfromrolla.com/webtech/faq/faqtoc.shtml#Beginner*

### ASP.NET

ASP.NET Web (the official Microsoft site) – *http://www.asp.net*
.NET Framework Overview –
                *http://hotwired.lycos.com/webmonkey/01/02/index3a.html?tw=programming*
ASP.NET on 4 Guys from Rolla – *http://aspnet.4guysfromrolla.com/*

### ColdFusion

ColdFusion (official Macromedia site) – *http://www.macromedia.com/software/coldfusion/*
ColdFusion MX Overview –
                *http://hotwired.lycos.com/webmonkey/02/34/index3a.html?tw=programming*
EasyCFM – *http://www.easycfm.com/*

### JSP

Sun's 'New to Java' section – *http://developer.java.sun.com/developer/onlineTraining/new2java/*
Download Tomcat for JSP – *http://jakarta.apache.org/tomcat/index.html*
Setting up a JSP development environment –
                *http://www.devshed.com/Server_Side/Java/JSPDev/page1.html*

### PHP

PHP – *http://www.php.net*
Setting up a PHP development environment –
> *http://www.devshed.com/Server_Side/PHP/SoothinglySeamless/page1.html*

PHP Beginner – *http://phpbeginner.com/index.php*
Installing and configuring PHP and MySQL on OS X – *http://www.entropy.ch/software/macosx/php/*
Building a database-driven web site using PHP and mySQL –
> *http://www.webmasterbase.com/article.php/228*

## Databases

### Access

Official Microsoft site – *http://www.microsoft.com/office/access/default.asp*
Access 2000 Tutorial – *http://www.fgcu.edu/support/office2000/access/*

### MySQL

The MySQL site – *http://www.mysql.com*
Beginning with MySQL – *http://www.devshed.com/Server_Side/MySQL/Intro/page1.html*
Setting up and configuring MySQL on OS X – *http://www.entropy.ch/software/macosx/mysql/*

### Microsoft SQL Server

Official Microsoft site – *http://www.microsoft.com/sql/default.asp*
SQL Team – *http://www.sqlteam.com/*

## Editors

### Windows

Homesite – *http://www.macromedia.com/software/homesite/*
NoteTab Lite and NoteTab Pro – *http://www.notetab.com/*
Dreamweaver MX – *http://www.macromedia.com/dreamweaver (also available for Mac)*
Web Matrix - *http://www.asp.net/webmatrix/default.aspx?tabindex=4&tabid=46*

### Mac

PageSpinner – *http://www.optima-system.com/pagespinner/*
BBEdit – *http://www.bbedit.com*

### Linux

Quanta – *http://quanta.sourceforge.net/*
Bluefish – *http://bluefish.openoffice.nl/*

## Firewall Software

Smoothwall (an excellent firewall product that can be installed on an old computer) –
> *http://www.smoothwall.org*

ZoneAlarm - *http://www.zonelabs.com/store/content/home.jsp*

# 16

- What and where to learn?
- Putting together a portfolio
- Getting help and advice

**Author: Rachel Andrew**

# Where Do I Go from Here?

I hope that, in the pages of this book, you have found inspiration and ideas to help you in your quest to become a 'web professional'. Economic slowdowns and dot com failures aside, there are still openings in this web business; they are just a little harder to find these days. The state of the economy makes it all the more important that you focus your skills and learn the right things to make sure that you look like the best candidate at a college or job interview, or to make your tender the preferred bid on a freelance job.

In this final chapter, I hope to point you in the right direction for the next stage in your journey. I'll talk about some of the paths you might follow from this point on, and discuss the pros and cons of these. I also want to introduce you to some of the places I hang out, the places where web professionals like myself hone our skills and keep up to date. The ability to keep learning and remain current with contemporary thinking will stand you in good stead throughout your professional life.

## Where Do You Want to Go?

You have probably realized by now that there is an awful lot more stuff that you could learn. You might be feeling rather concerned that you could never learn all these technologies and ideas, and don't even know where to start doing so. The first thing you need to realize is that very few people are real all-rounders. Many see themselves purely as designers, whose skills lie in creating amazing things in Photoshop and turning those into beautiful web pages. Other people have great JavaScript and CSS skills and spend most of their time creating DHTML for interfaces. Some people discover their talents lie in database design and implementation, and so leave the front-end design to other professionals.

# Finding Your Strengths

Specializing is all very well, but what might you specialize in? You should first gain a broad-based knowledge of the core technologies that make up web pages. This will include HTML and XHTML, CSS, some JavaScript, and an understanding of good design and information architecture. You will want to include in your basic skill set the ability to create simple graphics and optimize images and photographs within a graphics software package.

While the above might seem a lot to start with, these are skills you can gain simply by doing the job. The best way to learn how to build web sites is just to do it, and do it a lot. Build a site for yourself; build a site about your hobby; create a site for your daughter's Brownie pack, or some other local organization. They will probably be really glad of the offer and in the process of building these sites you will learn a huge amount about what goes into a web site. You'll learn how to use these technologies and, by putting them into practice, you will start to get a feel for what you really enjoy, and where you find your skills are strongest.

My own path into this industry began when I found myself out of work when I was pregnant with my daughter. I come from an arts background, as a dancer and choreographer, and my initial thought was that I would work towards becoming a web designer. As I started to teach myself it became apparent fairly rapidly that I am not a designer: graphics packages confound me. I can spend several days poking at something in Photoshop with the end result being rather strange and badly composed. However, I almost accidentally started writing a bit of JavaScript, then installed Linux and Apache on an old computer and taught myself Perl (a scripting language). When I decided to go back into employment, I did so as a webmaster, heading up a technical team really involved with the backend of web development.

I currently run my own web solutions company, (*http://www.edgeofmyseat.com*) developing some large intranet and extranet solutions, but much of my time is spent working for other agencies and designers, building web applications that they design the interface for, and adding database-driven functionality to static web sites. My foray into the world of web design stood me in excellent stead for this, as I am sympathetic to the work of designers, and don't ride rough-shod over their carefully composed pages, even though I rarely need to fire up Photoshop myself, these days! The point of this anecdote is that it is difficult to imagine where you might end up. I still have no idea what I'll be doing in two years time, since the Web evolves so rapidly. It is important that you keep an eye on the industry, and an open mind as to where you might end up, while you learn new skills – you might just surprise yourself!

The skills that you will need to learn, and the range of skills you will have to acquire, will also depend on what you want to do with your skills. For many, the lure of working freelance is what attracted them to this business in the first place. For others, their dream is to secure a position within an agency, working in a team with other designers and developers on large projects. You may well end up doing both of these things at different times in your career and, as someone who now works for herself, my experience as an employee working for someone else has proven invaluable.

# Being an Employee

> "When hiring web people, there are a few key things I look for. The first is a demonstrable enthusiasm for the Web. I need to know that the candidate understands how the Web works on both a technical and social level. They should understand what really constitutes good web design or development – meeting the needs of the users and surpassing their expectations.
>
> "The second thing I look for is proven knowledge of basic web languages. I don't care what tools the candidate knows backwards, so long as they have a good grounding in basic XHTML, CSS, and a reasonable grasp of JavaScript. Everything else follows.
>
> "The third aspect is the ability to learn. As the Web has grown, most designers and developers have taught themselves their trade by learning from others and experimenting. The Web is so fast-moving that this skill is essential. If you can teach yourself how to do something by following some tutorials on the Web or in a book and then trying it out, you're worth far more than anyone with letters after their name.
>
> Drew McLellan – http://dreamweaverfever.com

There are a range of web-related jobs within various companies and other large employers, such as web agencies, universities, "dot com" companies, and traditional companies who need in-house web professionals. These might include the likes of well-established brands, such as Amazon (http://www.amazon.com), who have a need for designers and developers. Searching on any job site will show you the variety of positions that are available and the skills required.

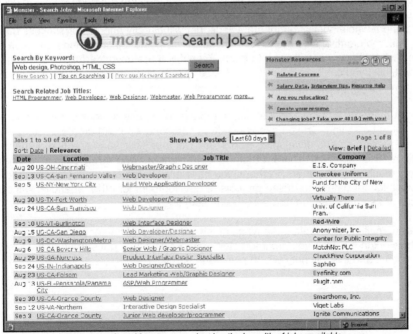

*An excerpt from Monster.com, showing the breadth of jobs available.*

The above screenshot extract is of the well-known site Monster.com (*http://www.monster.com/*). A search for '*Web design, Photoshop, HTML, CSS*' turned up a wide range of opportunities in a variety of different companies. Reading job adverts, even before you are in a position to start applying for them, is a good way to find out which skills seem to be most in demand, and the software that companies expect you to be proficient in. Finding out the most requested skills can help you to plan a road map for your own learning – whether you intend to teach yourself from books and online tutorials, or take a course through college or evening classes. Keeping focused on your goals, and the eventual job you want to be able to apply for successfully, will ensure that the skills you learn will be helpful in meeting those goals.

## Setting Up on Your Own

> *"As an individual freelancer, don't try to cover every kind of web site. Find your niche market and pursue. Also, stay in contact with other freelancers who do what you don't do (for example, web design, web developer, shopping cart expert, database guru). As potential opportunities arise, you can quickly form a 'team' to fit the project. Join several mailing lists to stay up on current developments and solutions."*
>
> *L. Michelle Johnson – http://www.grownmencry.com*

Freelancing and self-employment is certainly the way that a lot of designers and developers are earning their living. If you wish to go down this route, the skills that you will need to master are not only those professional ones that you will be paid for, but also the need to be able to pitch for a job, market yourself, keep accounts, be motivated enough to crawl out of bed in the morning and start work, and a whole host of peripheral things that will directly affect your success but have very little to do with the creative side of the Web. If you will be going it alone, then add these 'business' skills to the list of things you will need to learn. Even if you are a wonderful designer, your business will fail if you can't pay your tax bills, lose client's photographs, or forget to invoice people!

If you decide that your aim is to go it alone, then take some time to consider what it is you actually want to be selling. Do you see yourself as someone who can create a total solution for companies – designing and developing web sites? Do your skills lie in creating graphics, logos, and identities for companies? There are plenty of freelancers who rarely build an entire web site, but are very much web designers. Perhaps you have discovered that your skills are technical, and you will pitch for database-driven projects or development for other agencies without the in-house skills of database design and server-side scripting?

Read relevant mailing lists, look at the types of jobs on offer on freelance job sites, ask other people who work in the area you are interested in about how they got started and the skills they find most useful, and this will help you to plan your learning.

# Education

> *"Web designers at this stage in history must be people who enjoy living in a state of constant change. It takes a lot to keep up, to successfully learn and use the languages, tools, and vision necessary to the trade. Regular education is necessary and something that should be looked upon as a joyous aspect of the job, not a troublesome one."*
>
> *Molly E. Holzschlag – http://www.molly.com*

If you are going to succeed in this business, you are never going to be able to stop learning. I'm still learning as much every day as I was when I first got it into my head that this was something that I wanted to do. My personal list of things I want to learn, or improve my skills in, seems to increase daily. You could see this as a plus or a minus, depending on how much you like to study, but keeping your skills up-to-date will be a very important part of your professional career. If you start out with the attitude that learning new skills is not just something you do up to a certain point, but is an ongoing part of your career, you will find that you gain far more skills in a shorter time than you would ever imagine, and are someone who is attractive to employers and clients. You will be able to talk confidently about new technologies and the latest 'buzzwords' even if your knowledge is limited to something you read on a site the night before while you were trying to find out about the subject!

Once you have decided what your initial learning requirements are, then you need to figure out how to become proficient in those areas. Everyone is different. I, like many in the business, am totally self-taught, but other professionals have certifications and relevant degrees coming out of their ears. Some people learn well on their own, while others enjoy the push of learning alongside other students and having a tutor to ask questions of. One method is not better than the other, but one way may suit you better. Your choice will also depend on your current life situation.

## Traditional Education

If you decide on full-time education at college or university, you may have to choose between a three- and four-year course. There are some new media courses around, and there is also the route of formal computer science, if you want a good technical grounding. Many web designers also come through from more traditional design courses. A degree seems to be more common amongst 'real' designers, and if you are generally interested in design then this can be a very useful qualification, as it will allow you to move into different areas of the design world. Do investigate any degree or long-term course: ask to see work that has been done by previous students. A college that has had students who have gone on to do well for themselves will usually be only too happy to tell you, so see if you can find out what their graduates have ended up doing after leaving the college. You may even be able to find some information by searching the Web, since most people will state the college they attended in their resume.

While having a degree is often not very important to clients and to agencies, more traditional companies may not even look at your resume if you don't have one, so you may feel it is worth spending the time getting a degree-level qualification, depending on what you want to achieve in your career.

Many colleges and universities also offer part-time courses, evening classes, and summer schools on web design and development-related subjects. Classes can be a good way to learn to use software such as Photoshop and Dreamweaver, and you might be able to take a class to see how you get on with a particular bit of software before you take the plunge and buy yourself a copy. Many colleges also offer part-time business skills courses, which can be very helpful for anyone wishing to go it alone as a freelancer or set up their own agency.

## Online Courses

The Web is a fantastic source of free and low-cost information, tutorials, and reference material about all kinds of subjects. However, where it really excels is in the dissemination of advice from people who work in the business themselves. Search on Google (*http://www.google.com*) for the technology or skills you are trying to learn, and you will find site after site offering help, tips, and tutorials.

If you are short of free time in which to improve your web skills, or do not wish to pay for traditional courses, then you can teach yourself simply by dedicating some time each week to following tutorials and building your skills in the areas that you have chosen to learn.

## Certification

If you are interested in the more technical aspects of web development, you may be tempted to work towards one of the official certifications from Oracle, Microsoft, Sun, and so on. For an individual freelancer, these certifications are probably less important (unless you intend to specialize in Oracle, for instance). However, they do carry some weight with employers. You will often find that an employer will put you through the training needed to pass a certification examination and, if that is the case, go for it! However, if you pay for these courses yourself, you will find that they are very expensive. Without experience to back up the training, you may not find them very helpful in securing a role.

There are many centers and web sites that offer 'web master certification' and the like. However, unless the certification is to a known and recognized standard, then it is debatable how useful such qualifications are. If a course is within your budget and you feel it is helpful to you, then there is certainly no harm in doing it. Some clients and employers may be impressed to see that you have gained a certificate in a web-related subject, but it is certainly not necessary. There are many professional designers and developers who do not have such qualifications.

# Putting Together a Portfolio

Whether you wish to find employment with a company or work as a freelancer, you will need to be able to show potential employers or clients the scope of what you can do. How you present this is going to depend on the kind of work you are trying to get. If you are a graphic designer with skills in logo design and branding, as well as web site design, then you may want to have a 'paper portfolio' as well as web-based examples of your work. However, displaying examples of your work on a professional-looking web site will go a long way in displaying your talents as a designer or developer.

For example, take a look at Jeffrey Zeldman's company web site, Happycog (*http://www.happycog.com*). Examples of the company's work are displayed with a description of each project.

## Catch 22

**I need work to put together a portfolio, but I need a portfolio to get work!**

The examples of work in your portfolio don't necessarily need to be paid work, or things you have done in a full-time job. Earlier, I advised you to volunteer to do some sites for other people. These sites can then form a legitimate part of your portfolio. Working as a volunteer can also give you experience in working to a specification: try to be as professional as you can with web sites you create on a voluntary basis – draw up a specification, talk to the 'client' about what they would find useful on the site, and work with them to produce something they love. You will not only have made a contribution to a good cause, but you will also have improved your skills in planning and designing a site for someone else. You can describe this process when you talk to a prospective client or employer about the project and even write about it on your own portfolio site!

Make your own web site a good advert for your talents. When I was involved in hiring designers and developers, I would always do a quick search on their name to see what I could turn up, that they had put together. A well-designed and executed personal web site says a lot about the care that a person takes over their work, and their overall enthusiasm for the Web.

# Working for Yourself

Having made the decision to go it alone as a freelance designer or developer, and create your own company, how do you go about finding and keeping clients? What should you charge and how can you ensure that you get paid? All of these things could take up several chapters of a book, but here we will look at a few of the issues you will need to consider before you start. In the *Resources* section, at the end of this chapter, I have listed some places where you should be able to get more help and information.

**16**

# Charging for Your Time

In the US, it is illegal to engage in price fixing and therefore inadvisable to discuss pricing on an industry-specific mailing list or group. Because of the possibility of allegations of price-fixing, many lists explicitly ban such discussions. Of course, you can go to many freelance and small agency sites and find out exactly how much they are charging, but that is by the by! I only mention this because posting "*how much should I charge for my work*" to an international list is likely to get you chastised.

**!** Note: when determining the number of hours you will work, take into account all the non-chargeable time that you will incur: time to learn new skills, the time it takes to do your accounts and send out invoices, time spent going to the bank with checks, marketing time, and so on. If you know you can only devote thirty hours per week to actually working on your business, you could find that almost half of these hours disappear in non-chargeable tasks – particularly early on, when you need to actively market your skills to find clients.

Before you can come up with pricing that is appropriate for you, you will need to work out how much you need to earn to survive. Add up your living costs – rent or mortgage payments, food, bills, clothing, entertainment, and then add a little bit on top for contingencies. Next, look at the costs of running your business or working as a freelancer – computer equipment, business cards, postage, and expensive software packages. Work out an average monthly figure for these business-related costs. These figures give you a guide to how much you need to earn, to sustain your standard of living.

Once you have that, it is simply a job of working out how many hours you will work on chargeable projects each week (on average) and dividing the amount you need by the number of hours you will work. Remember that you will need to pay income tax on what you earn, so add this to the hourly amount.

# Getting and Keeping Your Clients

As someone who made the leap from employee to self-employed, I find myself frequently asked, by newcomers to the industry, how I get my clients. These are the tips I give to people, based on my own experience.

- Don't limit yourself to your locality – there is no reason at all why you need to only work for people you can go to and visit their offices. I have some local clients, but in the main they come from all over the UK (where I'm based), and also from the US and Europe. By communicating well through e-mail and telephone you can establish a good working relationship with someone you have never met.

- Establish a professional relationship – if you act like a professional you will find that you are treated like one. Make sure that all your correspondence, e-mail, and paper, reflects well on you or your business. You can appear to be a bigger company or more experienced than you are by always appearing professional in your contacts with clients or prospective clients.

- Be confident – if you are confident in your skills, that will come through to the client and give them confidence in you.

- Be able to think through the client's problem and offer ideas during a meeting. This is where being well-read on the latest technologies and ideas can really pay off.

## Help for New Businesses

There is a lot of help and information available for new businesses. This is often country-specific and therefore I shall refrain from citing too many examples, although I have added some more general references in the *Resources* section at the end of this chapter. Searching the Web for information will yield a whole host of useful advice. Your bank may well have a small business advisor who can point you in the right direction for help, and you may even qualify for grants and loans in order to help get you started. Your local library can also be a good source of local information and resources.

# Working for a Company

Even if you eventually dream of having your own business, working for a company can gain you a large amount of experience very quickly, especially if you are working alongside other web professionals. You also have the security of a real job and a paycheck each month, and don't need to spend so much time on business administration.

## The Kind of Jobs Available

In *Chapter 1*, you were introduced to the different kinds of roles available in the web industry. There are also a whole host of different types of companies who hire web designers and developers. While many designers set their sights on working in a design agency with other creative people, there are also opportunities within traditional business, as part of an in-house design and development team, and within academic institutions. You may decide that the stability of a traditional company is more suitable for your lifestyle, particularly if you have a family. Traditional companies can be more understanding of family life than a new media agency full of 19 year olds who can work in the office till midnight!

If you are trying to find your first job in the industry, you are probably looking for a 'junior' role. However, this doesn't mean you need to be young. You may well find that your immediate boss is far younger than you are if this is a second career for you! Junior web design and development roles tend to mean that you end up doing all the dull things on projects that no-one else wants to do, but they are a good place to prove yourself, and also to learn from more experienced professionals. Many companies take people on at a junior level with the aim that they will move up the ranks within the company. If you can prove to be interested, enthusiastic, and a fast learner, you may well find that it gives you the step on the ladder that you need.

## How to Find Jobs

The big recruitment web sites can be a good source of jobs. Searching for roles appropriate to your skills and experience will not only give you an idea of how much you are 'worth', but also allow you to send off your resume and a link to your portfolio to those that sound interesting. Many of the jobs are posted by recruitment agencies that may well then contact you in order to find out a bit more about you. They can then keep you on their books and send you to appropriate interviews. You do need to be wary of recruitment agencies, however:

While a good agency will help you with your resume and sell you to potential employers in order to get you interviews, there are agents who will send you to any interview they can think of. This sounds good until you end up sitting in front of an interviewer who thinks you are a Java programmer, and the only Java you know about is the cup of coffee you are going to have on leaving the place!

## Interviews

> "When you go for a job interview, don't forget that you're probably up against a dozen other faces that claim to have the same skills. Be sure to let the interviewer know that you are different and have something special to offer. Be proactive in the interview: try to pick up on any problem the interviewer mentions and offer advice as to how you would solve it. If you can help them out whilst being interviewed, half the battle is won.
>
> "If you're asked a question you don't have an answer to, tell the interviewer that you don't know the answer, but tell them how you would go about finding out. No one has all the answers, but the smart candidate knows where to look. Let the interviewer know that you are a smart candidate.
>
> "Remember, even if you're used to web companies having a fairly casual dress code, this might not apply to the place you are visiting for interview. Dress smart. At worst, you will look like you made more effort than was expected – and that's never bad. If you turn up under dressed, you'll look like you don't care about the job."
>
> *Drew McLellan – http://dreamweaverfever.com*

Once you get invited for an interview, try and find out about the company you are hoping to get a job with. If they are a design agency, then look around their own site and the sites on their portfolio to get a feel for the kind of work that they do. A common interview question is, "Why do you want to work here?" Being able to show that you have looked at the work they have done in the past and are enthusiastic about it, shows that you are interested in the company.

Other questions are often asked to get a feel for how you see yourself and your career. "Where do you see yourself in five years' time?" is a great chance to talk about the learning you have been doing and plan to continue doing in order to develop your skills. "Tell me something about a recent project that you have worked on" allows you to discuss one of your projects in depth. Come prepared, knowing what you will talk about, since interviewers need to know that the things they have seen in your portfolio were created by you, and that you can talk about the techniques you used and the problems that you solved in the process.

Many jobs, particularly within agencies, will require you to go out and speak to clients at times. As a designer, you probably won't be asked to go to meetings with clients alone, but it often makes it easier if a designer is present at the initial meetings, in order to answer questions from the viewpoint of the person who has the skill to make the client's ideas a reality. If this is likely to be part of the job you are being interviewed for, make sure that you come across as someone who could be let loose on a client.

At the end of the day, interviewers want to hire someone. However, they also want to know they are picking the right person. Even if you have a wonderful portfolio, you can't just rely on that. Interviewers for design and development jobs are very often the team leader, and will be working very closely with the person that they hire, so you need to make sure that you come across as someone who will fit into their team and be an asset to it.

# Getting Help and Advice

There is a lot of help out there for a newcomer to this industry. One of the advantages of moving into web design and development is that it is still a relatively new industry, so a large proportion of people are self-taught and know exactly what it is like to be new and wondering where on earth to start.

On a more general level, you may also feel you need to get help with business skills, interview techniques, writing your CV or resume, or your 'people' skills.

## E-mail Lists and Newsgroups

An **e-mail list** has a central address to which you send your e-mail, which is then duplicated and sent out to all of the other members of the list. These groups are generally hosted on list servers that have basic commands that allow people to sign up automatically and start posting to the list.

There are also a huge number of **usenet groups** dedicated to every topic you could ever want to discuss (and many that you would really rather not think about too deeply!). Usenet is a medium that goes back to before the Web, and is most readily accessed using a newsreader. Outlook Express has a newsreader interface, as do Netscape 7 and Mozilla. There are many other newsreaders available, if you enjoy this method of communicating.

You can also explore usenet groups and post to them from your web browser at Google groups (*http://groups.google.com/*). While Google groups is an excellent method of searching relevant groups for answers, it is far easier to follow the conversations in a newsreader, and it is worth taking the time to learn how to set up such software, as there is a wealth of information on usenet.

To read a wide variety of groups you will need to connect to a news server. Your ISP may well offer such a server with your dial-up or cable account. There are also dedicated servers such as Macromedia's news server (*news://forums.macromedia.com*).

 To find out more about usenet, visit Google's page on usenet basics at http://groups.google.com/googlegroups/basics.html.

E-mail lists and usenet groups can be an invaluable source of encouragement and information for newcomers and seasoned professionals alike. Many groups form tight-knit communities of designers and developers who will help test sites, solve problems, and offer support to each other through difficult times. While such groups can seem to be rather cliquey at first glance, that is often because people have been posting there for several years and 'know' each other well. The larger groups tend to have a constant influx of new members, who soon become part of the community.

Many groups have a web site or FAQ associated with them, and these are always worth a read before posting to the group. Often groups have certain rules or etiquette that you are expected to follow and, while most people are understanding of someone who is new to this type of interaction, it can get rather tiring having to explain the same rules over and over again. This is the reason that the popular lists will have published these ground rules. Many lists have one or more **moderators** (people who check mail before allowing it to reach the list). They may place you on a moderated status until you have made a few posts, so don't be surprised if your posts don't show up immediately. This is usually just to stop spammers or troublemakers from posting to the group. After a few posts, you will usually find yourself unmoderated (unless the whole list or group is moderated at all times).

## How to Ask for Help on a Mailing List or Newsgroup

If you are struggling with a problem, then a relevant mailing list or newsgroup can be a way to get some collective brains onto the issue. Often someone will have come up against this before and will be able to help you out quickly. However, you are more likely to get useful answers if you follow these simple rules:

- Try to solve your problem first and remember what you have tried, so that you can explain this in the e-mail.

- Check that you are posting to a relevant newsgroup. If the problem is JavaScript, don't post to an XHTML discussion list! There are plenty of general web-related lists where almost all subjects are on topic.

- If the group has archives, then search them before posting, as someone else may have answered or partly answered your problem. You can always refer back to that post if it goes some way towards helping.

- In your post, explain clearly what you are trying to achieve, the steps that you have already tried, and what happened when you tried them.

- If possible, give the group a link either to the page in question or, if it is a very specific element that you are struggling with, put it on its own on a page. This allows people to see more quickly the issue at hand.

- Be polite and friendly. The groups are populated by other web designers and developers who don't receive anything for helping you out.

- When you receive some advice, take it on board and act on it. If the advice doesn't solve the problem, then don't be afraid to come back and explain what happened. Again, show an example. Don't get frustrated with the person who is trying to help!

- Don't forget to thank people for their help.

In time, you will probably find yourself answering other people's questions. Hopefully, you'll remember the days when you were a newcomer and be happy to help other people get started. Being able to give something back to a community that has helped you get started, is one of the really satisfying things about being involved in these communities.

## Mailing List and Newsgroup Dos and Don'ts

- Do remember that your posts are read by the whole list. Even if you feel that the list is a safe community, you don't know who might be reading. Posting too much personal information to any list or group may not be advisable.

- Do read the list for a few days before posting, to get a feel for the way people tend to phrase questions or reply to others.

- Don't (as a rule) post in HTML, attach files, or embed anything into your posts.

- Do upload an example to your web space and post the URL if you are asking advice with a problem you are having.

- Don't quote masses of the previous post when you reply to someone. The technique of snipping means that you hit *Reply* in your e-mail client or newsreader, and delete everything but a few lines that explain what you are replying to. Then add your reply, usually under the quoted portion. This ensures that people can understand who you are replying to, but don't need to read the entire previous post again.

- Do remember that these lists are international and there may be people posting for whom English is not their first language. Try to be clear in your meaning – sarcasm and jokes often do not translate very well between cultures and languages. Use emoticons to make your meaning clear if necessary. See http://www.pb.org/emoticon.html for an explanation of the different emoticons used to convey meaning when using e-mail or usenet.

- Don't add a huge signature with the URLs of all your sites (including the one with pictures of your cat), a quotation, or your company's e-mail disclaimer to the bottom of all your posts. A signature is a good idea so that people know who you are, but no more than four lines is the usual requirement.

# The Web

The Web is, of course, full of helpful advice and inspiration from those who have been there, done it, and are still doing it. Many successful people within the industry have their own personal sites and give information, tutorials, and help freely to anyone who searches for it and comes across it. There are also, as we have already discussed, thousands of tutorial sites available. This advice can be invaluable – advice from real people who are working in the industry you are in, or want to be in. There is always something new to be learned and new ways of looking at things.

# Summary

In this chapter I have hopefully shown you around some of your options as a web professional. This has been based very much on my own experience and my conversations with other professionals. I have tried to offer general, multinational information here. However, you will need to do some of your own research into the specifics of your own local web market, particularly when it comes to setting up as a freelancer or beginning your own business, since laws change from country to country (and state to state, in the US, of course).

This chapter could be summed up by my own personal mantra for success in the web business:

**Never stop learning, and never lose your enthusiasm for the Web and for what you do.**

If you keep your skills up to date and truly love what you do, you have a good chance of success and you'll have a lot of fun along the way.

# Resources

Below is a selection of recommended resources: places I tend to visit when I want to brush up my skills or find out what current thinking is. There are many, many more worthwhile resources online for you to check out, so take these as a starting point and enjoy the journey!

## Training and Online Learning Resources

HTML Writers Guild – *http://www.hwg.org/*
W3Schools – *http://www.w3schools.com*
Webmonkey – *http://hotwired.lycos.com/webmonkey/*
A List Apart – *http://www.alistapart.com*
Web Developer's Virtual Library – *http://wdvl.com/*
Evolt – *http://www.evolt.org/*

## Small Business and Freelance Help

Pricing – *http://webdesign.about.com/library/weekly/aa102300a.htm*
Writing a Business Plan – *http://www.alistapart.com/stories/business1/*
Contracts – *http://www.webreview.com/2000/09_01/strategists/09_01_00_2.shtml*
Planning and running a web design business (huge resource list) – *http://www.websitetips.com/business/index.shtml*
Freelancing in the web world – *http://hotwired.lycos.com/webmonkey/98/44/index4a.html?tw=jobs*
Handling clients – *http://www.digital-web.com/features/feature_2000-10.shtml*

## Employment

35 ways to land a job online – *http://www.fastcompany.com/online/16/webjobs.html*
10 common mistakes in resumes and cover letters – *http://www.aiga.org/content.cfm?CategoryID=37*
Career Lab, cover letters – *http://www.careerlab.com/letters/*
Job Interview – *http://www.job-interview.net/*

## E-mail Lists

You might catch me on some of these lists.

Babble List – *http://www.babblelist.com/*
css-discuss – *http://three.pairlist.net/mailman/listinfo/css-discuss*
webdesign-l – *http://www.webdesign-l.com/*
Evolt lists – *http://lists.evolt.org/*

# Index

**A Guide to the Index**

The index covers the numbered chapters but not the Introduction and is arranged in word-by-word order (so that, for example, New York would precede Newark). Acronyms have been preferred to their expansions as main entries as being easier to recall.

# @allow_mail_to

**C**

# CSS (Cascading Style Sheets)

# CSS (Cont'd)

# DHTML (Dynamic HTML)

# events

# <ol> XHTML tag, ordered list

## U

Notes

# Notes

**glasshaus**

web professional to web professional

glasshaus writes books for you. Any suggestions, or ideas about how you want
information given in your ideal book will be studied by our team.
Your comments are always valued at glasshaus.

Free phone in USA 800-873 9769
Fax (312) 893 8001

UK Tel.: (0121) 687 4100        Fax: (0121) 687 4101

## Fundamental Web Design and Development Skills – Registration Card

Name _____

Address _____

_____

_____

City _____ State/Region _____

Country _____ Postcode/Zip_____

E-Mail _____

Occupation _____

How did you hear about this book?

☐ Book review (name) _____

☐ Advertisement (name) _____

☐ Recommendation _____

☐ Catalog _____

☐ Other _____

Where did you buy this book?

☐ Bookstore (name) _____ City_____

☐ Computer store (name) _____

☐ Mail order_____

☐ Other _____

What influenced you in the purchase of this book?

☐ Cover Design   ☐ Contents   ☐ Other (please specify):

How did you rate the overall content of this book?

☐ Excellent   ☐ Good   ☐ Average   ☐ Poor

What did you find most useful about this book? _____

_____

What did you find least useful about this book? _____

_____

Please add any additional comments. _____

_____

_____

What other subjects will you buy a computer book on soon?

_____

What is the best computer book you have used this year?

**Note:** This information will only be used to keep you updated
about new glasshaus titles and will not be used for
any other purpose or passed to any other third party.

**glasshaus**

web professional to web professional

Note: If you post the bounce back card below in the UK, please send it to:

glasshaus, Arden House, 1102 Warwick Road,
Acocks Green, Birmingham B27 6HB. UK.

*Computer Book Publishers*